Thinking in the Dark

Thinking in the Dark

Cinema, Theory, Practice

EDITED BY

MURRAY POMERANCE

R. BARTON PALMER

RUTGERS UNIVERSITY PRESS

NEW BRUNSWICK, NEW JERSEY, AND LONDON

LIBRARY OF CONGRESS CATALOGING-IN-PUBLICATION DATA

Thinking in the dark : cinema, theory, practice / edited by Murray Pomerance and R. Barton Palmer.

pages cm

Includes bibliographical references and index.

ISBN 978–0–8135–6629–0 (hardcover : alk. paper) — ISBN 978–0–8135–6628–3 (pbk. : alk. paper) — ISBN 978–0–8135–6630–6 (e-book (web pdf)) — ISBN 978–0–8135–7560–5 (e-book (epub))

1. Film criticism. 2. Film critics. 3. Motion pictures—Philosophy. I. Pomerance, Murray, 1946– editor. II. Palmer, R. Barton, 1946– editor.

PN1995.T44 2015

791.4301—dc23

2015002732

A British Cataloging-in-Publication record for this book is available from the British Library.

Visit our website: http://rutgerspress.rutgers.edu

Manufactured in the United States of America

For Gilberto Perez (1943–2015)
in respectful memory

CONTENTS

Acknowledgments ix

Introduction 1
R. BARTON PALMER AND MURRAY POMERANCE

1 Hugo Münsterberg: Psychologizing Spectatorship between Laboratory and Theater 7
JEREMY BLATTER

2 Vachel Lindsay: Theory of Movie Hieroglyphics 19
TOM GUNNING

3 Béla Balázs: Film Aesthetics and the Rituals of Romance 31
STEVEN WOODWARD

4 Siegfried Kracauer: The Politics of Film Theory and Criticism 42
JOHANNES VON MOLTKE

5 Walter Benjamin: Afterimages of the Aura 54
COLIN WILLIAMSON

6 Jean Epstein: Cinema's Encounter with Modern Life 66
SARAH KELLER

7 Sergei Eisenstein: Attractions/Montage/Animation 77
MATTHEW SOLOMON

8 Jacques Lacan: Giving All the Right Signs 89
DOMINIC LENNARD

9 Rudolf Arnheim: Cinema and Partial Illusion 101
NATHAN HOLMES

10 Roland Barthes: What Films Show Us and What They Mean 113
WILLIAM BROWN

11 Jean Rouch: The Camera as Provocateur 125
WILLIAM ROTHMAN

12 André Bazin: Dark Passage into the Mystery of Being 136
DUDLEY ANDREW

13 Gilles Deleuze: On Movement, Time, and Modernism 150
WILL SCHEIBEL

14 Stanley Cavell: The Contingencies of Film and Its Theory 162
DANIEL MORGAN

15 Michel Foucault: Murmur and Meditation 174
TOM CONLEY

16 Jean Douchet: *La Politique Hitchcockienne* 185
R. BARTON PALMER

17 Christian Metz: Dreaming a Language in Cinema 197
STEVEN RYBIN

18 V. F. Perkins: Aesthetic Suspense 208
ALEX CLAYTON

19 Jacques Rancière: Equality and Aesthetics 217
GILBERTO PEREZ

20 Michel Chion: Listening to Cinema 229
JONAH CORNE

21 Judith Butler: Sex, Gender, and Subject Formation 241
KRISTEN HATCH

Works Cited 253
Notes on Contributors 263
Index 267

ACKNOWLEDGMENTS

With special thanks to Dudley Andrew (New Haven), William Brown (London), Tom Gunning (Chicago), Michael MacDonald (Toronto), Tracey McVey (Coventry), William Rothman (Miami), Nick White (Toronto), Colin Williamson (Philadelphia), and Jason Steeves (Carpenter Centre, Harvard University).

We could not have succeeded in this project without the help of our families. The Palmer family, especially Carla and Camden, have always shown a much-appreciated tolerance for Barton's dedication to various scholarly pursuits. He is as grateful as ever for their continuing interest and support. At the Pomerance home, Nellie Perret and Ariel Pomerance have been tireless and generous in helping Murray with his efforts here. This book is therefore a labor of love.

To our compadrés at Rutgers University Press, our deepest respect and gratitude. These include Leslie Mitchner, Lisa Boyajian, Anne Hegeman, Jeremy Grainger, Lisa Fortunato, copyeditor Maria Siano, and John Barlett/Four Eyes Design for the cover design.

Thinking in the Dark

Introduction

R. BARTON PALMER
MURRAY POMERANCE

Chacun puisse traduire son âme dans le style visuel.

– Jean Cocteau, 1948

Most of the essays that make up this book engage with the ideas of prominent writers of film theory, which might be broadly defined as that area of inquiry in which the object of study is the medium itself, as well as the various social, economic, and cultural practices in which film plays a central role. Not specifically the content of a film, then, but the way in which that content is filmic, and what "being filmic" can mean. Some of the chapters here focus on a related area. They take up the work of thinkers best considered as cultural theorists whose writings, if they do not engage with the cinema directly, have often and repeatedly been invoked by those in film studies because they address issues (e.g., gender or aesthetics) that have come into importance in the discipline. It is hardly surprising that such a mixed and varied intellectual tradition came to exist and quickly flourish, given the widespread predisposition in the later nineteenth century toward an enlightened understanding of how the world and our experience come to be what they are. Unlike literature, architecture, dance, and the other high arts, however, film from its earliest years at the end of the nineteenth century, and well onward into the twentieth, was often derogated as merely fashionable, merely popular, and thus, low; and reflection upon it the stuff of chitchat rather than sophisticated thought. Theory, many might still say, is too grand a term for the cultural analysis, description, and advocacy that focus on film, modes of thinking that, unlike scientific theorizing, do not trade in hypothesis-building and data-supported arguments designed to establish empirical truth.

Film theory is perhaps more accurately described as serious writing about the cinema (including its critical evaluation) that in no way diminishes either its importance or its interest. If such thinking lacks scientific or even philosophical rigor, this body of commentary has nonetheless been an important part of the intellectual scene in North America and Europe for more than a century now. The advent in the early years of the twentieth century of the astoundingly popular new medium of film, and the establishment and flourishing of a world cinema culture soon thereafter, inspired many artists, public intellectuals, and scholars to offer their thoughts on what these developments might mean.

Early on, the cinema seemed to many intellectuals to be an art form with the capacity to change how we see the world and even to transform society. The cinema, in other words, was not just the most profitable and flexible of the different kinds of entertainment that emerged in the last decades of the nineteenth century, as leisure time on a mass scale became the inevitable target of marketizing forces. Just to make the obvious point, the amusement park, the vaudeville theater, and professional sports have provoked nothing similar in the way of intellectual curiosity and passion. For reasons explored by many of the figures whose work is considered in this volume, the cinema has proven to be the most influential of modern art/entertainment forms (with the possible exception, at least in part, of popular music). Because they are dependent on recording and are easily reproducible and transmissible, music and film have both readily attained and maintained an international presence, traveling easily between cultures. But only the cinema has, at least thus far, played an important role in political and cultural developments.

When the medium was barely a quarter of a century old in the early 1920s, films were enlisted to aid the radical transformation of a newly Soviet society following two revolutions and a bloody civil war, as state-sponsored productions were widely exhibited throughout the vast countryside in order to instruct a largely illiterate population about the new political order, its history and values. In every village and town, available buildings, including churches, were pressed into service as theaters, and there an oft-bewildered populace was offered stirring reenactments of recent history, even as important new programs (such as collective farming and industrial five-year plans) were accorded dramatic treatments that reflected and advocated for official policy. In Germany at the same time, the film industry established itself as a profitable entertainment business, but producers aiming for a certain prestige also permitted and encouraged its partial colonization by a high-culture artistic movement. Expressionism was politically tendentious and an important area of avant-garde practice within northern European modernism. Expressionist filmmaking transformed the model of the commercial feature film largely established by American commercial practice, making the cinema produced in Berlin, then the acknowledged cultural center of Europe, part of a transmedial, transnational artistic movement that affected music, the plastic arts, poetry, and even architecture. This German tradition demonstrated how the cinema could be accommodated within honored traditions of high art, and the capacity of the medium to do more than entertain a mass public with melodramas and comedies was also discovered by those involved in other "artistic" film movements such as cinematic Surrealism/Dada (which flourished in Paris during the 1920s) and cinematic Impressionism (whose practitioners were also active in Paris during the same period).

This volume is meant as an introduction to the practice of thinking about film, and introduces only some of many imaginable theorists. Legion are those, reflective and provocative, whose work we could not include for reasons of space. No doubt, this book would have been further enriched with chapters devoted to the cinema as addressed or implicated by such theorists as Louis Althusser, Alain Badiou, Jean Baudrillard, Maya Deren, Jacques Derrida, Hollis Frampton, Lev Kuleshov, Maurice Merleau-Ponty, Jean Mitry, Jean Narboni, Jean-Pierre Oudart, Vsevolod Pudovkin, Jacqueline Rose, Paul Sharits, Michael Snow, Dziga Vertov (Denis Kaufman), Paul Virilio, and Slavoj Žižek, among others. Some well-meaning witch is always neglected when invitations go out for the christening. We have only touched here on the rich and complex history of the cinema, which assumed substantially different forms as it spread globally and during a century of especially dislocating and radical historical change. It is hardly surprising that the film and cultural theorists discussed in this volume, writing from within distinct national experiences, offer contrasting and conflicting meditations about the nature of the medium, its place, real or desired, within modern culture, and its cultural functions, from reinforcing the status quo to changing how viewers see their world. Well-established before World War II, this informed conversation about the cinema only grew more immense with the expansion and growing sophistication of enthusiast film cultures in the postwar period, and these seem to have been the principal moving force behind the eventual academicization of film studies from the 1970s onward. Fifty years ago, no American universities offered courses of study of that area of popular culture then usually referred to as "the movies," but within a decade, responding to the growing acceptance, at least among the educated, of the cinema's importance as a sociological and cultural phenomenon, such programs began to appear; proving popular with students and academics alike, they quickly proliferated, in North America and in the UK as well, prompting the founding of a new scholarly field, whose place within conventional groupings of academic subjects is still evolving some forty years on, perhaps a signal that film studies has not yet congealed into a proper "discipline."

Like literary theory, which was also shaped decisively by the pedagogical needs of American university students, film theory has come by convention to include writings that are vastly different in terms of content and rhetoric. These texts have been transformed into an informal canon of masterworks that reflect developments in global film culture such as the emergence to preeminence in the 1950s of the Parisian journal *Cahiers du cinéma* (from 1953), whose first editor, André Bazin, was already a much read and greatly respected commentator on a series of historical or evaluative issues long before film study moved to the universities. Bazin wrote, however, not for today's students but for the mainly French enthusiasts who were his contemporaries. As we read the chapters that follow, it is worth remembering how, in a way similar to Bazin, each of these theorists was writing for a particular audience at a definable cultural node. The works of public intellectuals, academics, filmmakers, and journalists, mostly from Western Europe, became and remain the core of the "must-knows" of the field, but those of us who read them today for the first time are not, strictly speaking, members of the audience they were addressing, except in the very general sense that every great writer has for his intended audience all of humankind.

It is also often true with the thinkers in this volume that they did not all think of themselves as "film theorists" when they theorized about film. No doubt, many, perhaps most, of those authors from the first half of the twentieth century who are now studied as "film theorists" would be very surprised that this has become their posthumous intellectual fate. They could hardly have anticipated that the seventh art would become a subject area like philosophy or literature, or that their theoretical formulations would be echoed in the corridors of academic life and even—for some of them—reach an audience not pinned to professional scholarship at all.

If you scan the chapter titles for this volume, you will find there the names of major figures of this tradition: Bazin, Siegfried Kracauer, Walter Benjamin, Jacques Lacan, Christian Metz, Rudolf Arnheim, Sergei Eisenstein among them. Some of this group would even, perhaps, dispute the legitimacy of the field itself because they were more interested in the cinema's several connections with cultural politics, even the social transformation that the medium might achieve. Kracauer's major work, *Theory of Film* (1960), for example, is subtitled "The Redemption of Physical Reality," and his book offers an argument for a transindividual perceptual change, and hence social transformation, in which the cinema was destined by its very nature, or so Kracauer thought, to play a central role. "Modern man," he declares there, "lacks the guidance of binding norms . . . [and] touches reality only with his fingertips" (294). The cinema has the capacity to reconnect us to the particular, phenomenal real, eliminating the abstractness that is a dominant heritage of the Enlightenment and encouraging "direct efforts to revamp religion and establish a consensus of beliefs" (*Theory* 294). Not to forget, Kracauer was writing in a postwar era in which still fresh were the memories of a militant fascism that had come close to destroying the European culture in which he had been born.

The reformist, even evangelical strain of Kracauer's writing is to be found in the work of a number of his fellow "theorists." Yet American poet Vachel Lindsay, penning a book in 1915 (revised and reissued in 1922) that overflowed with the kind of enthusiasm for the cinema that was felt by many artists at the time, thought of himself as making "an appeal to our whole critical and literary world" about this exciting new medium (*Art* Preface). Russian director Sergei Eisenstein saw the cinema as uniquely qualified by its formal properties to play a vital role in the predicted triumph of the new Soviet state. Bazin was a fervent adherent of Personalism, Emannuel Mounier's humanist philosophy, with its traditional Christian endorsement of an individuality that also embraced limited forms of collectivism. Much like Kracauer, Bazin hoped that the cinema might be the engine of social change, a key force in the creation of a better society destined to emerge from the European wreckage of the postwar era.

In university film programs, although this was unthinkable only a decade or so earlier, courses devoted to "film theory" soon appeared as part of emerging curricula, an essential development as film studies established its academic credentials. This pedagogical development generated a need for textbooks that was quickly filled, with one or two thick volumes of reprinted materials (mostly journal articles and chapters from a few longer studies thought to be essential) soon dominating the field. With their selections of mostly translated writings, often presented with little information about the context in which these had been originally produced, such omnibus anthologies have decisively shaped the study of what was somewhat grandly known as theory, establishing a canon of approved and honored texts. Film theory texts are organized thematically, using labels such as "formalist," "realist," or "post-classical" to impose on their contents a rough sort of intellectual order. This grouping proves occasionally useful, but often at the cost of distortion and failure to simplify in an illuminating way. By forming and emphasizing categories such as these, by grouping theories under them, and by stressing to students the so-called importance of slotting theorists properly in one category or another, pedagogy has taken attention away from the work of the theorists and their living importance. Each author in this book is a person, and brings the rich experience of a life to his or her theoretical considerations of cinema. Categorization comes long afterward, as a kind of metatheoretical fetish, and is convenient to apprehend only for those who already grasp what they are meant to be trying to understand.

Thinking in the Dark offers a different, if complementary, model for the study of film theory centered on major figures rather than on specific texts chosen to illustrate a particular theme. We think that traditional forms of labelling are an inadequate way of classifying or grouping those who have written seriously about film. This volume is not designed to replace the reading of primary materials, which remains as essential in cinema studies as it is in the other humanities. Rather, the intention of the editors and contributors here has been to provide, for students and colleagues alike, informed and accessible discussions of those whose writings possess a continuing relevance to cinema scholars' intellectual labor. The intent of the contributors to this volume has not been to offer a summary in each case of the writings of a prominent thinker, but rather to sketch an overview of the thinker's approach and context, and then focus strongly on a particular issue that is illuminating and exemplary. So it is that we present, each through the eye and "pen" of a different film scholar today, twenty-one of the writers who have influenced today's film scholarship. We arrange them not in terms of metatheoretical categories but according to their years of birth, so that reading the book from start to finish should give some, albeit rough-edged, sense of the way thinking about film has grown and developed as it moves from one thinker to another. Film theory demands a continual thinking about and reassessment of the central figures who have come to constitute the field. The various chapters in this book anatomize and demonstrate the importance of these thinkers to the ever-emerging understanding of the cinema, both as an artistic medium and as a nexus of institutions and practices. A principal concern of the contributors has been to demonstrate through their application to selected films the continuing relevance of the ideas, values, or critical approaches to be found in the work of canonical film theorists.

Each chapter presents some of the theorist's influential ideas, and then uses them to approach one film from the classical era and one film from the period of the last twenty years or so. In this way, we come to learn how vital these theoretical materials can be for opening our exploration to old films and new ones, well-established films and those that may still be relatively unknown.

Each chapter is self-contained and focuses on the ideas of a thinker whose work has proven of substantial continuing interest and relevance, either because it grapples with issues that over time have proven to be quintessentially cinematic, or because it reflects important trends in the history of the medium itself. We hope and trust these essays will provoke, challenge, entertain, and shed light on what film is, was, and can be. As theory is always breathing and growing, perhaps, dear Reader, starting from these forays into the artistic, social, and political functioning of the cinema, you will move on to theorize moving pictures yourself.

1

Hugo Münsterberg

Psychologizing Spectatorship between Laboratory and Theater

JEREMY BLATTER

"It is arbitrary to say where the development of moving pictures began," *The Photoplay: A Psychological Study* (1916) begins, "and it is impossible to foresee where it will lead." Whether we locate the origins of motion pictures in the philosophical toys of the nineteenth century like the phenakistoscope or the zoetrope, in Eadweard Muybridge and Etienne-Jules Marey's chronophotographic studies of physiological movement, in Thomas Edison's kinetoscope, or in the Lumière brothers' cinématographe, the historical development of cinema as a medium and a cultural form may best be described as the piecemeal coalescing of perceptual theories, technological innovations, aesthetic experiments, and entrepreneurial efforts. The same observation holds true for the origins of film theory. It would be no more accurate to assign film theory a single founding figure than it would be to identify cinema with a singular inventor. Nevertheless, Hugo Münsterberg's (1863–1916) *The Photoplay* has come to be regarded by cinema and media studies scholars as the first rigorous study of film worthy of membership in the canon of classical film theory. Dudley Andrew called *The Photoplay* "not only the first but also the most direct major film theory" (*Theories* 14). Giuliana Bruno writes that Münsterberg "devised the first full 'experiment' in film theory" (90; see also Lindsay, *Art*; Sargent).

Not always was Münsterberg acknowledged as a pioneer in film theory. Indeed, it was only after *The Photoplay* was republished in 1970 that critics and scholars began referencing this work as the first example of academic film theory. The French film theorist and cineaste Jean Mitry is said to have remarked, "How could we have not known him all these years? In 1916 this man understood cinema about as well as anyone ever will" (qtd. in Andrew, *Theories* 26). Even Rudolf Arnheim, who in the 1920s studied psychology and moonlighted as a Berlin film critic, knew nothing of *The Photoplay*, despite his familiarity with Münsterberg's other writings ("Zum Geleit"). Unlike his early works written in German and translated into English, *The Photoplay* was written in English and not translated into German until 1996.

It would be misleading to say that *The Photoplay* had no initial impact on film discourse. Many reviewers praised Münsterberg at the time for his eloquent defense of film as a legitimate art and for the facility with which he analyzed the psychological mechanisms of filmmaking technique. After 1917, however, the book proved as ephemeral as the word "photoplay" itself, a term invented around 1910 to lend cultural prestige to the medium and attract new middle-class audiences hesitant to embrace what they often viewed as a low-brow vaudevillian type of entertainment (see Hansen, *Babel*). The most obvious and direct influence on *The Photoplay*'s long-term reception was the fact that it was eclipsed by Münsterberg's own dramatic death while lecturing at Radcliffe College in December 1916 and the subsequent entry of the United States into the First World War the following April. The impact of the war was not just important in terms of shifting cultural concerns. By 1914, Münsterberg had become a notorious figure in the eyes of an American public increasingly drawn into a riptide of anti-German sentiment (see P. Keller). Since the 1890s, he had taken it upon himself to promote mutual understanding between his beloved German *Heimat* and his adopted American home, but after war broke out in Europe what was initially tolerated as the benign cultural commentary of a Harvard professor interested in German–American relations was soon enough perceived as Teutonic propaganda. Symptomatic of this deeply politicized climate were false accusations that Münsterberg was a spy for the kaiser, followed by the scandalous offer of $10 million by a delusional Harvard alumnus in exchange for the professor's forced resignation (Hale 173).

This political context is important for another reason. The strain and anxiety that the war had brought him took its toll on his health and left him feeling alienated from his colleagues. According to his daughter, Münsterberg turned to the movies for a distraction, a break "from the wearing anxieties caused by the international stress" (M. Münsterberg 281). Why he chose film over some other form of entertainment is unknown, but it is likely that the German writer Hanns Heinz Ewers helped sway him in this direction (Schweinitz 13). In November 1914, Ewers had been Münsterberg's guest at the German-American Society in Boston and less than a year earlier had written the screenplay for the film *The Student of Prague* (1913). Like Münsterberg in *The Photoplay*, Ewers was an ardent defender of film as an autonomous art. In a private letter to Harvard president Abbott Lowell, Münsterberg suggested a "secondary motive" behind his turn to the psychology of film. "My name was so much connected with the war noise," he explained, "that I wanted to break that association by a new connection with a popular interest" (Münsterberg to Lowell).

While this background helps us understand the complex context in which *The Photoplay* was written and, to a certain extent, the cause of its delayed recognition, to understand the actual content of the book we must dig deeper into the author's intellectual biography and the tradition of experimental psychology in which he worked.

Before Münsterberg Went to the Movies

Hugo Münsterberg began his academic career at the University of Freiburg, where in 1887 he was appointed *Privatdozent* (private lecturer) in psychology. Having studied philosophy and experimental psychology under the eminent Wilhelm Wundt at the University of Leipzig, Münsterberg hoped to follow in his former teacher's footsteps by establishing his own psychological laboratory in Freiburg. As a *Privatdozent*, Münsterberg received no salary, only student fees, and initially no formal institutional support for his endeavor. Therefore, to realize his dream he relied on his family inheritance to finance the purchase of equipment that soon filled two rooms in the apartment he shared with his wife on Günterstalstrasse. Despite these limitations, Münsterberg's laboratory was in full swing by 1888, making it by most counts the fourth psychological laboratory in all of Germany.

Experimental research carried out by Münsterberg and his students was documented on the pages of the *Beiträge zur experimentelle Psychologie*, the laboratory's organ of publication. So impressed was William James by the experimental prowess on display in the first issues of the *Beiträge* that shortly after opening a new Psychological Laboratory at Harvard in 1891 he turned to Münsterberg to replace him as its director. Although by 1892 James had achieved stature akin to that of Wundt in Germany, he made no secret of his disdain for the tedium of experimental labor. In securing Münsterberg as director of the Harvard Psychological Laboratory for a three-year tryout, then as tenured faculty after 1897, James found in his precocious German colleague, only twenty-nine when he was appointed, long-desired relief from the responsibilities of an acting laboratory director.

As James's successor from 1892 to 1916, Münsterberg attracted considerable press and media attention. Psychology at the time was an exciting yet poorly understood new science and the Harvard Laboratory was soon reputed to be among the best on either side of the Atlantic. But for all the hoopla surrounding the young science the actual practice of experimental psychology in the late nineteenth century was self-consciously mundane and abstract. There was a widespread anxiety among psychologists that overblown or premature claims about the utility of their knowledge and techniques might undermine their credibility. This fear was compounded by the popular conflation of psychology with phrenology, mesmerism, and psychical research carried out by lay practitioners who often profited by making sensational claims about the ability to read human character and aptitudes from cranial topography, heal disease through hypnosis, and demonstrate telepathy and paranormal phenomena unverifiable by accepted scientific standards. Those psychologists who prematurely heeded the calls of commercial interests to put their skills to practical use were vulnerable to accusations of falling prey to base commercialism.

Such were the reasons why many academic psychologists through the 1890s upheld the image of their laboratories as cloistered spaces for disinterested research where ascetic scientists plumbed the depths of the mind purely for the sake of knowledge. In his first decade as director of the Harvard Psychological Laboratory, Münsterberg steadfastly affirmed the ethos of pure science by confining experimental work to what today we would call basic research. Given this constraint, useful applications for psychological knowledge and techniques were discovered only serendipitously as experiments designed to solve practical problems were strictly proscribed. Most experiments thus focused on isolating certain senses or mental faculties such as attention, memory, imagination, or emotion in complete abstraction from the everyday contexts in which they are employed.

To illustrate this method let us look, for example, at the human faculty of attention, a faculty which, as discussed later in the context of *The Photoplay*, was central to Münsterberg's understanding of the cinematic close-up. One common experimental technique for studying attention involved the use of what psychologists called a "puzzle picture." The puzzle picture is an image that by design includes certain objects or figures not immediately visible within a depicted scene. An object might be discovered hidden in the background, outlined in negative space, or otherwise camouflaged. By giving such puzzles to test subjects under controlled conditions in a laboratory the psychologist aimed to collect objective data, such as the time taken to identify certain objects, as well as subjective data, such as test subjects' observations about their experience of the task. Taken together, these pieces of information might give one hope of discovering something about qualities that quickly grab the attention versus those which elude it, and the means by which objects formerly overlooked may in a moment of recognition suddenly occupy the center of one's field of concentration.

As with most of his colleagues, Münsterberg's attitude toward this work was that of self-conscious restraint. Although it is easy to see how such an experimental technique as was used to study attention might be applied to the purposes of advertising, for most psychologists in the late nineteenth century venturing down such a path meant risking scientific credibility. The prejudices that checked psychologists' private and professional activities are apparent in Münsterberg's earliest film essay, "Why We Go to the 'Movies,'" which appeared in the December 1915 issue of *Cosmopolitan*. There he wrote, "I should have felt it as undignified for a Harvard Professor to attend a moving picture-show, just as I should not have gone to a vaudeville performance or to a museum of wax figures or to a phonograph concert." It was thus only while "traveling a thousand miles from Boston," he continued,

> [that] I and a friend risked seeing *Neptune's Daughter*, and my conversion was rapid. I recognized at once that here marvelous possibilities were open, and I began to explore with eagerness the world which was new to me. Reel after reel moved along before my eyes—all styles, all makes. I went with the crowd to Anita Stewart and Mary Pickford and Charles Chaplin; I saw Pathé and Vitagraph, Lubin and Essanay, Paramount and Majestic, Universal and Knickerbocker. I read the books on how to write scenarios; I visited the manufacturing companies, and, finally, I began to experiment myself. Surely I am now under the spell of the "movies," and, while my case may be worse than the average, all the world is somewhat under the spell. ("Why We Go" 23–24)

Becoming a film enthusiast was one thing, studying the movies as a psychologist something completely different. Psychologists through the turn of the century adopted a serious, even effete pose, and were reluctant to apply their science to practical life. However, in the first decade of the twentieth century this began to change. Walter Dill Scott of Northwestern University brought advertising psychology a respectability unimaginable in nineteenth-century scientific circles; William Stern co-founded an Institute of Applied Psychology in Berlin; Clark University and Teachers' College made educational psychology a fixture of pedagogical training; and the Psychology Department at Columbia University introduced a research fellowship financed by the Advertising Men's League of New York.

Keeping abreast of these developments, Münsterberg announced in 1908 the founding of a special department within his laboratory devoted entirely to the new field of applied psychology. Based on research carried out in this department, Münsterberg would publish influential books on the application of psychology to virtually every context of daily life, from the classroom, courtroom, and clinic to the market, factory, and movie theater. Only within this new regime conducive to applied psychology was Münsterberg able to justify his work on film.

The Photoplay: A Psychological Study

As an extension of works on applied psychology, *The Photoplay* followed a familiar model. The basic idea was to adapt experimental methods and tests designed with fundamental research questions in mind to the kinds of practical questions directly relevant to everyday life. For example, investigations into memory were revised with an eye to producing results of pedagogical value, studies of mental fatigue modified to test worker productivity. In *The Photoplay*, this takes the form of four core chapters organized around psychological functions: Depth and Movement (i.e., basic perception), Attention, Memory and Imagination, and Emotions. With each of these classic categories of psychological inquiry, Münsterberg aims to demonstrate what role it plays in film spectatorship and what techniques are used to exploit it.

"Depth and Movement" appropriately begins by asking what, psychologically speaking, it actually means to view a moving picture. "To begin at the beginning," he explains, "the photoplay consists of a series of flat pictures in contrast to the plastic objects of the real world which surround us" (45). That we perceive depth and movement in these flat images, however, does not imply that what we see is an illusion. "Differences of apparent size, the perspective relations, the shadows, and the actions performed in the space" (50) all combine to communicate dimensionality from the vantage point of the spectator. "*Depth and movement alike come to us in the moving picture world,*" he elaborates, "*not as hard facts but as a mixture of fact and symbol. They are present and yet they are not in the things. We invest the impressions with them*" (71; emphasis original).

In the three following chapters, Münsterberg moves from the fundamentals of film perception toward the analysis of discrete filmmaking techniques such as the close-up, cut-back, and the flash-forward, and the construction of narrative through editing. The chapter "Attention," for example, unpacks the significance of the close-up as a means of guiding the spectator's gaze toward details of dramatic or symbolic importance. In one example Münsterberg describes a scene in which a slip of paper falls unnoticed from the pocket of a criminal as he takes his handkerchief out of his pocket. While in theater this detail might be missed by the entire audience, captured in close-up on the big screen that scrap of paper becomes endowed with special significance.

The manipulation of attention, however, is not only achieved through the close-up. The absence of the spoken word also heightens our attention to the subtle play of gesture and facial expression. In his chapter on "Emotion," Münsterberg explores in greater detail how the "enlargement by the close-up on the screen brings this emotional action of the face to sharpest relief" (113). Unlike stage actors who, limited by their fixed distance from the audience, must rely on speech and histrionics to communicate emotion, screen acting encourages greater naturalism and expressive nuance by means of close-ups and the use of multiple takes.

While music and sound effects may shape the spectator's experience, Münsterberg asserts that film is first and foremost a visual medium and it is in the moving pictures that its true power lies. For this reason he expresses skepticism about the potential role of the spoken word in film. Although in 1916 the technology of synchronized sound was only in its earliest experimental phase and *The Jazz Singer* (1927) still a decade away, Münsterberg's prescient sensitivity to the problem anticipates many criticisms of the talkie by filmmakers and critics alike, from Charlie Chaplin to Béla Balázs.

In relation to the faculties of "Memory and Imagination," the cut-back and flash-forward are considered. Imagine a scene, for example, in which a soldier, huddled in the trenches, grips his rifle as a barrage of hostile fire passes overhead. Cut to a blissful summer afternoon from the man's childhood, then back to the trenches. In such a sequence Münsterberg argues that the cut-back represents "an objectification of our memory function" (95). Similarly, if the scene next jumps ahead in time to Armistice Day where soldier and wife are seen reunited, then we have the objectification of imagination, the hopeful image conjured in the mind's eye of a peaceful future. The photoplay in this way transcends space and time in much the same way that in our daily lives, filled with disparate stimuli, distant memories are triggered and future events imagined. As Münsterberg writes:

> The photoplay can overcome the interval of the future as well as the interval of the past. . . . In short, it can act as our imagination acts. It has the mobility of our ideas which are not controlled by the physical necessity of outer events but by the psychological laws for the association of ideas. In our mind past and future become intertwined with the present. The photoplay obeys the laws of the mind rather than those of the outer world. (96–97)

One reason *The Photoplay* has remained so relevant is that it not only outlines a technical vocabulary of filmmaking that persists to the present day but demonstrates an acute awareness of the bearing of technological developments on film aesthetics. For example, Münsterberg takes great care in distinguishing the implications of live musical accompaniment from a carefully composed soundtrack. Remarkably, despite writing as early as 1916 when the technology for sound synchronized with a moving image was only in its infancy and the talkies still a decade away, he nevertheless appeared fully aware of the potential to "connect the kinematoscope with the phonograph and to synchronize them so completely that with every visible movement of the lips the audible sound of the words would leave the diaphragm of the apparatus" (202–203). However, Münsterberg contended that on aesthetic grounds this was a great mistake because the introduction of voice would compromise the "visual purity" of the photoplay. Synchronizing voices, he argued, was simply driven by the desire to imitate theater, and no art was worth the name if it was merely imitating another. The photoplay must be respected as "an art in itself," defined by its own representational techniques. Those techniques, such as the close-up to activate attention and reveal the physiological subtleties of facial expression, the flash-back to evoke memory, and the flash-forward to project an imagined future, are all called upon to communicate the art of film in the absence of, not in addition to, the spoken word. Therefore any effort at "conservation of the spoken word," he writes, "is as disturbing as color would be on the clothing of a marble statue" (203). Whether or not Münsterberg was aware that ancient Greek and Roman statues were indeed ornately colored is not important; what is important in the metaphor is the emphasis on silence, the defining limitation of the art.

Music was important, since without it the spectator's attention would drift and his eyes become overtaxed in the absence of nonvisual sensory stimulation. Of course, not all photoplay music was equal. Münsterberg bemoaned the meandering house organist whose improvisational accompaniment often contradicted the activity or tone of the scene onscreen. The mechanically synchronized soundtrack in this way offered greater precision and control over the spectators' experience.

Charlie Chaplin's *City Lights* (1931), made as the sound revolution was burgeoning but emphatically shot without a "talking" sound track, resonates with Münsterberg's concerns. Chaplin was one of the great directors of the silent era who, like Münsterberg, believed that the nature of film was visual and nonverbal. While *City Lights* was shot as a silent film, it did feature a synchronized soundtrack with music composed by Chaplin himself (not the least memorable part of which is the song "Smile"). By comparison, Michel Hazanavicius's *The Artist* (2011) plunges into the problem by showing a performer from the silent days as he confronts the shocking novelty of sound film. Analyzing these two films side-by-side allows us to see how they both reflect on the nature and visual grammar of silent film and also how they deal with the psychological implications of new film technologies in shaping how films are made and seen.

City Lights

City Lights begins with an establishing shot of a city street crowded with pedestrians eagerly attending to a wildly gesticulating figure barely visible against the backdrop of a large monument concealed by a white covering. The gesticulating man turns to the masked object with a revelatory sweep of the arm. Cut to our first title card: "To the people of this city we donate this monument; 'Peace and Prosperity.'" With the scene now established we see our stout, charismatic mayor offering his dedicatory speech. Then comes the punch line. In lieu of mere musical accompaniment (or the actual voice of the mayor) we hear instead the kazoo-like caricaturing of speech produced. A female speaker follows the mayor. Hearing the same effect but in a higher pitch for her, we cut back to a shot revealing a hitherto unseen microphone on the stage. Among the earliest theories of silent film Münsterberg's *The Photoplay* offers a unique prism onto *City Lights* and *The Artist*, as both films idealistically invoke an obsolescent style to reflect on the nature of their art amid the changing technologies and techniques of production.

The sudden appearance of the microphone may be read in two ways. First it is comedic acknowledgment of the very technology Chaplin has chosen to ignore by leaving speech out of this film. As is evident thus far, everything we need to understand the plot has been perfectly communicated through gesture and mise-en-scène alone, and the microphone in frame is a superfluous object. At the same time, as diegetically speaking the microphone is presumably present for the purpose of a radio broadcast it also forces us to compare these two very different means and mediums of communication—the spoken word and the visual language of film. Whereas the spoken word is limited by linguistic boundaries, the language of gesture combined with the carefully constructed shot and eloquently edited scene could potentially transcend the curse of Babel. That the third figure to "speak" on stage resembles Leon Trotsky, the Marxist leader of the international Left, may also be an allusion to film as an international language. This would be consistent with Chaplin's political views combined with his conviction that film could unite the masses through its universal comprehensibility. Put differently, by drawing our attention to the mediation and mediums of communication, Chaplin offers his protest to the technological determinism of an industry that uncritically adopts new technologies without any consideration of aesthetic questions. As Münsterberg argues, the goal of the photoplaywright ought to be the "creation of plays which speak the language of pictures only" (200) emancipated from the "linguistic crutches" of the written and spoken word.

From this opening scene the real story of *City Lights* begins with a close-up of a basket brimming over with flowers that cross-fades to the face of an attractive young woman (Virginia Cherrill) selling flowers. We soon discover that she is blind. We cut to Chaplin's Tramp walking through traffic and dodging a police officer by passing through the backseat of a stranger's vehicle and exiting onto the sidewalk in front of the woman. Hearing the car door slam, the woman implores the Tramp to buy a flower, thinking him a wealthy man. For the Tramp, it is love at first sight.

In light of Münsterberg's conception of the close-up, the thrust of attention toward the flower basket before fading to our heroine links the interpretation of this image of beauty and innocence in the spectator's mind with the blind woman. In psychological terms, this is a form of "suggestion." As a commentary on the fate of silent film, *City Lights* constructs a deeply psychological argument about how the power of silent film lies in the heightening of visual cognition by omission of the spoken word. Indeed, it is the great irony of the film that it is a sound, the slam of a car door, that deceives the blind woman into thinking Charlie the Tramp is a rich man stepping out of his vehicle. Meanwhile, never hearing the sound the audience becomes privy to the truth. Then, in the

FIGURE 1.1 The Tramp falls in love with a blind woman selling flowers on the street. Charlie Chaplin with Virginia Cherrill in *City Lights* (Charles Chaplin, Charles Chaplin Productions, 1931). Digital frame enlargement.

famous final scene where the Tramp and the blind woman, now with her sight restored, reunite, it is through the isolated sense of touch that he is finally recognized by her. When she kindly insists that he take the coin she offers, and places it in the palm of his hand, his identity is suddenly revealed. In close-up we see his hand warmly clasped in hers and are reminded of their first meeting when their hands first met in exchange of a flower for a coin.

Using Münsterberg's *The Photoplay* as our guide we discover in this scene Chaplin's virtuosic skill in manipulating the psychology of the spectator. First, we have the emphasis on three isolated details: the exchange of a single flower, a coin, and the touch of hands. Each of these three elements also belonged to the scene of their first meeting. This association is encouraged by a close-up that draws our attention to the meeting of their hands, tilting up to Charlie biting his nails on the same hand in which he holds his flower and anxiously waits for her recognition. The close-up in this way simultaneously suggests the association with their first meeting as well as revealing the psychological process by which the formerly blind woman comes to recognize Charlie's identity. At the same time, this scene also serves as a persuasive appeal to the silent film as a powerful form of nonverbal communication.

The Artist

Whereas *City Lights* might be read as a meditation on the uncertain aesthetic implications of synchronized sound on the art of film, *The Artist* returns to the lost art of silent film in order to raise related questions about the fate of film and the shift toward 3D in the digital age. *The Artist* tells the story of silent-film star George Valentin (Jean Dujardin), beginning in 1927 at the pinnacle of his career (which also coincides with the rise of the talkie). In a foreshadowing of his demise, Valentin falls in love with the young actress Peppy Miller (Bérénice Bejo), whose career he launches after discovering her at one of his premieres. However, as Peppy's star rises as a leading lady in the less artistically ambitious talkies, Valentin's career begins its dramatic descent as he stubbornly (in the eyes of Hollywood execs) clings to an increasingly antiquated mode of filmmaking.

The growing tension between Valentin's artistic pretensions and the advent of sound comes to a head after he is called off the set by his producer to watch test footage of their studio's first experiment in "talking" pictures. After the short screening, Valentin stands up in nervous laughter, but before he can exit the room he is stopped in his tracks by the words of his producer: "Don't laugh, George! That's the future." To which Valentin can only reply, "If that's the future, you can have it!"

From the screening room we cut to the reflection of Valentin in his dressing room vanity mirror. The ominous music from the previous scene has now faded to complete silence. Valentin takes a sip of water as the camera slowly moves back. Then, suddenly, the silence is broken. We hear the sound of his glass meet the surface of his vanity table. Surprised by the sound, his attention darts to the glass. Again he touches the glass and hears the sound. At first he responds with childlike curiosity. Wonderment, however, turns into panic when he discovers he has no voice. As Valentin gets up we hear the sound of his chair shift against the wood floor. Screaming into the mirror he falls back in fear, startling his dog whose bark draws his attention. The ring of a telephone then shifts his gaze and we cut to a canted angle close-up of the rotary phone. Here we have the purest expression of Münsterberg's filmic conception of attention, with the attention-grabbing stimulus coming notably as a sound. As each sound is heard in relative isolation, the effect in essence mirrors aurally what is achieved visually by means of the close-up.

Outside his dressing room, Valentin turns toward the sound of a giggling dancer, then another, then three, then a dozen, passing him by on the studio lot. Next, the sound of the breeze and the graceful fall of a feather. However, when the feather reaches the ground we hear the sound of an explosion. In close-up Valentin awakens. It was all a dream. The ability to capture the subjective imaginings of the dreamer is described by Münsterberg as one of the innate

FIGURE 1.2 In a dream sequence, silent film actor George Valentin (Jean Dujardin) discovers he has no voice in *The Artist* (Michel Hazanavicius, Studio 37/La Petite Reine, 2011). Digital frame enlargement.

strengths of the filmic medium. Like the flashback that transports us to the past and the flash-forward that brings us to the future, the dream sequence reveals the subjective thoughts and feelings of a character in the form of his dreams.

The message of this scene is clear. Like Chaplin during the production of *City Lights*, Valentin is haunted by the possibility of being displaced by the talkie. Curiously, however, the sounds that terrorize him were increasingly present in theaters, given the transition to sound. In *The Photoplay*, Münsterberg describes varied sound effects already employed in many movie theaters. "We hear the firing of a gun, the whistling of a locomotive, ships' bells, or the ambulance gong, or the barking dog, or the noise when Charlie Chaplin falls downstairs" (205). In the 1910s and 1920s however, theater managers performed sound effects live, sometimes using patented devices, as a kitschy ploy to bring in audiences. For Münsterberg such effects were unwelcome "intrusions" in that their aim was mimetic, not aesthetic. In this way we might interpret Valentin's reaction to these sounds as not merely his projected fear of the talkies, but as the response of an artist to a technology that threatens the very nature and integrity of his art.

2

Vachel Lindsay

Theory of Movie Hieroglyphics

TOM GUNNING

The Art of the Moving Picture can be considered the first American book of film theory, perhaps even the first such book internationally.[1] I caution film history students to never use the word "first," since so many facts in early film history remain unknown. But there is little question that Vachel Lindsay's book, finished in 1915 and published early in 1916, was the first book-length work to offer a theory of the new medium. This priority, coupled with the fact its author was a well-known poet, probably rescued it from obscurity. Every discipline wants an origin and Lindsay supplies a somewhat unruly one for film theory. Lindsay also wrote a series of articles on film during 1917 for *The New Republic*, a journal of progressive politics and culture (see "Movies"; "Progress"; "Queen": "Train"; "Venus"). In the 1920s he wrote a sequel to his book, which was never published in his lifetime. Myron Lounsbury edited the manuscript and published it with commentary in 1995 as *The Progress and Poetry of the Movies*. These works develop ideas set out in *The Art of the Moving Picture*, which remains the central text for Lindsay's theory of film.

Born in Springfield, Illinois, Lindsay (1879–1931) studied art in Chicago and New York. One of his teachers, the painter Robert Henri, advised him to pursue poetry, inspired by hearing him recite (and underwhelmed by what he saw of his visual art). Initially his poetry brought him no great success. Envisioning a renewed American democracy founded in Populism, Lindsay embarked on long walking tours. He "bartered his poems for bread" (to paraphrase the title of one of his books), reciting his lyrics to farmers or small-town entrepreneurs in exchange for a night's hospitality. Lindsay took three such "tramps" between 1905 and 1912, inaugurating a tradition of trying to get in touch with the true America directly, from the wanderings of the Depression (such as folksinger Woody Guthrie's) to the road trips of the 1950s and 1960s (Jack Kerouac's *On the*

Road, Peter Fonda and Dennis Hopper's *Easy Rider* [1969]) (for an account of one such tramp, including a fine biographical essay by Robert F. Sayre, see *Adventures*).

His account of these "tramps" drew the attention of Harriet Monroe, editor of the Chicago-based magazine *Poetry*, which was fostering a revolution in modern verse. In 1913 *Poetry* published one of Lindsay's poems, "General Booth Enters Heaven," about the founder of the Salvation Army, set to the rhythm of the bass drum that this missionary group used to attract converts from the heart of the slums. Lindsay would recite this and other poems (especially "The Congo") in a style that borrowed syncopated rhythms from jazz and ragtime, college football cheers and revivalist preaching, chanting and singing lines and often accompanying himself on a tom-tom or tambourine. He became something of a sensation, and even attracted the attention of President Woodrow Wilson who had him recite before his cabinet. However, Lindsay soon found his style of enthusiastic bombast out of synch with the evolution of modern poetry. Many younger poets (like Ezra Pound, who also published in *Poetry*) found his verse increasingly embarrassing. As the Progressivist political agenda of radical reform was abandoned after World War I, and the Populist celebration of rural life declined in the Jazz Age of the '20s, Lindsay seemed anachronistic. Health and money problems hounded him throughout the decade and he committed suicide in 1931.

Lindsay preached "the Gospel of Beauty," a utopian vision that linked social reforms to a new democratic aesthetics. He believed architecture and city planning could overcome the crassness and inhumanity of an America increasingly based in capitalist profit and industrial expansion. Lindsay combined elements we now see as antithetical. He believed in Prohibition, and saw the movies as a "substitute for the saloon." He argued for racial equality, yet his poem "The Congo: A Study of the Negro Race," intended as a plea for racial tolerance, now seems riddled with racial stereotypes. He was a socialist, but promoted utopian rural communities rather than the organized industrial production that characterizes Marxism. He was strongly influenced by Christian missionary movements, but devised a "private theology" which incorporated Swedenborgian, Buddhist, and Hindu beliefs, and awaited an apocalyptic renewal based in his native Springfield that would include the resurrection of Johnny Appleseed. In some ways he anticipated the New Age thinking and utopianism of the 1960s. His thought is often naïve, perhaps a bit mad, but always included a vital sense of humor.

Movies were relatively new in 1916. Invented in the 1890s, for their first decade movies offered a gradually fading novelty, mainly shown in vaudeville houses. After 1906, small theaters appeared across the country that showed movies at a price working men could afford (and take their family)—a nickel—hence the term "nickelodeon" (nickel theater). Tapping a new audience for commercial entertainment, thousands of nickelodeons appeared by 1908; a small city like Springfield had at least a dozen by 1910. Patronized by the working class, nickelodeons alarmed guardians of official culture, some of whom wanted to close them down as immoral and unhealthy. However, a few intellectuals and artists, like Lindsay, saw movies as a vibrant force in American culture. Promoters of the movies defended them as "democracy's theaters," and this appealed to Lindsay's progressive social sensibilities. Just as he hoped reform of civic design would rescue American culture from crass commercialism, Lindsay wanted to celebrate the movies and to "uplift" them, to raise them to an art.

The Art of the Nickelodeon

Lindsay's book is frankly rather odd. In contrast to most film theorists, he projects a personal, even eccentric, voice. We are constantly reminded that the author is a poet, and that he thinks of poetry as a realm of fanciful imagination. Lindsay's mission might be described as re-enchanting modernity, seeing the innovations of technology from a fairytale perspective, so that electricity, locomotives, city lighting, and the new urban architecture of plate glass could be envisioned as what he calls "a picture of fairy splendor." Movies played an essential role in Lindsay's re-enchantment, offering a means of awakening audiences to the wonder contained in modern daily life. But Lindsay was also aware that for the most part modernity was headed in the opposite direction from enchantment, toward the standardization of a commodity culture. Especially in the 1920s, he felt that Hollywood was engaged in a struggle between the possibilities of a new vision and the routines of an industry dedicated to profit, which was destroying the promise of the new art form.

The first principle of Lindsay's theory appears emblazoned in his title: "The *Art* of the Moving Picture." Like a political orator, Lindsay proclaimed: "Let us take for our platform this sentence: THE MOTION PICTURE ART IS A GREAT HIGH ART, NOT A PROCESS OF COMMERCIAL MANUFACTURE" (*Art* 45). Claiming movies as a "great high art" may not seem radical today, but in 1915 it was. The U.S. Supreme Court ruled in 1915 that motion pictures could not claim the protection of the First Amendment, since movies were not a mode suitable for the expression of ideas. Against this grain, Lindsay not only claimed movies as an art form but argued they should receive broad institutional recognition and support. Art museums and universities, he declared, should establish collections of films for use in teaching film as an art form, something not realized until the formation of the Museum of Modern Art's film department in the 1930s.

In 1915, movies were undergoing radical redefinition and transformation. Lindsay wanted to shape this transformation. During the nickelodeon era, films had rarely lasted more than fifteen or twenty minutes; a nickelodeon program included three to five separate films. Around 1913, films began to stretch to "feature length," lasting an hour or more. Lindsay was ambivalent about this change, feeling that longer films contributed to eyestrain and mental exhaustion.

He praised the shorter films for their artistic economy: "The best of the old one-reel Biographs of Griffith contained more in twenty minutes than these ambitious incontinent six reel displays give in two hours" (*Art* 73–74). In 1915, Lindsay in some ways was looking back to a vanishing era: he is the theorist of the nickelodeon era.

The nickelodeon provided a space in which primarily working-class communities met and conversed with each other before—and even during—the film (Hansen, *Babel*; Rosenzweig 191–208). Lindsay advocated "A Conversational Theater" where film would be accompanied by the "buzzing commentary of the audience" rather than an orchestra. He hoped to reformulate the community viewing of the nickelodeon for a new era and raise it to a level of critical discourse (*Art* 224–225). Like many of his recommendations, this rubbed against the grain of the movies' dominant development. The audience for the new picture palaces that began to appear across the country in 1913–1915, elbowing out the smaller nickelodeons, were kept quiet by uniformed ushers. The nickelodeon gave Lindsay his fundamental vision forged in the earlier mode of reception. The movies offered an aesthetic experience that challenged dominant elitist forms of culture based in reading and the printed word, through a new form of picture-writing immediately understandable, even by children or illiterate immigrants. This new visual communication, Lindsay claimed, should form the basis of a new democratic art. Lindsay's book contains not only an early appreciation of "the art of moving pictures" but a theory, not always fully articulated, of film's new means of communication and power over an audience. It offers a theory of film language and of the psychology of the spectator, two topics which will dominate later film theory.

The Primitive and Hieroglyphics

Lindsay's theory expresses less simple nostalgia for the nickelodeon than a vision of cinema as the modern avatar of ancient and primitive impulses. Rachel O. Moore first isolated the crucial role that the "primitive" plays in much of film theory and saw Lindsay as its earliest example. Moore claims film theorists have used the trope of the primitive to explain the unique modes of signification of the cinema and its magical effects. Paradoxically, this return to the primitive comes through modern technology. Moore explains: "Above all, Lindsay shares with other great primitivists a particularly modern notion that the primitive (in this case the primitive art form he calls the photoplay) produces a step backward and a step forward at the same time" (58). Lindsay understood this. Stressing the novelty of Edison's invention of moving pictures (first named the "kinetoscope": the view of motion) Lindsay proclaimed, "And the invention, the kinetoscope, which affects or will affect as many people as the guns of Europe, is not yet understood in its powers, particularly those of bringing back the primitive in a big rich way. The primitive is always a new and higher beginning to the man who understands it" (*Art* 290).

Bringing together new technology, a democratic audience, and a new form of picture-writing, the movies promised to tap and transform this primitive energy.

Lindsay located the means of transforming primitive energy in his central theoretical concept: the hieroglyphic. Hieroglyphics form the most seductive and elusive of Lindsay's concepts, rightfully the center of later commentary. The hieroglyphic has been described as anticipating Marshall McLuhan's theory of the end of print culture, as cueing McLuhan through the provocative claim, "Edison is the new Gutenberg. He has invented the new printing" (*Art* 252; for an early comparison to McLuhan see Kaufmann's "Introduction" to *Art*). Lindsay's description of the cinema as a new form of communication, based in hieroglyphics, has some resonance with McLuhan's claim of historical transformations of media. However, many differences exist (including Lindsay's and McLuhan's contrasting attitudes toward cinema—although they were dealing with very different periods). But both thinkers make a strong differentiation between writing based in the phonetic alphabet and the system of hieroglyphics.

Interest in hieroglyphics began in late antiquity, when the Egyptian system of writing, which used pictographs, was no longer understood. Attempts to decode hieroglyphics (which were actually a system of writing that was partly phonetic and partly based in ideograms) claimed that they concealed a mystical system of allegories. This mystical understanding of Egyptian hieroglyphics persisted for as long as the writing eluded translation, which was accomplished only in 1822, by Champollion with the aid of the Rosetta Stone. To a certain extent, translation demystified hieroglyphics. However, the dream of a form of writing that replaced the abstract figures of the alphabet with a series of pictures fascinated scholars and poets. The Romantics, from the German poet Novalis to Edgar Allan Poe, maintained a mystical belief that a form of writing existed that held magical powers and revealed deep secrets of nature (see Irwin; Iverson). An awareness of Chinese ideograms, which also have a pictorial basis and correspond to ideas rather than sounds, expanded the understanding of the plurality of writings and their poetic possibilities. The Chinese ideogram directly inspired Lindsay's contemporary (and antagonist) Ezra Pound's theory of Imagist poetry. Ideograms would also be taken up and applied to cinema by Soviet filmmaker and theorist Sergei Eisenstein.

For Lindsay, hieroglyphics provided the bridge between modern technology and primitive energies. He said in the '20s: "Remember we are establishing a new alphabet or a very very old one" (*Progress and Poetry* 246). The occultists and Romantics had been fascinated by the mysterious nature of Egyptian hieroglyphics, their obscurity. For Lindsay the picture writing of the cinema was revolutionary due to its clarity: the cinema used pictures that everyone could understand.

As Miriam Hansen has claimed, for Lindsay the cinema offered a universal language, accessible to all (77–78). Although Lindsay had studied Egyptian hieroglyphics, he eccentrically believed that their imagistic quality allowed them to be directly understood; he claimed a layman could understand the Egyptian hieroglyphic text known as *The Book of the Dead*, if he or she had been watching enough movies! Although taken literally this claim is absurd, it represented Lindsay's belief in communicating through moving pictures. This is a major step in film theory, even if the more scientifically argued theory of Hugo Münsterberg in *The Photoplay: A Psychological Study* and Eisenstein's more linguistically sophisticated analysis of montage would take it further than Lindsay could.

"The invention of the photoplay," Lindsay said, "is as great a step as was the beginning of picture-writing in the stone age. And the cave-men and women of our slums seem to be the people most affected by this novelty" (*Art* 199). Comparing slum-dwellers (who had made up the greatest proportion of nickelodeon audiences) to "cave-men," Lindsay indicated the primitive appeal of the movies, accessible to the uneducated, even the illiterate. This appeal could become a means of transformation as "the cave-man reader of pictures is given a chance to admit light into his mind" (244). Movies would provide the medium for social transformation that Lindsay called "the Gospel of Beauty." Lindsay saw in the popularity of movies "an astonishing assembly of cave-men crawling out of their shelters to exhibit for the first time in history a common interest on a tremendous scale in an art form" (235).

For Lindsay the cinema introduced a revolution in which word and book culture would be replaced by an art and language of pictures. "A tribe that has thought in words since the days when it worshipped Thor and told legends of the cunning tongue of Loki, suddenly begins to think in pictures" (*Art* 213). Thinking in pictures—hieroglyphics—formed the basis of Lindsay's film theory, conceiving of the movies not merely as a way to represent the world but as a new system of thought. The main inspiration for movies, he claimed, should come from pictures rather than words. He argued for a minimal use of intertitles (words appearing on the screen), if not their entire elimination. Further, he argued into the '20s that the movies should be considered primarily as a pictorial art, avoiding the dominant models of the novel or the stage and instead obeying what he called "not dramatic logic but tableau logic" (186).

He also stresses the "moving" in "moving pictures." The cinematic hieroglyphic is an image whose structure and context allows it to substitute for words. The flow of images defines their significance, as the viewer moves from one image to the next, thus creating a new syntax specific to film. Lindsay never used the word "editing," which had not yet entered into the vocabulary of film criticism. But he refers to the patterns of alternation between images and refers to them as "conversations." Here lies the essence of his concept of thinking in pictures. Images integrate with each other, creating in the viewer a conversation in which communication no longer needs words but can articulate meanings simply through the succession of images. Lindsay saw motion pictures as the leader in a broad transformation into a modern hieroglyphic culture including billboards, comic strips, and magazine advertising. In the 1920s Lindsay clarified this concept in this way:

> This way of thinking from picture to picture, of leaping from vision to vision, without sound, without gesture, without the use of English, with as little use of type as possible, this tendency increasing every hour must be ruled by the motion picture, if it is to have any direction and leading, because the film art is so much more powerful than all the rest, by reason of the occult elements of motion and light. (*Progress and Poetry* 183)

Lindsay underscored the method of pictorial communication that moving pictures share with modern culture, as well as cinema's unique power of movement and illumination. He described the new modern American culture as "speed-mad" and saw the movies as the medium that could keep up with this dangerous energy and perhaps tame it. Films could penetrate into the most primitive aspect of human consciousness and illuminate and stimulate viewers. "Though the picture be the veriest mess, the light and movement cause the beholder to do a little reptilian thinking" (*Art* 236). Films grabbed viewers more primordially than any other medium, both visually and viscerally, unleashing a new power: "The key-words of the stage are *passion* and *character*; of the photoplay, *splendor* and *speed*" (193).

The Art of Moving Picture contains a fanciful section that proposes film scenarios based on the pictorial associations of specific Egyptian hieroglyphics, and recommends writers could devise film scenarios by arranging sets of hieroglyphics. Thinking in pictures highlights a rule of cinematic narrative that Lindsay is one of the first to describe: that a story needs a network of visual images to convey its plot and to enthrall its viewer. Lindsay explained hieroglyphics as clearly expressed visual meanings in one of his reviews for *The New Republic* of the 1917 Mary Pickford film *A Romance of the Redwoods*. In this western directed by Cecil B. De Mille, Pickford plays Jenny, a spunky young woman, who discovers the identity of a notorious bandit, Black Brown, and then reforms him. Lindsay describes how the story is conveyed through the use of objects that become significant hieroglyphics:

> Now note the hieroglyphics. The arrow hole in the uncle's bloody papers, a black-snake whip, Jenny's little derringer, Brown's six shooter, the gambling paraphernalia, the silk hat of the boss gambler, the dancing shadows on the doorways, all enable these episodes to be vividly given with few printed words on the screen. . . . At breakfast everything from griddle cakes to an apron is picture-writing to tell the finely graded progress of

> Jenny's conquest of the tough. . . . Later, doing Brown's mending, the lady finds a handkerchief mask, with eyeholes complete. This mask is as much the headline hieroglyphic of Brown as the derringer is of Jenny. . . . Meanwhile Black Brown with this wicked gold buys her a doll, in humorous allusion to her size, but actually the symbol of his tenderness for her, the third outstanding hieroglyphic of the piece. ("Queen")

Movie hieroglyphics visually convey information crucial to the plot through objects (the mask which reveals Brown is a bandit), or aspects of character (the derringer, which shows Jenny's determination to defend herself in the wild west); or define a key emotion of the film (the doll, which Lindsay reads as revealing Brown's love for Jenny). Such use of hieroglyphics may sound more like advice to screenwriters than film theory, but Lindsay makes an essential theoretical point too often forgotten: that films tell stories visually and that this involves a new way of thinking for the spectator, following a picture language, more immediate and more complex than words.

The power of hieroglyphics explains Lindsay's much-repeated claim that objects and even landscapes often become the most important actors in films. The magic of moving pictures animates the inanimate: "It is a quality, not a defect, of all photoplays that human beings tend to become dolls and mechanisms and dolls and mechanisms tend to become human" (*Art* 53). This apparent paradox is explained by the ability of the hieroglyphic method to give human beings not simply the appearance of life and motion but a significance that tends to objectify them. Likewise, by becoming significant, things seem to take on a life of their own. One wishes that screenwriters today, rather than figuring out "plot points," might use Lindsay's theory and build their scripts from images, as much as from characters and dialogue.

Describing his exercise in scenario writing through hieroglyphic arrangements, Lindsay indicates that hieroglyphics have two meanings, one literal and one more abstract (*Art* 200). The ideal screenplay will intertwine the more common literal meanings with occasional but deeply significant abstract or mysterious significance. D. W. Griffith emerged as an ideal filmmaker for Lindsay, equally able to use the closer framing, that is such a key element of film syntax, to emphasize a literal point in the plot (e.g., the bandit's mask) or to strike a more mysterious allegorical meaning, such as the close-up of a spider's web that Lindsay describes in Griffith's Poe pastiche *The Avenging Conscience* (1914) as an image of the cruelty inherent in nature (152–153).

Applied Hieroglyphics

Applying film theory to specific films sometimes seems elusive, but Lindsay's ideas were firmly rooted in the way films work. His books offered pioneer exercises in film analysis as much as film theory. The longest section of *The Progress and Poetry of the Movies* gives a detailed analysis of the 1924 Douglas Fairbanks film *The Thief of Bagdad* that not only describes the film's style in detail but introduces the method of the shot-by-shot analysis of sequences. *The Art of The Moving Picture* analyzes a number of key films, including Griffith's *The Battle* (1911), *The Avenging Conscience*, and *Judith of Bethulia* (1914). His *New Republic* articles provided detailed reviews of several films. Hieroglyphics provides not only a theory of silent film but a method of analysis.

Take almost any silent film and isolate the hieroglyphics and you will see the usefulness of Lindsay's methods. Think of the doorman's coat in *The Last Laugh* (1924), the Odessa steps in *Potemkin* (1925), the gold tooth in *Greed* (1924), the rocking cradle in *Intolerance* (1916). These are not just significant images but keys to their films' meanings and structures. As a tool of analysis, a hieroglyphic plays several roles. First, it stands out as an image, emphasized through composition and repetition. Second, it carries a strong significance, partly visualizing the plot (what Lindsay calls its literal meaning) but also carrying a freight of metaphor (Lindsay's "abstract" or "spirit-meaning"), opening it up to further interpretation. In this way an ordinary object in a film becomes complex. As Lindsay claimed, "The more fastidious photoplay audience that uses the hieroglyphic hypothesis in analyzing the film before it, will acquire a new tolerance and understanding of the avalanche of photoplay conceptions, and find a promise of beauty in what have been properly classed as mediocre and stereotyped productions" (*Art* 209).

Consider a central hieroglyphic of DeMille's *A Romance of the Redwoods:* the doll. When a group of vigilantes discover Brown's identity as a stagecoach robber, they come to his cabin to lynch him. Jenny pleads for his life, but the lynch party is unmoved and lock her in a storeroom. There she sees the doll Brown had given her. She strips off its clothes and emerges displaying them to the lynch mob as an indication she is about to become a mother. This claim of pregnancy is tricky, since it indicates premarital sex (although in fact the viewer knows Jenny has remained chaste). Hieroglyphics are often inspired by censorship. No dialogue title spells out Jenny's claim of pregnancy. It is conveyed entirely by the doll clothes and the reactions of the vigilantes, a perfect example of images replacing words. But more occurs here, a skein of associations and connotations that the viewer intuits directly and that the method of hieroglyphic analysis can unravel. The doll initially referred to Brown's view of Jenny as a "little girl," both in stature and youth. Stripping it and displaying its clothes as the sign of maternity, she resolutely becomes a woman. She declares not only her love for Brown by saving his life with a lie but her resolve to become his wife and form a family with him. Jenny is no longer playing house, but has grown up. A clichéd plot resolution, perhaps, but accomplished with imagistic economy and beauty.

But are hieroglyphics relevant to films made after the silent era? Or are they simply a visual sign system that compensates for the lack of spoken dialogue in silent film? Lindsay admitted the role silence played in fostering the new picture-language of film. So, are hieroglyphics relevant in the sound era? I would claim: absolutely. The strongest directors of the sound era, such as Alfred Hitchcock, were masters of hieroglyphics. As Jean-Luc Godard has claimed, we may forget the plot of Hitchcock's films, but we remember "a glass of milk, the

FIGURE 2.1 A glass of milk: a Hitchcock hieroglyphic in *Suspicion* (Vanguard/RKO, 1941). Digital frame enlargement.

sails of a windmill, a hairbrush, . . . a row of bottles, a pair of glasses, a sheet of music, a bunch of keys" (4:82; my translation).

These unforgettable objects featured in Hitchcock's films certainly convey turning points in his plots, but they also point beyond literal meanings to a network of visual associations. They are Hitchcock's hieroglyphics. Lindsay's concept remains central to our experience of films; filmmakers continue not only to work within the modes of picture-thinking that Lindsay was perhaps the first to describe but to expand and explore new pathways in this visual terrain. I will close with a brief consideration of a film I consider one of the most powerful films of the past decade, Terrence Malick's *Tree of Life* (2011).

Tree of Life

Tree of Life follows a family in 1950s Texas, focusing on a period from the birth of their first child to about a decade later. Interwoven with this very elliptically presented chronicle is a prologue dealing with the origins of the cosmos, visualizing the elements (water, air, earth, and fire) and the evolution of life, from single cells through diverse animal forms. This sequence blends violence and beauty with microscopic and macrocosmic scales of shots. Throughout the all-too-human family drama, Malick's imagery reminds us of the elemental forces of nature, now framed within a domestic context: light filtered through windows and curtains, candles held by human hands, and especially a tree in the family yard on which the boys climb and swing. Malick's cutting rarely plays out extended dramatic scenes but rather jump-cuts, juxtaposing gestures and shots imagistically. We are compelled to see these shots not simply as elements of a dramatic scene that fit together seamlessly but as resonant images reaching beyond the immediate situation, like bits of sense-memory recalled suddenly.

Malick's film appears less as a narrative based in a novel or stage play (although it is rich in character, incident, and setting) than as a series of visually heightened images. It seems to fulfill one of Lindsay's prophecies of the movies in 1916, that film could respond to new movements in poetry and produce a cinema of Imagism (*Art* 267–268). Malick's images take on the qualities of hieroglyphics, not simply as symbols but rather carrying the complex of meanings and sensations that an image composed of light and movement can summon up in the viewer. Rather than the explicit communication of a specific meaning that Eisenstein claims the juxtaposition of montage allows, we might return to Lindsay's idea of a conversation between images. In *The New Republic* Lindsay described the intercutting of different historical periods in *Intolerance*, as a conversation:

> Babylon is shown signaling across the ages to Judea, and there is many a message that is not printed out in the film. . . . And in like manner the

FIGURE 2.2 Boys climbing in Terrence Malick's *Tree of Life* (Cottonwood, 2011). Digital frame enlargement.

> days of St. Bartholomew and of the crucifixion signal back to Babylon sharp or vague or subtle messages. The little factory couple in the modern street scene . . . seems to wave their hands back to Babylon amid the orchestra of ancient memories. ("Progress" 76)

In *Tree of Life* Malick expands the context of a family drama into a conversation with the nature of the cosmos, orchestrating personal and element memory through the unique devices of the cinema—not only visualization, but the syntax of images and their rhythms of light and movement.

Lindsay's utopian hope for the cinema lay not only in the mastery of picture-writing for storytelling but in the new art form as a medium of vision: "We have maintained that the kinetoscope in the hands of artists is a higher form of picture writing. In the hands of prophet-wizards it will be a higher form of vision-seeing" (*Art* 299). Few filmmakers would acknowledge this aspiration, but I think it offers one way to understand Malick's film, and envision the possible scope of Lindsay's film theory.

NOTE

1. This is a reprint with an introduction by Stanley Kauffmann of the 1922 revised edition. The revised edition added a new foreword by George William Eggers and a new opening chapter by Lindsay (pages 1–35 of this edition). It cut some of the opening of the original 1916 edition (basically the first seven pages). The bulk of the book is substantially the same in the 1916 and 1922 editions. The 1916 edition is available online from Google Books.

3

Béla Balázs

Film Aesthetics and the Rituals of Romance

STEVEN WOODWARD

Part of the pan-European Jewish intelligentsia of the early twentieth century who were a driving force in both cultural modernism and Marxist-inspired politics, between 1919 and 1945 living in exile from his native Hungary in Vienna, then Berlin, and later Moscow, Béla Balázs (1884–1949) wrote in many different fields and forms—poetry, drama, fairy tales, journalism—before becoming one of film's first great theorists. As noted by Gertrud Koch, he was philosophically grounded in the *Lebensphilosophie* (philosophy of life) of Georg Simmel and Henri Bergson, animated by Marxist thinking and the politics of the short-lived Hungarian Soviet Republic in which he played an important role, and immersed in the culture of popular film as a critic for newspapers in Vienna and Berlin. Even before the Soviet theorist-filmmakers, he championed the movies as "a material realization within contemporary popular culture of revolutionary ideals" (Carter xxiii), though he was far more catholic in his range of tastes, and more lucid and less polemical in his theorizing.

Balázs published three books of film theory at three different moments in the development of the movies, between 1924 and 1948 (another volume appearing only in Russian in 1945 was subsequently revised into the third book). For each, he was faced with the daunting problem of the shifting nature of the medium prompted by such technical developments as the coming of sound and the increasing veracity of color, each of which rebooted the already developed "form-language" of the cinema. *Visible Man* (*Der sichtbare Mensch*, 1924) appeared in the silent period and begins with a defense of theory. *The Spirit of Film* (*Der Geist des Films*, 1930) was published shortly after the introduction of the talkies, as Balázs felt a renewed urgency to prove that film's "'purely visual' values are among its best" (131). His final book, *Theory of the Film* (*Filmkultúra: A film müvészetfilozófiája*, 1948; English translation 1952) appeared after World War II, when Balázs realized that while film had proven itself to be "*the* popular art of our century," its aesthetics, its form-language, remained largely unknown and unexamined by its audience, who were therefore "at the mercy of perhaps the greatest intellectual and spiritual influence of our age as to some blind and irresistible elemental force" (17).

Known today by students of film theory only through short excerpts from chapters 6 through 8 of that final book—his only writing available in English until very recently—Balázs appears as a formalist and, correspondingly, as a harbinger of auteur theory; the political dimensions of his theory are totally elided. Admittedly, there is a strong strain of formalism throughout his work. *Visible Man* proposes that film, despite its photographic basis, can only be an art to the degree that it is "unfaithful to nature," for "Art actually consists in reduction" (*Visible* 78), sometimes to one sensory field, like sight, and even to one element within that field, as with painting's emphasis on color. Furthermore, the filmmaker must harness not the reproductive but the productive power of the cinema. Balázs wrote most persistently and extensively about three particular spheres of cinema's productivity: the close-up, set-up (by which he means both mise-en-scène and cinematography), and montage. His last book would circle back to exactly the same terrain: "What are the effects which are born only on the celluloid, are born only in the act of projecting the film on to the screen? What is it that the film does not reproduce but produce, and through which it becomes an independent, basically new art after all?" (*Theory* 46). The answer is multiple: new subjects are opened up by the very mobility of the camera; camera angle and shot length offer expressive views of a subject; the combination of shots through montage releases the "latent meaning" of the individual shot and produces rhythmic effects and associations (*Spirit* 123); and the whole procedure creates a powerful and shifting viewer identification with characters. Balázs covered all of these ideas—many of which we might now consider the truisms of film analysis—in considerable detail in each one of his books, often repeating verbatim passages from one book to another, sometimes offering a slightly different formulation (often in response to a critical exchange with another theorist).

What makes Balázs's books more than just a survey of film's "form-language," as he called its range of medium-specific signifying practices, is an imperative that guides the whole, an overarching principle beyond the three productive spheres: filmmakers must reveal the "physiognomy" of things, make the world animate, reveal a human meaning in all of creation, meld the objective with the subjective. The image always conveys an intention, is never purely objective, so that even the most mechanical image "produced with no particular goal in mind . . . testifies to an inner attitude, even if it be one of dull inertia or inner blindness" (*Spirit* 115), as is typical of the commercial cinema. "The artist's gaze, in contrast, sees meaning, and his images acquire symbolic overtones, become metaphors and allegories through the camera set-up" (*Spirit* 115). Today, Balázs is mostly associated with that imperative and with his theory of the close-up, in particular his idea that the close-up of the human face presents us with a "silent soliloquy" through its "microphysiognomy."

However, to understand the broader, political scope of Balázs's theory, we need to understand the source of this imperative in a notion of cultural and linguistic evolution that underpins his whole schema, that links his ideas to those of dialectical materialism, and that was first expressed in the titular chapter of *Visible Man*. Here, he claims that the origins of language are in expressive movements, not sounds. The movements of our tongue and lips were originally just one small part of a full range of bodily expressivity, with the sounds produced being only "a secondary phenomenon, one subsequently exploited for practical purposes. The immediately visible spirit was then transformed into a mediated audible spirit" (11). After 500 years of print-based culture, a secondary mediation of the audible spirit, we have almost entirely lost the expressive dimensions of the body, with the exception of our face, which "has now come to resemble a clumsy little semaphore of the soul, sticking up in the air and signalling as best it may" (10). Instead we are bound by language-based abstractions (for Marx, reifications) that cannot hope to convey the full range of the human spirit, for "the language of gestures is the true mother tongue of mankind" (11). Neither dance nor sport can reacquaint us with that language. Only the movies by virtue of their silence are forced to excavate that lost language in the actors' performances as they are mediated through set-up and arranged in montage, with extraordinarily utopian consequences: humanity will be delivered from its alienated state and will be united by a shared language. The movies hold out the hope of delivering us back to a universal kinship: "The cinematograph is a machine that in its own way will create a living, concrete internationalism: *the unique, shared psyche of the white man* [original emphasis]. We can go further. By suggesting a uniform ideal of beauty as the universal goal of selective breeding, the film will help to produce a uniform type of the white race" (14).

Amazingly, the Jewish socialist Balázs clearly had no apprehension of how the fascistic means he invokes toward the desired end of universal kinship would play out across Europe in the next few decades. (He was equally, appallingly pragmatic about the global hegemony of Hollywood, seeing it as necessary to realizing film's utopian promise of a "redemption from the curse of Babel" [*Visible* 14].) More than twenty years later, Balázs simply suppressed the emphasis on white universality, speaking in *Theory of the Film* more ambiguously of "the development towards an international universal humanity" (45). For Balázs, human experiences expressed in bodily gestures were "not rational, conceptual contents" (*Theory* 42), but he did ultimately insist, "Let no one think that I want to bring back the culture of movement and gesture *in place of* the culture of words, for neither can be a substitute for the other . . . fascism has shown us where the tendency to reduce human culture to subconscious emotions in place of clear concepts would lead humanity" (43; emphasis mine).

For Balázs, though, the cinema would always embody the culture of movement and gesture. Synchronized sound did not integrate into the existing cinema a culture of words, but simply overwhelmed it. Thus, from his first to his last book, Balázs emphasizes the visual dimension, in particular those aspects of the cinema that offer the surest route to recovering the lost universal language: the close-up, especially of the human face; and the world seen physiognomically, whether through expressionism (using distortions of cinematography or mise-en-scène) or impressionism (depending upon selective shots with strong associations), or through montage.

Already in *Visible Man* Balázs delineates the specificity of the new medium in terms of the close-up, "film's true terrain," which acts as a "magnifying glass" to reveal the "individual cells of life" and as an instrument to enable us to hear "the individual voices of all things which go to make up the great symphony" (38). Despite his reference to a "magnifying glass," Balázs is not speaking of a minute scientific mapping of the objective world. His point is that the close-up is a focalized view. It is "the art of emphasis," expressing "not so much . . . a good eye as . . . a good heart" (39), the love of the narrator for the small thing that in everyday life goes unnoticed or unheeded. Indeed, the enthusiasm of audiences for the cinema stems from their awareness that "*what matters in film is not the storyline but the lyrical element*" (33; original emphasis).

That lyrical element can come from the way the filmmaker frames an object or even more powerfully frames a performer's face in close-up, since the face still instinctively, unconsciously speaks the lost universal language. Overcoming the slow, sequential nature of the lyric poem, the close-up of a face can give us the "harmony" of complex emotions in an instant, the "legato" of their fleeting transformations, and is far more "polyphonic" than words can ever be (34). Thus, Balázs ends *Visible Man* by celebrating an actress, not a filmmaker, in the most superlative terms: "It is Asta Nielsen, and she alone, who is capable of restoring our faith and our conviction" (87), as in *Absturz* (Ludwig Wolff, 1923) in which she conveys "trembling hope, mortal panic, eyes shrieking for help so loudly that you feel deafened; then tears flow—visible, real tears—pouring down her emaciated cheeks, which suddenly wither before our very eyes, and we witness the death of a soul" (90). For Balázs, the aesthetics of such film practice cannot be separated from the politics: Nielsen's restoration of a visible expressivity of the soul is a powerful counter to the abstracting tendencies endemic to literary culture and capitalism. Any narrative that allows for such moments of spiritual revelation is inherently progressive, if not revolutionary.

Indeed, all things have a spirit that the camera can and must reveal. In the section of *Visible Man* entitled "The Face of Things," Balázs explains that the ability to perceive "*the living physiognomy that all things possess*" (46; emphasis in original) is the natural state of children, but adults perceive these "faces" only when they are pushed out from behind the "veil of our traditional, abstract way of seeing" (46). Film can and must restore the "mysterious play of expressions" of things through either "naturalistic expressionism" that distorts the world through composition alone or the "object world's demonic play of features," as in films like Robert Wiene's *The Cabinet of Dr. Caligari* (1920) (47). Employing some degree of expressionism is an imperative for all filmmakers, he insists: "No director today can still tolerate a lifeless background, a neutral milieu; instead, he attempts to animate the entire screen with the same mood that animates the faces of his actors" (47). However, he allows for an alternative approach to an expressionistic rendering of the physiognomy of things: impressionism, which offers carefully selected, naturalistic fragments, leaving the viewer to complete the picture and "imbue the scene with his own momentary mood" (51).

The Docks of New York

In principle, Balázs should have been extraordinarily responsive to the silent films of Josef von Sternberg, the Austrian-American director renowned not for the plots of his films but for their unparalleled lyricism embodied in meticulous lighting and composition. Von Sternberg shared Balázs's belief in the need to animate the entire frame, insisting that "the greatest art in motion picture photography is to be able to give life to the dead space that exists between the lens and the subject before it" (325). He also shared Balázs's belief in the crucial role of cinema in recovering the spirit of things, observing in a 1968 Swedish TV documentary: "This will be known as the age of the cinema. . . . We have become familiar with the world; we know how people act and how people think."

Sternberg's body of films played a crucial role in defining the age of the cinema, especially during his "Paramount Period" between 1927 and 1935. *The Docks of New York* (1928) in particular was singled out by Andrew Sarris as the pinnacle of silent-film form (19). Essentially a *Kammerspielfilm* limited in setting to the boiler room of a ship and a bar and rooming house beside the East River (all built on set), the action of *The Docks of New York* is slight. On shore one night, Bill Roberts (George Bancroft), a brash and virile ship's stoker, saves from drowning and then marries a desperate prostitute, Mae (Betty Compson), leaves her the next morning, then unexpectedly returns later that day to prevent her imprisonment by submitting to his own.

Sternberg is able to convey the inner drama of undemonstrative characters through the expressionist and impressionist methods defined by Balázs, while consciously avoiding close-ups, which Sternberg viewed as neither unique to the cinema nor as important as camera movement and shifting viewpoint (30).

Take, for example, the impressionistic scene of Mae's attempted suicide as she leaps into the harbor, which Balázs praised for its novel rendition, crucial to its tragic effect:

> We at one point see only water, and in its reflection moonlight, clouds, the shadows of the night. Then a further shadow glimpsed in the reflection of the water. The shadow of a woman as it falls upwards from the depths of the mirror towards the surface. A great splash, and the shadow disappears amidst the shadows of the night. The mirror shot here encapsulates atmosphere and becomes poetic. (113–114)

Although Balázs makes no other reference to this film (and only one other, negative reference to Sternberg's other work) in his three books, *The Docks of New York* is charged with many of the productive techniques that Balázs identified, only a few of which can be mentioned here. Being studio-bound, the film necessarily depends heavily on impressionistic fragments. The arrival of Bill's ship is conveyed through a brief montage: an anchor dropping into the sea; a hand setting the engine-order telegraph to "Finished with Engine"; weary, soot- and sweat-soaked stokers ceasing their coal shoveling; mooring lines being guided around bollards. For Balázs, the choice of such fragments must serve the narrative *and* awaken metaphorical associations in the audience. In this case, the fragments point simultaneously to rest and entrapment, the opposing notions that will animate Bill's behavior in relation to Mae. As in so many of Sternberg's films the theme here is the foundering of sovereign masculinity on the reefs of an irresistibly alluring, erotic, and mysterious femininity.

Docks forcefully employs long shots. Despite the theoretical weight that he gave to the close-up, Balázs acknowledged the expressionistic effectiveness of longer shots, like the medium shot which "shows only the characters' immediate surroundings . . . [and thereby] enables a character to illuminate himself, as it were, with the emanation of his own soul. His milieu becomes a visible 'aura,' his physiognomy expands beyond the contours of his own body" (*Visible* 51).

Here, in Figure 3.1, for example, once Bill has rescued Mae from the water, we see him carrying her through the night and fog in a long shot, the steady passage of the unwavering man with the unconscious woman rendered all the more impressive by the murk, nets, and poles through which he navigates even if it foreshadows his willing entrapment at the film's end. Sternberg uses camera movement to similar effect, often tracking with Bill as he moves through barroom or dockside. Bill controls both space and narrative (until the closing long shot of Mae left alone in the courtroom). Balázs had noted this effect of the tracking camera in a section of *The Spirit of Film* entitled "Montage without Cutting": "When the camera follows a single figure over an extended period, the images that pass by in the background become a subjective montage of that person's impressions" (139).

FIGURE 3.1 Animating "dead space": Bill's path is littered with murk, nets, and poles, giving the substance of the world an expressive physiognomy. George Bancroft in *The Docks of New York* (Josef von Sternberg, Paramount, 1928). Digital frame enlargement.

So brilliant was Sternberg's formal control over the lurid story that *Docks* received enthusiastic responses in Paris in its regular showings at the depressing Vieux Colombier, a sometime experimental theater: "Its popularity has not adversely affected the appreciation of it by the studious minds of the avant-garde," wrote the *New York Times*. "It fulfills their requirements, somewhat obscure to this reviewer, of rhythm, plasticity and unity" (Gilbert 15). Yet, at precisely this moment the movie industry was undergoing a monumental upheaval, the movies a painful metamorphosis. In *The Spirit of Film*, Balázs tries to accommodate himself to the coming of synchronized sound, casting it as a crisis rather than a tragedy, a technological opportunity that might, like the cinema camera itself, open up "*new objects* of representation" (184). Those "new objects" might include the "many-voiced orchestra of life" (185) that we now know only as noise, or silence that we would hear in the sound cinema as "a screaming hush" (190–191). Contrapuntal use of image and sound (an idea perhaps borrowed from the 1928 "Statement on Sound" co-signed by Eisenstein, Pudovkin, and Alexandrov) "should awaken ideas and associations in our minds that the silent image on its own might have failed to arouse" (198). Asynchronous or offscreen sound could expand our sense of space beyond what we see in the visual image (205). In *Visible Man*, Balázs had envisioned the "absolute film" in which montage works to link images by irrational association, without recourse to narrative. Now he could imagine an "absolute sound film" that would "give form in far richer and more subtle ways to the psychic world of internal ideas than could the silent film" (200). By contrast, "speech has so far brought to cinema more difficulties and far fewer benefits" (203). Camera set-up in the talkie has been reduced to a "primitive level"; montage rhythms have been disrupted as shots must be held until dialogue is complete; actors must focus on clarity of speech rather than the far more evocative expressivity of gesture (203). And even worse, "The triviality of [the actors'] words nullifies the human depth of their gaze" (204).

When he published *Theory of the Film* eighteen years later, Balázs claimed that there had been so little development in the sound film that he could mostly quote verbatim what he had written in the previous book, framing it with a far gloomier view: "What I then foretold as a threat, is now already accomplished fact. On the other hand what we hoped and expected from the sound film has not been fulfilled" (194). That view is nevertheless belied by the more particular observations that follow, for he now admits how the richly meaningful combination of photographed things accompanied by the sounds they make provides "the whole chord of expression, the exact nuance. Together with the sounds and voices of things we see their physiognomy. The noise of a machine has a different colouring for us if we see the whirling machinery at the same time" (205). Even dialogue may be productive, expressive rather than exclusively rational since

> speech . . . is an instinctive expression of . . . emotions and is just as independent of rational intentions as is laughing or weeping. Live men and women don't say only things that have reason or purpose and it is not their rational utterings that are most characteristic of them. We must not forget, even in the sound film, that speech, apart from everything else, is a visible play of features as well. (227)

However, only poets might be able to craft such speech, keeping it appropriately "weightless" (229), its significance carried in neither denotation nor tone, but instead in the shot's "whole atmosphere" (230).

WALL-E

One could argue that Balázs's dream of the perfect synthesis of sound and image, dialogue and visual expressiveness did not materialize until long after his death, in computer animation, particularly in the work of Pixar, and nowhere more completely than in *WALL-E* (Andrew Stanton, 2008), the company's ninth feature film. By definition, the computer animation is entirely produced rather than reproduced: animators and sound designers build a filmic world in a digital domain that can draw freely on the associative principles that shape the "absolute sound film." Admittedly, *WALL-E* is still controlled and directed to a great degree by a conventional narrative, but that narrative reflects Balázs's idea that the movies will act as a spiritual restorative. The story concerns two robots in the near future who, far from being unconscious automata, become more and more humanly expressive using only their "faces" and "hands" and, for dialogue, only the sounds of each other's names. They fall in love and save humanity as a result. Indeed, WALL-E learns to be human by watching a movie musical. The film is as much about redemption through the mysterious passage of courtship as *The Docks of New York*, but with a reverse polarity: the "woman" in this case, a perfectly ovoid robot with the acronym EVE (Extraterrestrial Vegetation Evaluator), has to be swayed from her single-minded directive so she may recognize the value of a mystical union, made all the more irrational by the fact that the individuals involved are robots.

Balázs wrote explicitly about animation in his second and third books, *The Spirit of Film* and *Theory of the Film*, noting that cartoons like *Felix the Cat* and *Oswald the Lucky Rabbit* count as "absolute films" because their characters in action exist only in film (*Spirit* 174), even if cinematography and montage play no real part. Likewise, Balázs saw tremendous possibilities for the sound cartoon, especially in a counterpoint of image and sound, as with Mickey Mouse's spit hitting the ground to the sound of a drumbeat and a skeleton (presumably of Disney's *Skeleton Dance* [1929]) producing from his own ribcage the sound of a xylophone (208). The sound cartoon can reveal to us, like the physiognomies of the visual image, "our own sound associations, the irrational links between our visual and auditory conceptions . . . we shall continue to make many curious discoveries about the profound interconnections between sounds and forms in these grotesque *jeux d'esprit*" (208).

FIGURE 3.2 The language of gestures is the true mother tongue of mankind. WALL-E first sees and becomes entranced by EVE in *WALL-E* (Andrew Stanton, Pixar/Disney, 2008). Digital frame enlargement.

Most of Pixar's computer-animated films have been built on precisely these *jeux d'esprit*, focused as they are on giving plausible anthropomorphic life to the inanimate or bestial world through the intricate interweaving of physiognomic visual detail with "auditory conceptions," from *Luxo Jr.* (1986), which focuses on the "behavior" of a "young" table lamp and was made primarily to showcase Pixar's Image Computer and rendering software, through to *Monsters University* (2013). And where in montage and camera effects the drawn cels of traditional animation were limited, Pixar's digital films are unfettered, allowing extraordinary, impossible camera angles and movements through three-dimensional space, dynamic montage, and effects of sound direction and dimension through multi-channel recording (Balázs bemoaned the lack of directionality and dimension of the monaural sound of the cinema of his time).

Carefully avoiding the potential for complete disorientation that digital animation enables, the opening sequence of *WALL-E* exploits the fact that we are always ready to see the world physiognomically. "Put on Your Sunday Clothes," an exuberant and passionate song from the 1969 musical *Hello, Dolly!* (directed by Gene Kelly), accompanies a camera that travels through the cosmos, arriving at an Earth encircled by a thick cloud of orbiting debris. A series of other inhuman perspectives on a decimated and apparently unpopulated planet follows. So far, we could be watching *Koyaanisqatsi* (1982) with an ironic soundtrack. Crucially, however, the song becomes diegetic as we realize that there is something below, an indistinct object kicking up a trail of dust as it moves with speed and purpose. A ground-level shot provides a street view of a desolate city of high-rises in sharp focus, with that object speeding through the foreground, too large and unfocused to decipher. Now we see the "thing," some kind of robot at work, in a series of close-ups as it gathers garbage with caliper-like hands, drags it into a belly-space, and squashes the material with a whole-body effort into a neat ejectable cube. Picking up the cube, it speeds off and we see, for the first time, something decidedly organic appear: a cockroach emerges from a can with an expressive chirrup, turns to watch the robot, then quickly follows it. After the brief series of austere opening shots, we have immediately found a physiognomic focus in the film, being encouraged to identify robot and cockroach as humanlike characters because of the way their anatomy and apparent intentionality are articulated through focalized shots, expressive sounds, and analytical editing. The idea that this robot is a character rather than an object is quickly reinforced by what follows: he finds an object he likes, a hubcap in a compressed cube, grunts appreciatively, and then yanks it out; he then admires it in the rays of the late-day sun, and raises his eyebrows. Seeing the sun descending, he decides to call it a day, switching off the diegetic music using control buttons on his body and hanging his Igloo cooler on his back. He invites the cockroach onto his outstretched hand and, after a little chuckle from the bug's ticklish intrusion into his innards, speeds off home. WALL-E, a Waste

Allocation Load Lifter–Earth-Class, has been half-transformed by all of these narratological strategies into Wally, a likeable working-class guy, impressively strong for his size, with a dedication to, but not obsession with, his job, and a complete lack of prejudice.

Championing the emotional expressivity of goal-driven robots like WALL-E over the soulless idylls of a porcine human race who have destroyed the planet and now drift through space and time on the spaceship *Axiom*, Pixar's extraordinary film seems to include a scathing satire of the mindless inertia into which we have been lulled by our consumer-capitalist utopia, even as it generates massive profits for Disney, Pixar's parent company and the film's distributor. That the film nevertheless fully realizes Balázs's cinematic ideal should alert us to the key tension in his theory, between aesthetics and politics, between formal concerns and social ones, a tension that he often simply glosses over with the energy of his prose and his optimism about the medium. As Gertrud Koch puts it, Balázs was caught between championing film as a representational medium for ideological critique and pushing for the expressive autonomy of film, even though such an attitude often entailed "a politically conservative cultural criticism" ("Physiognomy" 169).

Regardless, reading his three volumes of lucid and compelling theory is to be reminded of how film, through a range of techniques and procedures of which we are barely conscious today, quickly seduced audiences, effecting a revolution in the way viewers saw the world and themselves, a revolution that continued long past those formative years of film practice that Tom Gunning has labelled the cinema of attractions. Balázs makes point after point that reminds the jaded twenty-first-century viewer of all the remarkable specificity of film, the extraordinary resources that its practitioners in a "romance" of expanding perceptions with its "primitive" audience, discovered in film's first half-century and that have since become largely invisible behind the verisimilitude of sound-, color-, and now digital-cinema. Especially in reading the first two books, published in English for the first time only in 2010, one stumbles constantly over ideas many would associate with, if not attribute to, Rudolf Arnheim, Sergei Eisenstein, Siegfried Kracauer, or Walter Benjamin, thinkers whom Balázs frequently anticipated and, in many cases, knew personally, quarreled with, or directly influenced. Writing for a broad audience with clarity and urgency at a time when the creation of a new European social order seemed within reach, Béla Balázs pitched his writing not as abstract formulation but as a productive force in that project.

4

Siegfried Kracauer

The Politics of Film Theory and Criticism

JOHANNES VON MOLTKE

Steven Spielberg's *Lincoln* (2012) begins with a much-discussed sequence during the last months of the Civil War. In tightly framed images, we enter the fray of a gruesome, muddy battle scene comparable in its visceral impact to the memorable opening of *Saving Private Ryan* (1998). Gradually, a voiceover transports us to a military encampment, where we first encounter Lincoln himself (Daniel Day-Lewis), conversing with soldiers about the rights of African Americans and about his address at Gettysburg two years earlier—most of which the soldiers recite back to its orator. The sequence is hardly subtle (it's Spielberg, after all), but it effectively sets the tone and establishes the political theme of the film, which will be concerned not just with the passage of the Thirteenth Amendment but also with the historical function of civil war as a threat to democracy *and* as an opportunity for the abolition of slavery.

Lincoln

The Civil War scenes are only a prologue to the intrigue proper, which begins in January 1865. An intertitle informs us that two months have passed since Lincoln's reelection and that the country is in the fourth year of the war. We cut to a dark image of a figure looking off into the distance, blurred by visual effects that evoke water and rapid movement. Eventually, we realize that these are dream images: in voiceover, Lincoln relates the impression of standing on a ship moved "by some terrible power at a terrific speed" with no one else aboard. "I am very keenly aware of my aloneness," he concludes as we finally enter the diegetic space of the film, where Lincoln is recounting the dream to his wife, Mary Todd (Sally Field), late one evening in the White House. Mary proceeds to interpret the dream for him, connecting it to the amendment that Lincoln wants to pass before the war is over.

As the film's second beginning, so to speak, the dream sequence efficiently introduces several central plot lines: we meet Lincoln in the domestic setting that supplies the foil for the historic politics, but also as a pensive man very much alone and beset by awful dreams; we find Mary tracing her headaches to an earlier assassination attempt, thus effectively laying the groundwork for the film's ending; and we are introduced to the subject of the Thirteenth Amendment to the Constitution, to which Lincoln will devote his efforts during the course of the film. The scene introduces the figure of Lincoln in a more structural sense as well, as the mediating third term between the two poles of civil war and democracy that the battleground sequence had set up. Given his recent reelection, Lincoln seems to have a mandate supported by the people ("No one's ever been loved so much," Mary tells him) and thus appears vested with virtually limitless authority: "You might do anything now," says she, entreating her husband not to waste that power "on an amendment bill that's sure of defeat." Though he may be troubled by dreams, and although he may sound "meek" in Daniel Day-Lewis's controversial impersonation, Lincoln commands the historical moment with executive powers greater than ever before.

The dark, sepia images of the dream are striking. Lincoln appears in them as a ghost-like, solitary figure hurtling across a strange, sparkling seascape. Prominently positioned at the beginning of the film, this sequence appears to draw on an altogether different aesthetic register than the remainder of *Lincoln*, offering a brief glimpse of expressionism in the somber realism of the historicizing mise-en-scène. In fact, to anyone familiar with the work of F. W. Murnau, the expressionist inspiration for these images should be unmistakable: if Lincoln here vaguely recalls the hero careening across the sky on Mephisto's coat in Murnau's *Faust* (1926), he surely appears to have leapt from the iconic scene in *Nosferatu* (1921) in which the vampire speeds from his home in the Carpathian mountains toward the German town of Bremen on a ghost ship.

FIGURE 4.1 The all-powerful president in Steven Spielberg's *Lincoln* (Dreamworks SKG/Twentieth Century Fox, 2012). Digital frame enlargement.

Writing about *Nosferatu*, the German-born film critic, historian, and theorist Siegfried Kracauer (1889–1966) held the film's "most impressive episode" to be "that in which the spectral ship glided with its terrible freight over phosphorescent waters" (*Caligari* 79)—a description one senses Spielberg or Tony Kushner, the film's screenwriter, might have read in preparing the dream sequence. Might Kracauer help us read that sequence in turn?

Kracauer was a prolific film critic during the Weimar Republic, penning over 700 reviews and countless pieces on literature, art, and culture for the influential, left-liberal *Frankfurter Zeitung* before he was forced into exile by the Nazis in February of 1933. However, he would not comment on Murnau's 1921 film until much later, when he reencountered it in the screening room at the Museum of Modern Art during the 1940s. Having arrived in the United States in 1941 after eight difficult years of exile in Paris, Kracauer had taken up a position as "special assistant" to Iris Barry, the curator of MoMA's recently established Film Library. Here, with the help of grants from the Rockefeller and Guggenheim foundations, Kracauer first undertook some work on Nazi propaganda films and newsreels and then went on to write *From Caligari to Hitler: A Psychological History of the German Film*.

Devoted principally to the years of the Weimar Republic, Germany's first democracy between 1918 and Hitler's rise to power, *From Caligari to Hitler* advances an argument about the socio-political significance of cinema. Films, Kracauer claims, reflect the "psychological dispositions" of a nation. As a medium that involves both collective production and reception, he argues, the cinema reveals unconscious tendencies in society: it is a medium in which the "collective mind" can be witnessed "talking . . . in its sleep" (*Caligari* 162). The task of the critic, then, becomes to decode these films like dreams and to reveal the unspoken tendencies inscribed into not only plots but mise-en-scène, iconic motifs, and other stylistic aspects as well.

Reviewing the cinema of the Weimar Republic in this vein from the distance of exile, Kracauer diagnosed a set of collective dispositions that he traced principally to the middle class, a subject that he had studied previously in a series of path-breaking essays later published in his book *The Salaried Masses*. In films from the immediate postwar era—most famously in Robert Wiene's *The Cabinet of Dr. Caligari* (1920)—he finds an inability to respond to the "shock of freedom" after the end of World War I and imperial rule in Germany. Instead of promulgating lasting democratic forms, Kracauer contends, the German middle classes appeared paralyzed, captivated by the false alternative of authoritarian rule or chaos. The cinematic "symptoms" that lead him to this diagnosis include everything from the prevalence of instinct and the irrational in films scripted by Carl Mayer (*Scherben* [*Shattered*, 1921], *Hintertreppe* [*Backstairs*, 1921], *Sylvester* [*New Year's Eve*, 1923]); to the emphasis on claustrophobic, confining spaces in the predominantly studio-bound set designs of Weimar cinema

(*Caligari*, *Der müde Tod* [*Destiny*, 1921]); to recurring motifs such as fairgrounds with their circular and spiraling patterns (*Berlin-Symphony of a Great City* [1927], *M* [1931]); to the era's titular protagonists from Homunculus to Dr. Mabuse.

Drawing heavily on the work of the psychologist Erich Fromm, Kracauer describes the mentality that he finds reflected in Weimar films as an "escape from freedom," a flight that leads inevitably from rebellion to submission and thence to the adulation of authority, whether in the guise of former monarchs (an entire cycle of films was devoted to the exploits of Frederick the Great) or of the various monsters that we now associate with expressionist film. As Kracauer puts it in the conclusion to the book, the rise of Hitler was presaged by "conspicuous screen characters now [come] true in life itself. Personified daydreams of minds to whom freedom meant a fatal shock, and adolescence a permanent temptation, these figures filled the arena of Nazi Germany" (*Caligari* 272). Among these figures, Nosferatu looms large. For Kracauer, Murnau's *Dracula* adaptation exemplifies the "tyrant films" of the Weimar Republic in the wake of Robert Wiene's expressionist masterpiece. Under this rubric, Kracauer includes a number of films that resolve the reigning political alternative between tyranny and chaos in favor of "blood-thirsty, blood-sucking tyrant figures looming in those regions where myths and fairy tales meet." German audiences are drawn to these figures, Kracauer argues, under a "compulsion of hate-love" (*Caligari* 79).

Kracauer's method in *From Caligari to Hitler* met with mixed reviews when it was published in 1947, and the book has drawn its fair share of criticism over the years. It has been faulted for being overly "reflectionist" in that it assumes a direct, mirror-like connection between cinema and social reality rather than accounting for the complex operations of representation and mediation in the cinema. The book has also been critiqued for adopting an "anticipationist" and teleological line of argument that, with the benefit of hindsight, reduces the historical process to a seemingly straight line leading "from" a 1919 film "to" Hitler. And *Caligari* has been considered overly "essentialist" in its recourse to notions of a "collective mentality" and a particularly German soul. This is not the place either to pursue or to refute these criticisms, but it may be worthwhile briefly to historicize Kracauer's project, the better to evaluate the relevance and applicability of the various critiques.

Three considerations seem particularly important. First, we should recall that Kracauer's interest in cinema as a repository of social meanings was pioneering in its day. Although traces of such thinking could be found in writings by Béla Balázs, the early Rudolf Arnheim, or Sergei Eisenstein, few critics articulated the socio-political function of cinema as coherently as Kracauer did in *From Caligari to Hitler*. Secondly, one should read the book as much for what it says about the writer's presence in American exile during wartime as it says about his past as a film viewer and critic in the interwar years in Germany.

Viewed from this perspective, *From Caligari to Hitler* does not simply mount an "anticipationist" narrative in hindsight but also intervenes decisively in contemporary debates in the United States about the origins of totalitarianism, the threat of homegrown anti-Semitism and fascism, and the nature of the authoritarian personality. Thirdly, however much we may wish to critique Kracauer's "symptomatic" readings of films as the dream images of a nation, we should note the ways in which his approach has long since become the lingua franca of film criticism. Theodor W. Adorno commented after Kracauer's death that his way of writing about film had become "anonymous," by which he meant that it had been widely accepted and entered common usage (Adorno). In the United States, to take but one example, Kracauer's assumptions underwrote an ambitious (if ultimately short-lived) film project at the Library of Congress, which was designed to enable future Kracauers to study American history by watching films at the National Archives in much the same manner in which Kracauer himself had reconstructed German mentalities and Weimar political history by re-viewing the films of the era at MoMA (see Jones).

Today, many of Kracauer's assumptions, pioneering at the time, are written into the DNA of film criticism. The basic claim of *From Caligari to Hitler* that films mirror a nation's "psychological predispositions" and provide clues to political tendencies is operative whenever critics tie a particular film to national mentality or map historical developments onto film history. Take, for example, the way some of the leading American film critics traced Barack Obama's presidency to American films that paved the way. Jim Hoberman considered *WALL-E* and *Milk* (both 2008) "prescient" for the way they articulated the "longing for Obama (or an Obama)," and Manohla Dargis and A. O. Scott looked at half a century's worth of movies to chart the ways in which the changing function of leading African American characters prepared Obama's election. Although they caution that these films could hardly be said to prophesy the present moment (thus steering clear of the anticipationist argument by Kracauer, whom critics had dubbed the "prophet in retrospect"), Dargis and Scott echo not only the spirit but even the letter of *From Caligari to Hitler* when they suggest that the American cinema offers "intriguing premonitions, quick-sketch pictures and sometimes richly realized portraits of black men grappling with issues of identity and the possibilities of power. They have helped write the prehistory of the Obama presidency"(Dargis and Scott). In a subsequent article, indeed, the two principals of the *New York Times* film section go on to flesh out the "Obama-inflected Hollywood cinema" that J. Hoberman had already anticipated: George Clooney appears to be the "quintessential Obama Era movie star," and *The Avengers* (2012), in which Nick Fury (Samuel L. Jackson) must do some community organizing to galvanize a fractious group of individuals, is "the exemplary Obama Era superhero movie" (Scott and Dargis).

Unsurprisingly, then, Scott and Dargis also establish a connection between Obama and Lincoln (the man), *Lincoln* (the movie), if not a wave of "Lincolnmania." However, before we follow contemporary film critics in spinning this associative web any further, we should recall that Kracauer's book about Weimar cinema not only asserts a link between film characters and historical personae, or even between film and society, but also takes a political stance on that link, indicting both German society and its films for the profoundly illiberal turn that led to the rise of Nazism. *From Caligari to Hitler* is a book that couples its knowledge of subsequent outcomes with a deep worry about the fragility of democracy and of cinema's utopian promise as a democratic art form.

Reading *Lincoln* through *Caligari*, then, would involve more than simply finding the parallels between the protagonist of the biopic and the political figure, the way Kracauer linked the mad scientist in Wiene's film to Hitler or Dargis and Scott find echoes of Obama in Hollywood's "Lincolnesque" characters. It would mean also reading for the film's historical unconscious, for the "secret history involving the inner dispositions" (*Caligari* 11) of the society that produced it. Contrary to what some of Kracauer's critics have claimed, *From Caligari to Hitler* does not reduce films to their stories or leading characters but considers them to be full of "visible hieroglyphs": formal and thematic motifs that can range from a recurrent image (a man placing his head in a woman's lap in many Weimar films) to cinema's affinity for "huge mass displays, casual configurations of human bodies and inanimate objects and an endless succession of unobtrusive phenomena" (*Caligari* 7). These hieroglyphs acquire relevance in the type of "symptomatic" reading that Kracauer seeks to model. In this vein, we might ask of *Lincoln* how Daniel Day-Lewis's much-discussed voicing of the sixteenth president signifies, how the film's domestic politics mirror the political procedural, or what to make of the overall darkness of the film's cinematography.

Why, indeed, do we often see Lincoln roaming the White House late at night, appearing suddenly in staff quarters and conducting consequential presidential business in the wee hours of the morning? Or, to rephrase this in terms of the dream images that set the stage for the action at the beginning of the film: what are we to make of the vampiric undertones of this historical story? For the figure of Lincoln seems haunted in ways that were made explicit in the title of Timur Bekhmambetov's *Abraham Lincoln: Vampire Hunter* (2012), which hit screens contemporaneously with Spielberg's film. Like the proverbial vampire who survives his own death, Lincoln still haunts the present, and the history of slavery remains in tangible ways undead despite passage of the Thirteenth Amendment that *Lincoln* celebrates.

In view of Kracauer's reading of *Nosferatu* as an exemplary figure in a longer "procession of tyrants," however, another dimension of the vampire imposes itself. For Kracauer, Nosferatu incarnates the authoritarian character that threatens the very fabric of democracy. Even if we do not adopt Kracauer's teleology and posit a totalitarian endpoint; and even where—as in *Lincoln*—the cinema appears to return to the primal scene of American democracy, the latter's investment in the values of compromise and equality (articulated forcefully in Kushner's screenplay) is undercut by the protagonist's titanic executive authority. As the film makes clear, Lincoln operates as a wartime president, and as such he is "clothed in immense power," a view he himself forcefully asserts in a cabinet discussion. As the camera slowly zooms in on him, the president schools his cabinet in a bit of political theory: "I *decided* the constitution gives me war powers. No one knows just exactly what those powers are. Some say they don't exist. I don't know. I decided I needed them to exist to uphold my powers to protect the constitution, which, I decided, meant that I could take the rebel slaves from them as property confiscated in war."

In a term popularized by one of the recent successors to the office Lincoln held, the second president Bush, Lincoln is "the decider"—a sovereign who emancipates the slaves at the cost of a war that endows him with the power to ignore the judiciary and preempt the legislative. In decisive gestures, Day-Lewis's Lincoln cuts through the deliberative discourse of his cabinet members, slamming his hand on the table and seizing the moment that bloodshed has "afforded" him. The president charts the course between ending the war and securing the amendment or waging war and sending his cabinet officers out to procure the necessary votes behind the scenes. While we get to see the necessarily messy business of democracy in the process, the need to cajole and compromise, we are never left in doubt about the genius of Lincoln's leadership as the true anchor of that process.

The "meek" voice and the hunched gait are in this sense not only historically "accurate" details, authenticated in interviews by presidential historians. Rather, they serve an ideological function as smoke screens behind which Day-Lewis barely conceals the terrifying power of the wartime president. Reading the effect of the actor's performative decisions as "visible hieroglyphs," we might trace a line with Kracauer from Spielberg's and Kushner's hagiography of Abraham Lincoln to far more current threats to American democracy, such as the expansion of executive power spearheaded by Dick Cheney during the Bush years in the wake of 9/11 and arguably expanding well into the Obama administration and its counterterrorist policies. Scott championed *Lincoln* as a "rough and noble democratic masterpiece" that was to be numbered among the "finest films ever made about American politics." Against other critics, he defended the film as a successful, even radical representation of the messy business of democracy, and a corrective of sorts to its equally symptomatic predecessors, *The Birth of a Nation* and *Gone with the Wind* (Scott). But he missed the film's more ominous undertones, which the opening dream sequence and Kracauer's reading of the vampire in a different era of film history allow us to detect.

Young Mr. Lincoln

In this respect, Spielberg's Lincoln is not far removed from John Ford's. Although the latter's famous *Young Mr. Lincoln* (1939), with Henry Fonda in the title role, focuses on a different moment in the president's biography, it, too, underlies the seemingly celebratory portrayal of its protagonist with an unconscious and far more sinister dimension. Such, in any case, was the claim of a famous article by the editorial collective of *Cahiers du cinéma*. Devoted to exemplifying a method that is certainly inspired more by Althusserian Marxism and Lacanian psychoanalysis than by Kracauer's ideology critique, the *Cahiers* collective text on "John Ford's *Young Mr. Lincoln*" may nonetheless be said to have assumed Kracauer's heritage after the latter had become "anonymous," and without reference to the German critic's work. Like Kracauer, the editors deliberately set out to relate films to ideology, to *read* them and thereby complicate their apparent, deceptive transparency. Invoking Kracauer's friend Walter Benjamin, they note the complex, mediated, and decentered relationship between films and their socio-historical context. As critics, they seek to "make the films say what they have to say within what they leave unsaid, [and] reveal their constituent lack" (*Cahiers du cinéma* 8). Consequently, in their reading of *Young Mr. Lincoln* the *Cahiers* group points out the astonishing "total suppression of Lincoln's political dimension," a fact that constitutes the political dimension of Ford's film, in turn (17).

Focusing on the early years of Lincoln's career as a lawyer, on his brief courtship of Ann Rutledge (Pauline Moore), and on the tumultuous events surrounding a murder trial of two brothers, *Young Mr. Lincoln* appears interested in the young man before he becomes the historical figure as which he is monumentalized in the film's final shot of the Lincoln Memorial. But, as the *Cahiers* editors note, the film operates in the future anterior, anticipating the president that young Mr. Lincoln will have become. In this sense, Ford both assumes and disavows the spectator's knowledge of the historical character, making the suppression of Lincoln's abolitionist politics—the ostensible subject of Spielberg's/Kushner's *Lincoln*—all the more glaring. In place of history and politics, the editors note, the film offers a moralizing discourse on the Lincoln myth and instrumentalizes it for the historical present of Roosevelt's New Deal. Nominally a biopic of the "pre-political" young Lincoln, the film in fact speaks to the New Deal's increased emphasis on federal government over states' rights, U.S. isolationism on the eve of World War II, economic reorganization after the Great Depression, and a deepening chasm between Democrats and Republicans—always a welcome opportunity to dust off the Republican party's nineteenth-century hero.

Ford's hero, like Spielberg's, is a personable, judicious man, a figure of identification and admiration. But here again, an uncanny dimension creeps into the acting and mise-en-scène, making Lincoln less a guarantor of liberty and equality than a (future) president invested with an awesome power to decide, to adjudicate right and wrong ("By gee, that's all there's to it," young Lincoln muses after spending some time with Blackburn's legal commentary under a tree: "right 'n' wrong"). As a lawyer, Lincoln appears to be omniscient and omnipotent in the film, with the power to short-circuit the legal process of reason and argumentation by pulling the truth out of his hat at the last minute (in the form of an almanac). More significantly, perhaps, plain Abe Lincoln clearly has a terrifying dimension that the editors describe as his "castrating power," and which they detect in the recurrent motif of Fonda's "empty, icy, terrifying stare." Or, to reprise Kracauer's terminology: Lincoln, ostensibly the personification of American democracy, is endowed in this film, as in Spielberg/Kushner's, with an undeniably authoritarian streak. In ways that Kracauer had critiqued in important essays on Hollywood already during the 1940s ("Hollywood's Terror Films"; "Those Movies with a Message"), that streak unsettles the ideological "message" of the film, an effect that is only magnified if we consider it through the lens of *From Caligari to Hitler* and its insistence that film motifs encode tendencies whose real effects are to be sought in the socio-political arena.

FIGURE 4.2 Lincoln on the brink of history in John Ford's *Young Mr. Lincoln* (Twentieth Century Fox, 1939). Digital frame enlargement.

In suggesting that the *Cahiers*' famous reading of *Young Mr. Lincoln* owes an implicit, subterranean, or "anonymous" debt to Kracauer's method in *From Caligari to Hitler*, and that the latter can help illuminate the more recent *Lincoln* film in turn, I do not wish to claim any direct influence or applicability of Kracauer's "psychological history" of German film. To do so would be to overlook the fact that Kracauer went on to write another major book on film that appears to complicate any such triangulation. Although he had reiterated his commitment to "a fusion of sociological and aesthetic approaches" to film throughout his American exile (*Siegfried Kracauer's American Writings* 226; see also von Moltke), toward the end of his life it seemed to many that Kracauer's politics and his investment in a critique of ideology had fallen by the wayside. *Theory of Film: The Redemption of Physical Reality*, the final book to be published during his lifetime (*History* appeared posthumously three years after his death in 1966), shifts the definition of cinema to a concern with realism. Here, the astute critic of the "mass ornament," of social alienation and capitalist rationalization from the Weimar years (see *The Mass Ornament*), and the incisive commentator on illiberal manifestations of cinema from the early New York years appeared to have yielded to a quasi-theological perspective on film's power to "redeem" physical reality, as Kracauer puts it in the book's subtitle. This theological motif, which has deep resonances with the work of Walter Benjamin, centers principally on cinema's ability to record and reveal aspects of our reality that otherwise would go unnoticed and remain unseen. By contrast to our routinized, everyday perception, Kracauer argues, the cinema picks out details and makes them meaningful through close-ups. Where we remain caught up in the bustle of everyday life, the cinema grants us fresh perspectives on habitual movements or on the configurations in which we move, from the life of the street to that of the crowd. Kracauer derives these powers of the cinema from the inherent "affinities" of film, the way it gravitates, differently from other media, toward the staged, the fortuitous, the flowing, the fragmentary, the transient, or the indeterminate in life.

This list reflects the forms of cinema that Kracauer's late theory favors: films that retain documentary qualities, that eschew tightly constructed "classical" narrative forms in favor of open-ended, episodic, or "paratactic" arrangements, and films that do not overburden their subjects with artistic pretensions or verbal explanations. In this sense, *Theory of Film* is very much of a piece with the film historical moment in which it was published, when *cinéma vérité* was pioneering new ways of insinuating the camera into political and ethnographic situations, and the various New Waves were experimenting with ways of exploding the ossified conventions of classical Hollywood. By the same token, *Theory of Film* dismisses certain cinematic forms that are situated at the greatest remove from realism, such as fantasy and (more importantly for our present concern) the historical film: forced by definition to stage their subject and dress up their actors in period costumes, history films such as *Lincoln* exist in a flatly "uncinematic area" (*History* 80). In Kracauer's theory, they conflict with the medium's affinities for the unstaged and for endlessness.

And yet, Kracauer's views were, if not more nuanced, then at least more complex in ways that may yet prove productive for thinking about Ford's and Spielberg's films. First, we may note that the dismissal of historical films in *Theory of Film* hardly captures Kracauer's complex and lifelong engagement with historiographical issues, from an early essay on photography ("Photography") through his posthumous book on history where, indeed, he posits a strong correlation between "camera reality" and "historical reality" that would require us to reevaluate the flat-out claim in *Theory of Film* that history is "uncinematic." Further, as far as Hollywood was concerned, Kracauer was doubtless suspicious but not roundly dismissive, as his ongoing interest in American movies from the 1920s through the 1950s suggests. Far worse than the routine fare churned out by Hollywood, he thought, were pretensions to classical notions of artistic value, for example in adaptations of canonical literature or Shakespearean drama. In keeping with the methodological premises elaborated in Kracauer's Weimar essays and in *Caligari*, Hollywood films minimally retained a diagnostic value; and some could certainly live up to his vision of cinema as a "redemptive" medium.

That vision entailed nothing short of a renewal of our capacity to experience the world, and thereby to reconstitute an integral sense of subjectivity, memory, and the freedom to act. As Kracauer and other critics from Theodor Adorno to Leo Löwenthal and from Hannah Arendt to Dwight Macdonald and Robert Warshow held at the time, these capacities had been stunted in the recent history of war, totalitarianism, and the terror of the camps, which had reduced humans to bundles of atomized reactions devoid of any continuity of experience out of which to constitute a coherent sense of self. Film, with its affinities for the overlooked, seemed to Kracauer to provide a vital resource for regaining one's senses and reconstituting experience. In this sense, his *Theory of Film* may be read as a political project in its own right, and as a hopeful response to the questions concerning cinema's function as a democratizing medium, which *From Caligari to Hitler* had still answered in the negative. Throughout his career as a film critic and theorist and spanning the seemingly dissimilar projects of the two major monographs, Kracauer had prized cinema's ability to "ferret out minutiae" (*Caligari* 7) and thereby readjust our vision to the world and to things we ordinarily overlook or do not perceive. This utopian aspect of cinema, I would suggest in conclusion, should not be pitted against its ideological dimensions, which Kracauer had analyzed in *Caligari*. To adopt a principle that Kracauer articulated in his posthumous book on history, and in keeping with the two different perspectives developed in his history of Weimar cinema and his theory of film, respectively, we may argue that utopia and ideology exist "side by side" in any given film.

Reading for these different aspects becomes a matter of perspective. If *Caligari* led us to emphasize the vampiric nature of Lincoln in Spielberg's and Ford's films, *Theory of Film* prompts us to complement that perspective with a cinephile's eye for cinematic details that hold significance beyond their function in a given plot (however tightly constructed) or as part of the mise-en-scène (however heavily staged). In this perspective, even historical biopics such as Ford's or Spielberg's remain repositories of gestures, details, and ultimately of *experiences* that spectators have with the moving image. In keeping with Kracauer's "affinities," these experiences relate to film's ability to intimate a life that extends beyond the dimension of the screen. Returning to the opening that precedes the expressionist dream images in *Lincoln*, we might note, for example, how the Civil War extends beyond the boundaries of the frame that plunges us *in medias res*. Or we might note the fortuitous moments even in Ford's tightly controlled blocking, when a gangly, awkward Henry Fonda untangles himself to meet Ann Rutledge or goes through a series of undecided gestures before sticking his hands in his pockets to sum up his political principles at a political rally. In such moments, the ideological function of political myth-making is joined by the utopian promise that *Theory of Film* attributes to the cinema: its ability to reconnect us to an alienated world and make us "experience things in their concreteness" (296).

5

Walter Benjamin

Afterimages of the Aura

COLIN WILLIAMSON

Walter Benjamin's (1892–1940) relationship with cinema studies has long reflected the waves of fragmentation, searching, and (re)discovery which characterized his own experience of modernity. From the 1910s through the 1930s, the German-born cultural theorist and literary critic wrote prolifically in the light of astonishing technological, commercial, and artistic developments, as well as in the shadows of World War I, the rise to power of fascism, and the outbreak of World War II. Some of Benjamin's most well-known work on mass culture and modern life—including his famous essay "The Work of Art in the Age of Mechanical Reproduction" (1936)—was written under desperate circumstances between his flight from Nazi Germany in 1933, when he began a life in exile, and his tragic suicide in 1940. His writings are sometimes labyrinthine, but his brilliant insights into everything from poetry, politics, and history to architecture, painting, photography, and film have moved fluidly across disciplines, inflecting central discourses in art history, cultural studies, and cinema and media studies.

Despite being a prominent figure in classical film theory, Benjamin never offered a rigorous or even sustained "essentialist" theory of film. Nor does his work on film lend itself easily to categorizations like "formalist" or "realist," which were developing in film theoretical and critical discourses at the time Benjamin was writing. And, although his work bridges the pivotal transition to synchronous sound, he was relatively silent on the acoustic properties of the cinema. Benjamin's theoretical engagements with film were primarily in the service of a much larger intellectual exploration of the experience of modern life.

Guided by the question of film's relationship with modernity, Benjamin was mainly in dialogue with early critical theory and members of the Frankfurt School, such as Max Horkheimer, Siegfried Kracauer, and Theodor Adorno.

In the 1930s, these theorists were instrumental in launching a Marxist critique of mass popular culture and the ways in which media operate in the context of capitalism, what Adorno and Horkheimer in *Dialectic of Enlightenment* (1944) call the "culture industry." Film was of interest because, as a technology of illusion, it could transform audiences into passive consumers of commodities—for example, individual films, fashion, merchandise, etc. The cinema was sometimes criticized in this vein for reproducing the alienations, deceptions, and complacencies of consumer culture at the expense of audiences' active, critical, and liberating engagements with society. Benjamin's reflections on film are ambivalently positioned in relation to such a critique, but this was the critical landscape in which he was drawn to exploring the social functions of the cinema. As Miriam Hansen explains, along with Adorno and to an extent Kracauer, Benjamin "[was] more interested in what cinema *does*, the kind of sensory-perceptual, mimetic experience it enabled, than in what cinema *is*" (*Cinema and Experience* xvii; emphases in original).

Eschewing the ontological question "What *is* cinema?" raises the question of what Benjamin *does* for film theory. What do his writings on film *enable*? Some of Benjamin's most potent and penetrating observations about film and related media—in essays like "The Work of Art," "Little History of Photography" (1931), and "On Some Motifs in Baudelaire" (1939)—have preoccupied and eluded cinema scholars for decades. This endurance stems from Benjamin's rich insights into how film weaves together the (dis)enchanting, transformative, and revelatory powers of art, science, and technology. Although unraveling the complexities of these insights is no small task, there are at least three prominent threads in his writing which clarify how Benjamin sees the cinema broadly as "an interlocutor for modernity" (Casetti 10): the experience of shock, the revolutionary potential of the camera's mechanical vision, and film's relationship with art.

One of Benjamin's central concerns is the cinema's affinity with "the increasing atrophy of experience" in modern life, particularly as it relates to the perceptual shocks of urban environments ("Motifs" 159). Like the sociologist Georg Simmel, Benjamin was drawn to the emergence in the nineteenth century of a modern experience characterized by fragmentation, disorientation, distraction, and alienation. At least since the 1850s, the rapid expansion of industrial and technological changes fostered an acute awareness of how city dwellers were subjected to an ever-increasing barrage of audiovisual stimuli. The tumult of crowds, traffic, cars, and trains, and the proliferation of newspapers, advertisements, photographs, and eventually motion pictures—what Jean-Louis Comolli called the nineteenth-century "frenzy of the visible" (122)—produced an array of constantly changing and oftentimes violent sense impressions. According to Simmel, the chaos and unpredictability of city life corresponded with a compensatory dulling or deadening of experience, a "blasé attitude," which developed to safeguard individuals against the nervous exhaustion and persistent shocking of the visual system (on cinema and nervous shock, see further Fischer, "Shock").

For Benjamin film was an important medium for reflecting and transforming these effects of industrialization and urbanization. In his essay on Baudelaire, he claims that "technology has subjected the human sensorium to a complex kind of training. There came a day when a new and urgent need for stimuli was met by the film" (175). Film fulfilled this need with its capacity for spatial and temporal manipulation (e.g., montage), its early affinities with the thrills of amusement parks and stage magic spectacles, and its rapidly flickering images. The cinema also worked the shock experience of modern life into a powerful "modern aesthetics of astonishment" (Gunning 128), which manifested in the kinetics and playfulness of trick films, animated films, and special effects films, as well as in certain avant-garde filmmaking practices. The "complex kind of training" embedded in the cinema's shock effects has inspired some scholars to align Benjamin with the idea that film played a key role in shaping actual changes in the human perceptual system brought about by the changing landscape of the modern world. This idea is the basis of the so-called "modernity thesis," a term elaborated and debated by scholars like David Bordwell, Noël Carroll, Charlie Keil, Ben Singer, and Malcom Turvey interested in film's relationship to the idea that the human perceptual apparatus changes over time. Benjamin speaks to this when he claims, "During long periods of history, the mode of human sense perception changes with humanity's entire mode of existence" ("Art" 222). The broader import of this idea is that perception is historical, that it has a changing cultural context. But arguably, the more productive idea for Benjamin is that film is a powerful technology for mediating human experience by offering a modern way of seeing the world.

The cinema's related capacity to allow audiences to see the world anew informs a second unifying idea in Benjamin's work: *the optical unconscious*. With an eye to the wonders of scientific uses of chronophotography, magnification, and slow-motion and time-lapse photography, Benjamin saw in film—and earlier forms of instantaneous photography—the revolutionary potential of optical devices to transform the conditions and habits of unaided visual perception. In "Little History of Photography" he observes that the photographic image confronts the viewer with aspects of reality that are ordinarily invisible, unseen, or unnoticed. As Benjamin explains,

> It is another nature which speaks to the camera rather than to the eye: "other" above all in the sense that a space informed by human consciousness gives way to a space informed by the unconscious. Whereas it is a commonplace that, for example, we have some idea what is involved in the act of walking (if only in general terms), we have no idea at all what happens during the fraction of a second when a person actually

> takes a step. Photography, with its devices of slow motion and enlargement, reveals the secret. (510)

In this space, "secret" phenomena, like the automatic, unconscious movements of the human body, take place and become newly visible through the mechanical eye of a camera. The optical unconscious is also a contingent space opened by the vision of a machine that, lacking consciousness, offers up the fullness of reality automatically, directly, and indiscriminately (510–512).

The revelatory potential of the optical unconscious is inflected by Benjamin's critical-theoretical associations, as well as his interest in the atrophy of experience linked to modern life. In "The Work of Art," he claims that

> our taverns and our metropolitan streets, our offices and furnished rooms, our railroad stations and our factories have us locked up hopelessly. Then came the film and burst this prison-world asunder by the dynamite of the tenth of a second, so that now, in the midst of its far-flung ruins and debris, we calmly and adventurously go travelling. With the close-up, space expands; with slow motion, movement is extended. The enlargement of a snapshot does not simply render more precise what in any case was visible, though unclear: it reveals entirely new structural formations of the subject. (236)

In other words, the mechanical eye of the cinema can free the human sensorium from habit and dullness, free reality of the mediations of appearances, language, and consciousness, and place audiences in immediate contact with "another nature." Benjamin characterized this nature as "other" because the cinema affords a way of seeing that renders the modern world uncanny, that is, makes the familiar strange. By revealing the unnoticed, the unseen, and the imperceptible, film enables a depth of perception that can lead to a critical consciousness of the modern world.

If through the optical unconscious Benjamin explored how the cinema stages a potentially emancipatory encounter with reality, it is through film's relationship with art that he developed one of his most elusive ideas: *the destruction of the aura.* The "aura" is a concept Benjamin used to think through the implications of film and photography for theorizing art and aesthetic experience in the twentieth century. In "The Work of Art" he frames the aura with remarkable ambiguity as an "[artwork's] presence in time and space, its unique existence at the place where it happens to be" (220). Similarly, in "Little History," he describes the aura as a "strange weave of space and time: the unique appearance or semblance of distance, no matter how close it may be" (518). Benjamin's invocations of "presence" and "uniqueness" are intentionally broad. Although he is primarily interested in the aura of an artwork, Benjamin claims that objects, human beings, and even natural features like a mountain range can also have an aura. The aura is manifested as an emanation of physical, geographical, temporal presence.

To claim that a "traditional" work of art like a painting has an aura is to point to something like the painting's embeddedness in tradition, which is to say the "original" artwork's accumulation of a unique history by way of its singular presence and transmission through space and time. The uniqueness of the original artwork guarantees its authenticity, "the essence of all that is transmissible from its beginning, ranging from its substantive duration to its testimony to the history which it has experienced" (221). According to Benjamin, techniques of mechanical reproduction—lithography, letter-press, and later photography—initiated the decline of the auratic dimension of art because media like photography and film do not abide by the same principles of authenticity. "From a photographic negative," he explains, "one can make any number of prints; to ask for the 'authentic' print makes no sense" (224). A photographic print or a film is not a unique object; rather it is always already a copy without an original.

The aura has many layers which extend beyond the scope of this chapter, but an important point of gravity in Benjamin's concept is that, like the optical unconscious, the "destruction" of the aura harbors emancipatory potential (see further Petersson and Steinskog). In "The Work of Art" he traces the relationship between art and aura to its ritual function in ancient magical and religious contexts where artworks acquired value as cult objects by being "unapproachable" and thus maintaining a distance from reality (243). Cinema distinguished itself by replacing this distancing cult value with a culture of exhibition and display, in which works were brought near to viewers wherever they lived. As Benjamin explains, "[F]or the first time in world history, mechanical reproduction emancipates the work of art from its parasitical dependence on ritual. To an ever greater degree the work of art reproduced becomes the work of art designed for reproducibility" (224). Unlike the cult object, in other words, film is both a medium of mass reproduction and a medium of the masses capable of offering audiences a collective experience of reality. It also fulfills what Benjamin calls a modern "desire . . . to bring things 'closer'"—captured by the famous promise of early travelogue film companies to place "the world within your reach"—and a related willingness to sacrifice the uniqueness of a work of art for the copy without an original (223). With the emergence of the cinema, therefore, the work of art becomes a commodity.

Sunset Blvd.: The Cult of the Star

The decline of the aura did not occur without leaving traces, afterimages that haunt the cinema and continue to shed light on Benjamin's ideas about technology, art, and the modern experience. In "The Work of Art," for example, he admits that, even with the emergence and proliferation of a mechanical art of film, "cult value does not give way without resistance" (225). One enduring manifestation of this resistance is the phenomenon of the cinematic star.

Consider the case of Billy Wilder's *Sunset Blvd.* (1950), a classic film noir about the nature of the Hollywood star's life as an image elevated to the status of cult object. In structure, the film is a memory recounted by a dead man, struggling screenwriter Joe Gillis (William Holden), who encounters the once-famous silent-film star Norma Desmond (Gloria Swanson). Norma has shut herself away in the decadent ruins of a Hollywood mansion in a desperate attempt to preserve her star image as it was before the transition to synchronized sound made her a relic of silent-film history. Joe becomes trapped in Norma's increasingly delusional world when he agrees to help write a screenplay that will serve, she hopes, as the vehicle of her return to stardom. Norma gradually descends into madness and eventually shoots and kills Joe in a moment of jealousy triggered by his romantic relationship with a young aspiring scriptwriter, Betty Schaefer (Nancy Olson).

Woven into this narrative is a deep fascination with what Benjamin describes as the alienation of the film actor from his or her own aura, a loss of the quality of having a unique existence or singular "presence in time and space." Norma is unable to cope with the death of her stardom at the end of the silent era, and with the autonomous life of her star image. Her struggle revolves around the fact that, as Benjamin explains, in contrast to the stage actor whose presence with the audience preserves her aura, the film actor is separated from his or her audience by the camera. For the viewer, the camera replaces the live presence of the actor with the phantom presence of his reproduction as a moving image. Thus, Benjamin explains, "for the first time . . . man has to operate with his whole living person, yet forgoing its aura. For aura is tied to his presence; there can be no replica of it" ("Art" 229). To convey this loss of the aura Benjamin invokes the concept of the double. "The feeling of strangeness that overcomes the actor before the camera . . . is basically of the same kind as the estrangement felt before one's own image in the mirror. But now the reflected image has become separable, transportable" ("Art" 230–231).[1] Rather than being unique in space and time, the film actor is a series of infinitely reproducible images.

Norma's eventual madness stems from the strangeness and difficulty she experiences as an aging actress trying to maintain a connection with her younger star image thus mechanically separated and reproduced. Wilder uses the idea of Norma's aging to heighten and dramatize the more general sense any actor can have of not belonging to his or her image onscreen. To overcome the sense that she has become a mere shadow of her double, Norma fills her mansion with a massive collection of photographic portraits of herself in various "celestial" roles from her cinematic past. Early in the film Joe is unsettled by Norma's relationship with her star image and remarks hauntingly in voiceover: "She was still sleepwalking along the giddy heights of a lost career, plain crazy when it came to that one subject: her celluloid self, the Great Norma Desmond. How could she breathe in that house so crowded with Norma Desmonds, more Norma Desmonds, and still more Norma Desmonds?" Joe's astonishment and his criticism are aimed not simply at the collection of photographs—the unending series of Norma Desmonds—but also at how Norma has become a fan of her cinematic double.

Norma's preservation of "her celluloid self" is a grotesque version of the "cult of the movie star," which Benjamin saw as a kind of afterimage of the aura. In his view the emergence of the cinematic star was a "response" to the loss of the aura as it pertains to the mechanical reproduction of the actor just described, and to the idea of film as art more broadly ("Art" 231). If the cinema destroyed the aura of traditional works of art, the cult of the star—the immense magnification of personality, the widespread familiarity with the star face—was an attempt to restore the aura in the age of mechanical reproduction. A star, for example, is an actor elevated by the film industry and by film audiences—for beauty, talent, or some "unique" or "original" quality of their persona—to the status of a divine being, a celestial figure with cult value. Being thus distanced from audiences, stars are adored and admired by their fans, who might "commune" with a star by writing letters, collecting autographs and photographs, or repeatedly viewing a star's films.

With the loss of her own fans, Norma, a perverse case, enacts these rituals of devotion herself. In one of the film's most striking scenes, she and Joe watch a projection of a silent film in her mansion. The film, *Queen Kelly* (1929), was in fact directed by Erich von Stroheim, who plays Norma's butler, Max, in *Sunset Blvd.*; it also features a young Gloria Swanson playing the title role. The bottom of the screen is lined with photographs of Norma, which form a kind of altar on which *Queen Kelly* is projected. Norma's (Swanson's) reverence for her own image flickering like a ghost on the screen is mirrored by the young Norma (the young Swanson), who is praying and gazing up behind a pair of devotional candles. The layers of doubling in this bizarre scene of worship visualize the cult dimension of the star phenomenon (Norma the star is worshipped like an idol) and the dialectical relationship between stars and their reproduction as images. As Edgar Morin explains, "[The star as a person] is nothing since her image is everything. She is everything since she is this image too" (53).

Morin's idea that the star, "like the gods," is "everything and nothing" (88) resonates with Benjamin's criticism that the cult of the star is at best a simulation of the aura. The veneration of the star, Benjamin explains, "preserves not the unique aura of the person but the 'spell of the personality,' the phony spell of a commodity" ("Art" 231). It is "phony" because the cult object (the star) is not a unique person per se (the "real" Norma) but that person's mass reproduction

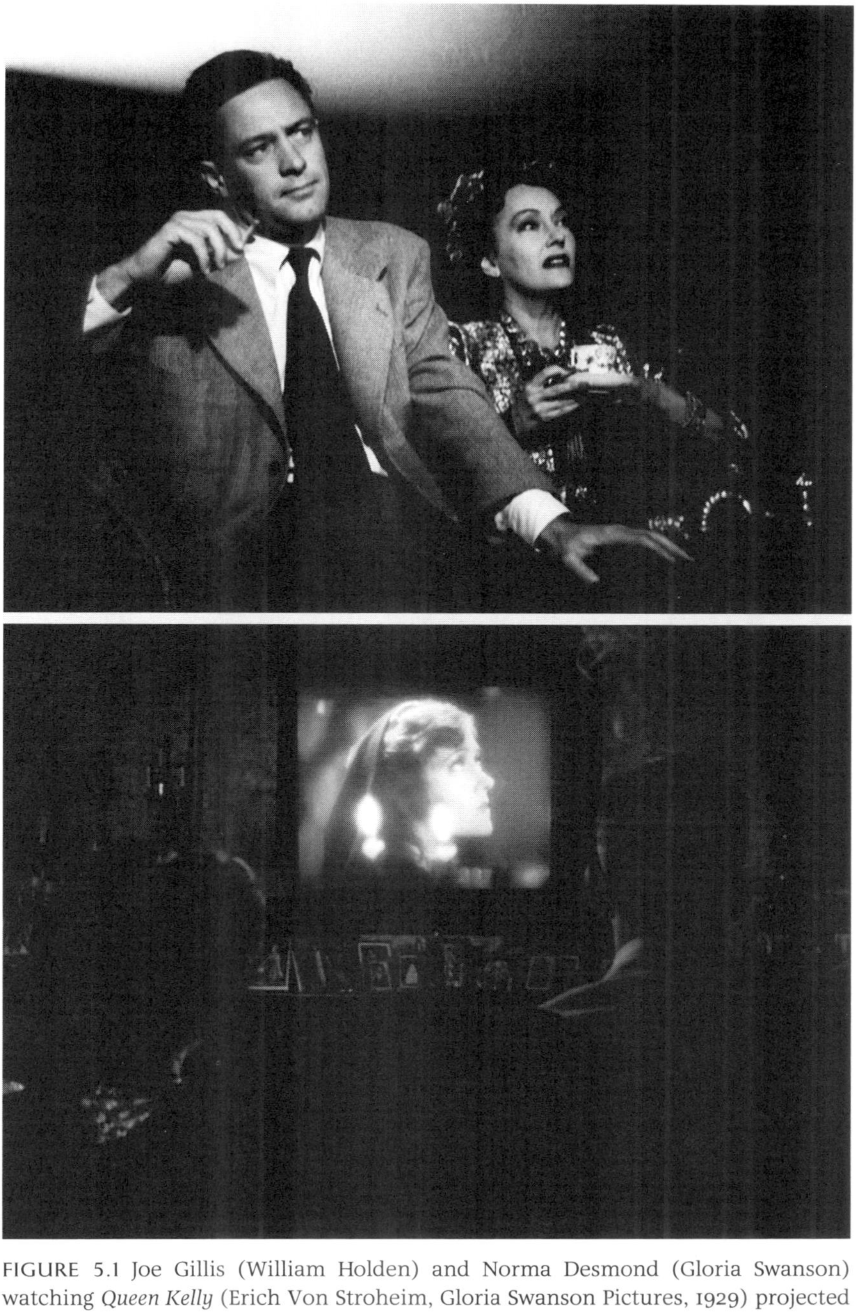

FIGURE 5.1 Joe Gillis (William Holden) and Norma Desmond (Gloria Swanson) watching *Queen Kelly* (Erich Von Stroheim, Gloria Swanson Pictures, 1929) projected on a screen in a sitting room of Norma's mansion in *Sunset Blvd.* (Billy Wilder, Paramount, 1950). Digital frame enlargements.

as a series of images (the "cinematic" Norma). We see Benjamin's critique reflected in the way Norma is under the spell of her own star image. She has preserved her cult value only by shutting herself away in her mansion and surrounding herself with photographic doubles. Sometimes she is visited by other aging stars like Anna Nilsson and Buster Keaton, "dim figures" and "waxworks" from the silent era, as Joe remarks. The world she inhabits is thus a phantasmagoric one, literally a house of mirrors and a house of wax, haunted by ghosts of the silent screen.

Norma's illusion culminates in a now-famous scene from the end of the film. After murdering Joe she descends the grand staircase of her mansion to meet the police and news reporters who have come for her arrest. Mistaking the reporters' cameras for a movie set under the direction of her old friend, Cecil B. DeMille, she announces, "All right, Mr. DeMille, I'm ready for my close-up." Norma advances toward us—the audience of *Sunset Blvd.*—and, through a dissolve, she visualizes Luigi Pirandello's idea, quoted by Benjamin, that in the cinema the actor's "body loses its corporeality, it evaporates . . . flickering an instant on the screen, then vanishing into silence" ("Art" 229).

A.I. Artificial Intelligence: Digital Phantasmagoria

The emancipatory potential which Benjamin saw in film is deeply embedded in a discourse of failure that is, in an important way, inseparable from his historical moment. World War I, for example, had exposed the realities of humanity's capacity for mass-scale, self-destructive uses of technology. Shortly thereafter, the Nazis' use of film and mass spectacle to aestheticize the political power of fascism confirmed the endurance of dangerous affinities between technology, ritual, and cult. But Benjamin's writings are also importantly about *possibilities* of the cinema—as a space of revelation, collective experience, and critical engagement—which continue to resonate with questions about how digital technologies are reflecting and shaping the human experience in our contemporary moment.

A rich site for exploring how Benjamin's ideas illuminate and are illuminated by digital cinema is Steven Spielberg's *A.I. Artificial Intelligence* (2001). Set in a future in which humans have made astonishing advances in the mechanical simulation of life, the film revolves around the dream of a young automaton child named David (Haley Joel Osment) to become human. David is adopted by human parents as a substitute for their terminally ill son, Martin (Jake Thomas), who has been cryogenically frozen. When Martin is unexpectedly cured, reanimated, and returns home, the two boys compete for the love of their mother, Monica (Frances O'Connor), who is ultimately forced to return David to his manufacturer where he will be destroyed. Unable to let him meet this fate, Monica frees David and he embarks on a quest to find the Blue Fairy, the character from his favorite bedtime story, *Pinocchio*, whom David believes will transform him from a machine into a "real boy" so that he might finally be loved by his human family.

David's quest for the real is useful for teasing out some resonances between Benjamin's ideas about mechanical reproduction and digital cinema culture. David is an artificially intelligent electro-mechanical device. He believes that he is unique, that he has the qualities of an original, authentic work of art. When Martin points out that David is merely a sophisticated toy (like the cinema) with no history, no memories, and, we might say, no aura, the automaton begins to question his authenticity and seeks answers from his creator, Professor Hobby (William Hurt). In a powerful sequence set in Hobby's Manhattan laboratory, David encounters another mechanical "David" for the first time. Unlike Norma in *Sunset Blvd.*, David reacts not with adoration but with horror: "I thought I was one of a kind!" He then destroys his double, exposing the internal machinery which produced its illusion of life, and wanders into an assembly room filled with more Davids, all inanimate and in various states of completion. Like a hall of mirrors, David's doubling is pointedly cinematic. As Benjamin explains of the cinema: "By making many reproductions [film] substitutes a plurality of copies for a unique existence" ("Art" 221). David's experience is precisely one of his own plurality. His realization is that he is a machine and a mechanical reproduction, one industrial commodity in an endless series of copies. Not only is no original to be found, but to seek one out, as Benjamin would have it, "makes no sense."

FIGURE 5.2 David (Haley Joel Osment) in the assembly room of Professor Hobby's Manhattan laboratory surrounded by other automaton "Davids" and an unassembled animatronic face, from *A.I.* (Steven Spielberg, Warner Bros./Dreamworks SKG/ Amblin, 2001). Digital frame enlargement.

The idea that David finds himself caught in a series of potentially infinite doubles stages a discourse on simulation that manifests prominently at the end of the film. Distraught and disillusioned by the revelation that he is not unique, David falls from Hobby's tall building and plunges into the sea. At the bottom of the ocean he finds himself face to face with a statue of *Pinocchio*'s Blue Fairy preserved among the ruins and debris of a long-lost Coney Island. David hopelessly entreats the statue, as one might a god, to make him real. After his battery dies, he remains submerged in this wondrous encounter for 2,000 years until he is discovered and reanimated by incredibly advanced androids that have inherited Earth from an extinct human race. It is unclear whether David has "awakened" in the future or in his own fantasy. Hobby implies the latter when he suggests at the beginning of *A.I.* that David will be an unprecedented scientific innovation, "a robot that dreams." Ultimately, the film suggests, the boy lives out the remainder of his mechanical life in an enchanting (posthuman) world in which it has become impossible to distinguish between reality and illusion.

It is significant that the scene of David's ambiguous waking dream is, of all possible places, Coney Island, the amusement park that emerged with the cinema in the 1890s. In addition to reproducing the shocks, thrills, and disorientations that drew Benjamin to the cinema, Coney Island was a mass-mediated world apart, a kind of virtual reality comprised entirely of a series of dizzying electrical and mechanical spectacles. Like the cinema, it was celebrated, criticized, and experienced as a collective space of leisure, entertainment, and play—an "environmental phantasmagoria" (Kasson 49) that offered visitors an escape from the realities of their working lives by immersing them in a world of simulations. Jean Baudrillard, elaborating on Benjamin, has called this world an endless "play of illusions and phantasms," a "hyperreality" (12).

The "hyperreal" dimension of the Coney Island in which David finds himself is compounded by the fact that what appears in this part of *A.I.* is actually Spielberg's computer-generated simulation of the phantasmagoria that was Coney Island. Captivated by the "spell" of this digital phantasmagoria—a simulation of a simulation—David embarks on a new adventure. Through his interaction with androids which read his memories by projecting them like cinematic images, David is introduced to an animated version of the Blue Fairy, who grants him his wish and makes him "real." In the final sequence of the film, David is temporarily reunited with his mother Monica, who embraces the automaton boy in an act of love, thus confirming that he is unique. Being long dead, of course, Monica is apparently simulated as a clone or as a figment of David's imagination. Either way her love is a simulation, which suggests that David can be unique only in a dream world where even his aura, like that of the Hollywood star, is a simulation.

The postmodern ambiguity of David's fate—is his world real or is it all a robot's dream?—captures an anxiety linked largely to the astonishing innovations in digital imaging technologies of the 1990s. At the time of *A.I.*'s release, the computer-generated images and digital effects of which Spielberg made extensive use were fueling powerful discourses on the potential for electronic media to produce exceptionally convincing simulations, undetectable as simulations, like a perfect automaton. The idea of a perfect digital simulation corresponds with how electronic images can conceal their status as products of human labor so well that they appear with an uncanny "effortlessness" (Sobchack), like magical objects conjured out of thin air.[2]

Although he was critical of such powerful displays of illusionism, it is likely that Benjamin would have reflected on digital cinema, or at the very least on Spielberg's film, with the same kind of optimism with which he imagined the possibilities of early cinema. Consider that as an automaton David represents a history of philosophical toys that enchant and astonish but also promote curiosity, skepticism, and debate by playing with and confusing the boundaries between human and machine, reality and reproduction. David performs the kind of critical engagement afforded by the automaton's game of perception—is he real or fake, and how does he work?—by questioning and investigating his own status as a simulation. As a metaphor for film—that other mechanical simulation of life—David points to how, even in the context of digital images, the experience of the cinema is animated by a similar game of perception and the *possibility of critiquing the illusion*, which for Benjamin was of utmost importance.

Exploring Benjamin's resonance with our contemporary moment in this way is possible largely because his work on mass culture and modern life is kaleidoscopic. He wrote broadly in a wandering, fragmentary, and dialectical style with a tendency toward contradictions and ambiguities. As Hannah Arendt explains, his writings are like elusive reflections or afterimages of "the *flânerie* in his thinking" (43). This quality has given Benjamin's ideas a distinct mobility, as though in thinking he has strolled every boulevard and alleyway of his—and our—culture. Beyond the material discussed here, his influences are visible in everything from phenomenology, apparatus theory, and the work of Gilles Deleuze, Giorgio Agamben, and Guy Debord, to contemporary discourses on memory, globalization, immersion, play, and even video games. However elusive and unsystematic, his theoretical engagements with film function like a critical space in which we are invited to "calmly and adventurously go travelling" so that we might rediscover the cinema.

NOTES

1. With regard to the dialectical presence and absence of the screen actor, André Bazin makes the strikingly similar claim that the cinema "is a mirror with a delayed reflection" (see Bazin, *What Is Cinema?* 1:97).
2. By "magical object" I mean to invoke a discourse cultivated by Benjamin and others—like Adorno and Karl Marx—on the commodity form as a kind of "phantasmagoria," that is, an illusion that masks the techniques and technologies with which it is created.

6

Jean Epstein

Cinema's Encounter with Modern Life

SARAH KELLER

The writings of Jean Epstein (1897–1953) on cinema constitute a richly complicated set of ideas about the cinema's role as an art. Because his thoughts developed nearly in tandem with his initiation as a film director, his thinking about the cinema and his film practice mutually inform each other. Epstein's films compile visually striking images that coincide with his sense of cinema's capacities for expression. Looking at a few key phases of Epstein's writing about the cinema over thirty years of engagement with it demonstrates consistent obsessions even across the emergence of several different styles in his filmmaking. I want to focus briefly here on three aspects of his writings—his notions of *lyrosophie, photogénie*, and the expressive capacities of film sound—to provide a sense of how his work allows for and even promotes a cinema that simultaneously mobilizes narrative and non-narrative elements as a way of presenting and representing modern subjects.

Epstein begins writing about cinema shortly before he makes his own first film (*Pasteur*, 1922). His invitation to direct that film arrived thanks to the success he sustained in his publication of three related volumes in 1921–1922, *La Poésie d'aujourd'hui: un nouvel état d'intelligence* (*Poetry Today: A New State of Intelligence*, 1921), *Bonjour cinéma* (*Hello, Cinema*, 1921), and *La Lyrosophie* (1922). *La Poésie d'aujourd'hui* begins in the realm of literary concerns, taking up the dictates of poetry before turning to the ways in which cinema addresses similar issues: in particular, Epstein focuses on the capacities of a form that does not take narrative as its basis, positing a mode that would solidify the artistic ambitions of cinema and offer an alternative for meaning-making that does not depend solely on the demands of character motivations, causation, or a narrative arc. *Bonjour cinéma*, following closely on this first book, includes some of Epstein's most familiar works, including the widely anthologized "Magnification." It puts the theoretical ruminations of texts of that ilk side by side in mosaic fashion with poems, fan bills, musical notations, and images of his favorite actors in films. In both its form and content it offers an alternative to analytical, logical structures of meaning. *La Lyrosophie* then introduces foundational theoretical ideas that, as Katie Kirtland suggests, serve as "the armature upon which he constructs his film theory" (281)—though these ideas are manifested with different ends in mind elsewhere (for example, we see them reemerge in his writings on the paradoxes of discontinuity and continuity inherent in the cinematic apparatus, which he discusses in detail at the beginning of *L'Intelligence d'une machine*). *Lyrosophie* is the idea that modern life's attendant fatigue holds out the promise of reconfiguring modern beings' relationship to time, space, and perception. By suppressing a learned and potentially faulty logic of the too-conscious mind, fatigue offers access to the fuller potential of the mind. Importantly, the book also describes a relationship between a scientific logic and a subjective, emotive logic, arguing that the two are parts of a larger intellectual process, with affect encompassing a broader range of activity in fact, since it is the means by which one must come to discern even scientific knowledge. Illustrating this concept with a range of examples, Epstein suggests that language and ultimately the cinema also work through this doubling:

> The *lyrosophie* of language thus succeeds in giving a double sense or even a double series of senses to each verbal expression. One comprises a rational, logical, stable meaning for which the possible variations are rather limited. The other is formed by affective meanings, which the logical meanings bring along after them. These affective meanings are infinitely more complex, more and differently specific, and more unpredictable. Thanks to them, the word is clearly much richer and more largely expressive. . . . It is more intelligent in that it offers the opportunity to understand more things, but it runs the risk of not making understood the one thing it hoped to say among the many things it can say. (181–182; my translation)

The tension between the specific, denotative, intentional meaning of words and their unpredictably connotative or allusive meanings has ramifications for Epstein's film theory in terms of how images do double duty as both logical and affective meaning makers. (It also explains why Epstein may have often chosen a thin or melodramatic plot structure—for example in *Coeur fidèle*, 1923—through which his images might be allowed room to resonate in that way.) *La Lyrosophie* emphasizes the balancing act between logic and affect: "Each word in its adult form possesses two sides: it is intelligible on one hand and moving on the other. These two qualities generally depend on each other and are therefore, in this way, contradictory" (*Lyrosophie* 167–168). His theory of film depends on this balance, so that images might serve a narrative purpose, pushing forward the drama by providing motivations and consequences, while simultaneously dwelling upon (even becoming arrested by) multiple resonances engendered through this "double series of senses."

For Epstein the cinema therefore serves as a kind of deliverance—not an escape, but a complex and potentially multivalent conveyance for meaning akin to the process of thought, which (for Epstein) is seldom straightforward. When confronted with an image, the spectator must navigate the push and pull between the way it functions narratively and the other meanings it activates in the process.

Intimately connected to *lyrosophie*, Epstein advocated for *photogénie*, the concept within his theory that has received the greatest amount of attention. Taking up the term from fellow film critic/theorist Louis Delluc in the early 1920s, Epstein developed the idea of *photogénie* within the context of French film theory and criticism of the interwar period, which aimed to raise cinema to the status of an art form. As Richard Abel has put it, such initiating early theorists "used the theoretical or critical essay as a speculative instrument—which soon became a model—to generate or provoke insight, new ideas, and action" (97). Through the ranging speculations of this type of essay and their resulting insights, theories such as Epstein's developed and were accordingly often marked by conjecture or contradictions.

Photogénie is a notoriously elusive yet provocative idea. It readily takes hold in the imagination as describing something familiar about a certain experience of film, but it has also been plagued by the charge of being notoriously difficult to pin down. This does not negate the work Epstein accomplished toward articulating its terms. As early as *Bonjour cinéma*'s "Magnification," he adumbrates *photogénie*'s qualities, noting its fleeting but puissant ability to arrest the attention: "Until now, I have never seen an entire minute of pure *photogénie*. Therefore, one must admit that the photogenic is like a spark that appears in fits and starts." *Photogénie* fixates on anticipation and a process of becoming: "Even more beautiful than a laugh is the face preparing for it. I must interrupt. I love the mouth which is about to speak and holds back" (Epstein, "Magnification" 236). Interestingly, Epstein's writing frequently mimics the function of *photogénie*: it interrupts the flow of his thought (as in the lyrosophical mode) and leads outward from the center of the image he describes to become, possibly, many other related things, ideas, and feelings. While the object filmed (or written about) exists in this semi-inchoate state, it has enormous potential to increase in significance beyond the way it serves the narrative. In a later essay that goes the furthest toward defining *photogénie*, "On Certain Characteristics of *Photogénie*," Epstein considers how a prop as ordinary as a revolver might well serve an important function in the plot but is also "no longer a revolver, it is the revolver-character, in other words the impulse toward or remorse for crime, failure, suicide. It is as dark as the temptations of the night, bright as the gleam of gold lusted after, taciturn as passion, squat, brutal, heavy, cold, wary, menacing. It has a temperament, habits, memories, a will, a soul" (317). While the first descriptions tend toward functions that might also serve the narrative, at least obliquely (leading toward familiar plot devices and themes such as "crime, failure, suicide"), as he continues Epstein allows the meanings that accrue to the revolver to become more and more affective and abstract.

A photogenic mode accomplishes such connotative resonance through an emphasis on specific cinematographic devices. Through these devices, as Stuart Liebman has argued, *photogénie* shares qualities with the Russian formalists' defamiliarization of objects and images: "Close-ups and camera movements (especially rapid, whirling ones), among other filmic procedures, extracted things from their ordinary contexts; their removal often suspended denotations, refashioned referents, and thereby broadened the scope of connotations" (85). Superimpositions, for example, are also a favored device in Epstein's cinema, involving a simultaneity in the construction of the image that brings forth the potential for *photogénie.*

Throughout his thirty years of writing about the cinema Epstein revisited, extended, and complicated these notions that serve as the beginning of his theorizations. For instance, in *L'Intelligence d'une machine* he elaborates on the role of the close-up in generating photogenic, lyrosophical, disjunctive yet evocative effects: "The close-up further undermines the familiar order of appearances. . . . So many rigorous and superficial classifications presumed of nature are but artifices and illusions. Beneath this mirage, the multitude of forms proves essentially homogeneous and strangely anarchic" (2–3). One of the clearest moments in the development of his thinking is reflected in the upheaval that ensued when the coming of sound changed some of the fundamental terms of the medium. His writings about sound serve as a rich, early foray into its potential for film aesthetics. The aural correlative to *photogénie,* aptly dubbed by Epstein *phonogénie,* also maintains the balance between moving things forward and holding them back, primarily by soliciting the filmic auditor's attention parallel to and in excess of narrative concerns. For instance, after using slow-motion sound in his film *Le Tempestaire* (1947), he argues for the extension of a double sense of meanings available through this type of experimentation: "The thing is, the ordinary data we receive from hearing are themselves confused, unstable, fleeting, and do not lend themselves to logical examination, definition, or ordered signification. While it is often ineffable, a mere noise may still directly cause a psycho-physiological shock which puts the subject in a state of instantaneous, intense, thoughtless emotion" (Epstein, "Close-Up" 366). Together, the sound and image work in counterpoint for and against the smooth delivery of narrative. They thus have the power to access the whole being of the modern subject that both does and does not fully attend to the stimuli provided by the film.

All of these ways of soliciting the double meanings available through the film image and soundtrack provide insight into not only Epstein's own films but many other works, from the classical canon with its frequent narrative excesses and solicitation of attention to things outside the narrative proper (deferring the steady flow of narrative information, however fleetingly, as in the glorious lighting of Marlene Dietrich in Josef von Sternberg's *Blonde Venus* [1932]), to experimental films that depend on accessing multiple registers for their meaning, to post-classical films that depend on a tension between the two in order to provide a fresh cinematic experience. Briefly, let us turn to examples in these last two categories, to see how Epstein's theory might enhance a spectator's experience of such films.

Meshes of the Afternoon

Maya Deren's first film, *Meshes of the Afternoon* (1943) (made with her then-husband, Alexander Hammid), readily demonstrates several Epsteinian principles. Not altogether surprisingly, Deren's own theorizations about film, the most extended of which appears in her work *An Anagram of Ideas on Art, Form, and Film*, reflect certain of the traits of experimental theorization contained in Epstein's *Bonjour cinéma* and certain of his themes concerning the purview of cinema more generally. Her notions of simultaneity, surprise, and "vertical" investigations of the film image in particular correspond with Epstein's notion of the constant tension in the film image between denotative and connotative meanings (see further Deren, "Symposium"; S. Keller; Nichols).

Meshes of the Afternoon features Deren and Hammid as the lead characters, and follows a very loose narrative thread. It opens with a sequence wherein Deren's unnamed character walks up a path, enters a house, and looks around at a number of objects (a phone off the hook, a knife stuck in bread) before settling down to sleep in an armchair. This sequence of actions then repeats three more times, and in each iteration another Deren collects in the house until there are four in total: three others who meet to determine the fate of the first one, who continues to sleep in the armchair. The film is thus redolent of the logic of dreamscapes, where repetition (the manufacturing of multiple Derens) and rumination on odd or seemingly emotionally charged details delays forward movement. Still, the narrative, such as it is, depends on this recursive logic. In her publicity materials for the film, Deren called it "a film concerned with the inner realities of an individual and the way in which the subconscious will develop an apparently casual occurrence into a critical emotional experience" (Deren to Dorman). The film effectively has it two ways: it moves forward and circles back, rendering its images both reflective of the "inner realities" and grounded in the actions that are doomed to repeat in various forms. It maintains the story of its protagonist by showing her constantly stymied progress through the film's terrain.

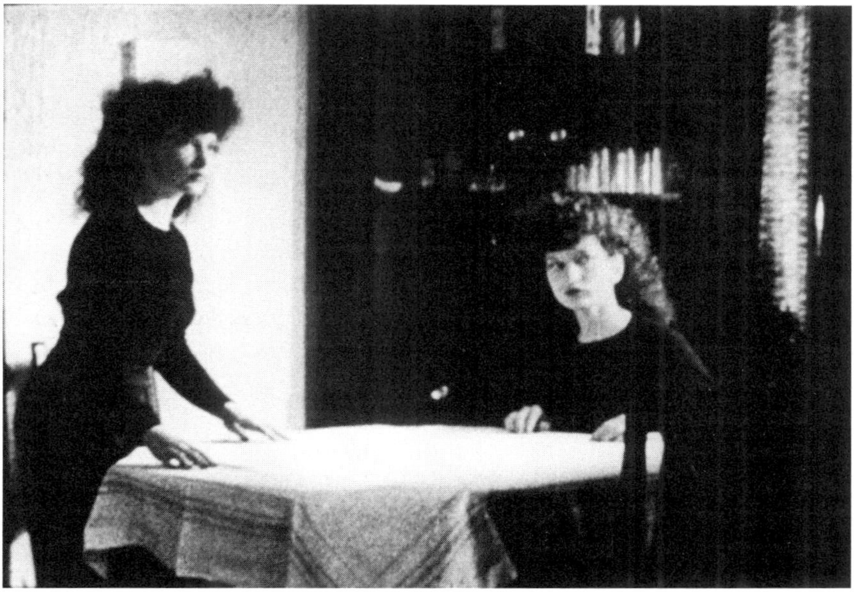

FIGURE 6.1 Multiplying figures in *Meshes of the Afternoon* (Maya Deren, 1943). Courtesy Anthology Film Archives.

In a letter from 1953, written in response to a communication from a fan (Dorman to Deren), Deren articulates the intentions of *Meshes of the Afternoon* in terms that echo Epstein's theory:

> *Meshes of the Afternoon* is, indeed, a kind of time study. It is based on the idea that, like a sound, so an event or image, once created, vibrates perpetually, outward, in the atmosphere. And if action, instead of developing normally, got stuck like a phonograph record, so that instead of developing the images, or if the event became reiterative . . . well, what would happen if those three images, which were actually one, confronted each other in time? (Deren to Dorman)

From this description of the simultaneity of an image's development and stoppages, Deren goes on to address the metaphor of the vertical and horizontal constructions of a film text in such a way that renders them parallel concepts to Epstein's "double senses": she sees them as "a competent metaphor for the distinction between dramatic or narrative structure on the one hand, and poetic structure on the other" (Deren to Dorman).

Meshes of the Afternoon's first image readily demonstrates this distinction, as well as the tension that ensues between these structures. A mannequin arm lowers from the top of the frame to drop a (fake) flower on the sidewalk where shortly afterward Deren's character will come upon it. What is the status of this shot? It happens before any narrative that one might speak of exists, and it contains a number of resonances that lead outside of the film: for example, associations with the symbology of the flower (a poppy), or with Deren's photographs of mannequins in her "Experimental Portraiture" series, made with Hammid in 1942. At this early stage, we cannot know what the narrative function of this shot is, if any, even if later shots allow it to accrue significance in retrospect. However much Deren claimed to want to distance the film from Freudian meanings in particular, the props populating the film have strong a priori symbolic associations attached to them: mannequin, key, bread, bed, telephone, flower, window, mirror, knife. They inspire reflection rather than forward movement, and exist on their own terms even as they assist narrative meaning.

Melancholia

Precisely the same may be said for the opening shots of a very different film, Lars von Trier's *Melancholia* (2011). After a prologue through which, as Kristen Whissel convincingly argues, the major themes and concerns of the film are introduced in a series of "effects emblems," the film centers on the relationship between two sisters, Justine (Kirsten Dunst) and Claire (Charlotte Gainsbourg), Justine's wedding and illness, and the possibility of an apocalyptic collision of Earth with another planet (see Whissel 171–184). After the prologue the film is divided into two parts, one for each sister, with the first detailing Justine's failed wedding party at the golf course of an estate owned by Claire and her husband John (Kiefer Sutherland) and the second concerning how each character deals with the imminent collision of the rogue planet Melancholia with Earth. This two-part narrative unfolds in a fairly conventional way, so that despite some quirks mainly having to do with Justine's melancholia, the characters act according to clear motivations, which drive the plot forward to an ultimate form of closure (the end of everything).

While that narrative treats sensational subject matter (for example, paranoia and suicide) and includes some visually stunning shots (as when homemade hot-air balloons are released into the night sky or Justine and Claire are seen in a bird's-eye shot riding horses through the estate grounds), it is the opening prologue of sixteen shots that serves as the film's most unique and arresting feature. An effort to account for the status of these relative to the whole film demonstrates how presciently Epstein's theory anticipates the way a range of narrative (and non-narrative) strategies emerging out of a spectacular digital idiom might come to shape the cinema. The subject matter of these images falls into categories: footage of the estate grounds rolling with rich greens under luminous skies; Hubble-style space footage of Earth and Melancholia; allusive shots suggestive of paintings or shots from other films;

and some shots that fall into multiple categories at once. All of these images take the form of tableaux (sometimes giving the impression of terraria) that set the film's themes and narrative elements into (extremely slow) motion.

In a *New York Times* article on the film shortly after its release, Manohla Dargis focuses exclusively on these shots—the "overture" that she dubs "a masterpiece in miniature that is a palimpsest of literary, artistic and cinematic allusions" ("This Is How the End Begins" MT1). She elaborates on the specific qualities of the images and suggests a representative sampling of their ensuing resonances. The difficulty of doing this in a sequence so elaborately constructed and allusive results in Dargis's complicated descriptions for each shot, even necessitating three entries to more fully describe the first shot. Her initial comment describes the way the image looks: "The movie opens with a fade from black to a close-up of Justine's head, with a bit of her neck. Her eyes are closed, and her head is slightly to the left of the center of the frame." When she gets to the dead birds that "begin falling from the sky like stones," she adds by way of interpretation: "an intimation of the disaster(s) to come." Dargis's second item is reserved for the soundtrack, which features the calculated use of a sensuous Wagnerian motif:

> On the soundtrack the exquisite prelude to Wagner's opera *Tristan and Isolde* (completed 1859), begins to play. Wagner described the opera as 'one of endless yearning, longing, the bliss and wretchedness of love; world, power, fame, honor, chivalry, loyalty and friendship all blown away like an insubstantial dream,' for which there is 'one sole redemption—death, finality, a sleep without awakening.' (MT1)

The Wagner adds affective meaning within the scene, and it leads outward to other referents, for example the composer's own pronouncements as referenced by Dargis, or Marcel Proust's *Remembrance of Things Past*: "If the pianist wanted to play the ride from *The Valkyrie* or the prelude from *Tristan*, Mme. Verdurin would protest, not because she did not like that music, but on the contrary because it made too strong an impression on her" (*Swann's Way* 196). *Tristan und Isolde* has multiple histories and resonances. Many have considered that its key quirk, both its confounding quality and its genuine originality, rests in its harmonic suspensions, its refusal to resolve. Melodies build, retreat, repeat, and ultimately remain open and unresolved, undercutting the film's depiction of the end of everything. Dargis's final comment about the first shot of the film makes precarious the film's balancing act of openness and closure, underlining the balance between poetic/allusive resonance and narration building toward conclusion. Fixating on the choice of "Justine" for the name of Dunst's character, Dargis notes the literary reference to the Marquis de Sade's novel as well as von Trier's other films, in particular *Breaking the Waves* (1996), in which the similarly mystical prescience of a young woman plays an important role. Dargis thus begins to register the many layers of meaning upon which the opening shot alone operates. The extreme slow motion through which the shots unfold allows plenty of time for such reflection.

In fact, notwithstanding the final, empty black image of the film, read by some critics as a depiction of the nothingness in the aftermath of Earth and Melancholia's collision, *Melancholia* as a whole permits and even encourages a sense of irresolution in light of the multiplicity of allusions it evokes. For one example, reference to Ophelia both in one of Claire's painting books and the fourteenth shot of the overture (depicting Justine floating down a river in her wedding dress) might allow the film to be read as Justine's psychodrama rather than any real occurrence. For another, a painting by Pieter Bruegel the Elder, *Hunters in the Snow* (1565), first seen burning in the opening prologue, points to the tripartite construction of meaning inherent in all of these shots: it alludes to a part of the narrative (a *narrative/thematic function*); it incorporates its own meanings outside of anything having to do with the cinema (a *self-contained/non-narrative function*); and it reflects the larger cinema of which von Trier considers his work to be a part (an *externally resonant/allusive function*). The *narrative/thematic function* operates by creating a link between this shot in the prologue and a moment later in the film, when in a fit of pique Justine changes all the art books in Claire's study from abstract impressionists to representational paintings, many of a desolate or gruesome nature, including the Bruegel. The *self-contained/non-narrative function* derives from the fact that this painting, depicting hunters returning, weary, from the hunt and without a bounty to compensate for their trouble also resonates with its own allegorical, cycle-of-the-seasons meanings that take one temporarily out of the narrative proper; finally, the *externally resonant/allusive function* becomes discernible in von Trier's clear admiration for and reference to the work of filmmaker Andrei Tarkovsky, who used this same painting in *Solaris* (1972). (Other shots corroborate this referent by echoing shots from other Tarkovsky films, including *The Sacrifice* [*Offret*, 1986].) The painting opens up a pathway for multiple meanings to accrue, in what Maya Deren would call the "vertical" investigation of a moment that temporarily leaves the drive of narrative and causality behind in favor of a place for reflection.

If there is a narrative impulse when we first see the opening sixteen images, it is necessarily sublimated. One *cannot* read these shots narratively at first; only retroactively might one read narrative meaning into the shots. The film maintains a restive balance between, in Epstein's phrase, "poetic meaning" and narrative. The balance is indeed a tricky one, and the spectator has some say in the question of which has greater emphasis. Whissel addresses exactly this question in her elegant argument about the prologue. Providing a crucial corrective for reading the sequence through the recent anachronism of dubbing such CGI-laden spectacles part of an "attractions" mode,[1] she argues that

FIGURE 6.2 Bruegel burning in *Melancholia* (Lars von Trier, Zentropa, 2011). Digital frame enlargement.

the von Trier shots, arresting though they may be, are not divorced from narrative concerns. For instance: "several of the shots in the prologue externalize the internal emotional and psychological states described or experienced by the protagonists in later scenes and are, therefore, inseparable from the development of character" (179). While acknowledging the way one might and probably should read these shots as tied into the narrative dynamics of the film as a whole, I want to propose that their role is not limited to this function, nor are the shots absolutely inseparable from character. Indeed, it is precisely their ability to be both narrative and not narrative that makes their role in the film compelling.[2] If we read them retrospectively, they gain in narrative meaning, but they cannot lose entirely the sense of being separate from that meaning, the way one necessarily first confronted them. Considering the significant visual differences between the way they appear in the prologue and how they function at points in the narrative further opens up a gap that the film seeks not to close but rather exploits, reminding the viewer of Epstein's "affective meanings [that] are infinitely more complex, more and differently specific, and more unpredictable" (*Lyrosophie* 181–182). These shots might well have resonance for narrative, but they simultaneously transport the spectator to a space outside of it.

Melancholia's opening images are excessive and opulent: their colors (green, gold, blue) are often richly saturated, and their presentation in slow motion demands heightened attention. However stunning and sensuous they may be, a suspicion persists that these images might also represent a less conservative aesthetic than the Romanticism it seems to embrace suggests. The hyper-Romantic Prelude to *Tristan and Isolde*, a musical theme repeated throughout the film and especially tied to both the planet Melancholia and Justine's character, complements the narration and the lush imagery while simultaneously underscoring the film's potential critique of such visual opulence: as such, it constitutes a form of *phonogénie*. The way von Trier uses Wagner recalls Justine's sarcastic response to Claire's suggestion that they greet the ending of the planet with a glass of wine on the terrace: "How about a song? Beethoven's Ninth, something like that?" In case her sarcasm doesn't register, Justine tells Claire exactly what she thinks of her plan: "I think it's a piece of shit." The film's strategies—grand music and glorious, sumptuous, provident images—are called into question even as they work on spectators. But if the spectator is meant to align with Justine's apparently nearly omniscient perspective on the end of all things, then this scathing evocation of grand music to accompany the apocalypse suggests that von Trier also attempts to have it both ways: a visually and aurally sumptuous condemnation of sumptuousness. This reading is strongly inflected by the way the film asks the spectator to immerse herself in narrative devices it seems constantly to be commenting upon, providing a buzz in the mind not unlike that which always accompanies shots of the planets, as if in providing deep space for reflection on the film's themes a distracting hum should ever draw one back to Earth.

As Richard Abel's introduction to the period of Epstein's development of film theory suggests, "Disruptive of space and time, story and spectacle, *photogénie* contained the potential for a modernist aesthetic" (111). Its disruptions, interrupting the flow of narrative in a brief fit and start, allow the image to yield its other associated meanings simultaneous with whatever the narrative might be up to. Epstein's film theory, which embraces multiple possibilities, can help us to better understand how films of many sorts create meaning. It allows the kind of absorption required by a narrative flow *and* provides space for interruptions that lead elsewhere into a multiplicity of meanings. In short, Epstein's theorizations signal a way to navigate this multiplicity and allow it to reflect the simultaneously divided and focused center of modern experience.

NOTES

1. The "cinema of attractions," a concept theorized by Tom Gunning and André Gaudreault, argues that a mode of spectacle features solicitation of the spectator and an overall aesthetics of display featured in early cinema (prior to circa 1906); Whissel agrees with critics who wish to preserve the historical specificity of this mode, arguing that it does not take on the same form in more contemporary digital spectacles, especially those in blockbuster films that make ample use of such effects.
2. Whissel makes a related argument when she highlights the "dynamic emblematic assemblage," dependent on a "mosaic" of messages, despite her sense that these "are ultimately integrated into the narrative" (182).

7

Sergei Eisenstein

Attractions/Montage/Animation

MATTHEW SOLOMON

Sergei Mikhailovich Eisenstein (1898–1948) is often understood primarily as a theorist of film editing, or *montage.* Montage is undoubtedly central for Eisenstein's thinking about cinema as well as for his film practice, but Jacques Aumont notes at the outset of his book *Montage Eisenstein* that "there is no unitary 'concept of montage' that comes to theoretical fruition over the course of his career—at least not in the limited, rationally defined, and constant form by which one could characterize a true concept" (viii–ix). Thus, Aumont considers the more general "*principle* of montage" in Eisenstein's writing (viii–ix). The principle of montage, in countless manifestations and seemingly limitless possibilities and applications, dominated Eisenstein's intellectual biography and filmography. This chapter juxtaposes Eisenstein's principle of montage with two related concepts, *attractions* and *animation*, both of which are dependent upon it.

Reading Eisenstein can be daunting and intellectually bracing. The range of his learning and the ambition of his theoretical aims are both staggering (if not always entirely consistent), while his sheer enthusiasm for ideas comes through, even in translation, in an affective way that is quite consistent with his own theorizing. Further, the structure and style of his prose often reads like a cinematic montage sequence. Eisenstein's writing may have mimicked some of the characteristics of his filmmaking, but the converse is also true: Eisenstein's work as a filmmaker is effectively inseparable from his theoretical writing. Oksana Bulgakowa emphasizes that "Eisenstein's analytic matter (which emerged from psychology and psychoanalysis, anthropology and etymology, linguistic, mathematics and geometry, literature, theater, art and music theory) and his artistic practice had been united all his life" ("Evolving Eisenstein" 38). Eisenstein was a bibliophile who read voraciously in several different languages, including Russian, English, French, and German. Reading was a continual source of inspiration and he found ideas that he could use in countless unexpected places.

As Bulgakowa suggests, consideration of Eisenstein as a film theorist must simultaneously engage with his films, which provided a working laboratory for developing and testing ideas while also later serving as objects for critical self-reflection and self-investigation. Eisenstein developed his ideas across an extensive corpus of writing, much of which remained unpublished during his lifetime. His writings have become progressively more and more available in English, but many of the later works exist in various states of incompleteness. Some, like what he wrote on Disney—considered here—were only partly developed, and thus include fairly long sections that are little more than notes. Frustratingly skeletal and digressively ruminative at times, these incomplete works contain some highly suggestive ideas that Eisenstein himself never made fully cogent.

Eisenstein's most important initial ideas about cinema actually took shape as part of his work in theater, which was the source of his interest in biomechanical acting as well as the context for his formulation of the concept of the "attraction." Like Orson Welles, whom Eisenstein called "one of the most interesting and promising figures in the Western cinema" in 1943 (Letter to Alexander Korda), Eisenstein turned to filmmaking in order to make films that could be screened as components of live theater productions. The film known by the title *Glumov's Diary* was but one "attraction" in the 1923 production of Alexander Ostrovsky's play *Enough Simplicity for Every Wise Man* that Eisenstein directed for the Proletkult Theatre.[1]

Eisenstein had originally intended to become an architect and engineer like his father, but, as he recalled, "Theatre became the subject of my constant attention and enthusiasm" ("How I Became" 284). When he was nineteen, writes Peter Wollen, "The Revolution . . . smashed the co-ordinates of his life, but it also gave him the opportunity to produce himself anew" (*Signs* 19). When in 1917 classes at the Petrograd Institute of Engineering were cancelled on account of the Revolution, Eisenstein joined the Red Army and later formed a military theatrical troupe. With the Revolution's end in 1920, he abandoned his studies of civil engineering and moved to Moscow to study Japanese. Soon, he joined with Moscow's Proletkult Theatre, working initially as a set designer.

Attractions

As a child, Eisenstein was fascinated by the circus, which proved to be a crucial inspiration when he went to work in theater. He and his collaborators sought nothing less than "abolishing the very institution of theatre as such and replacing it by a showplace for achievements in the field at the *level of the everyday skills of the masses*" in order, he wrote, to "liberate theatre completely from the yoke of the 'illusory depictions' and 'representations' that have hitherto been the decisive, unavoidable and only possible approach" ("Montage of Attractions" 29, 31). The eccentric modes of performance seen in the circus as well as the modular arrangement of the circus show into distinct acts (and separate rings) were equally important for Eisenstein. Instead of conceiving of a play as a self-contained linear narrative performed by actors simulating the behavior of characters, Eisenstein wanted to harness the directness and energy of the circus.

In the 1923 production the *Wise Man*, "Clowns and 'noise bands' assaulted the audience, under whose seats fireworks exploded. At one point a screen was unrolled and a film diary projected" (Wollen, *Signs* 21). All of these different "attractions" were meant to get the audience to react. Theatrical production thus became a matter of training and programming the proper sequence of "attractions" in the manner of a well-ordered variety show dedicated to ideological ends. Eisenstein emphatically claimed the concept of the "attraction" as *his* initial intervention in Soviet art, writing in his diary, "The attraction is *my* invention" (qtd. in Bulgakowa, *Biography* 39; emphasis in original). Adapted to cinema, attractions formed the basis of Eisenstein's first feature, *Strike* (1925).

Like many industrial films of the time that show how products are made step by step, *Strike* shows a process—that of planning, organizing, and executing a labor strike. Set partly in a factory, the film is structured as a series of attractions, among which are a fight between two men as they struggle to keep their balance atop a board teetering back and forth on another man's back and the clownish antics of a group of lumpenproletarians who live in large barrels buried in the ground. The most notorious of *Strike*'s attractions are shots of violence: a soldier on horseback dropping a baby to its death from a high balcony and the slaughter of a bull in close-up, which Eisenstein cross-cut with acted scenes of the strikers slaughtered by mounted soldiers. Much of the film's action is staged along the axis of the camera to directly address—and often confront—the viewer of the film. *Strike* ends with an extreme close-up of the eyes of a factory worker who committed suicide earlier in the film after being wrongfully accused by the management of stealing a micrometer. He stares directly at us, imploring the audience to "Remember, Proletarians!" An intertitle reminds viewers of the places where a number of strikes had been violently suppressed in Russia during the early twentieth century.

Strike generated vigorous critical controversy. Particularly outspoken in his criticisms was Eisenstein's rival Dziga Vertov, whose film *Cine-Eye* (1924), credited collectively to his Kinoks group, vied with *Strike* for the gold medal at the 1925 Paris Exhibition of Art and Industry (Bulgakowa, *Biography* 54). Vertov accused Eisenstein of having borrowed the Kinoks' methods while betraying them at the same time through what he described as "a whole series of qualities and particulars which are taken not from 'life as it is,' but from the so-called theatre of fools" (125)—a clear potshot at the eccentric performances and theatricalized attractions of *Strike*. Eisenstein retorted by insisting that his film had nothing in common with Vertov's, phrasing his response in a series of staccato sentences that resemble one of his montage-lists:

> The *Cine-Eye* is not just a symbol of *vision*: it is also a symbol of *contemplation*. But we need *not contemplation but action*.
>
> It is not a "Cine-Eye" that we need but a "Cine-Fist."
>
> Soviet cinema must cut through to the skull! It is not "through the combined vision of millions of eyes that we shall fight the bourgeois world" (Vertov): we'd rapidly give them a million black eyes! ("Materialist Approach" 59; emphasis in original)

For Eisenstein, "a work of art (at least in . . . theatre and cinema) is first and foremost a tractor ploughing over the audience's psyche in a particular class context" (56)—like the eponymous sea vessel in his film *Battleship Potemkin* (1925), the prow of which bears down on us (cannons pointed directly at the viewer). Like a tractor, a film should be engineered to be functional, its value as a work of art based entirely on its usefulness in the class struggle. It is the combination of attractions through montage that is particularly crucial. While Eisenstein's two essays on attractions propose montage at the level of the "moment" and the "action," he subsequently focused increasingly on montage between and within individual shots.

Montage

For Eisenstein, the shot is the basic unit of cinema, but it acquires meaning only insofar as it is placed into relationships with other shots. Eisenstein insisted, "montage is conflict," and film editing was like the "series of explosions in an internal combustion engine" ("Beyond the Shot" 88). Consistent with this analogy, his idea of montage often entails a certain degree of repetition for the purposes of emphasis. In *Strike*, for example, it takes a man six successive shots to simply put on his trousers, which he wriggles into with evident difficulty while grimacing sleepily. Eisenstein claims in "The Montage of Film Attractions" with regard to another sequence of *Strike*: "The accumulation of the details of conflicting objects, blows, fighting methods, facial expressions and so on produces just as great an impression as the detailed investigation by the camera of all the phases in a logically unfolding process of struggle" (42). As in the Odessa Steps sequence in *Potemkin*, the temporal sequence of, and spatial relationships between, successive shots are quite secondary to the overall impression produced through a series of attractions.

Eisenstein's contemporary Vsevolod Pudovkin says, "Montage, like living language, uses words, whole pieces of exposed film—and sentences—combinations of those pieces" (78). Eisenstein, however, proposes that Japanese hieroglyphs, or "ideograms," are a more apt comparison. While studying at the Lazarevsky Institute of Oriental Languages for the Proletkult Theatre, he "memorized 1500 words, 150 characters" (Bulgakowa, *Biography* 19) and put his knowledge of Japanese characters to work in writing the postscript to a book about Japanese cinema by Naum Kaufman. In it, Eisenstein quickly dismisses Japanese silent film as "quite unaware of montage" and therefore un-cinematic, but identifies "cinematic features of Japanese culture," including Kabuki theater, portraits by the printmaker Sharaku, haiku poetry, and what he describes as "copulative" hieroglyphs, which combine two characters:

> The point is that the copulation—perhaps we had better say the combination—of two hieroglyphs of the simplest series is regarded not as their sum total but as their product, i.e. as a value of another dimension, another degree: each taken separately corresponds to an *object* but their combination corresponds to a *concept*. The combination of two 'representable' objects achieves the representation of something that cannot be graphically represented.
>
> For example: the representation of water and an eye signifies 'to weep,' the representation of an ear next to a drawing of a door means 'to listen,' a dog and a mouth mean 'to bark.' ("Beyond the Shot" 82–83; emphasis in original)

Eisenstein returns to this analogy (and the same series of copulative hieroglyphs) in "The Dramaturgy of Film Form," contending "*montage is not an idea composed of successive shots stuck together but an idea that* DERIVES *from the collision between two shots that are independent of one another*" (95; emphasis and capitalization in original). For Eisenstein, montage collisions took place at multiple levels between and within shots and could thus be carefully orchestrated.

Just as Japanese characters provided a telling example of how "the collision of two factors *gives rise to an idea*" ("Beyond the Shot" 87, my emphasis), Eisenstein aspired to "intellectual effects" generated by intellectual montage. "At the same time, however," writes Wollen, "he moved away from the role of montage as the agent of reason (as exemplified in his project of filming Marx's *Capital*) toward its capacity for arousing emotion, toward ecstasy as the final goal" ("Perhaps. . . ." 46).

If in 1929 Eisenstein hesitated to use the word "copulative" to describe the calligraphic combinations that produced certain Japanese characters, he showed no such reluctance in making the metaphor between montage and reproduction explicit in *The Old and the New* [also known as *The General Line*], a film he completed the same year. That year, he also noted, "Very many people have remarked on the extraordinary physiological quality of the effect of *The General Line*" ("Fourth Dimension" 113), pointing to an effect that he attributed to the film's use of overtonal montage. After "Fomka," the prize bull, arrives at the collective farm, the peasants stage a wedding ceremony and bring out "The Bride," a heifer, swathed in garlands and ribbons. The nuptials are consummated immediately in a sequence that cross-cuts between shots of the bellowing Fomka and shots of his mate, udders quivering, as he canters and then gallops toward her. The tempo of the editing quickens as he nears, climaxing with a rapid montage of explosions and rushing water. The next scene shows Fomka grazing in a meadow with frolicking calves. The attraction is carnal, a bestial analog for the cream separator sequence that comes earlier in the film. In that famous sequence, Eisenstein uses a protracted montage of spinning mechanical motion, flickering facial close-ups, and white spurting liquid to depict the benefits of collectivized agriculture as a joyful, long-anticipated communal ejaculation. Years later, Eisenstein quoted a magazine article's description of the sequence at some length:

> Suddenly, right before our eyes, milk condenses and turns to cream!: Eyes sparkle, teeth shine through breaking smiles. A joyfully smiling, peasant girl, Martha, stretches out her hands to capture the flow of cream, vertically streaming toward her; cream splatters all over her face; she bursts into a fit of laughter, her joy being sensual, almost animal in nature. One almost expects her to cast off all her clothes in a frenzy of passion to wallow naked in the flood of well-being produced by the spouting torrents of cream. (*Nonindifferent Nature* 40)

This long quotation is part of Eisenstein's analysis of "pathos," which he describes as "a state of continuous 'ecstasy,' a continuous state of 'being beside oneself'" (38). An analogous state could be stimulated cinematically, Eisenstein proposes, through pathos constructions like these, compositionally and rhythmically parallel to the physiological experience of ecstasy.

Animation

Eisenstein's pursuit of pathos struck at visceral forms of experience shared by humans and animals alike—attractions that do not require specific cultural knowledge, much less cognition. Analogies between people and animals serve as an important form of characterization in Eisenstein's films from *Strike* all the way through to *Ivan the Terrible*, where specific characters are presented in terms of their animal totems. Many animated films take the identification of humans with animals even further, through forms of graphic anthropomorphizing that are of course utterly impossible in live-action films. In the extended study of Walt Disney that Eisenstein worked on during the 1940s (never completed, but published posthumously in fragmentary form as "On Disney"), Eisenstein pays particular attention to the "unity of man and animal" on which Disney's entire oeuvre is founded (133). For Eisenstein, this unity is "a return to pure totemism and a . . . reverse shift . . . towards evolutionary prehistory" (148). Eisenstein argues that Disney has such great appeal for viewers because his films make manifest the prehistoric animal origins of human civilization, harkening back to some of the very earliest modes of representation and storytelling: "The more ancient the epos, the less man is separated from animal, the closer he is to him, and the more abundant and splendid the comparison with beasts and animals" (135).

But for Eisenstein, an even more primordial attraction of Disney's films is the way they sometimes depict an unbounded capacity for metamorphoses. What Eisenstein terms "plasma appeal" is based upon "the omnipotence of plasma, which contains in 'liquid' form all possibilities of future species and forms" (149). It is this quality of "plasmaticness," "the ability to assume dynamically any form," that fascinates Eisenstein (101). "For those who are shackled by hours of work and regulated moments of rest, by a mathematical precision of time, whose lives are graphed by the cent and the dollar," the infinite possibilities of pure protoplasm, Eisenstein argued, offer a figurative revolt (88).

Naum Kleiman notes that Eisenstein "followed the [Disney] studio's every new release" (79), but I have found no mention of Disney's *Dumbo* (1941) in anything that Eisenstein wrote that has been published in English. The film nevertheless has several homologies with ideas discussed by Eisenstein. *Dumbo* is set largely in a circus and includes a number of "attractions" performed under the big top. Performances like the "pyramid of ponderous pulsating pulchritudinous pachyderms" and Dumbo's high-dive into a pail of water absurdly exaggerate recognizable circus stunts, comically substituting lumbering elephants for agile humans. Yet, these attractions are yoked to a sentimental, even lachrymose plot that cannot be reconciled with Eisenstein's ideological goals. If anything, *Dumbo* works to counter the political aims of agit-cinema: the drunken clowns we hear enthusiastically congratulating themselves for a great performance (when Dumbo is in fact the star of the show) have often been seen as "malicious caricatures of striking Disney Studio cartoonists" (Michael Wilmington qtd. in Denning 403). Clown make-up conceals their faces and they are visible only as shadows on the tent in which they remove their costumes and swill booze. Faceless and caricatured, the shadow figures file out of the tent singing, "We're Going to Hit the Big Boss for a Raise."

But, as they're leaving one clown knocks a bottle of bubbling alcohol into a water barrel with his rear end. Dumbo and his friend Timothy J. Mouse unknowingly drink from this and their accidental intoxication provides a narrative pretext for the film's most plasmatic sequence, which is accompanied by the song "Pink Elephants on Parade." Timothy and Dumbo both start hiccupping yellow bubbles that float through the air while retaining their shape. Dumbo blows a cubical bubble and an enormous bubble that assumes the shape of an elephant. This pink elephant-bubble blows another pink elephant-bubble from its trunk, which in turn produces another and another, soon morphing into a parade of shape-shifting, color-changing, and often entirely abstract elephants. At first, the pink elephants share the frame with Dumbo and Timothy, but this soon gives way to a series of arabesque kaleidoscopic frolics against a black background. The parade of pink elephants assumes a variety of colors and patterns that vary in size, form, and detail. Species merge freely as one elephant becomes an elephant-camel and then an elephant-cobra, and finally a belly dancing elephant-human. Metonymy gets literalized when the elephant-human becomes a giant blinking eye. Distinctions between mechanical and living things are effaced as pairs of conga-dancing elephants transform into speeding trains and racecars with elephant features. A waterskiing elephant is pulled in circles by an elephant-shaped boat as groups of elephants sled along an undulating path through the frame. These pink elephants are perfect illustrations of Eisenstein's definition of plasmaticness—each "a being of a definite form, a being which has attained a definite appearance, and which behaves like the primal protoplasm, not yet possessing a 'stable' form, but capable of assuming any form" (101). The choreographed chaos of color, form, and movement of "Pink Elephants on Parade" abates only when the pink elephants descend from the sky and settle into the shape of clouds behind the tall tree in which Timothy and Dumbo are both asleep, having somehow soared to the topmost branches the night before.

The gray elephants of earlier, more sober circus scenes are also noticeably malleable. As the last elephant loaded on the circus train is unceremoniously stuffed into a boxcar, her body gives way like a squashed beanbag. So, too, do the enormous bodies of the elephants that pile on top of one another in the pyramid of pachyderms. Their tails and trunks often prove remarkably elastic, as in the sequence when Mrs. Jumbo manages to cradle Dumbo with her trunk through the bars on the window of the circus wagon in which she has been locked. When the clowns talk about raising the platform for the circus finale and one says Dumbo might get hurt if they do, another clown retorts that elephants don't have feelings since "they're made of rubber."

The elephants in *Dumbo* do indeed appear to be made of rubber, an important material that was in dangerously short supply—at least in its natural form—during World War II on account of combat in southeast Asia and the south Pacific. As it is animated, elephant skin repels water and is also fairly elastic, as we see when Dumbo's mother gives him a bath and when a heckler pulls on one of his floppy ears, which snaps back into place like a rubber band.

When Dumbo weeps, as he does several times, the tears bead off of his cheeks and slide down his trunk.

Eisenstein applauded the anthropomorphizing in Disney's films as an atavistic return to primitive thought as well as an utter disregard for seemingly unbroachable categorical differences. Dumbo's triumphant flight under the big top at the end of the film suggests a combination of an elephant, a bird, and an airplane that is consistent with Eisenstein's account of the protean possibilities depicted in Disney's films: "A departure from one's self. From once and forever prescribed norms of nomenclature, form and behaviour. . . . And, of course, in comic form. Seriously, as in life—and especially in American life—there is no such thing, it does not and cannot occur" ("On Disney" 94). When, plummeting rapidly to the ground after dropping the magic feather, Dumbo spreads his ears and flies, it is an individual triumph for the "little guy." But this is also a moment when the categorical distinction between an elephant, the largest and heaviest of the land-based mammals, and a bird, a class of animal species that can take flight, is obliterated. As Dumbo soars, the sound is an airplane engine, and Dumbo swoops like a dive-bomber, vacuuming peanuts from a cart, firing them at the other elephants in machine-gun fashion, and effacing the distinction between a living thing and a machine. It is also presented as a victory over fascism: the montage of print media that follows includes not only the newspaper headlines "Elephant Flies!" and "Wonder Elephant Soars to Fame!" but also the magazine cover "'Dumbombers' for Defense!" which shows a formation of elephant-shaped airplanes, at once mechanical and organic, soaring in flight.

The Adventures of Tintin (2011) lacks the plasmaticness that Eisenstein praised so ecstatically in Disney. Part of this is no doubt the consequence of the film being produced digitally in 3-D. From the beginning, one can see that *The Adventures of Tintin* does not look at all like the hand-drawn cel animation of classic Disney films. While the credits sequence of *Dumbo* is based on the colorful, but resolutely static and two-dimensional, artwork of lithographed circus posters, the credits sequence of *The Adventures of Tintin* mimics the graphic style of Hergé's drawings in his series of Tintin books, dynamically putting them in motion in the receding planes of stereoscopic 3-D. The films that follow conform to these distinct respective aesthetics: While *Dumbo* never aspires to verisimilitude, *The Adventures of Tintin* achieves an unprecedented—and often uncanny—level of visual realism through an exacting attention to detail in the appearance of the settings and a close adherence to the lifelike articulation of the movements of characters (and, to a lesser extent, the movements of animals, which always appear to move slightly slower and more jerkily than their real-life counterparts).

The detail, movement, and depth of *The Adventures of Tintin*'s three-dimensional photorealist animation is itself put into relief by the film's incorporation of a variety of two-dimensional images in its mise-en-scène, including

FIGURE 7.1 An elephant roosts like a crow in *Dumbo* (Ben Sharpsteen, Walt Disney Productions, 1941). Digital frame enlargement.

posters, paintings, illustrations, mirrors, and maps. The difference between two and three dimensions is the basis of one of the film's initial gags, where Tintin is having his portrait painted by a sidewalk artist who looks just like Hergé (and has a panel of portraits of a number of other characters in "The Adventures of Tintin" book series). The artist shows Tintin his painting—the iconic portrait of Tintin that became a logo for the book series as well as the larger international Tintin franchise—and says, "I believe I have captured something of your likeness," to which Tintin replies, "Not bad, what do you think . . . ," as he pauses and holds up the picture, turning toward the viewer and making eye contact for a split second before ending his sentence, " . . . Snowy?," and looking around for his sidekick white dog. Asking us what we think from the start forces us to acknowledge the categorical difference between *The Adventures of Tintin* and other animated films.

While Disney's anthropomorphized animals wear clothing and generally conduct and comport themselves like people, this is not at all the case in *The Adventures of Tintin*, where Snowy's onscreen feats rarely if ever exaggerate what a well-trained animal actor like Rin Tin Tin could have done in comparable situations; and where comic book characters move like the human performers upon whom they were modeled through motion capture technology. Unlike Disney's animals, which often display a supple plasticity of bodily form, everyone (and everything) in *The Adventures of Tintin* looks (and sounds) remarkably solid and stable—even though we fully realize that it is all entirely virtual, existing only as colossal quantities of data and an inestimable number of pixels. Though the facial features of most of the characters are distorted to mimic the style of Hergé's drawings, these distortions, neither monstrous nor incongruous, are burnished with detail and endowed with lifelike movement, resulting in what Eisenstein regrettably described as the "subordination to the inviolable order of things" entailed by conventional modes of proportional and perspectival representation ("Beyond the Shot" 85–86). The only monstrous distortions of physiognomy in *The Adventures of Tintin* are presented as optical illusions caused by environmental impediments to normal vision: the distorted face of Captain Haddock, seen first through the curvature of a whiskey bottle and then again momentarily through a distorted point-of-view shot after he blows whiskey-breath in Tintin's face.

The animation of water and fire in several of the more spectacular scenes of *The Adventures of Tintin* could justly be described as plasmatic—certainly more plasmatic than fire and water appear in *Dumbo*—but this elemental plasticity does not extend to representations of living things. Characters retain their bodily form even as their bodies impossibly defy the laws of gravity and human survival. Their inelasticity is all the more noticeable in relation to the one sequence of the film that highlights elasticity because it is an animation of an actual piece of elastic. In a scene adapted directly from panels of Hergé's *The Secret of the Unicorn*, the detectives Thompson and Thompson attempt to apprehend a pickpocket by using a length of "industrial-strength elastic" fastened to a wallet on one end and the inside of one of their coat pockets on another. The gag works on film, but it is scarcely more striking than in the static images of the book (Hergé 30–33) since the elastic appears for only a few seconds of screen time as a perfectly straight thin red line.

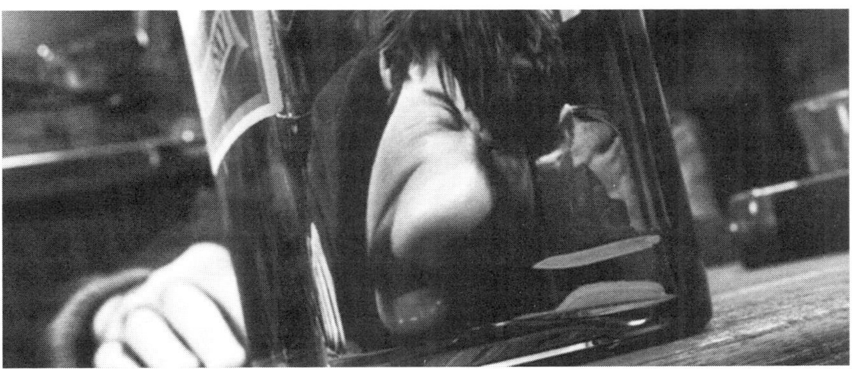

FIGURE 7.2 Captain Haddock seen through a whiskey bottle in *The Adventures of Tintin* (Steven Spielberg, Columbia/Paramount/Amblin, 2011). Digital frame enlargement.

Compared with the supple, seemingly inflatable 'toons in *Who Framed Roger Rabbit?* (1988), or the flexible, unendingly stretchable Elastigirl in *The Incredibles* (2004), Tintin and all of his cohorts appear remarkably rigid and inflexible, despite the fluidity with which their movements have been digitally articulated. Computer-generated images produce a series of dizzying sequences involving airplanes and cranes at the end of *The Adventures of Tintin*, but in the final analysis, animation is never used for the much more modest task of creating plasmaticness. This, Eisenstein argues, is the most compelling use for animation. If digital animation will indeed lead the way for the future of cinema, we might be wise to follow Eisenstein in looking back to its potential to generate primal protoplasm as much as its ability to produce stunning attractions.

NOTE

With thanks to Vincent Longo for sharing his Welles research with me, and to Charlie Solomon for his feedback on possible film choices.

1. This short film can be seen among the "special features" on the most recent DVD edition of *Strike* (Kino Lorber, 2011).

8

Jacques Lacan

Giving All the Right Signs

DOMINIC LENNARD

Much of the work of French psychoanalyst Jacques Lacan (1901–1981) focuses on modes of *looking*. Lacan dissects how one looks at potential romantic partners; how one understands visual impressions of one's own body; how one is placed in the world as an "object" that is subject to the gaze of others. Arguably his most significant contribution to psychoanalysis is his theory that independent subjectivity is founded partly via one's first experience of seeing oneself in a mirror, a moment that conveys the impression of a distinct and autonomous "self": in Lacan's hypothesis, the infant is thrilled and obsessed by a kind of "screened" image. Thus, it is hardly surprising that Lacan has been of particular interest to scholars of cinema.

Lacan seems naturally to offer us a vocabulary of ideas for interpreting the behavior and deep motives of filmic characters. His ideas have also proven useful more broadly in analyses of cinema's representations as manifestations of primal psychological conflict or fixation, and in discussions of how film images reinforce dominant gender roles. Drawing on the "Mirror Stage" of human development, Christian Metz has argued that cinema's representations provide an image of oneself that repairs the disunity that afflicts one's most primal experience of the body. Focusing more directly on gender relations, Laura Mulvey influentially applied to cinema Lacan's notion of the "gaze," a mode of spectatorship in which the viewer effectively looks for signs that confirm his or her position within a structure of "normative" sexual roles. The usefulness of Lacan's theories to filmic analysis has been demonstrated more recently in the work of Slavoj Žižek, whose work often emphasizes what remains outside a world of meaningful objects and associations, what cannot be definitively structured by or understood through "reality" as we know it (see for instance his documentary, *The Pervert's Guide to Cinema* [2006]). Taken as a whole, Lacanian psychoanalytic approaches often draw attention to the conflict between the primal forces of one's earliest "self" and the requirements of "identity" in a broader social world.

Building explicitly on the work of Sigmund Freud, Lacan considered himself a Freudian; yet whereas Freud's work was remarkably accessible (partly in an attempt to legitimize the controversial discipline of psychoanalysis), Lacan's writing style is notoriously obscure. Elizabeth Grosz refers to Lacan's writing as "stretching terms to the limits of coherence, creating a text that is difficult to enter and ultimately impossible to master" (17). The difficulty of Lacan's concepts and the complex network of ideas and traditions in which they are enmeshed lead me to focus on a few core ideas in necessarily brief but—I hope—clear and useful detail. First I will address the Mirror Stage of human development; then three "orders" of experience—Symbolic, Imaginary, and Real—that dominate Lacanian psychoanalysis; and lastly Lacan's account of heterosexual relations as governed by the "phallic signifier." I move on to demonstrate how some of these Lacanian tools might be applied practically to analyze two films, Otto Preminger's noir classic *Laura* (1944) and Darren Aronofsky's more recent thriller *Black Swan* (2010), both of which deal with the desire, sexual identity, and idealized representations that are at the center of much of Lacan's writing.

The Language of Desire: Some Key Lacanian Concepts

It is important briefly to reiterate the work of Freud from which Lacan's thinking extends (see, as well, Freud; Bowie 1–16). Freud's account of the child's psychosexual development is, for the male child, structured around the Oedipus complex, which describes a traumatic event that effectively "founds" heterosexual identity. The Oedipus complex arises from the child's close relationship to his mother, whom Freud assumes (in accordance with the patriarchal society in which he lived and wrote) is the primary caregiver. The child takes the mother as his first love object and experiences hostility toward the father as an intruder. The complex is resolved when the son comes to believe that the mother is "castrated": having discovered his penis as a site of pleasure, he realizes that the mother does not possess this same organ and fears that his own is somehow under threat. The male represses his attraction to the mother, henceforth identifying with his father, a shift of allegiance that provides the male child's initiation into both patriarchy and heterosexuality, while the mother nevertheless remains the model for future love interests. In Freud's narrative of female sexual development (considerably more controversial), the female's recognition that she, too, is castrated leads her to fix on the father as a love object who will become her model for future lovers. These theories have been subject to extensive comment and critique (see, for instance, Irigaray), as well as developments that hypothesize accounts of sexualities beyond this patriarchal heterosexual paradigm. However, it is from this basic narrative that much of Lacan's most significant work extends.

The Mirror Stage

In his famous essay, "The Mirror Stage As Formative of the Function of the I As Revealed in Psychoanalytic Experience" (*Écrits* 1–7), Lacan described an additional stage of development that prefigures the Oedipus complex, further elucidating the infant's developing understanding of himself as a being independent of his mother—a "missing link" that forges a distinct consciousness or "ego." The Mirror Stage occurs upon the child's discovery of his image in a mirror at the age of six months. He observes his reflection with great delight and pleasure, perceiving an image of wholeness and autonomy, forming an understanding that "that is me." This identification is driven by feelings of lack, of frustrating unfulfillment, that have begun to compromise the most primal, organic, and "full" experience of the world in which the child is born (the "Real," discussed further later). Lacan writes, "This act [of recognition] rebounds in the case of the child in a series of gestures in which he experiences in play the relation between the movements assumed in the image and the reflected environment, and between this virtual complex and the reality it reduplicates—the child's own body and the persons or things around him" (*Écrits* 1). Although a chimpanzee of the same age has an intellectual advantage over the human child, the mirror-image quickly loses its value for the ape. The child, however, retains his fascination with the image; he celebrates the realization of an autonomous "self." The recognition is, however, a kind of "misrecognition," an *illusion* of wholeness and autonomy: the child is still, at this stage of life, entirely dependent on adults for care and sustenance.

The specular image also evokes the body as a triumphantly unified and constant whole: it is not depicted as something *in process*. At this point the child begins to perceive and understand himself as an independent entity within a world of objects. However, this is a false location. It is through misrecognition that one's sense of self is developed. The subject perceives its thinking identity in a dislocated and falsely unified image of self. The link between mirrors and identity is frequently referenced in artistic works, consequently Lacan's narrative, in which the mirror heralds the idea of an autonomous, "symbolic" self, remains a popular way of analyzing such motifs (for a more comprehensive introduction to the Mirror Stage beyond Lacan's original essay, see Grosz 31–49).

The Real

What Lacan calls the Real is the most primal, unmediated zone of experience, prior to the acquisition of language or comprehension of representations. It is the domain of raw drives and sensations into which we are born, predating a coherent and unified sense of self or even bodily unity (and thus the Mirror Stage). Immersed in the Real, the infant experiences its body only as a fragmented and amorphous series of sensations; it cannot distinguish between itself and its mother and, accordingly, has no distinct conception of a world around it. Importantly, the Real is not the same as "reality" in the way that we conventionally understand it; for Lacan and his followers, "reality" is always experienced through imaginary identifications and symbolic representations. The Real is greater than, prior to, and independent of "reality."

The Symbolic

The Symbolic is the realm most closely describing "reality" as we conventionally perceive and understand it. It is the sociocultural landscape of social norms, roles, representations, and words. In Lacan's discourse, full and functional selfhood requires understanding a role and identity for oneself within the Symbolic Order—within a world of meaningful objects and associations. The Mirror Stage precipitates a tracing of desire onto roles and representations, thus paving the way for initiation into the Symbolic. In contrast with the primal world of the mother, the pre-Oedipal "Real," this Symbolic Order is associated with the father figure, who symbolizes the outside world of social structure, power, and hierarchy. In Lacan's theory, the father's world of language and representation leads to coherent selfhood by replacing the wordless and primordial space of the mother.

The Imaginary

The Imaginary is a state of associations and recognitions from which the subject never truly graduates. It is the always-in-process creation of meaning—of connection—over disorder and fragmentation, the realm of experience and connection between the self and others. The Imaginary describes the process through which we are urged to define and shore-up our identities through identification and reflective relationships. The Imaginary is provoked by our "lack," the loss of fullness of our initial state of being, the Real—by the persistence of feelings that we are never adequately "whole." For Lacan, the desire to refill or recapture this primal "lack" is at the center of all human desire.

The Phallus

Freud's castration thesis situated males and females as either having or lacking a penis. For Lacan, romantic relationships are always structured with reference to the phallus. The phallus is not merely the male organ explicitly, but a symbolized power and agency of which the penis is merely the original representative. In Lacan's narrative of romantic love, each partner strives for a subjective affirmation based on "possession" of the phallus, as either a correction of lacking or a reaffirmation of having. While the heterosexual female strives for a "phallic" male to legitimize her, the male requires a "lacking" female in order to affirm his own phallic power and completeness. As Elizabeth Grosz writes, in Lacanian theory "the subject demands a wholeness, unity, and completion, which it imagines the other can bestow on it" (137). Thus, Lacan argues that when gazing sexually at a woman, a male effectively "looks for" and eroticizes the signification of *lack*. For example, rather than trying to view a woman as a complete, exotic, "outside" object, the male voyeur is really trying to see "the object as absence . . . merely a shadow, a shadow behind the curtain. . . . What he is looking for is not . . . the phallus—but precisely its absence" (*Four Concepts* 182). In Lacan's thought, the male's phallic power can be meaningful only if there exists one who is perceived to lack it, thus, taken on its own the phallus may be considered an "empty signifier," a "neutral" term reliant for its coherence on shared meaning. Notably, feminist psychoanalytic scholarship has had much to say against this. As Grosz writes, "As the word suggests, it is a term privileging masculinity, or rather, the penis" (122). This debate is part of the broader question of whether psychoanalysis has historically merely described identity- and gender-formation within a patriarchal society, or whether it has actually been complicit in naturalizing patriarchy (see Grosz 122–125, 147–187).

Lacan's work focuses substantially on the construction and situation of a "self" within a world of "symbolic" objects, a world in which behaviors and identities have a representational function both socially and psychically. It posits the importance of the subject's understanding of himself or herself in a world of objects and associations that reflect and define his or her identity. Lacan thus places particular emphasis on psychoanalysis's similarity to linguistics—a study of representations. For Lacan and his followers, subjectivity and sexuality are far from "organic," asocial forces; they are developed through and dependent on representations and shared meanings. Thus, whereas Freud's work emphasizes the ego's battle with a fundamentally asocial "id," Lacanian theory focuses on the subject's negotiation of an identity within the "Symbolic Order."

Framing Romance: *Laura*

Otto Preminger's noir classic *Laura* plays out a curious series of events and associations that can be elucidated through Lacan's theory of heterosexual relations. After the eponymous Laura (Gene Tierney) is apparently murdered by a shotgun blast that obliterates all key identifying features, a detective, Mark McPherson (Dana Andrews), sets about quizzing the men who loved her. While skulking around the crime scene one evening, he falls in love with the dead girl via a glamorous portrait of her hanging in her living room. Shortly afterward, however, the living Laura strolls through the front door, thus revealing that it was all along a different girl lying dead on the carpet (the ex-girlfriend of Laura's most recent lover). This development adds the enchanting Laura herself to the list of suspects in the murder.

As the detective's fixation on the painting indicates, the male competition for Laura's devotion illustrates Lacan's account of heterosexual relations as a series of signifying practices in which the object of one's adoring gaze is ultimately "fictionalized"—a construction needed to complement and render meaningful one's own identity and phallic possession. For Lacan, romance is ultimately a game of signification: fundamental identity is irrelevant by comparison. McPherson develops his fascination with Laura purely through representations of her: anecdotes told by other men, the stylized painting produced by another male admirer, and the feminine artifacts through which he rummages in her apartment. Liahna Babener argues that when the real flesh-and-blood Laura shows up in the middle of the film, McPherson is in fact "threatened by [her] liberation from the secure confinement of death" (92), for that death has allowed him total and self-flattering control over what he perceives this beautiful woman to represent. McPherson is a pistol-carrying "tough guy" and veteran of a violent gun battle: an archetype of traditional phallic male power (including a generalized sexism that sees women as "dames"). Yet, his power is only assured through reference to some Other, and he fixes upon Laura. As in Lacan's theory, the phallic male needs his phallic status to be desired by one who "lacks" in order to feel affirmed. The portrait image works brilliantly. And when Laura appears in life, she threatens to invalidate McPherson's power by assuming a sudden and powerful agency as an object of desire for others.

In competition for Laura's interest and validation McPherson is up against other men, the most overtly narcissistic and self-serving of them being the aging journalist Waldo Lydecker (Clifton Webb). Lydecker offers a clearer example of striving for legitimization within a patriarchal Symbolic Order and using a woman as a prop for heteronormative male self-realization. At the beginning of the film, McPherson interviews Lydecker immersed in a bathtub. Despite the presence of his naked body, thus his physical "manhood," Lydecker provides a clear example of how phallic status and signifiers are symbolic, not literal, his manhood having been transferred into penetrating verbal capacity: his typewriter, posed on a stand so that he can type while bathing, hovers tellingly over his genital region. When the detective enters, Lydecker reads out a formal statement hammered out on this contraption, thus immediately demonstrating his male potency. In the interview, we learn that he had earlier verbally eviscerated a man with whom Laura was spending time after she stood him up; via flashback we see him enforcing his superiority while hunched naked over his typewriter, as if the sexual energy he would have expressed with Laura is channeled sadistically against his male opponent. Lydecker's newspaper column is a tool for symbolically castrating male rivals and perpetually reannouncing his patriarchal might. Accordingly, Lydecker's recounted relationship with Laura makes clear that he required her as an object for his own flattery and power. He read his articles to her, observing that "the way she listened was more eloquent than speech." Moreover, we later discover that Waldo had decorated Laura's apartment with antiques in the same style as his own, thereby fictionalizing her in the same way that McPherson does in constructing a "Laura" most validating to his own identity.

The young southerner who temporary deflects Laura's affection from Lydecker, Shelby Carpenter (Vincent Price), enacts a contrasting type of masculinity that curiously eschews patriarchal posturing. Shelby is a socialite who subverts the gender roles expected in patriarchal society by attaching himself to wealthy women. Shelby himself notes that he is "a natural born suspect just because [he's] not the conventional type." With Laura's aunt, Ann (Judith Anderson), he forms a socially shunned alliance that denaturalizes romance, exposing it as a social "act." As she applies her make-up, Ann tells Laura about wanting Shelby: for her, romance is a game in which ensnaring a validating Other is paramount. In his relationship with the older aunt who dotes on him, Shelby seems to reside in a kind of pre-Oedipal state of union with a mother figure, a primal position from which he has not yet graduated. However, his eventual desire for Laura signifies his emergent "adult" sexuality and places him in the same matrix of expected male behavior as other rivals for her hand. This is striving for status within the Symbolic Order.

Yet, Shelby's general refusal within the film to play the phallic male (thus his implicit questioning of dominant gender roles) makes him a source of irritation to other characters (especially Lydecker, who refers to him as "a male beauty in distress"), and means he is made a fool for the viewer, a kind of "prop" male, and for the aunt a phallic token to validate her identity within a patriarchal society. His union with a culturally disapproved Other means that his masculinity is not regarded as "legitimate" by the other men.

In this group of yearning men, it is Lydecker who turns out to be the killer. After Laura rejected him for Shelby, he conspired to kill her but accidentally gunned down the wrong girl. When Laura rejects Lydecker again—this time for McPherson—he creeps into her room to get the job done properly. He stalks up behind her, shotgun in hand, as Laura listens attentively to his voice on the radio (recorded earlier). That disembodied voice describes love as the "strongest motivator of human behavior," as "stronger than life," aggrandizing his past and pending aggression as the result of a "mythic" desire. Yet Lydecker's behavior and insecurity throughout the film clearly constructs his love as a symbolic request driven by feelings of masculine inadequacy. Having had his patriarchal role in the Symbolic unsettled by Laura's unwillingness to reciprocate his desire, Lydecker seeks to reassert his primacy. His shotgun is thus an exaggerated expression of his threatened masculinity, a symbol with which he intends to brutally subjugate the object of his desire. However, the aging journalist is

FIGURE 8.1 Taken by force: Waldo Lydecker (Clifton Webb) takes aim at Laura (Gene Tierney), the lover who has rejected him, in *Laura* (Otto Preminger, Twentieth Century Fox, 1944). Digital frame enlargement.

killed in a gun battle with Laura's chosen lover, Detective McPherson. Consequently, the film uses a traditional display of male power to restore and legitimize the Symbolic Order to which Lydecker has improperly and inarticulately sought access. McPherson's triumph and the restoration of order are in accordance with a patriarchal and heterosexist culture in which possession of the woman confirms the legitimacy of one's power and position.

Violent Reflections: *Black Swan*

In *Black Swan*, Nina (Natalie Portman), a starry-eyed ingénue ballerina with a renowned New York company, strives to impress her exacting director, Thomas (Vincent Cassel), enough to win the lead in the company's upcoming production of *Swan Lake*. Thomas's conception of the ballet demands one dancer to handle both starring roles, the innocent White Swan with whom a prince falls in love and her twin, the lustful Black Swan who stymies the union and precipitates her double's suicide. Nina is a natural for the virginal persona but is so prissily cute that she is only a long shot for the role of the seductive twin. Thomas derides the "frigidity" of her dancing and, during a private rehearsal, gropes and caresses an alarmed Nina, pressing his open mouth onto hers; but

FIGURE 8.2 Not (yet) the right girl for the part: Nina (Natalie Portman) is frightened by the sexuality of her dancing director, Thomas (Vincent Cassel), in *Black Swan* (Darren Aronofsky, Fox Searchlight/Cross Creek, 2010). Digital frame enlargement.

then he breaks derisively away, lamenting that he is the one seducing her rather than the reverse. She is visibly crushed. Thomas's prescriptions thus concern not merely the symbolic "role" of the narrative of the ballet itself but also the role prescribed by his sexual desire. He can believe Nina as sweet, but not as a temptress. In effect, he requires her to become a different version of "herself," and one who more explicitly craves his phallic sexuality. He needs to position her as a graspable object within a heterosexual network of desire. In Nina's quest to become this "ideal" self, her identity becomes increasingly fragmented and chaotic, and throughout the film she encounters a barrage of unpredictable and terrifying mirror images of herself. Thus, in *Black Swan* we see a particular emphasis on symbolic roles, on the location of oneself within predefined grids of representation, that a Lacanian theoretical lens can help to elucidate.

Awakening from a dream in which she imagined herself dancing as the Swan Queen, Nina stretches before a triptych mirror in an image that multiplies her. The first in a profusion of such imagery throughout the film—imagery that becomes increasingly unusual and traumatic, this first mirror placement indicates the connection between mirror images and an ideal, symbolic role (a role, she believes, her dutiful stretching routine will better position her to achieve). Presided over by the domineering Thomas, Nina's dance school is a patriarchal symbolic matrix par excellence, in which male-approved performances are desperately aspired to. The discriminating prescriptions of heterosexual male desire (and the women's internalization of those expectations) are indicated by the former lead dancer Beth (Winona Ryder), whose aging has forced her retirement and renders her the target of cutting jibes from the younger dancers.

Yet Nina cannot comfortably exist within this matrix of male desire, cannot position herself as a sexual object within the Symbolic Order, because, as the film goes to some lengths to demonstrate, she still lives in a maternal bubble of childhood. Her bedroom is almost preposterously infantile, the wallpaper a clutter of pink butterflies, and pink plush ballerina bunnies sitting propped on the windowsills. At one point her mother (Barbara Hershey) activates a music box at Nina's bedside before she goes to sleep (in her single bed). Later in the film, we see the mother depicted as an explicit stifler of Nina's sex life, too, when she forbids her to venture out with fellow dancer Lily (Mila Kunis) in search of male company (Nina disobeys) and dreadfully disrupts her attempt at masturbation. Nina's relationship with "mommy" strongly evokes the Lacanian mother–child dyad which prefaces patriarchal intervention and installment within the Symbolic Order (see Grosz 34). Nina's mother is a former dancer herself, and clearly uses her daughter as a conduit for her own unrealized desires. In Lacan's theory (which presumes a patriarchal society in which women are the primary caregivers), the mother and child exist initially in a kind of vortex of self-reflection, each defining the identity of the other. Yet this identity-position, in Lacanian theory, must be renounced in order for the subject to achieve successful integration within the Symbolic Order—the realm associated with the (here tellingly absent) father, governed by language, and also the realm in which one finds a stable and culturally approved heterosexual identity.

Black Swan's preoccupation with mirror imagery both reflects the practices of professional ballet training and bespeaks the role of externalized, apparently objective images of self in identity-formation. Throughout the film, Nina's world is increasingly subject to horrific fragmentation and confusion that reflect her personal insecurity within a world of symbolic objects and relationships. She is increasingly tormented by misbehaving reflections, which glare menacingly at her, heedless of her own actions. And one day in the subway, a girl she passes transforms momentarily into a living double of herself, a more darkly dressed and seductive incarnation who represents the Nina her director desires—a Nina who has positioned herself as an object for male attention. Nina's divided or incomplete self is clearly the result of the unsuccessful split between the infantile persona associated with her mother and the interruptive advances of heterosexual male desire. In Lacan's theory, the mirror is a kind of "gateway" to the Symbolic, a rejection of the earlier, purely absorbing relationship with the mother. In identifying with the mirror image, the child establishes an identity beyond the maternal world, eventually allowing integration into the Symbolic (and sexuality).

However, we must also note that through the demanding Thomas, the film gestures to the role of male desire in constructing this woman's "Imaginary": she desires identification as the prima ballerina, that is, as both the White and the Black Swan characters. The apparently objective "self," triumphantly autonomous, presented in the mirror is, for Lacan, a self located within a male-dominated

Symbolic Order. This "self" is never "organic" but is alienated and constructed because it is always located within a network of shared meanings and associations.

Nina is eventually awarded the prima role, signifying her ascendance in her male coach's approval. Yet, given her failure to completely let go of her virginal and pre-Oedipal self, Nina's desired and fascinating sexualized "self" begins rupturing from her body in monstrous extrusions—manifestations of the character of the Black Swan. The rupturing is Nina's inadequate integration into the symbolic and her discomfort with her new, patriarchally prescribed role. Moreover, despite having won the part of the Black Swan, Nina comes to feel that Thomas is trying to replace her with Lily just as she herself replaced the aging Beth. Falling further into bizarre fantasy, Nina imagines that during the actual performance of *Swan Lake* she stabbed Lily to death backstage with a shard of broken mirror. This paranoia, phrased as part of Nina's growing psychosis, nevertheless manages to suggest the ultimate interchangeability of women within the narrow roles that heteronormative male desire outlines for them.

Before the ballet's final act, Nina discovers a bloody and apparently self-inflicted hole in her own abdomen, from which she retrieves a shard of mirror. Still (and to the confusion of many viewers), she takes the stage, literally dying as she enacts the White Swan's suicide. At her death—concealed from the theater audience's sight—Nina appraises her own performance as "perfect" while the crowd roars. Thomas's long-awaited praise, that she is his "little princess," reinforces her "successful" performance in the role he had desired for her. Given the implausibility of Nina's dancing the entire final act with a gory wound in her midsection, we can safely read this scene as a hallucination (a few minutes earlier, dancing the Black Swan, she apparently sprouted wings without audience alarm). In having apparently "killed" herself, we might say that Nina has in fact killed the virginal, infantile incarnation of herself fostered by her mother. The work of Lacanian psychoanalyst Serge Leclaire is especially pertinent here; supplementing Lacan's narrative, Leclaire argues that stable selfhood within the Symbolic is dependent on one's "killing" the most primal image of selfhood, the image of the wonderful child projected by the mother (2–5). Nina has clearly been trapped in the world of her narcissistic mother, who is determined to produce an idealized facsimile of herself rather than allowing her daughter to develop an identity within the Symbolic Order—an identity within a broader network of identificatory relations. Throughout the film, Nina gradually throws off her maternal authority, explicitly rejecting her girlhood persona: "What happened to my sweet girl?" the mother pleads; "She's gone!" Nina shouts back. In fact, as Nina fantasizes killing Lily in the dressing room, her rival morphs into both Nina, and then Nina's mother, indicating the desire in which Nina feels trapped while blurring the identity between mother and child. In Lily's attempt to usurp her role Nina sees also the entrapping desire of her mother, who has sought to use her as a cipher for reinvigoration of her own dancing dreams—as her own mirror. In short, the final scene of *Black Swan* reveals that the true target of Nina's murderous violence was in fact "herself": an internalized, pre-Oedipal image of herself instilled in her by her mother.

Black Swan is a fitting film with which to conclude this introductory discussion of Lacanian ideas in that it brings to light some of the controversies of Lacanian theory for feminist and queer theorists. In *Black Swan*, as in a patriarchal and heterosexist society, to find a stable sexual identity the woman must accept her castrated status and locate herself within a symbolic inflected by patriarchy. The film also traditionally associates prolonged maternal care with psychological stagnation and eventually psychosis—a psychosis that could presumably have been prevented by formative patriarchal intervention. Yet, one might alternatively argue that through the hypersexist setting of the dance academy the film draws attention to a patriarchal network of meaning in which women are expected to perform to the standards of male desire. Thus, the advantage of Lacanian psychoanalysis for some scholars of gender and sexuality is its exposure of entrenched, but presumably changeable, networks of representation in structuring our identities. Biology does not necessarily mean destiny. Moreover, Lacan's thought suggests that the kind of female "madness" depicted in *Black Swan* cannot be considered pathological but reflects a traumatic restructuring of identity within the symbolic. Nina's psychosis is no more truly "inherent" than Waldo Lydecker's love for Laura: both can be traced to the prescriptive structures of a patriarchal Symbolic Order. Nina's victimization by her assigned role (even if phantasmal) is made bloodily explicit. As for Laura, almost destroyed as a token of male power, she finds what Hollywood noir frequently offered, a narrow escape.

9

Rudolf Arnheim

Cinema and Partial Illusion

NATHAN HOLMES

Watching Auguste and Louis Lumière's *L'arrivée d'un train en gare de La Ciotat* (1895), it is difficult to resist transporting oneself back to the late nineteenth century. What would the sensation of watching images in fluid motion feel like for the first time? Trying to grasp the past through this film, however, we may neglect its presently powerful aesthetic dimension. In contrast to such a historical gaze, consider the following description:

> Everyone has seen a railway engine rushing on the scene in a film. It seems to be coming straight at the audience. The effect is most vivid because the dynamic power of the forward-rushing movement is enhanced by another source of dynamics that has no inherent connection with the object itself, that is, with the locomotive, but depends on the position of the spectator, or—in other words—the camera. The nearer the engine comes, the larger it appears, the dark mass on screen spreads in every direction at a tremendous pace (a dynamic dilation toward the margins of the screen), and the actual objective movement of the engine is strengthened by this dilation. (Arnheim, *Film as Art* 60–61)

These words were written by the critic and theorist Rudolf Arnheim (1904–2007) in the 1930s, more than three decades after the Lumières' initial exhibition of the cinématographe. In the intervening years, film had morphed from scientific novelty and fairground attraction into mass entertainment, political tool, and, though some still had reservations, to art form. *L'arrivée d'un train* therefore signified the history of a manifold medium for viewers of the 1930s in much the same way that it does today. In this passage, however, Arnheim draws our attention to the way the camera's perspective converts a familiar view into a two-dimensional splash, a "dynamic dilation" like a drop of ink pressed between glass slides. If, in the here and now, we can sense something still powerful in the arrival of a train, is it not through the way that a carefully chosen position on a train platform one day a long time ago can now repeatedly offer a pulsating picture of modern transport?

Arnheim's remarks on the aesthetic possibilities of camera perspective and the reduced depth of cinematic motion highlight the approach taken throughout his most well-known collection of writings on film, *Film as Art* (first published in English in 1957). A practicing Weimar-era film critic trained in Gestalt psychology, Arnheim wrote film theory committed to exposing the dialectical relation of materials and form, what he called *Materialtheorie*. For Arnheim, the artistic potential of film was realized through the camera's technological affinity with expressive presentation—rather than duplication—of the physical world. In the main section of the book (adapted from his German-language book *Film* [1933]) Arnheim directs his materialist theory toward systematically dismantling the then-pervasive argument that "film cannot be art because it does nothing but reproduce reality mechanically" (8).

To advance a counter-argument, he catalogues the many ways that creative filmmakers had converted into artistic devices film's apparent disadvantages, the properties of film that contributed to peculiarly nonrealist representation. These included: the way that three-dimensional objects looked on the screen's two-dimensional surface; the necessity of lighting and the lack (at the time) of color; the delimitation of the film frame and the relative distance of the camera from objects; the way that editing could manipulate perceptions of time and space; and the absence of sense experiences like sound and balance. All of film's properties deemed unfavorable to the creation of lifelike illusion, properties that realist filmmakers would try to suppress or compensate for, were in Arnheim's view the primary resources of the film artist. For him, the role of the artist was not to copy the world but "to originate, to interpret, to mold" (157).

Arnheim thought that film art was constituted through a filmmaker's decisive mobilization of the camera's power to transform reality into images of unreality in order to shape an aesthetic world. In "The New Laocoön: Artistic Composites and the Talking Film," Arnheim would begin to speculate that cinema might be well served to move away from photography altogether, suggesting that it "will be able to reach the heights of other arts only when it frees itself from photographic reproduction and becomes a pure work of man, as animated cartoon or painting" (213). This statement would seem to lend support to the idea, more recently developed by the new media theorist Lev Manovich, that with innovations in computer animation techniques, photography is becoming much less central to the cinema than it was in the twentieth century (Manovich 295).

It is tempting to cast Arnheim as a formalist in the extreme. Yet he did not always think that film should leave photography behind. Reviewing the abstract animation works of Hans Richter, Viking Eggeling, Oskar Fischinger, and Len Lye in a 1965 essay, Arnheim sees a "museum collection of venerable curiosities," preferring instead the liquid blend of authenticity and mystery in Jacques Cousteau's underwater cinematography for *World Without Sun* (1964) ("Art Today" 26). This may seem a significant reorientation for a theorist associated with advocating form over representational realism, but in fact it hardly contradicts the patterning of core ideas in *Film as Art*, many of which are structured around the aesthetic procedures of the camera. A significant strand in the book's early chapters is the idea that the experience of film is the result of a perceptual split in which the image is understood as both referential and pictorial. As film viewers we see an expanding black shape on the screen, but we also comprehend a train; film offers "the scene of a living action" but also a flat picture postcard. Arnheim calls this doubled experience—to which he returns throughout his writings—a "partial illusion . . . simultaneously the effect of an actual happening and of a picture." Partial illusion explains a camera-based image that both suggests and departs from profilmic reality, the world in front of the lens. On a two-dimensional surface, such as the screen, the presence of the train in *L'arrivée d'un train* is converted from a shrinking distance to a growing size. Physical proximity, which would be sensually discerned by noise, smell, and heat, is converted into a maximized visual presentation that shades into abstraction. This abstraction is partial because despite the fact that key components of the event have been removed, we still recognize the image's connection to actuality. Thus, although Arnheim's conception of the partial illusion rests in film's photographic basis, it points to how this basis links the real world to more indeterminate realms of visuality.

Arnheim was famously skeptical of synchronized sound and color processes (not to mention 3-D), taking positions that, while convincingly argued, conveyed an ineluctable shortsightedness in contrast to the more prophetic speculations of thinkers like Walter Benjamin or even André Bazin. However, recent scholarship has pushed for a renewed understanding of Arnheim's approach (see Higgins, ed.; Koch "Rudolf Arnheim"). Although to those familiar with film analysis, the early chapters of *Film as Art* may seem rudimentary, Arnheim models a straightforward precision that is lacking in many discourses on cinema. Moreover, closer examination reveals that Arnheim's approach is richer than commonly thought. First, his delineation of the film's partial illusion as an image both taken from reality and apart from it puts him in more direct dialogue with the ideas of Benjamin (on the optical unconscious), Jean Epstein (photogénie), Christian Metz (the film image's presence/absence), and theorists of filmic realism like Bazin (especially in "The Ontology of the Photographic Image") than traditional genealogies of film theory often grant. Partial illusion also troubles a simplistic transposition of realist and formative aesthetics onto opposing ends of a stylistic spectrum, in the way that it exposes how claims of filmic realism often overlook the elemental otherness of filmic representation. Finally, Arnheim's theory challenges more recent arguments that are centered on the demise of photochemical film and the ascendancy of digital image production.

Film as Art orients us to consider an experience of the photographic image that is dependent on camera optics and framing; technological assemblies that have remained relatively stable even as presentation formats and processes of registration have shifted from celluloid strip to digital chip. To highlight these and other insights latent within *Film as Art*, the following discussion will consider two films that creatively explore the advantages of cinema's partial illusion, Jacques Tati's *Play Time* (1967) and Michel Gondry's *Eternal Sunshine of the Spotless Mind* (2004).

Play Time

As a 70 mm widescreen, Eastmancolor production with a four-track stereo sound mix, *Play Time* would seem to emblematize the type of false techno-aesthetic progress of which Arnheim was famously skeptical. Yet the atmosphere of perceptual illusion and surprise that Tati creates depends on the basic principles of creative camera work outlined by Arnheim.

Play Time's loose narrative depicts a young American tourist (Barbara Dennek), Tati's famous self-caricature M. Hulot, and a small coterie of other characters interacting within a series of hypermodern Parisian environments: an airport, downtown streets, an office, a trade show, an apartment, and a restaurant/nightclub on opening night. All of these environments were sets designed by Tati and built specifically for the film. The time and effort expended on "Tativille," in an undeveloped area southeast of the center of Paris, might seem to suggest that Tati intended *Play Time* to be the film record of a spectacular architectural set construction. Yet Tati's satire of modern Paris often relies on optical effects involving the coordination of production design and camera perspective.

Play Time is largely filmed in deeply staged long shots, often from a slightly high or low angle, necessitating sets built deep and to a certain height. To some extent, Tati was following practices conventional to studio filmmaking, where sets are built for the camera, not the eye. Yet whereas studio films frequently used these effects to engulf the viewer in a simulated world, Tati deploys them to present a denaturalized view of Paris.

For example, early in the film a group of American tourists exit their bus on a busy street. A single shot shows them in the bottom left of the frame, a line of nearly identical glass and steel skyscrapers receding along the boulevard taking up the right half of the screen. The apparent height and dimensionality of the buildings is a perspectival manipulation; in fact, these are wooden and plastic facades, much smaller than the structures they model, and painted to force a sense of verticality. How does this design count, however, as a partial and not a complete illusion? For one, the white, gray, and black in the set, the costumes, and the props block an apprehension of this scene as natural, despite the fact that the slightly cloudy blue sky seems very real. The artifice of this gradient helps viewers see the scene as a picture rather than a duplication of an actual environment. Tuned by color, the viewer is guided to see the row of skyscrapers as similarly composed, their height and distance too mathematically uniform to be real.

Secondly, although it seems that Tati is reproducing Renaissance perspective, it's not entirely true that film realism is the resulting effect. In this shot and others in the film, geometric precision gives the impression of architectural drawings, a pictorial genre which typically portrays human bodies as a way to convey scale. Inasmuch as the tourists are characters at this point, they suggest a world of narrative action that is meant to interact with the space that Tati has designed. Cramped in the corner, framed against a bus and hemmed by traffic, these story-figures seem trapped within an inhospitable picture. Thus, Tati provides a double, or partial, image, one that is both a diegetic space and a picture-space.

Throughout *Play Time*, Tati exploits the array of possibilities offered by camera perspective to generate comic effects. A tradesman strolls up the sidewalk to a doorman to ask for a cigarette lighter and the doorman motions him in a different direction. Pulling away, the camera reveals that there is, and has always been, a glass wall between them. Here, deploying a simple reframing technique that Arnheim would call "delimitation of size of the image," Tati has produced visual surprise: men who appear to be on the same sidewalk with each other are in fact separated by glass. Later, during the Royal Garden restaurant sequence, a waiter appears as if watering women's floral chapeaux with champagne but is in fact filling glasses occluded by the hats. Another moment in the restaurant is more subtle: a bartender must contend with newly installed ornamental ceiling trim running along the length of his working area, constantly dipping his head to avoid it as he moves between customers and the bottles of liquor behind him. The exact placement of the trim in the bartender's work zone isn't immediately visually evident; it becomes present to the viewer only by watching his negotiated movements, and his growing annoyance with yet another of the restaurant's design flaws. Hence, bodily movement creates a gestalt effect that cues us to perceive an element of décor that otherwise we might have been unable to see. What starts for the viewer as a very neurotic bartender, constantly twitching and dipping as he moves around, becomes finally a sane and very competent man trying to work under insane conditions. These are just a handful of the visual effects that make up *Play Time*—the totality of which can only be grasped in multiple viewings—but they are representative of Tati's overall strategy of generating humor through comic visuals created via fairly basic camera procedures.

One of Tati's most ingeniously subtle framings occurs when Hulot visits the chic new apartment of his old friend Schneller (Yves Barsacq). The camera remains on the street outside the building, peering in through large plate-glass windows that give it a doll-house view. Because only street noise can be heard (the camera is in the street), the long-shot arrangement of action inside the apartment occasions what becomes pantomime, as the man proudly conducts a tour of his fashionable living room, introduces his wife and child, and demonstrates his wall-encased television set. As the sequence unfolds, the camera angle shifts to reveal identically furnished neighboring apartments in the building, one adjacent and two above. As with Schneller, the occupants of these units are also consulting television listings and turning on their own sets. M. Giffard (Georges Montant) arrives and enters the apartment adjacent to Schneller's. Both Giffard and Schneller have turned on their televisions and, because their sets happen to occupy two sides of the same wall, from a viewing position outside looking in, the families in both flats appear to be gazing at one another, all of them bathed in a cathode glare. Adjusting to an angle that uses the exterior façade of the building to conceal both the interior wall that divides the apartments and the two glaring televisions has created the bizarre impression that the two mirrored families are seated in front of, and being entertained by, each other. Each neighbor is alternately positioned as an audience, ostensibly for his television but, from the camera's perspective, for the goings-on on the other side of the wall. We can imagine the happenstantial comedies: Hulot and the Schnellers recoiling slightly as Giffard's wife inspects his broken nose; or the Schnellers asking their daughter to leave the room as Giffard begins to lazily undress; or the Giffards seeming to be engrossed in Schneller's lively recap of a skiing vacation. Once again, Tati creates a surprising image simply by shifting camera position and distance in front of a fixed setting.

This short sequence exemplifies a point Arnheim makes about film's ability to shift between characteristic and uncharacteristic views in order to create stirring visual effects (*Film as Art* 9–11, 42–46). A characteristic view, he explains, gives the perspective of an object's three dimensions, and an uncharacteristic view makes the same object more difficult to identify. From a characteristically oblique angle, a chair is shown as a three-dimensional assembly including legs, a seat, and a rising back. A more frontal view, however, would portray an unrecognizable pattern of perpendicular lines. A partial illusion swings perception between apprehension and indetermination. In *Play Time*, this oscillation propels a comic and conceptual universe: the neighbors are physically separated by apartment walls but visually conjoined in the appearance of a theatrical tableau. Their assumedly normal private behaviors, uncharacteristically viewed from a public perspective (raised from the sidewalk as if on a rostrum), playfully show them as audiences and performers, lookers and looked-ats.

FIGURE 9.1 As they watch their wall-encased television sets the inhabitants of a chic apartment complex appear to be watching each other in *Play Time* (Jacques Tati, Jolly/Specta, 1967). Digital frame enlargement.

Tati's artful use of camera angle in this sequence recalls an illustration given by Arnheim of a similar technique used in Abram Room's Soviet film *The Ghost That Never Returns* (1929). A man walking down a road stops to pick a flower and then turns angrily around. Cutting to a different angle, the man is shown gesturing from further away and this view now includes bars jutting vertically through the frame. The camera position reveals that he's just been released from prison. Arnheim is appreciative here of the unobtrusive manner by which the grating "brings itself into prominence and makes clear that it was not introduced without definite intention. It makes its entrance as if it were one of the actors" (*Film as Art* 49). While not so sudden, the effect in *Play Time*'s apartment sequence is similar. The metaphorical theatrical configuration that appears has not appeared in an artificial way, and yet there is clearly an intention (and creative result) in placing the camera and designing the home in this way. Seen from a particular angle—an angle that Tati would like us to see—these bourgeois apartments correspond with the glass and steel buildings of earlier scenes: they both divide themselves from the street and interact with it in surprising ways.

Play Time's ambivalence toward modernization comes most fully to the foreground in the final act. The dull gray walls of buildings are now covered with paper decorations, cars and costumes in primary colors are introduced, cheerful carnival music is heard, and the speed and variety of visual surprises increases while the American tourists circle a huge traffic roundabout. A window tilted back and forth momentarily throws a reflection of the tour bus up and down, providing optical delight for the tourists, who, as they ooh and ahh, perhaps suggest a model for the film's ideal spectator. And finally, Hulot's young tourist friend finds a small bouquet of lilies of the valley, the undulating stems and bells of which rhyme with posies of street lights that line the highway. Understanding *Play Time* through the lens of Arnheim's principles reveals that Tati's style, as much as the story it tells, is comprised of an ambiguity: although the film partakes of large-format presentation and uses emerging sound technologies, the bulk of its visual effects are derived from elemental camera techniques inherited from the silent era. Like the characters and world he portrays, Tati straddles the new and the old.

Eternal Sunshine of the Spotless Mind

Like the hypermodern France satirized by Tati and the era of synchronized sound resisted by Arnheim, the film industry of the present is preoccupied with gimcrack novelty. The contemporary rhetoric of digital visual effects frequently maintains that the pathway to visual fascination entails a departure from the exhausted traditions of photographic cinema, tendentiously perpetuating the industry-led view that newer is better. Modern filmmakers have proven that the ordinary features of the film apparatus are still sufficient to render extraordinary visions.

Eternal Sunshine of the Spotless Mind takes an ambitious tack in such a direction: in seeking to concretely visualize dreaming and mental states, it assembles film images to reorganize perceptions of time and space, partaking of a cinematic system of continuity only to disaggregate it. A science-fiction romance, *Eternal Sunshine* tells the story of a man, Joel (Jim Carrey), who enlists the services of the company Lacuna Inc. to delete his memories of his ex-girlfriend Clementine (Kate Winslet). The film depicts both Joel's waking life on the outskirts of New York City and a world inside his head as the deletion is under way, often switching rapidly between memories as well as moving backward and forward through events in the objective portion of the story. Matching this potentially baffling plot construction are visual effects that replicate mental processes such as fading memories, childhood experiences, and the surrealism of personal fantasy. A central drama of the film involves Joel's decision, from within his dream state, to counteract the procedure. The film's vivid figurations of his attempts to save memories from extermination literalize the mind's struggle to preserve impression and experience against the tidal flows of time.

The opening sequences of *Eternal Sunshine* depicting the meeting and budding romance between Joel and Clementine deploy a contemporary realist style that has been termed "intensified continuity": handheld, roaming camera movement and fast cutting conveying immediacy but generally following conventional continuity patterns (Bordwell, *Way* 121–138). As an aesthetic developed out of documentary filmmaking practices, intensified continuity connotes realism by implying a camera that records a spontaneously unfolding action. One short scene is illustrative. Clementine has invited Joel up to her apartment for a drink. Apartment interiors are standard topoi of continuity editing, conventionally organized using a master shot defining layout before moving to closer framings corresponding to the staging of social action and narrative development, and this scene roughly performs these patterns. The sequence opens with Joel sitting on a couch in Clementine's bohemian-eclectic living room. Shots of him looking around (he sees a shelf of homemade potato people) alternate with brief shots of Clementine preparing drinks in the kitchen. As Clementine brings the drinks into the living room she is united with Joel and they sit on the couch together. The conversation that follows is filmed in a shot/reverse shot pattern and the camera shifts its position along the traditional axis of action (necessarily so, since they sit on a couch that is against a wall) using both two-shots and individual close-ups.

Though as I describe it this scene may seem stylistically conventional, rapid cutting and tremulous cinematography blanket it in a superficial messiness that tends to obscure its controlled organization. As a nominally realist style that works to convey the impression of the mechanical reproduction of a scene as it happens, intensified continuity seems to be precisely the type of aesthetic that Arnheim might oppose. What Arnheim directs us to ask here is whether the filmmaker in this scene has channeled the properties of film into an artistic representation or works to suppress these properties in the name of a contrived naturalism. An answer lies within his understanding of the experience of montage.

Arnheim's description of the visual experience of the montage of a single scene immediately reconfigures conventional notions of continuity editing as a process of illusory integration:

> In scene 1 a man is discovered ringing the front doorbell of a house. Immediately following appears a totally different view—the interior of the house with the maid coming to answer. The maid opens the door and sees the visitor. Suddenly the viewpoint changes again and we are looking through the visitor's eyes—another breakneck change within a fraction of a second. Then a woman appears in the background of the foyer and in the next moment we have bridged the distance separating us from her, and we are close beside her. (*Film as Art* 27)

The construction of a scene from multiple angles and framings sustains Arnheim's principle of cinema's partial illusion. The montage of a single scene is possible, Arnheim explains, because of film's unreality: "If film photographs gave a very strong spatial impression, montage would probably be impossible. It is the partial unreality of the film picture that makes it possible" (28). As much as *Film as Art* offers a framework of evaluation it also models a defamiliarizing approach to film style.

Eternal Sunshine's scenes of intensified continuity are not merely functional, but internal to the film's narrative visualization. When Joel finds himself able to stand inside and watch his own memories unfold, and to move between them, spatial and temporal coherence becomes unmoored. Joel recounts to friends his failed post-breakup attempt to bring Clementine a Valentine's Day gift at the bookstore where she works, motivating a "flashback": as he strides away miserably in a reverse tracking shot, overhead lights dramatically shut off behind him, transfiguring a space that was initially framed objectively into an expressionistic environment. Suddenly, he passes through a doorway that returns him to the apartment where he had begun to relate the story. While cutting away from Joel's story in a standard fashion (using a voiceover to bridge the cut) the scene returns to Joel's original space of narration through what might be called an architectural splice: the apartment and the bookstore are shown as physically contiguous, but because we are familiar with the flashback procedure, we recognize that this contiguity is figurative and that the doorway is meant to represent a break between the episode narrated and its original diegetic location.

The scene discussed previously neatly initiates the viewer into an idiosyncratic visual language that will continue to build, a language in which temporal shifts (shifts in memory are essentially temporal) may occur spatially. The use of intensified continuity in early sequences is a prelude to, and prepares the viewer for, an overall structure that will begin to dispense with conventional methods of orientation to time and space, and alignments between plot-time and story-time. When Joel decides he wants to preserve memories, he must frantically outrun and hide from Lacuna's deletion technology (represented within the mise-en-scène by a glaring white spotlight) by pulling Clementine by the hand through a series of spaces representing distinct memories—a movie theater, Grand Central Station, apartment dinner parties, the kitchen of his childhood home. The potentially disjunctive experience of this ongoing chase is mitigated by the viewer's knowledge of Joel's need to escape and of the conventions of the filmic chase (using consistency of direction in shots of different spaces). Visual pleasure, on the other hand, inheres in the way that Gondry has elevated to narrative significance what Arnheim identifies as the basic freedom—derived from film's photographic heritage—of montage: the fact that "pictures may be displayed for as long or short a time as one pleases, and they can be shown next to one another even if they depict totally different periods in time" (26).

The many surreal images of *Eternal Sunshine* are based on simple incongruity: a bed sits on a beach, a thundershower takes place in a living room. Gondry achieves the majority of the film's "special" effects through camera perspective, editing, and production design rather than computer imaging. When Joel and Clementine hide from Lacuna in one of Joel's childhood memories, Joel is

FIGURE 9.2 Within a memory of his four-year-old self, Joel (Jim Carrey) grasps for ice cream while Clementine (Kate Winslet) takes on the guise of Mrs. Hamlyn, in *Eternal Sunshine of the Spotless Mind* (Michel Gondry, Focus/Anonymous Content, 2004). Digital frame enlargement.

played by both a child actor (Ryan Whitney) and Carrey, both dressed in identical patterned pajamas. Oversized props and painted sets create an appearance of scale from the child's point of view, even though Carrey's presence obviously disturbs this view. Like the other images in the film, this image is not incongruous for its own sake but to motivate the story. Here is a different sort of visual partiality, an image that serves a narrative function by involving us in the illusory world of the story, but that also offers pictorial splendor by presenting a marvelously absurd depiction of a man-sized child's milieu.

Partial illusion names film as a phenomenon wherein semblance falls into perceptual play, where images of the familiar veer into formal abstraction. Because this concept designates both filmmaking practice and spectatorial activity, Arnheim's theory must be understood as outlining both the aesthetic and cognitive dimensions of film—a way of making film and a way of experiencing it. *Film as Art* is, as he says, a book of standards, a set of guidelines on which creative practices may be based.

Arnheim's standards may be accused of a normativity that straitjackets artistic experimentation, or a parochial formalism that ignores the way that the properties of media are subject to historical change. Yet by examining film's perceived constraints to show the abundant possibilities afforded by the medium, Arnheim exposed the blindness of technological progress. He saw innovations, such as sound and color, as unnecessary supplements to an art that had not yet begun to exhaust the possibilities of the camera itself. But although the history of cinema would become littered with the technology-driven imitation of life that Arnheim abhorred, it is also possible, using his methods, to discover filmmakers like Tati and Gondry who, interested in the possibilities of sound and color, produce miraculous images by very deliberately placing and moving their camera. Inasmuch as contemporary filmmaking remains an art of camera lens and camera placement despite the advance of digital technology, the insights contained within *Film as Art* remain vital.

The sustained vitality of *Film as Art* also rests in how it models a way to describe the experience of seeing moving images. Everyday life in the twenty-first century, as in the twentieth, is pervaded by moving images. The difficult task of reflecting on this fact involves the struggle to find expressive language that originates, interprets, and molds in order to stand apart from an engulfing media environment. In the 1957 foreword to *Film as Art*, Arnheim wrote:

> Shape and color, sound and words are the means by which man defines the nature and intention of his life. In a functioning culture, his ideas reverberate from his buildings, statues, songs, and plays. But a population constantly exposed to chaotic sights and sounds is gravely handicapped in finding its way. When the eyes and ears are prevented from perceiving meaningful order, they can only react to the brutal signals of immediate satisfaction. (6–7)

This statement applies as much to Arnheim's theoretical writings as it does to the partial illusion endowing the art of film. Film theory's description of film experience must also be partial, reverberating experiences and ideas in order to help us find our way.

10

Roland Barthes

What Films Show Us and What They Mean

WILLIAM BROWN

Roland Barthes's method of structural analysis, as well as his concepts of the readerly and the writerly text, the death of the author, and the *punctum*, are relevant to and have at times been taken up by film studies (see, for example, Pomerance 107ff). However, in this essay I am going to elaborate upon Barthes's slightly overlooked distinction between denotation and connotation to demonstrate how, when we watch films, we often unthinkingly conflate what we actually see with what it supposedly means. To do this, I shall look at moments from two films, Sofia Coppola's *Marie Antoinette* (2006) and Joseph L. Mankiewicz's *Guys and Dolls* (1955), arguing that precise explanations that elaborate how we get from what we see to how we understand it are the foundation of good film scholarship.

Barthes: Key Ideas

Roland Barthes (1915–1980) was a prolific thinker and writer who authored some twenty books between the late 1950s and 1980, when he was killed in a traffic accident in Paris. Various texts have also been published posthumously. One of his first major publications was *Mythologies*, which remains one of his best known works today. In *Mythologies*, Barthes dissects aspects of popular culture, in particular advertisements, in order to show how in order to sell products advertisers draw upon not truths but myths. Barthes analyzed the way images often function not simply in a neutral fashion but as signs with meanings above and beyond what we actually see. For this reason, Barthes is associated with the study of signs, or what is often referred to as semiotics.

Barthes is also associated with structuralism and, latterly, poststructuralism. In a series of works on literature, starting with *Writing Degree Zero* and culminating perhaps in *S/Z*, his analysis of Honoré de Balzac's novella *Sarrasine* (1830),

Barthes identifies how language plays a key role in storytelling. Much as the images in advertisements are not simply neutral and devoid of meaning, literature is not just the telling of stories in a neutral fashion. A specific deployment of language allows an author not just to recount stories but to invest them with meaning. That is, there is more than a narrative/story in a novel; a novel also tries to pass off as realistic a certain set of values that, typically, reflect the dominant, bourgeois ideology within which it is produced. In identifying how language functions in literature, Barthes thus helped us to understand how literature is structured: hence structuralism.

However, while Barthes believed that stories were structured—deliberately or otherwise—he also felt that the identification of an underlying structure did not necessarily exhaust a story's (potential) meaning. That is to say, literature might well be put together deliberately but there is no "final" interpretation of a text to be made. Barthes makes this clear through his concept of the "death of the author," elaborated in a 1968 essay of the same name. The author is "dead" first because we can never get inside authors' heads (even if they are alive and we can interview them) in order to work out what precisely they meant when they wrote a particular text. Secondly, the author is "dead" in the sense that he is not a mystery figure who identifies the final meaning of a text. Instead, the meaning of a text is established through its contact with a reader. Barthes further establishes this idea in *S/Z*, where he distinguishes between the "readerly" and the "writerly" text. The "readerly text" does not challenge a reader; it draws upon no complex ideas but instead appeals only to the reader's preexisting knowledge (think, if you will, of Dan Brown). A writerly text, meanwhile, is much harder to understand, and requires the active participation of the reader in understanding what the text means, or rather might mean. We have a paradox here: a writerly text places particular emphasis on the reader, while also reaffirming the presence of the writer, meaning that the so-called "death of the author" is not some apology for texts without human authors (such as, I might suggest, those written by computers); on the contrary, it is a means to affirm a type of writing the authorship of which requires and demands attention and participation from the reader. The reason that we see Barthes progress from structuralism to poststructuralism is that while language might be a key element in constructing literary narratives—if not *the* key element (they are "structured")—the meaning of that language, and thus also of the narrative, perhaps still escapes being definitively pinned down, especially when the writer deliberately adopts a harder-to-understand, or "writerly," style. In other words, Barthes moves beyond ("post")structuralism.

Even though he was writing about advertisements and stories, it seems obvious that Barthes's ideas might apply to the study of film, since like an advertisement film adopts images. Film is also a form commonly used in a narrative fashion for telling stories. That said, no idea from Barthes circulates in film studies as much as his concept of the *punctum*, developed in his late work on photography, *Camera Lucida*. The *punctum* is an effect that a photograph can have on a viewer, akin to the "writerly" style of linguistic composition: it presents to us something that eludes easy definition, but which instead encourages a much more engaged response from the viewer. However, contrary to the ideas circulating in Barthes's work on literature, the *punctum* is an essentially nonlinguistic response to an image. This we can compare to the *studium*, which is the equivalent of a "readerly" image that is easy to understand, and about which we perhaps feel we need not think twice. To be clear: it is not that a photograph is either a *studium* or a *punctum*. Rather, every photograph possesses aspects of the *studium* (we can just look at it without spotting anything of interest, just seeing in the photograph something banal and/or everyday), while also possessing the potential for the *punctum* (we might find something odd, intriguing, or shocking). Indeed, how much of either *studium* or *punctum* an image possesses depends as much as anything on how (and how hard) we look at it. It is important to add that particular to photography is the fact that the *punctum* also conveys a sense of the past coexisting with the present. Writing *Camera Lucida* in the aftermath of his mother's death, Barthes describes seeing a photograph of her as a child, in which there are details that make her seem present to him once again, even though she is not there. This is a deeply personal response—indeed, most people looking at the photograph would see in it only a little girl, not a girl that would become Barthes's mother. This personal response pierces/punctures Barthes (hence the name, *punctum*). And this personal response is also one that relies on what is called the indexical relationship between a photograph and reality. This indexical relationship is based upon the fact that a photograph is evidence of what was in front of the camera at the time of the image's taking, much as a fingerprint is evidence of someone's touching an object in the past. We do not necessarily know when the image was taken (although we can guess from appearances and background details, even if the photograph is not necessarily time-stamped as a digital image today would be). Nevertheless we see the photograph as evidence of the past existing in the present, which in turn imbues the viewer with a sense of loss, because he knows that the past depicted here has irretrievably gone forever.

The *punctum* is useful for film studies, since it functions as a means for understanding both the effects of home videos of one's own past—like Barthes contemplating images of his dead mother, we might feel an inexplicable sense of loss when in home movies we see relatives who have since died or images of ourselves in childhood—and the effects of early films more generally (I see an actuality film of life in, say, Paris [for example, the Lumières' *Parade of Ostriches* (1895)] and am filled with a strange sorrow as I realize that all of the participants in the film are now dead). What is more, since the *punctum* also points to the moments when a film evades our linguistic capacities, suggesting an engagement with film that is less intellectual and more physical, it can be evoked when discussing the love for tiny details during film viewing that often goes by the name of cinephilia. So, I can write at length about what a film supposedly means, yet say nothing of that moment when the actor half-smiles and turns away, and which is the most memorable and hard-to-explain moment of my actual viewing experience.

Marie Antoinette

Given that the *punctum* evades linguistic description—Barthes describes it as a general process, but cannot truly put his finger on the experience, and does not reproduce in his book the photos of his mother because he knows that the effect of those photos on him will not be the same as they will be on other viewers—it perhaps seems odd that I wish now to emphasize, via denotation and connotation, precisely the linguistic response to film.

There is more to be said about the complex relationship between language and affect, or between intellectual and physical responses to photographs and to films, but this is not the task of the present chapter. Instead, having sketched out Barthes's key ideas, and having hinted at their value for the study of film, I wish now to discuss the distinction between denotation and connotation. The difference between the two concepts has already been intimated earlier. If when we see an advertisement the images in fact convey values in addition to simply their own contents, then we have already a difference between what is denoted in the image (what is shown) and what is connoted (what the image supposedly means). Similarly, the structuralist project as a whole is designed to show that language itself is perhaps never neutral, itself always connoting as much as it denotes. In other words, when we look at an image, there is a difference between what we see (what is denoted) and what the image apparently means (what is connoted). Writing in *Image, Music, Text*, Barthes explains it thus: "'imitative' arts comprise two messages: a *denoted* message, which is the *analogon* itself, and a *connoted* message, which is the manner in which society to a certain extent communicates what it thinks of it. This duality of messages is evident in all reproductions other than photographic ones" (17).

For Barthes, photography, because of its indexical link to reality (it is an *analogon*), is a *message without a code* (17)—or so it would seem. For, Barthes goes on to argue that

> there is a strong probability that the photographic message too—at least in the press—is connoted. Connotation is not necessarily immediately graspable at the level of the message itself (it is, one could say, at once invisible and active, clear and implicit) but it can already be inferred from certain phenomena which occur at the levels of the production and

> reception of the image . . . [a] photograph is not only perceived, received, it is *read*, connected more or less consciously by the public that consumes it to a traditional stock of signs. (19)

Let us look at how Barthes's argument applies by analyzing an image from Sofia Coppola's *Marie Antoinette.*

The title character (Kirsten Dunst) is in an exceptionally ornate light blue silk dress, lying down on a *chaise longue*, staring directly at the camera. When I show this image to my students in class, I typically ask them what they can see in the image, and common responses include wealth and decadence. In other words, students pass over what is denoted (I've given a very cursory description above) and instead explain to me what is connoted. How is this so? This is so because wealth does not have a color, or a shape, or a material existence such that we can describe what it looks like denotatively. Wealth is, in other words, an abstract concept. So, too, is decadence. If someone sees in this image either decadence or wealth, by definition they can only be referring to what is connoted by the image, not what is denoted. Yet one of the major tasks of any film student or scholar is to be able to explain how an image comes to convey its meaning. That is, how an image manages to connote what it does. And we do this by looking at what the image denotes and by describing it in such a way that the relationship between what is denoted and what is connoted becomes clear. Let us do this in relation to the image before us.

Although it is out of focus, we can see through the window behind Marie seeming classical architecture, replete with big windows and a mixture of (reddish) brick and sandstone around the windows. Dispensing with a detailed

FIGURE 10.1 An early morning for the queen: Kirsten Dunst in *Marie Antoinette* (Sofia Coppola, Columbia, 2006). Digital frame enlargement.

history of architecture and glasswork, we can perhaps know simply from experience that the two types of brickwork coupled with the large windows suggest wealth (this is why basement flats are the cheapest—because they let in less light). Inside the window itself, we see the gold-edged window frame, together with detailed patterns in gold on the panel below the window and to the left of the window. The curtains also seem thick and warm and laid with detailed, golden designs, while the chair has an intricate level of detail in the wooden flourish at its top. Again, we do not need to be experts on interior design to understand why these details signify or connote wealth as long as our socialization makes possible that we recognize that they do: the more intricate are the details of a window frame, of a panel, of a set of curtains or of a chair, the more work will have gone into them. The more work has gone into them, the greater their value, meaning that only wealthy people can afford them, especially when they include what appears to be gold, a substance that is expensive as a result of its scarcity. Similarly, to have matching windows, panels, curtains, and chairs is a sign of wealth, for we know that matching sets often cost more than individual, separate items that do not create a coherently designed whole. Visual coherence, difficult to achieve, costs money.

Moving forward, Marie herself is wearing a (blue) silk dress with white embroidered edges. Her skin seems to be fair and without blemishes, while she wears a necklace and has dyed blond hair that is also adorned, in this case by feathers. While I am no expert on dresses or dyes, I know that silk is a relatively rare fabric, while blue, a color not commonly found in nature, is a sign of opulence. (Readers studying the black-and-white photograph will please trust my description.) As a dye blue is therefore harder to manufacture than, say, red (there are far fewer blue than red flowers, for example). Marie Antoinette's jewelry, her dyed hair (something hardly commonplace in the eighteenth century), and the feathers in her hair also connote wealth, as do the champagne bottle, the fan, the candelabra, and various other details in her surround, populating the image. By describing what the image denotes, we can work out how it connotes wealth—or at least the notion of wealth as we have it.

As for decadence, this is connoted through various other details that the image denotes. There is an empty champagne bottle on the table by the *chaise longue*. Champagne, not wine, not water. Not only is champagne expensive but it also induces drunkenness—and the bottle is empty. We do not know from this image whether Marie Antoinette has drunk the bottle alone or with company, but the implication is that she has been partying—and partying in an extravagant fashion. What is more, the candles are burned down nearly to their wick. This suggests that the party lasted long into the night. Furthermore, Marie Antoinette is herself in a horizontal position, suggesting that she may be about to sleep or has been sleeping. In short, she never made it to her real bed. And since she is fully clothed, while she might already have arisen, gotten dressed, and lain down on the *chaise longue* simply because she is hung over or tired, more plausible seems the possibility that she stayed up all night drinking, never made it to bed, and never even managed to get undressed to sleep. Combined, these denoted elements connote the idea of decadence, a kind of unreasonably lavish attention to one's own pleasure and satisfaction.

Finally, our Marie Antoinette is staring directly at the camera. Here we move into a slightly more specialized realm of signification, or connotation. For, Marie is calling attention to herself by looking directly—unusually—at us, the viewers. The direct look at us/the camera, then, seems to suggest a refusal on Marie's part to apologize for her decadent behavior: "This is me," she seems to say, "and I can look you in the eye, even if you disapprove of my partying all night and being super rich and profligate with my money when (as we might discover from the full film itself) people for whom I am supposed to be responsible are starving (such that they will rise up against me and seek my execution)." In effect, the denoted look to the camera connotes a troublesome lack of shame, which in turn might reinforce the decadence of Marie Antoinette's behavior.

In sum, then, we have a lot of information conveyed to us in what is only one still image from one film. This information might be summed up succinctly as "a rich and decadent world." However, part of the skill to develop in film studies is the ability to closely describe what one sees, and one does this by paying attention to what one sees, or what is denoted, and working out the links between this and what is connoted. In doing so, one sees precisely that the meanings of images are, as Barthes argued, often coded; that is, images use common signs or signifiers in order to give easy meanings to what we see. Talking about trick effects, Barthes says that

> they intervene without warning in the place of denotation; they utilize the special credibility of the photograph—this . . . being simply its exceptional power of denotation—in order to pass off as merely denoted a message which is in reality heavily connoted; in no other treatment does connotation assume so completely the "objective" mask of denotation. (*Image, Music, Text* 21)

In some senses, most movie images—especially those in narrative fictions—can be considered "trick effects." As per the empty champagne bottle and the gilded window frame, the "easy" meaning of the image from *Marie Antoinette* (richness and decadence) relies in fact upon a long history of architecture, interior design, metallurgy, embroidery, furniture manufacturing, interior lighting via windows and candles, clothing design, dying, alcohol making, and more, all as received and to some degree understood by the audience. These are cultural codes so longstanding and ingrained in us that we do not think twice about them when we see an image such as this one; this is simply, directly, and plainly a rich and decadent character. Yet that this meaning is constructed through the synthetic processes of architecture, interior design, lighting, alcohol manufacture, and so on, suggests that even if "naturalized" (that is, we do not think twice about it), the meaning we make, via the associations of those processes with wealth, is anything but "natural" (even if it utilizes natural resources like gold).

Not only do our powers of description help us better to identify how a film means what it does, then, but they also help us to identify how meaning comes into the world as a whole, and how meaning is, as Barthes suggests, constructed through cultural—often bourgeois—norms. In understanding how the world is constructed in the image of the bourgeoisie (not that of the working classes or various other groups who do not easily belong to the bourgeoisie), we achieve a position of knowledge whereby we might begin to change that world. In this way, paying attention to images and what they denote becomes a political act: now that I can change the world—by seeing how the supposedly "natural" nature of wealth and decadence is in fact built upon coded signs—I become a politicized being. Film studies, then, helps humans not just to understand films, but potentially to change the world.

Guys and Dolls

I have sometimes heard responses to the sort of analysis I provide earlier along the following lines: "But I just want to sit back, relax, and enjoy watching films. I don't want to have to pay attention to them so much. And I also don't want to have to describe images in exhaustive detail. This just takes the fun out of watching films." I could not disagree more. While written film analysis does require strong language skills on the part of the film student, as a keen turn of phrase needs to be cultivated in addition to a good eye for detail, the work increases one's viewing pleasure. Let us elaborate further the value of developing these skills, moving past the notion that ("over-")analyzing a film "spoils" it somehow.

Films more often than not function not just in the structural fashion suggested by Barthes—images connote cultural codes via signs—but also in the poststructural fashion. That is, often the harder one looks at a film the more details emerge. The film does elude the linguistic capacities of the viewer, inducing a real sense of cinephilic wonder or joy. Indeed, to appeal to a given truth that under other circumstances might well bear closer scrutiny: the more one puts into film analysis, the more one will get out of it. Perhaps I can convey a sense of this through a brief consideration of a sequence from Joseph L. Mankiewicz's classic musical *Guys and Dolls*.

The film tells the story of Sky Masterson (Marlon Brando), a New York crook who gets into a bet with his old friend Nathan Detroit (Frank Sinatra) that he can bring on a date to Havana none other than Sergeant Sarah Brown

(Jean Simmons), a sister from the ultra-puritanical Christian Save a Soul Mission. Sky wins the bet (though he will later tell Nathan that he lost it), and catches a plane down to Cuba for the night with Sister Sarah. The date goes very well and Sky and Sarah end up falling in love with each other (although the fact that, even as embodied by the attractive Brando, Sky is a crook and a gambler means their union will be delayed once they get back to New York).

The Havana sequence begins with Sky and Sarah standing in a square, with Sarah reading from a guidebook about the origins of the church in front of them. It is for the most part Spanish baroque, built of native limestone. Sky insists to Sarah that she put down the book and instead take in the beauty of her surroundings; the guidebook does not mention the beauty of the moonlight, says he, nor the music that we hear playing—a lilting romantic melody for guitar and male voice. Sarah continues to read from the book (standing on cobblestones that are supposed to be approximately four centuries old), before the two walk away, over a bridge and past a tramp to a bar/restaurant where in the next scene we will join them.

In this short sequence in the square, we have a sense in which *Guys and Dolls* is explicitly a film about how connotation arises from denotation. It does this by drawing explicit attention to the film's mise-en-scène: Sarah discusses the church and the cobblestones, while Sky mentions the moonlight and the music. That is, Sarah and Sky do the viewer's job not only of explaining to us what we see and hear, but also how to interpret it. For, in watching this sequence, we do not *actually* see a baroque Spanish church dating from 1674 and reconstructed between 1704 and 1724 (as the scripted "guidebook comments" indicate), nor do we *actually* see any moonlight. Instead we see a film set that is made to look like a baroque Spanish church and a lighting scheme that is made to seem like bright moonlight.

On one level, *Guys and Dolls* uses Sky and Sarah to make the viewer skip from denotation (seeing a film set) in order to get to connotation (seeing Havana, in particular Havana on a romantic night, with beautiful music and strong moonlight). However, on another level, in making this process of meaning-making/connotation so obvious, in making the set design so palpable for us, *Guys and Dolls* also undermines this process. The question becomes: why would the film (this film, any film) do this? And the answer can be reached through a consideration of the tramp figure, whom Sarah and Sky pass on that "bridge." The tramp is not present in the image by accident; neither did a real tramp nor an actor dressed as a tramp stumble into the image during filming, with Mankiewicz and his crew deciding to let him go and to carry on filming regardless. Instead, the tramp is deliberately there, and so asks to be interpreted as part of the scene.

Tramps typically represent downtrodden members of society, even castaways, who out of choice, out of a lack of opportunity, or as a result of other

FIGURE 10.2 Sarah (Jean Simmons) passes by her so-called charity work to the lure of booze in *Guys and Dolls* (Joseph L. Mankiewicz, Goldwyn, 1955). Digital frame enlargement.

problems, have become homeless and jobless and who must find support from the alms of others. The existence of tramps in Havana might also have come about as a result of the longstanding socio-economic imbalances arising from colonialism and the exploitation of indigenous peoples and imported slaves for the benefit of wealthy Europeans and white colonists. Indeed, it is perhaps as a result of these longstanding, ingrained, even "naturalized" economic imbalances in society (there are a very few very rich people, and many struggling poor people) that a country might decide to hold a revolution, one of the aspirations of which is/was to bring about greater economic and social equality throughout its population. *Guys and Dolls* was made in 1955, four years before the end of the Cuban revolution in which president Fulgencio Batista was displaced by the revolutionary Fidel Castro. It was also made at a time when, in spite of the country having long since rid itself of a Spanish colonial presence, Cuba was undergoing intensified economic exploitation in the form of its dependence on the United States. This exploitative relationship is suggested in the film by the very presence of Sky and Sarah and by the way in which Havana is treated as simply an overnight playground in which rich tourists can spend money. In other words, the church (a legacy of colonialism) and the characters (contemporary, imperial tourists) themselves point to why the tramp is in the scene. And the tramp also suggests that even if one colonizes or tries to create a state of economic dependence in a country like Cuba, one cannot control such a place, one cannot entirely determine its socio-political, economic, or cultural meaning. In this way, the tramp "exceeds" the romantic scene that Sarah and Sky are enjoying (tramps begging for money do not normally feature on romantic dates in movies), and points not only to the colonial/imperial domination of Cuba in the past but also to the imminent end of the revolution that promises to demonstrate that Cuba itself will not be what Spain or the United States have wanted, or want, it to be.

While the film demonstrates how images are deliberately structured so as to have meaning, it also skillfully demonstrates the way in which that meaning will be undermined: the tramp both interrupts the romance of the moment and points to a history of economic exploitation—he "interrupts" a greater, more diffuse romance. If on one level the tramp functions as a coded sign, on another he points to the way in which film exceeds language altogether, and thus also deserves a poststructuralist framework *in addition to a structuralist one* in order to be fully understood. Exceeding language, it also exceeds the lingo of set design and scripted "reality," the superficial presentation of "Havana" as Havana. Thus, significantly, Sarah's book does not capture the magic of the square. Sky points to the way in which language, via Sarah's guidebook, cannot capture romance, just before the tramp demonstrates how romance itself is a construct. That this all takes place in a scene so self-consciously fake brings down the entire system of meaning-making that is cinema, pointing to the way in which cinema's true power is in always exceeding the very meaning it purports to create. In this way, the harder we look at any cinematic image, the more meaning we may find, but in all likelihood the more images will become elusive. In other words, that which exceeds language/meaning is incessantly in the image.

Conclusions: Why Study Film?

There is much more to say about *Guys and Dolls*, in particular the Havana sequence that continues once Sky and Sarah have passed the tramp. For example, there follows a scene in which teetotal Sarah drinks milkshakes that, unbeknownst to her, have Bacardi in them; she likes the taste so much that she ends up drinking Sky's milkshakes, too, and so becomes drunk. All this is taking place in a story about "good" Sarah trying to convince "evil" Sky to be a better person. One has to wonder whether the sequence directly inspired Paul Thomas Anderson to use a milkshake analogy in *There Will Be Blood* (2007), when priestly Paul (Paul Dano) confronts evil Daniel Plainview (Daniel Day-Lewis) in order to try to convince him to be a better person, too. I hope to have shown here that the close analysis of a film, especially understanding how images connote through what they denote, can enrich our understanding of film. I have used Roland Barthes's concepts of denotation and connotation in order to do this. Even though they do not and perhaps cannot explain the totality of our experience of viewing films, these concepts certainly remain useful tools for us when as film scholars we confront the necessity of writing revealingly about films. Indeed, it is my contention that the more attention one pays to what a film denotes, the more one will find that the denotation in fact eludes a precise mapping onto what the film ostensibly connotes. The sequence discussed from *Guys and Dolls* self-consciously and paradoxically points to precisely this fact.

The film's use of a (coded) tramp to unsettle the other coded images in the sequence (a romantic date for rich Americans) suggests why the film is to be considered a masterpiece. It uses the process of connotation being derived from denotation to undermine this very process itself. In order to better understand how film might elude language, though, it is certainly of use to understand—via Roland Barthes—how description and the use of coded signs is also core to cinema. We must keep our eyes open. We must describe accurately how meanings arise in films. And then we may enjoy how all films begin to escape easy understanding. Film studies thus marks the road to true cinephilia.

11

Jean Rouch

The Camera as Provocateur

WILLIAM ROTHMAN

Jean Rouch (1917–2004) is widely recognized as occupying an important place in the history of cinema as a missing link between postwar Italian neo-realism and the French New Wave, especially for his *Chronicle of a Summer* (1961), a pioneering experiment in what he called "*cinéma-vérité*." Most of his work remains unknown by film scholars, due largely to the continued unavailability of all but a handful of the more than a hundred films he made in over fifty years of filming possession ceremonies of the Songhay of Niger, the subject of his own ethnographic publications, and the Dogon of Mali—the people studied by Marcel Griaule and Germaine Dieterlen, his mentors—whose traditional rituals are triumphs of mise-en-scène. Rouch's work among the Dogon culminated in a series of films about the epic *Sigui* ritual, staged every sixty years to commemorate the origin of death among humans; and two feature-length films, *Funeral at Bongo: The Old Anaï (1848–1971)* (1972) and *Ambara Dama: To Enchant Death* (1974). The films Rouch made in Africa were the crucible in which he forged his profound ways of thinking about cinema. To pigeonhole them as "ethnographic" would be to fail to acknowledge both their artistic achievement and the potentially fruitful ways of thinking about their medium that these films exemplify in their procedures and forms and articulate verbally in their poetic but theoretically rigorous voiceovers. They present theoretical ways of thinking that earn Rouch a place in this volume, all the more so because they serve as a reminder—as do the late works of Jean-Luc Godard, for example—of the theoretically significant fact that cinema can be—and has been—not only an object of study for film theory but also a vehicle or medium of film theory itself.

In the concluding sequence of *Chronicle of a Summer*, Rouch and his codirector, Edgar Morin, walk the corridors of the Musée de l'Homme in Paris, conducting a postmortem of an event that has just taken place. They have just screened a rough cut of their work-in-progress to the men and women who were in it, and led a heated discussion of its strengths and weaknesses. In that discussion, Marceline maintained that when she strolled through the Place de la Concorde followed by Rouch with his camera, and in a monologue to her dead father spoke in a child's voice about the day the Nazis rounded up the Jews in her neighborhood, she was only acting. No matter what she thinks, Rouch insists, Marceline did not act this scene; she was really living it. Morin adds, "Or if she did [act that scene], it was her most authentic side."

Close-Up

Abbas Kiarostami's *Close-Up* (1990) epitomizes Rouch's theory that the camera acts as a catalyst that allows film "to reveal, with doubts, a fictional part of all of us, which for me is the most real part of an individual," as he put it in a 1971 interview (Esnault, qtd. in Eaton 51). *Close-Up* revolves around Hossain Sabzian, a poverty-stricken man who was jailed after he pretended to be the famous film director Mohsen Makhmalbaf and entered the home of a well-to-do Tehran family, promising them a prominent role in his "new film." Kiarostami read a magazine story about the case and persuaded the clerical judge to let him film the trial. Since some scenes present events that occurred before filming began, they obviously had to be staged. The trial sequences, though, are hybrids of fiction and nonfiction that inextricably intertwine documentary footage and reenactments that may or may not hew closely to the actual trial.

At one point, Sabzian asks Kiarostami to convey to Makhmalbaf that his new film *The Cyclist* is "part of him." He feels it is "part of him"—the "most real part"—because he recognizes his own suffering in the suffering of that film's protagonist, Nasim (Moharram Zaynalzadeh), who is forced by poverty to earn some money by riding a bicycle continuously for a week. Even (and perhaps especially) in the scenes—all reenactments—in which he is impersonating Makhmalbaf, Sabzian's words seem heartfelt. In order to be believable in the role of Makhmalbaf, after all, he has to speak with an eloquence befitting the artist he so admires. His belief that within his own heart he has what the creator of *The Cyclist* has within his, helps Sabzian to find within himself a capacity for eloquence that might never have been revealed had he not pretended to be Makhmalbaf.

In one of *Close-Up*'s most poignant scenes, Sabzian, sensing the jig is up, speaks one last time in his role as Makhmalbaf. As if explaining to himself why he has returned to that house despite his premonition of being arrested, he says, "This morning, looking out the window, I felt so close to nature and the mountains. One must be in touch with the colors of nature to remove the rust covering one's heart." Then he slips into—out of—then back into—a mode of quotation (presumably from a classic Persian text) before putting the moral into his own words: "I asked, 'Why are you hiding your face from me?' She replied, 'It is you who are hidden.' Human beings hide their true selves. 'You yourself are the veil, for my face is revealed.' That's the issue: To uncover that true face." Makhmalbaf himself—or Rouch, for that matter—could not have said anything more profound, or more apt, than these sage words scripted by Kiarostami for Sabzian to speak. This man is playing himself playing a famous film director, yet with the camera as witness he seems genuinely to be speaking for himself, speaking as himself, speaking to himself, speaking to us. I, for one, am convinced.

Convinced of the sincerity of the defendant's contrition, the judge persuades the aggrieved family to forgive him. Sabzian confides to Kiarostami that he is more interested in acting than directing. The filmmaker asks him, point blank, "Aren't you acting for the camera now?" He replies, thoughtfully, "I'm speaking from the heart. This isn't acting."

He really believes he isn't acting—unless, of course, he is only acting when he says this. By provoking this man to ask himself whether he is acting, Kiarostami provokes us to ask ourselves, first, whether we believe that he is acting and, second, what we believe the relationship is between acting and "speaking from the heart." Sabzian goes on to quote Leo Tolstoy, who said that real art is "the inner experience cultivated by the artist and conveyed to his

FIGURE 11.1 Sincerely, it seems, Hossain Sabzian is addressing the filmmaker behind the camera in *Close-Up* (Abbas Kiarostami, Kanoon, 1990). Is he acting? Digital frame enlargement.

audience." He adds, "I think I could be an effective actor," as if unaware of how effectively he has conveyed his "inner experience" throughout the film already. Kiarostami challenges him further by asking, "Then why did you pretend to be a director instead of an actor?"

"Playing the part of a director is a performance in itself. To me, that is acting."

"What part would you like to play?"

"My own."

"Haven't you already done that?"

This last question reduces Sabzian to silence because it reveals him trapped in a contradiction. If acting is pretending, it isn't acting that the camera has been provoking him to do. But if acting is conveying "inner experience" by "speaking from the heart," he has been acting throughout the film. Like *Chronicle* before it, *Close-Up* offers strong evidence in support of Rouch's theory that film, the medium of the visible, is capable of conveying an individual's "inner experience," capable of making visible the invisible.

What Makhmalbaf has in his heart is what he has in his own, Sabzian believes; indeed, it is what all human beings have in theirs. That is what makes it possible for a film like *The Cyclist* to have the power to move everyone. Yet, as Kiarostami's filming conveys—and enables him to convey—so heartbreakingly, Sabzian's "inner experience" is his and his alone. Similarly, Marceline was not the only Jewish girl the Nazis separated from her parents that day, yet the "inner experience" that haunts her, which in a sense she has in common with others, is also utterly particular to her. This is part of what Rouch understands it means for her to be an individual, to have or be a "self." In this respect, *Close-Up* perfectly illustrates Rouch's understanding that to reveal the "most real part" of an individual, as he believes film has the power to do, is to reveal at once what is particular to that individual and what that individual has in common with others—indeed, with *all* others. Sabzian takes what is universal to all human beings as *suffering*. Ralph Waldo Emerson thought of it as a power or agency—at once receptive and creative, like a movie camera. He called it "Intellect." Henri Bergson, one of Emerson's devoted readers, called it "*élan vital*." In his narration for *Ambara Dama*, Rouch calls it "life strength," even as the film theorizes that there is a close connection, both logical and causal, between the fact that the possession of "life strength" is universal among human beings and the fact that we are all fated to die.

Why does Rouch refer to this "most real part" of an individual as *fictional*? If it is real, how can it be fictional? Rouch never tired of saying that he did not film reality as it is but reality as filming provokes it to become, a reality in which the invisible is rendered visible. It is this new reality, which comes to be only because of the making of the film and which has no existence apart from the projected world itself, that a film like *Chronicle* reveals and creates, documenting a new truth, a *cinema* truth. *Cinéma-vérité*.

But *Chronicle* also lies. As Rouch remarks in the 1971 interview, "We contract time, we extend it, we choose an angle for the shot, we deform the people we're shooting, we speed things up and follow one movement to the detriment of another movement. So there is a whole work of lies" (Esnault, qtd. in Eaton 51). At the time he and Morin made that film, he adds, these lies were "more real than the truth" to them. He still stood by *Chronicle*'s demonstrations of the camera's power to provoke reality to reveal itself. But he had developed a new method of filming—he called it "one take/one sequence"—that enabled him to forgo the classical conventions that for all its revelations also made *Chronicle* a "work of lies."

Rouch-the-Camera

In *Turu and Bitti: The Drums of Yore* (1971), a ten-minute film that is a veritable paradigm of the "one take/one sequence" method, the entire film consists of a single continuous take that lasts the duration of the camera magazine. Except for Rouch's first-person narration, nothing is added after the fact, nothing edited out, no effects created in post-production, no "lies" told of the kind *Chronicle* tells. Rouch walks with the camera on his shoulder into a Songhay village in which a possession ritual is under way. He focuses his camera on the dancers who have been trying for hours to become possessed by the invisible spirits whose help they need to bring rain for their crops; then on the drummers trying to make music that will help entrance them. Just when it appears that nothing is going to happen he finds himself moved to return his camera to one of the listless dancers. Suddenly, the dancer's demeanor changes in a transformation seemingly precipitated by the attention of the camera—a moment that epitomizes Rouch's theory that the camera's very presence, when it is doing its mysterious work, has the power to provoke reality to reveal itself.

Convinced it was his filming that precipitated this possession, Rouch wrote "On the Vicissitudes of the Self: The Possessed Dancer, the Magician, the Sorcerer, the Filmmaker, and the Ethnographer," an essay that offered a theory as to how the camera's presence could have had this effect, not only on the Songhay mediums (who were possessed when the camera came closest) but also on the spirits (who possessed the mediums precisely then). Of course, we in the West are unlikely to believe that such "spirits" as Kure, the hyena god, really exist. But what do the mediums believe the camera to be that they understand its presence to be capable of provoking them to abandon themselves, so as to enable invisible spirits in whose existence *they* believe to take possession of their bodies? How can they so much as imagine that invisible gods are provoked by a camera into manifesting themselves?

According to the essay, the Songhay believe that when a dancer becomes possessed, he or she is approached by an invisible spirit carrying an animal skin that the spirit wraps around the dancer's head, both capturing and protecting the dancer's "self." Then the spirit enters the body of the dancer, who is now in a deep trance. When it is time to leave, the spirit lifts off the animal skin, liberating the medium's displaced "self." As he was filming *Turu et Bitti*, Rouch suggests, he fell into a "ciné-trance" comparable to the trances of the mediums. Walking with camera on shoulder, he became the being that Paul Stoller, in an eloquent account of the film, calls "Rouch-the-camera" (193). Rouch-the-camera walked among the villagers gathered for the ceremony, and also among invisible spirits, who recognized him as belonging to their realm as well as the realm of the visible. Evidently, invisible spirits and human dancers alike wanted Rouch-the-camera to be present—observing, filming, provoking—at the moment of possession.

Viewed through a camera viewfinder, the world is reduced to its surfaces, as it is when film images are projected. In this sense, we can think of the camera as an instrument that skins the world alive. It sounds fanciful to put it this way, but when Rouch became Rouch-the-camera, his "self" was literally wrapped within the skin of the world, freeing him to become possessed by the spirits of the individuals he was filming—each a "self," each capable of being a medium.

Who or what *is* Rouch-the-camera? A clue can be found in the fact that we speak of the individual a photograph is of, as the subject of that photograph. That its "object" is also its subject suggests of the photograph that what is in it is what it is about, and that the object of this study participates actively in this study. When Rouch enters into a ciné-trance and becomes Rouch-the-camera, what is in the frame of the viewfinder—the visible world of people and objects, the world in which spirits are invisible—reveals itself to him as a subject, an active participant in creating the world on view. Rouch theorized that the viewfinder becomes a kind of crystal ball in which the entranced filmmaker sees what to everyone else is invisible: the world as it is fated to appear on the movie screen, a world in which the filmmaker's invisible "self" reveals itself in the visible. When *Turu et Bitti* is projected on a movie screen, Rouch's own invisible "self," the "most real part" of him, is revealed.

"Whatever the mechanism, the paramount fact of possession is that the medium's [self] is displaced," Stoller writes, "and the paramount fact of the filming of *Turu et Bitti* is that Rouch entered a 'ciné-trance of one filming the trance of another.'" Without support from Rouch's words he adds, "Ciné-trance, however, is entered only by filmmakers who practice cinema-vérité, who hunt for images in the real world" (168–169). All filmmakers "hunt for images in the real world"—where else are they to find them? It is one of Rouch's profoundest theoretical insights, gleaned from his study of the way the Songhay understood these matters, that the concept of possession is a key—perhaps *the* key—to the camera's mysterious ability to provoke individuals to reveal the "most real part" of themselves.

Vertigo

This theoretical insight is capable of illuminating a wide range of films, perhaps all films, not only films we might associate with the term "cinema-vérité," much less films shot by the "one take/one sequence" method. One that immediately springs to mind is *Vertigo* (1958), usually thought of as a story about obsession but no less a story about possession. In the first half of the film, Scottie Ferguson (James Stewart) falls in love with a woman he believes to be Madeleine (Kim Novak), Gavin Elster's wife. She seems to fall into deep trances during which—or so Scottie is deceived into believing—she is possessed by the spirit of Carlotta Valdez, a nineteenth-century woman who went mad and died by her own hand. In the second part of the film, we learn that the woman Scottie believed to be Madeleine, now dead, was really Judy Barton from Kansas, who had taken part in Elster's elaborate plan to murder his wife. Perhaps not all of her trances were phony; we cannot know. In particular there is a moment in the redwoods when, strolling with Scottie—who is in love with the "her" who is only a creation of Judy's acting—Madeleine seems transfixed by a cross-section of a giant sequoia and pointing to one of its rings, as if entranced, says in a faraway voice, "Here I was born." Pointing to another, she says, "And here I died." Who or what is really speaking these words—Judy, pretending to be Madeleine possessed by the ghost of Carlotta, or Carlotta herself, a ghost, speaking through the medium that Judy has become in a trance that is real?

As *Vertigo* makes clear, there is a close logical connection between possession and obsession. As he is obsessed with the woman he knows as "Madeleine," Scottie's will is no longer his own, not because he is possessed by her but because he is obsessed with possessing her. The Madeleine he loved, aloof and elegant, is Judy's fiction, but the Judy who wears sweaters too tight and too much make-up isn't this woman's "true self" either. Judy, too, is a fiction, a character who so perfectly denies her "inner Madeleine" that she could have been created for just that purpose.

The actress or star we know as "Kim Novak" plays or incarnates this woman in both of her guises. In a so-called fiction film, it is the prevailing fiction that the characters, not the actors, are real. Yet *Vertigo*, no less than *Chronicle* or *Close-Up*, is also a "document" of real encounters between the camera and the individuals it filmed. Unlike Marceline or Sabzian, Kim Novak is not playing or simply being herself. Neither is she impersonating an individual she is not, since Judy has no reality apart from the film; it is only Kim Novak's incarnation of her—or Judy's incarnation *as* Kim Novak—that makes Judy real. Pretending to be Madeleine or simply being—or pretending to be—herself, Judy Barton *is* Kim Novak or, rather, she is the woman Kim Novak really becomes—the woman the camera's presence provokes Kim Novak to become—in *Vertigo*'s world. The camera's presence provokes Novak not to pretend to be an individual she is not but to reveal a part of herself that is no less real for being fictional. The Madeleine with whom Scottie falls in love, the Madeleine who in *Vertigo*'s world is only Judy playing a role, is just as real, in the same way, as the Judy who plays her. We can say that Kim Novak becomes possessed by Judy, as long as we keep in mind that within *Vertigo*'s world, it is Judy who is possessed by Kim Novak.

That Rouch himself never tried to think through how the concept of possession casts light on fiction films is not a reason to doubt the concept's potential fruitfulness for thinking theoretically about cinema in general. It only testifies to Rouch's own ever more focused commitment to what he called "shared anthropology." He eventually became less interested in thinking about the camera's ability to provoke individuals to reveal the "most real part" of themselves. That is because he became less interested in thinking about individuals.

Rouch regularly screened his footage for the Songhay and Dogon villagers he filmed, and questioned them about events he had captured with his camera. Their answers helped him film in ways that enabled him to ask new questions and receive new answers. His goal was to help these "ethnographic others"—the traditional objects of ethnographic study—to become subjects who shared in the pursuit of knowledge. And screening his films to Western audiences was his strategy for winning converts to his filmmaking procedures. Making films to beget films, he hoped to further his radical practice of "shared anthropology" whose goal was to transform anthropology, with its claims to know others with scientific objectivity, into a practice at once scientific and artistic, a practice no less rigorous for acknowledging the unknowable, unsayable value of breaking down the walls that separate what we know from the way we live. He believed there were no such walls in traditional African societies, so that tapping into the knowledge inscribed in Songhay and Dogon rituals was the key to advancing toward his goal.

Rouch's way of filming, which he devoutly wished others to emulate, was also a way of thinking and living that embraced the magical, the strange, the fantastic, and the fabulous, and promised freedom from the alienation, the joylessness, to which we would otherwise be consigned by Western society where the individual is privileged—a condition Rouch increasingly saw as an affliction.

Funeral at Bongo

Funeral at Bongo: The Old Anaï (1848–1971) "documents" the spectacular funeral dances occasioned by the death—at the age of 122!—of Anaï Dolo, a revered elder. There is a passage in which the participants reenact the 1895 battle between the Dogon and their French colonizers that left Anaï seriously wounded. At one point, dancers aim their archaic rifles directly at Rouch behind the camera: Rouch being French was a fact that wasn't lost on them, or on him. But pointing their guns at the camera had another symbolic meaning as well. A soul separated from its body is vulnerable, the Dogon believe, and also dangerous. However much the dead man's spirit wanted to stay in the village, it had to be made to leave, even if this meant frightening it away. Pointing their guns at Rouch as he was filming underscored that these Dogon villagers associated the camera with the invisible spirit of the dead Anaï, as if Rouch-the-camera, too, was to them a disembodied spirit, vulnerable and dangerous, haunting a world in which he was homeless, longing to rest in peace, yet reluctant to sever ties with the living.

When dancers perform the "dances of burial" in the public square, Rouch tells us, they are making visible the "system of the world" that finds expression in every facet of Dogon society. In these dances, which reenact the life of one individual, the history of the Dogon people, and the creation of the universe, the invisible plays essential roles as characters and audience: dead souls, ancestors, gods. In filming Anaï's funeral, Rouch wasn't interested in conveying any individual's "inner experience." His challenge was to convey the full dimension of a reality in which, in the Dogon worldview, there are no walls separating the visible and the invisible, the living and the dead, the present and the past, the individual and the collective. To Westerners, such a reality is a distant dream. But in the Dogon world, as *Anaï* envisions it, that dream is reality. If this vision is also a fiction, as surely it is, it is a fiction that enables the "most real part" of the Dogon world—and the "most real part" of Rouch's art—to reveal itself.

In the Dama ritual that *Ambara Dama* documents, dancers wearing tall masks reenact the first death of a human being. They reenact, as well, the performance of the first Dama ritual, which was meant to empower the soul of the first man who died to follow the long path to the land of the dead, but which led to the contagion that caused death to spread so widely that it became universal—a necessity, not a mere possibility for all human beings. At the heart of *Ambara Dama* is a passage in which Rouch, drawing his words from Marcel Griaule's writings, reflects on the "inner experience" of the beholders of the ritual, linking it with the role the original Dama played in spreading death. At the very moment the dancers "enchanted the dead through their masks, they themselves were enchanted. The funeral choreography enchanted people of the mask society to the point where they provoked the contagion of death. Displayed in museums, shorn of pulsing drumbeats, Dogon masks retain little if any of their power to enchant." All this time, the camera has been lingering on the mask of one of the dancers, but in an extraordinary gesture Rouch slows down the image (and the sound track, lowering the music's pitch two octaves and dulling its pulsing beat)—not to enhance the spectacle, but to spare us its dangerous, potentially deadly, power.

At the end of the film, the masks made for this Dama festival are taken to a cave where, Rouch says, "their fatal charm" will operate only "against those who enter their forbidden doorstep." He goes on:

> In five years, at the next Dama, these masks will be replaced by new ones. Formerly, old masks used to disintegrate in the caves. Today, the Dogon sell them to museums or amateurs who do not suspect that they spread death. But a mask without music and dance is only a piece of wood. However, in caves where masks are resting, men have tried to recover their dangerous strength. On the walls, they have painted in red, white, and black—paintings only initiated elders can decipher.

Rouch's camera discovers in these paintings a tangible sign of the true dimension of the Dogon world. To those who know how to read them, the paintings make visible the "system of the world." And the film's images of the paintings, in their own way, make visible the world as a whole, as do all film images. Those who "left in the red earth the mark of their fingers" have departed "on the long path to the country of death," Rouch says, "but a part of their life strength is left here, in these paintings, and they will transmit it to all the masks to come." In transmitting their power to enchant, they will transmit their power to endow those who behold them with "life strength." They will also transmit their death-dealing power. When the Dogon perform the Dama ritual, reenacting the origin of death and thereby accepting their own participation, they acknowledge their own implication in the "system of the world" that makes death a reality for all human beings. And with this ending, Rouch's film accepts its own participation—Rouch acknowledges his own implication—in the reality that we are all fated to die.

That the camera's mysterious powers reveal it to have such a deep and intimate affinity with death is another of Rouch's profound insights (this one gleaned from the Dogon worldview) that have far-reaching implications for our understanding of a wide range of films, although in this case, too, his single-minded focus on "shared anthropology" kept him from being moved to think them through. Here again, *Vertigo* immediately comes to mind.

In *Vertigo*'s devastating climax, Scottie holds a different Judy in his arms. Looking once again like the Madeleine he loved, he now knows she *is* the woman he loved, a woman who never really existed. He awakens to the reality that whoever or whatever she may be, this is the woman he loved then, the woman he loves now, the woman he will always love. Yet Judy is suddenly provoked by something to open her eyes. A glint in her eye makes it clear that her gaze is drawn toward the camera.

That what provokes her to look toward the camera is not something she *literally* sees is made clear when Hitchcock cuts to her point of view, where we at first see—nothing. Only after a moment does a shadowy figure emerge, barely perceptible, out of the blackness. Judy seems to know what she will see before

FIGURE 11.2 What provokes this woman to open her eyes and look toward the camera? Kim Novak and James Stewart in *Vertigo* (Alfred Hitchcock, Paramount, 1958). Digital frame enlargement.

she sees it, as if she envisions it in her mind's eye before her gaze and Hitchcock's camera, in concert, provoke this specter into revealing itself. I cannot doubt that she immediately recognizes the apparition as the shadow of death, death coming to claim her. She wants to live. But what she sees, or envisions, when the camera provokes her to look in its direction, causes her to die.

Vertigo is Hitchcock's meditation on the fatal revelation, provoked by the camera, that for Judy the death that was her fate—a fate she was doomed to have in common with Carlotta Valdez and Madeleine Elster—was the "most real part" of herself. *Vertigo* thus has profound affinities with *Ambara Dama*, Rouch's meditation on the Dogon view that death became a necessity for all human individuals—the "most real part" of themselves, in effect—because human beings, possessing "life strength," had the power to *create* death. It is because we have an appetite for life that we must die.

Along with *Psycho* (1960), *Vertigo* is Hitchcock's darkest meditation on his understanding—virtually identical to that of Rouch—that the camera is an instrument of taxidermy. As I put it in *Hitchcock: The Murderous Gaze*, "The camera fixes its human subjects, possesses their life. When they are reborn on the screen, creatures of the film's author, life is not fully breathed back into them. They are immortal, but they are already dead" (346). In Emerson's view, individuals are free to participate actively in the authorship of their own lives. The characters in *Vertigo* do not have such freedom. The story of Judy's life had already been written. And it ends as it must. The same can be said of the Dogon villagers who participate in the Dama ritual that *Ambara Dama* documents. But the condition that Hitchcock envisions as tragic is an inalienable part of the "system of the world" Rouch would have us accept and, in a joyful spirit, embrace.

12

André Bazin

Dark Passage into the Mystery of Being

DUDLEY ANDREW

André Bazin (1918–1958) grew up in the very midst of existentialism. He knew Sartre personally. He also interacted with Gabriel Marcel, Sartre's rival as a popular philosopher and playwright, whose chief books, *The Mystery of Being* and *Homo Viator* (Latin for "Man the Traveler"), signal in their titles Bazin's attitude toward life and art. Never holding forth about ultimate meaning, completely uninterested in dogma, Bazin, like Marcel, felt that we are all travelers in a mysterious world. We should put faith in our five senses, our intelligence, our imagination, and in our access to civilization's legacy of the sciences and the arts. He was, in short, a humanist, believing we must strive for increasingly clear and comprehensive views of the physical and social universe, so that we can properly—that is, ethically—play a role in it. Yet his humanism was tempered by his appetite for science, by his interest in the way the world works without man at its center. Undoubtedly influenced by the phenomenology that Maurice Merleau-Ponty was expounding at just this time, he considered our vision of things to be inevitably partial, intermittent, and a construct consisting not just of what our eyes sense but of what our mind, memory, and other senses suggest is hidden from direct sight (for an overview of Bazin's philosophy see Andrew, "Ontology"; Dalle Vacche).

A Philosophy of Life

We may live surrounded by darkness, but we may share with others whatever we do see, as well as our perspectives. Moreover, science and art augment and stabilize our knowledge, testing and recording various kinds of encounters with the world. Scientific discoveries and artistic breakthroughs form plateaus of understanding on which we stand to gain different and larger vantage points. Bazin was twenty-two when the cave paintings in Lascaux, France, were discovered. He cites them at the beginning of *What Is Cinema?* as evidence of a universal drive to defeat time. As toolmaker and artist, *Homo sapiens* eventually developed cinema, a marvelous flashlight prompting more profound explorations of the caverns of our ignorance, caverns that give onto ever larger chambers.

As it reveals some of the physical and social contours of our existence, cinema may not be our subtlest or most accurate instrument, but it is ubiquitous. Bazin was optimistic about cinema, believing, with Roberto Rossellini, in its capacity to prepare the ground for a reconstructed social world based on a more common understanding of the natural world and of human behavior and needs. It's not only high-minded movies that open up what we know; genre films do so as well, since they repeatedly probe some dirty or cluttered corner of experience. Each film directs light either toward what is already well-lit (the clichés that most films repeat) or toward the irregular contours at the dim edges of experience (avant-garde works).

Every film presumes a totality of which it delivers slivers and sections that we are meant to connect into a story or line of reasoning. Bazin's adherence to cinema as the medium of our time stems from its way of blending—in different ratios—perception and imagination. From film to film, he calculated the weight of what is shown and the greater weight of what is left unseen; he sketched a film's implicit design and laid out the consequences of that design. He took the position of phenomenology, that every experience supplies only a certain number of elements (and in cinema these are mere traces) but always implies a totality, which in the case of fiction we call a world.

Every world can be looked at from several perspectives. In cinema we speak of the filmmaker's and the viewer's perspectives, but also triangulate these through the values and sometimes the points of view of characters who relate to each other and to circumstances changing around them. Bazin rose to the challenge of films like Renoir's *Rules of the Game* (1939), where such relations are dizzying in their complexity, but he also "philosophized," if we can call it that, whenever a film moved him to interact with it. And films could move him in myriad ways, from the faces they presented, to the desires behind those faces, and the trajectories (call them plots) launched by desires. A trajectory is a pathway through the fictional world. It leads the spectator toward what is deemed important, often isolating people and things in close-up, while filtering out other people and things beyond the frameline. A trajectory also speeds the film along through ellipses in time, or by providing explanations in flashback.

Now Bazin was particularly attentive to the clutter of unbidden perceptions and elements that crop up to the side of a film's chosen pathway. He may have preferred cinema to literature because of the happenstances that a filmmaker cannot control and that register the inertia of the world as it slows the momentum of the artistic imagination. So, to him cinema was not entirely an art, and human values were not entirely its goal. Its technological basis establishing a partly nonhuman relation to the world, cinema invites a reconsideration of existence altogether. Isn't this precisely what it means to philosophize? Some films seem to provoke, and perhaps enact philosophy.

Dark Passage to Utopia

One clear candidate is Delmer Daves's *Dark Passage* (1947), starring Humphrey Bogart and Lauren Bacall. Reviewing it, Bazin signaled three aspects that made the film stand out: the destiny driving its plot, the attention devoted to its San Francisco setting, and the face of Bogart (Bazin, "Passagers"). A philosophy of cinema and of life can be extracted from his observations.

The Face

Of these three aspects, the third might seem least important, until we remember how important the face is in Bazin's theory. "The neo-realist filmmakers . . . endow their films with a sense of the ambiguity of reality. Rossellini's purpose when filming the face of the boy in *Germany, Year Zero* is the opposite of that of Kuleshov when working with a close-up of Mozhukhin. Rossellini wants to preserve the face's mystery" (Bazin, "Evolution" 37). Bogart's face may have been well-known but for Bazin it remained fundamentally unknown, ambiguous. The touching eulogy he composed for Bogart carries a subheading, "The Face of Death." Here he describes the actor as growing into the death mask he seemed to wear already in *Dark Passage* (Bogart died ten years afterward). For he "epitomized the immanence of death, its imminence as well . . . [his face represents] the corpse on reprieve which is within each of us" (Bazin, "Death" 98). In *Dark Passage* this face is withheld for over an hour, until plastic surgery turns Vincent Parry into "an older-looking guy," that is, Humphrey Bogart. The surgeon, operating clandestinely and without a license at 3 A.M., talks like a make-up artist: "You'll look older. I hope you don't mind a few scars." We scrutinize his features because he does so himself in a mirror, noting what Bazin calls "his visible stigmata" emerge from the bandages. This face is designed to look weathered, after having gone through the beatings and hard drinking as the face of Sam Spade and Philip Marlowe. Bogart was born (and is here reborn) immersed in a dirty world. As Bazin says, "He's a stoic who has absorbed a lot of punches . . . a man not defined . . . by his courage or his cowardice, but above all by this existential maturity which gradually transforms life into a stubborn irony at the expense of death."

Bogart's stubborn irony is expressed in the distinctive timbre of his voice, something Bazin doesn't mention.[1] Together face and voice embody, literally, a state of existence, a way to pass through a murky world where things seem stacked against him. We're not far from Albert Camus, or better from Ernest Hemingway and William Faulkner, a fact Bazin would note in declaring Bogart to be "in the cinema the first illustration of the 'age of the American novel,' where tough luck characters are 'sources of ambiguity' who have 'internalized death'" ("Death" 100–101), not only the place where we are all headed but the only place from which any life can be judged (see, for an earlier, and perfectly titled, discussion of this existentialist dictum, Bazin, "Saint").

Bogart in fact was on set for only half the shoot, because whip pans simulate his character's head turning, and an unsteady track mimics his gait. *Dark Passage* was an audacious experiment in first-person perspective, following MGM's *Lady in the Lake* (1947), by six months.[2] And it was far more successful with the critics and the public, because it provided the additional suspense of waiting for Bogart to appear at last on the other side of the camera. For the first hour he talks to himself or answers those around him in a rare example not of "voiceover" but "voice with" . . . that is, voice with the camera's look. The shower head spouts water toward the camera, as would happen in *Psycho* (1960). A hand puts a razor on the basin and brings a towel up to cover the lens (Vincent Parry's face). The same stunt hand (it needn't have been Bogart's) turns on the phonograph, just as a knock is heard and a woman's voice (Lauren Bacall's) asks for Irene. The camera jerks up to focus on the door as Bogart says clearly, "That's Madge's voice," though we can't tell if this is audible or internal. The camera moves to the door's peephole, but doesn't open it. Nevertheless—and breaking with point-of-view rules—the picture dissolves to a close-up of Madge (Agnes Moorehead) in the corridor. She hears Bogart's voice now muffled by the door, telling her to go away. As she leaves, image and sound return to the other side of the door and to Vincent Parry's perspective. The camera swivels to quickly mount the circular staircase so that it—and he—can catch a glimpse of Madge leaving. This bravura traveling shot lasts over a minute, as it passes into the upstairs bedroom (the door swinging open before it), then rushes straight ahead to the window where two stunt hands jut out to spread the blinds enough for us to see Madge looking back from the street. The shot continues in real time, tracking to a dresser and opening the drawer to reveal Irene's scrapbook that stunt hands page through until a close-up on a newspaper clip explains her obsession with Vincent Parry, the man looking at it. The view finally changes when Irene bursts in and says, "I thought I heard someone talking in here."[3]

Shots like this abound, the script concocting occasions for the presumed body behind the lens to make its presence felt, as when a hand reaches out for a light and brings it toward the camera. But once he has been released by the doctor back on the streets, we finally have Bogart in front of us, photographed from the outside; yet, like Irene (Bacall), we must wait for the bandages to come off. She peels these slowly (excruciating because of the suspense more than the pain), until, in front of that mirror, Bogart can look at himself and approve, just as Bacall does. It is indeed Humphrey Bogart. All this occurs so far into the film

FIGURE 12.1 Bogart hidden and revealed in *Dark Passage* (Delmer Daves, Warner Bros., 1947). Digital frame enlargements.

it could be deemed a climax, not of the drama of escape but of the drama of identity, which is the real experiment of the film. Voice joins face to render a person in depth, a man with a past in other films and an off-camera life that is very public, since everyone knew that Bacall and Bogart were romantically involved at the time.

Vincent Parry's new face is meant to be anonymous, the face of no one alive, so that he cannot be easily tracked. Yet he is given Bogart's face, a visage so famous it inspired Michel Poiccard (Jean-Paul Belmondo) in *Breathless* (1960), when that escapee was also being tracked down. Cities make one feel anonymous, yet under surveillance.[4] *Dark Passage* represents this existentialist anguish; it thematizes identity, guilt, and the otherness (the "hell," Jean-Paul Sartre would say) of other people and a deeper otherness within ourselves.

Destiny

While the mystery of the neo-realist face may be seen in Bogart's, the loose neo-realist plot is the opposite of the "mystery story" that makes up *Dark Passage*. Neo-realism can afford to abjure montage, whereas *Dark Passage* requires a good deal of editing before Vincent Parry can make it through the birth canal of the plot to be reborn in a seaside Peruvian Eden.

In a two-part examination of the *policier*—and calling on Aristotle to distinguish it from tragedy—Bazin first analyzed what he called the "physics" of its mechanism (plot) before turning to the "chemistry" of its substance (character). I have begun with the chemical makeup of *Dark Passage*, because this film's distinctiveness lies precisely in the chemistry of its hero, or rather in the way the film almost scientifically tests that chemistry through an experiment with the special effect of plastic surgery. Bazin identified the noir hero by a peculiar molecular combination involving elements of both criminal and detective, and he held up Humphrey Bogart's Philip Marlowe as an unalloyed example (see "Le film policier"). Vincent Parry is not so clear a specimen but, once given a new face, he feels transformed from someone who is technically a criminal on the run (condemned as such) into a detective hunting down the real killer. With his original face he feared every person he ran into, every knock at the door; he cowered upstairs and peered from behind the blinds, sure that he was being spied upon. But with a new face, and as Humphrey Bogart, he starts acting like Philip Marlowe: "I've got to prove who killed him," he says. Now it will be he who turns the table on the blackmailer when the latter knocks on his hotel door. Bogart wrests the gun from him and forces answers from him in a brutal interrogation. Next, he knocks on Madge's door and corners her. Both his tormenters wind up in panic, falling to their deaths from a great height.

Like all noir heroes, Parry plays hide and seek in a murky world. "Caught within the ambiguity of events, it's not he who is immoral; rather it is morality that gives way under his footsteps. For duty and crime appear to be desperately relative notions when seen under the light of a series of actions that are always duplicitous and perpetually disguised" (Bazin, "Grandeur").

Vincent Parry's "destiny" moves in but one direction through *Dark Passage*. After an establishing shot of San Quentin, the film is on the move aboard a truck heading away from the prison. Ten fingers emerge from one of the barrels on the back of the truck. They grasp the edge of the barrel and rock it off the truck, rerouting destiny, rolling the escapee to the bottom of a gully. A tunnel shot from the barrel is followed by his POV as he clambers back up the hill and offers himself up to a chance encounter, hitching a ride with the first car coming along. Does he deserve this second chance? Apparently framed for the death of his wife, in fact he feels some guilt for having wished her dead. His marriage had been a prison even before San Quentin. Now he hands himself a future, but one he can scarcely control. For the car he boards would whisk him to his demise, if he didn't overcome the driver, a blackmailer, and take a chance with the next person to come along, Irene Janson. Like some guardian angel, Irene has taken fate into her hands, too, and provoked what appears to be this haphazard encounter. He hides under a tarp, as they drive through a tunnel leading to the Golden Gate Bridge, past a close call at a roadblock and into the safety of her art deco apartment.

Afraid to leave, effectively imprisoned once again, Vincent Parry's nightmare scenario begins as figures from his past return to knock on the door and stalk him from the street. Even Irene's genial boyfriend (who is also the former lover of Madge) poses a threat every time he phones or comes around. Taxi drivers might turn Parry in. A plain-clothes cop slowly approaches him from the far end of the diner where he is the only other customer, and badgers him mercilessly, escorting him onto the street where he is lucky to escape again. Every step Parry takes finds him running from scrutiny. Even when his two nemeses, the blackmailer and Madge, literally fall out of the picture, he must remain out of sight, guilty now of four murders he was in fact at least partially responsible for. After he manages to purchase a bus ticket to a town in Arizona where he may be able to cross the border to freedom, he must first endure the depot's waiting room, with the police combing the place. Then, inspired by two travelers he overhears confessing their loneliness and looking at each other hopefully, he dials Irene from the phone booth to dictate a better fate for them both, a life together far away. "I'll be waiting for you," he says, "if you could see your way clear." He has put "You're Marvelous" on the jukebox, the song that played when Irene had first explained her presence in his life: "Oh, I don't believe in fate or destiny or any of those things. But I guess it was something like fate to get me to go out there to Marin County. Or because I was thinking of you." A talisman, this recorded song comes back to reassure Bogart and Bacall each time they feel threatened, until at last it is played live, on cue, when, in the final shot, Irene stands before him as the image of a dream fulfilled. And it will be "love ever after," with neither rivals nor inconstancy, for Vincent Parry is not just a lover; he is the surrogate as well for Irene's father, his near double, a man who languished until death in San Quentin, though innocent of the murder that sent him there. Irene's scrapbook, together with her phonograph record, contain Vincent Parry's destiny. He couldn't go wrong.

San Francisco, Open City

Bazin deflated the pretentions of the *policier.* He appreciated the intricacy and rigor of its narrative form, as well as the urban milieu it exploited. But he found trivial its recourse to fate and destiny, at least in comparison to tragedy, because these films aimed to be realistic rather than mythic. Film noir is surely the *policier's* most interesting sub-genre, but he felt it reached a summit in *The Big Sleep* (1946), with most later noirs mainly exploiting one gimmick or another.

Dark Passage features two gimmicks: first-person point of view and outdoor shooting. These work at cross purposes, however. Sticking so close to a hero with few things on his mind beyond survival, the film's visual scope is deliberately limited. Many props common to the genre crop up: cigarettes, lighters, taxis, whiskey on the counter, the diner, the fleabag hotel, stylish apartments, the phonograph, the phone booth, even muddy shoes, and of course, the pistol. Since it is nearly exhaustive, this list is not particularly long, as the plot requires little in addition. The cast is similarly small, and conventional. Except for the blackmailer, the main characters are interlocked well before the opening scene. Madge had tried to seduce both Vincent Parry and Bob, who later became Irene's boyfriend. Irene went to the trial where Parry was convicted because the case was similar to that of her father. There she must have met Bob, accompanying Madge at the time. In sum, Daves moves this handful of people around a couple of locations and amid a limited number of standard props.

Yet *Dark Passage* goes out of its way to feature San Francisco, providing vistas of San Quentin Island, the Golden Gate Bridge, Filbert Street and its famous wooden staircase. Bogart climbs those stairs to reach Irene's "Streamline Moderne" apartment, the famous Malloch building on Montgomery Street. Then there are the views we get during a few taxi rides and on the picturesque trolley that effectively gives us a downtown tour, as we pass ordinary citizens going about their shopping and their business.

But since theirs is not Vincent Parry's business it isn't ours either, and few viewers notice what is given to see. Of all genres, the policier keeps to the narrowest of pathways since whatever shows up on the path is either evidence or a red herring. Bazin was naturally fascinated that an urban realist trend (best exemplified in *Call Northside 777* and *The Naked City* [both 1948]) had come to widen the genre's appeal, but he ultimately determined this to be merely "a formal, not a profound influence of neorealism" ("Grandeur"), since the American films invariably fall back on the sort of simplistic moralism that the better Italian ones abjure.

Still, as in *Bicycle Thieves* (1948), ordinary folk on the periphery of *Dark Passage*'s vision and drama come to the hero's aid. His musician friend George offers him a place to stay; a cabby sympathizes enough to lead him to the plastic surgeon. These men are loners. George lives in a tenement by himself, afraid to disturb the neighbors with his horn. The cabby talks on and on, but mainly about how lonely it is to drive a cab. The surgeon has been disbarred and works out of a back alley. "I don't know you and you don't know me," he tells the bandaged Parry who slips back into the cab just before dawn. The cabby says the same thing. Everyone lives alone with the possibility of camaraderie cut short. As for families, the ones we hear about are nightmarish. Husbands admit they are ready to murder their wives, evidently preferring solitary confinement.

But then in the waiting room of the transit center, sitting amongst hapless transients, Parry overhears a drab mother with two youngsters talking aimlessly to a stranger down on his luck at the other end of the bench. Upset with the brusque treatment they've received, the man remarks, "There was a time when people used to give each other a helping hand." The mother sighs in reply, "Sometimes I get so tired; nothing to look forward to at all." He then looks at her kids and says, "At least you've got these." They gaze at each other in mutual sympathy, and he continues, "You know, we've got something in common, being alone."

This stray homespun lament, seemingly out of a Frank Capra film, strikes Parry, who has until now paid attention only to his survival. Prudently, Delmer Daves doesn't move in for a close-up of his star's reaction, but keeps him in the second plane until this conversation motivates him to get up, put "You're Marvelous" on the jukebox, and make the phone call that sets his future in motion. All of them then board the bus, Parry sitting behind this smiling family-in-the-making.

The *Cahiers du cinéma* critics who followed Bazin proclaimed a special place for films that stage a tightly organized drama within a wide and open world, particularly when unrelated occurrences in that world are given a chance to affect the drama. *Dark Passage* is far too calculated to allow the reality of San Francisco to change the rhythm, let alone the events of its plot, the way Rossellini, just two years earlier, had allowed the unpredictability of postwar life in Rome to break into the melodrama of *Open City*. But *Dark Passage* pointed in the direction that Nicholas Ray would take in *They Live by Night* (1948) and later in *On Dangerous Ground* (1951). It pointed toward the New Wave use of noir plots set in Paris, as in Godard's *Breathless* and François Truffaut's *Shoot the Piano Player* (1960, taken from a David Goodis novel, just like *Dark Passage*). It also pointed to Eric Rohmer, who succeeded Bazin as editor at *Cahiers du cinéma* and remained an ardent advocate of his ideas. Most of Rohmer's minutely calculated scripts were shot in sequence on real locations, where happenstance played the wildcard in his moral tales, comedies, and proverbs. More than a production technique, this amounts to a genuine philosophy, one he imbibed from Bazin.

4 Months, 3 Weeks, 2 Days . . . and Sixty Years Later

Bazin's enthusiasm for *Dark Passage* was restrained; for despite experimenting with first-person narration and a live urban setting, this is a classic Hollywood production of the first order. And it came out just as Bazin was trumpeting a shift away from such classic (reassuring) entertainment to the modern "cinema of discovery," epitomized by Rossellini's *Paisà* (1946), which was shot the same year as *Dark Passage*. In *What Cinema Is! Bazin's Quest and Its Charge*, I make the case for the continuity of this aesthetic from Rossellini through the New Wave and up to our own day. Against digitally enhanced confections like *The Fabulous Destiny of Amelie Poulain* (*Amélie*, 2001), I held up Cristian Mungiu's *4 Months, 3 Weeks, and 2 Days* for daring to descend with the flashlight of cinema into the darkest of passages.

More rigorously than Daves, Mungiu restricts his camera to his main character and what she encounters. No voiceover underlines what counts as we track her increasingly desperate steps; no one assists us across the ellipses that allow sixteen hours of a single, traumatic day to unroll in 110 minutes. Ten lengthy scenes, each shot mainly in long take, are joined by Ottilia's (Anamaria Marinca) furtive movements between locations. The spectator is lashed to her side, barely fathoming what she is up against or thinking.

The second shot takes us down the hallway of her dormitory, as she ducks into the shower room to meet a colleague, then knocks at a door where cosmetics, candy, and cigarettes are available; she stops outside a room to pity a kitten

FIGURE 12.2 The camera tethered to the wary Ottilia in *4 Months, 3 Weeks, and 2 Days* (Cristian Mungiu, Mobra, 2007). Digital frame enlargement.

being sheltered by a student we never encounter again and then takes a message for her roommate, Gabi (Laura Vasiliu), relayed by the dorm's concierge who calls out from the far end of the long corridor. The first of several virtuoso long takes, this one establishes the gray temporality of innumerable dull days in socialist Romania. Against such monotony, there arises an intense drama on the second day, third week, and fourth month of Gabi's secret pregnancy.

Ottilia risks jail when she books a hotel room for the abortion from suspicious desk clerks. At an anonymous crossroads she encounters the even more suspicious abortionist, Mr. Bebe (Vlad Ivanov). His piercing indirect questions pull her into an ugly and mysterious moral drama. This is Ceausescu's Romania, 1987, where citizens are kept ignorant and under surveillance. Ambiguity and menace grow within each excruciatingly long take, especially during her negotiation with the abortionist, so elusive that few spectators know when (and what) deal has been made; and then the abortion procedure itself on the plastic bag covering the bed linens, viewed from first to last.

Spectators may argue over the ethics of abortion, but the sex Mr. Bebe extorts from Ottilia is an undisputable atrocity; though unseen (indeed because unseen), it constitutes the hollow at the center of both the social and the filmic system, a moral black hole. Mungiu inserts this ellipsis as a blind spot in the film, just as the entire day is one about which—Ottilia says in the last line of dialogue—she and Gabi will never again speak. Silence and obscurity prevail, as do Ottilia's viewing angles. The camera ducks secretively into a tawdry hotel, and seems to keep its head down while moving through nearly deserted streets in obscure light. Bits of dialogue provide hints of motives and suggest interconnections between people we never meet but whose roles we guess.

4 Months unrolls as a series of evasions and prevarications. Yet shockingly, and against our wish, we are made to look at the unavoidable, the bloody fetus on the bathroom floor. This hideously red mass—the stain of the Real, Lacan would call it—lies in the belly of this gray film. For an awful moment, and against the rules Mungiu established, we are left alone with it. Then Ottilia wraps the towel around it, empties her bag to stuff it in, and carries it into the dark city, looking for a way to dispose of it. The film's most elaborate and relentless tracking shot follows her into dark alleyways where she avoids encounters with lone men and barking dogs. Almost corralled by fences, she slips through a dingy door and up several flights of stairs of an anonymous building. Without a cut we watch her move to the service balcony and send the contents of her bag down the chute. We hear it rattle down and thud into in the Dumpster below. Her expression lost in the obscurity, Ottilia remains stark still as if the chute were a gravestone, below which lay her ideals and self-respect. Finding Gabi alone in the fluorescent light of the hotel restaurant, she decrees the vow of silence. She can only stare in disgust at the mass of meat (mutton, calves' brains, and marrow) a waiter brings her ashen friend. Meanwhile, against a translucent glass wall in the background, vague shapes of merry-makers, and a few belligerent guests, carouse at a wedding reception. In a final, accusative gesture, Ottilia glances up to catch and hold our eye. This final flourish brings with it the full force of modern cinema: the freeze frames that conclude Ingmar Bergman's *Monika* (1953), Truffaut's *400 Blows* (1959), and Godard's *Breathless*. It also highlights the difference of *4 Months*' dystopic modernity from the classic final image of *Dark Passage*, where two beloved movie stars lock eyes in a warm and charming nightclub, their future assured.

A Philosophy of Cinema

These two films take the camera's condition of limited perspective almost as a philosophical premise. They virtually eliminate reaction shots and parallel scenes, since these would put the main characters' perspectives in perspective, so to speak, positioning them in a larger field. However, there is no "larger field" when you start with the camera as the eyepiece of subjectivity. For better or worse, we experience the world with Parry and Ottilia, both of whom, it turns out, have reason to stay out of sight. These films exude the Sartrean sense of radical isolation, doubled by incessant surveillance that overtook Paris's Latin Quarter during the Occupation. Bazin grew into adulthood while curfews, checkpoints, informers, and dark nights were the norm. Yet Sartre's views of cinema didn't convince Bazin. The sedentary notion of consciousness—consciousness as the "seat" of perception and reflection—was less appealing than Gabriel Marcel's idea of human beings thinking on their feet as they travel incessantly through a world that often appears hostile and is always mysterious (Bogart's and Ottilia's situations exactly). Marcel's Christian existentialism made room for glimpses of "revelation" within the obscurity of existence, even for moments of putative "grace." Both words apply to Bazin's belief in the cinema's extraordinary potential.[5]

As an analogue of the quest for knowledge, the camera is capable of registering more than humans perceive, in fact; hence it humbles us before an indefinitely rich cosmos that outlasts our encounters with it. Increasingly sensitive lenses and microphones alert us to types and quantities of matter and energy beyond the spectra and limitations of our eyes and ears. Yet the camera has its own obvious limits, too: it displays a rectangular visual field from a single position, doing so in two dimensions and with variable focus and clarity depending on lighting conditions. To achieve a wider view of a place or a situation, a camera's "take" must be supplemented with complementary views that are pieced together—edited, we say—to comprise or construct something that no single person or camera can see all at once. Hence a limited *view on* the world which, we might trust, becomes a *version of* a world we either believe or not. Every fiction film plays with this asymmetry, some directors (take Alfred Hitchcock or Peter Haneke) doing so diabolically.

The mobile long take expands the trusted view, since it captures a situation that develops within its field. Bazin highlighted the importance of this possibility, because it puts the spectator in a state of acute anticipation, just as we should be before life itself, where "things may come up" to change an initial situation. Situations (a key term for Sartre) are the way humans organize their perceptions so that they can grasp them and act within them. But just as the camera senses more than the eye perceives, so every field is full of things extraneous to our situation. In Bazin's philosophy, the world is precisely what is "extraneous" to the plot that develops within it. The world exists before and beyond the meanings we forge in negotiating it. Certain long takes (Bela Tarr's, for instance) submerge whatever the characters may be up to under that weight of the world's persistence.

Bazin applauded any film that found a way to deliver the complexity of a situation, including a film like *Potemkin* (1925) that does so through montage. But he especially appreciated films whose quest to attain a view of a situation could be felt as it occurred. Where montage produces a relation that has been decided upon or noticed in advance, films in which characters and camera interact in time exhibit the struggle to come to a significant view in their very mise-en-scène. Thanks to the technological aspect of cinematography, the world that the camera registers (the "scène" of the mise-en-scène) retains a solidity and an ambiguity above and beyond the meanings and projects that characters or even the filmmaker try to ascribe to it. Conceiving cinema as a quest in this way makes it as much a philosophical practice as an artistic one.

In signaling a return to cinema's rapport with a (post-)ontology of "the real," Thomas Elsaesser starts with Bazin only to invoke philosopher Jean-Luc Nancy who has turned to cinema because it offers to reach beyond art and beyond the human.

> [Jean-Luc] Nancy takes Deleuze's version of Bazin's neo-realist aesthetics and turns it on its head. [Nancy's] Heideggerian philosophical move is to argue that . . . letting go of meaning actually gives us the world, and the cinema can thus be a means for freeing ourselves from this obsession with meaning—not by representing the world but by presenting it in its self-evidence and self-sufficiency: "The evidence of cinema is that of the existence of a look through which a world can give back to itself its own real and the truth of its enigma." (Nancy 44; see as well Elsaesser)[6]

Both our films allow us to conceive of just such a "look" at the world, because their central characters are so frantic to understand what might immanently happen to them that they are, until the last moment, literally myopic, short-sighted. Watching (with) them, but watching to that last moment, we recognize that the world is indifferent to their particular plights. We need supply only a small measure of irony for Bogart and Bacall's final kiss to seem so far-fetched, so distant from the nightmare of *Dark Passage*, that it evaporates into Neverland leaving us to consider the world we have looked at as "world moving of its own motion, without a heaven or a wrapping . . . a world shaken, trembling as the winds blow through it." This is the world that Nancy, channeling Heidegger, would restore via the "look" of cinema (Nancy 44). As for Ottilia and Gabi, in the end, looking down at that plate of meat, they vow not speak again of their horrific day, relieved to return to the silent meaninglessness of routine, letting the world's thickness—another name for its *greatness*—bury the sordid plot that briefly took over their lives.

Eric Rohmer, in thinking of what the greatness of the world meant to Bazin, claimed that at the bottom of his friend's philosophy one would find not Sartre but Martin Heidegger, not *Being and Nothingness*, but *Being and Time* (Rohmer to Andrew; Rohmer, "Révolution"). The long takes of *4 Months, 3 Weeks, and 2 Days* impress on us the traces of *being* (beyond meaning) and the anxiety of *time* (beyond plot) that are available in every film. More directly than the traditional arts, cinema keeps us alert to the "truth of the enigma" of the world it engages; at its best, it does not flinch in groping forward in the ambiguity and mystery of Being.

NOTES

1. Perhaps Bazin was obliged to watch a dubbed version of *Dark Passage*, and so would have missed our richer experience of the moment at the mirror when Bogart's familiar voice, so imperturbably knowing, at last is conjoined to his stubbly face.
2. Actually Orson Welles was set to try this experiment even before *Citizen Kane* with *Heart of Darkness*, a 1939 project scuttled when World War II interrupted shooting in Africa. Welles was to have played Mr. Kurtz, while Marlow would be portrayed by only the camera.
3. This apparent traveling "shot" is actually a three-shot sequence with an invisible cut at the bedroom door and a micro-dissolve at the venetian blinds, giving the effect of uninterrupted movement in real time. In addition, Irene's line underscores our inability to distinguish Bogart's internal monologue from his voiced expressions. Creating subjectivity in narration is a result of tiny material techniques like these.
4. Perhaps the deepest cinematic meditation on this theme is Hiroshi Teshigahara's *Face of Another* (1967), which was drawn from a 1951 existentialist novel by writer-philosopher Kobo Abe.
5. "Philosophy/cinema" can be more than speculation. Marcel's disciple in philosophy and Bazin's friend Amédée Ayfre used the terms "ambiguity" and "revelation" as early as 1951 (see "Neorealism"). Even beyond this intermediary relationship, Bazin knew Marcel and even participated with him on a radio program about cinema in 1948.
6. Elsaesser in addition draws on Laurent Kretzschmar, who traces Nancy's *Évidence du film* to Heidegger's notion that a primordial "there is" precedes beings and meanings.

13

Gilles Deleuze

On Movement, Time, and Modernism

WILL SCHEIBEL

The beginning of the 2000s inaugurated what might be called a "Deleuzian turn" in English-language film theory, as thinkers increasingly came to the cinema with questions of affect, phenomenology, sensory perception, and embodied experience, engaging either directly or indirectly with the ideas of French continental philosopher Gilles Deleuze (1925–1995). Books such as *The Cinematic Body* (1993) by Steven Shaviro and *Gilles Deleuze's Time Machine* (1997) by D. N. Rodowick set the precedent for a new generation of scholarship (see, for examples, Del Río; Kennedy; MacCormack; Marks; Martin-Jones, *Deleuze and World*; Martin-Jones, *Deleuze and Cinema*; Murray; Pisters, *Matrix*; Pisters, *Neuro*; Powell, *Deleuze, Altered States*; Powell, *Deleuze and Horror*; Redner; Rushton, *Cinema*; and Sutton). I would direct Deleuzians old and new, interested in film, to that recent material.

This chapter comes from a position more generalist than specialist, and is thus written for film critics and students interested in Deleuze. Rather than "using" film texts to explain his discourse on cinema, it draws out a practical aesthetic framework as a model for film criticism to sketch a line of further inquiry: how the movement-image of classical cinema regulates the time-image of modern cinema in mainstream American films produced after World War II. I have restricted my purview to canonical concepts from his two volumes on the ontology of cinema, *Cinema 1: The Movement-Image* and *Cinema 2: The Time-Image*, published in France in 1983 and 1985, respectively.

Following the "screen theory" of the 1970s and early 1980s—which through the linguistics of Ferdinand de Saussure, the Marxism of Louis Althusser, and the psychoanalysis of Jacques Lacan mounted a critique of textual politics and the cinematic apparatus—the turn to Deleuze might seem like a strange direction in poststructuralist film theory, since Deleuze was neither trained in the history of cinema nor a professional film critic. Further, the interventions of cultural studies in the mid-1980s and 1990s were not involved in the philosophies of aesthetics where Deleuze might have played a role. He studied cognition and film form, but was by no means a cognitive psychologist or neoformalist. His prose is notoriously difficult and his arguments did not enter the same dialogue of ideological critique that helped cinema studies gain recognition to become accepted as a legitimate academic discipline in the humanities. The romantic cinephilia, the director-centered methodology, and the privileging of Hollywood and European art cinemas that characterize *Cinema 1* and *2* might lead one to bracket Deleuze with the film critics at *Cahiers du cinéma* in 1950s Paris rather than to include him among his contemporaries in either philosophy or film theory.

However, as a philosopher, Deleuze saw film as a vehicle for exploring unique concerns with image, movement, and time with which he had long been preoccupied and with which film theory is finally coming to terms. As Rodowick observes:

> Deleuze is quite sensitive to the ways in which contemporary culture is becoming fundamentally an audiovisual culture. For him, the semiotic history of film is coincident with a century-long transformation wherein we have come to represent and understand ourselves socially through spatial and temporal articulations founded in cinema, if now realized more clearly in the electronic and digital media. Film theory and history have a key place in both social theory and semiotic theory, a place that has been slighted in the recent history of philosophy. (*Time Machine* xiii)

Authorship was crucial for Deleuze, not as much because of a high *auteurist* tradition that informed his writing as because he understood film directors as philosophers working *through* film, positing new modes of thinking, seeing, and feeling in the world—a cinematic consciousness or, rather, a consciousness that led to the developments of cinema.

Deleuze's intellectual project is therefore one of film-philosophy, what his translators Hugh Tomlinson and Robert Galeta refer to as "a practice of creation of concepts, a constructive pragmatism." To the degree that "philosophy itself is not a reflection on an autonomous object," they maintain that "Deleuze does not set out to provide another theory *of* the cinema" (xv). By this they mean that Deleuze does not "apply" concepts to cinema the way Laura Mulvey, for example, applies Jacques Lacan in her influential feminist challenge to visual pleasure and narrative cinema. Tomlinson and Galeta describe Deleuze's contribution to the field as "philosophical invention, a theory of cinema as conceptual practice. . . . Philosophy works with the concepts which cinema itself gives rise to" (xv).

What Deleuze offers film scholars is a language, obscure as it may be, to deal with the haptic and visceral qualities of mediated image and sound—the pleasures for which psychoanalysis does not adequately account. Steven Shaviro takes psychoanalysis to task, indeed, for asking the theorist to distance herself from the film, an "object" of study, through a "reflex movement of suspicion, disavowal, and phobic rejection," without acknowledging the pleasures in which she may be implicated, with which she may be complicit, or to which she may be subordinate (10). With his occasional collaborator Félix Guattari, Deleuze helps Shaviro interrogate what we have been taught to resist (or repress): "a rising scale of seduction, delirium, fascination, and utter absorption in the image" (10). Regarding the fetishism and scopophilia under Mulvey's analysis, Shaviro insists that she formulates an Oedipal, phallic paradigm of film spectatorship that remains "totalizing and monolithic," her thesis so "all-encompassing" it precludes "whatever potentials for resistance and subversion, or Deleuzian 'lines of flight,' *are* latent within mainstream narrative film" (12). We need not deny the pleasure a text may afford us, lest we regard cinema merely at the level of representation, as a function of dominant ideology and hegemonic institutions. Instead of writing ourselves into detachment from the image, we might take up Deleuze's investments in the transformative power and possibilities of cinema.

From Movement-Image to Time-Image; or, "Time Out of Joint"

Cinema is a time-based form of image media. As such, movement and time are two of its most fundamental and deceptively obvious properties, and also the main issues Deleuze seeks to address in his *Cinema* volumes. Deleuze had already written on literature, theater, music, and painting, but he seemed most fascinated by the screen art of cinema (Bogue 2). Of all the great French thinkers, he has been called the only true film lover (Serge Toubiana, qtd. in Bogue 1), and was the first philosopher to write a two-volume film book (Colman 1). Here, he proposes a loose and open taxonomy of "cinematographic concepts" (*Cinema 1* ix), or "images of thought" re-created or re-presented by cinema (Tomlinson and Habberjam xi). It derives from a variety of philosophical sources, from Aristotle and Plato to Spinoza, from Kant, Hegel, and Nietzsche to Henri Bergson, Charles Pierce, and Michel Foucault. The cinematic reference points are equally diverse: Luis Buñuel, Robert Bresson, Sergei Eisenstein, Abel Gance, Jean-Luc Godard, D. W. Griffith, Werner Herzog, Alfred Hitchcock, Ingmar Bergman, Akira Kurosawa, Fritz Lang, Jean Renoir, Alain Resnais, Roberto Rossellini, and Orson Welles (to name just a small sample, representing the range of filmmaking movements and periods Deleuze covers in the vast scope of his project).

Deleuze contends, "The cinema seems to us to be a composition of images and of signs, that is, a pre-verbal intelligible content." His classification system outlines "types of images and the signs which correspond to each type" (*Cinema 1* ix), rejecting not only the notion of cinema as a language but also cinema as the rapid succession of separate still images perceived as movement through persistence of vision. *Cinema 1* is primarily devoted to the movement-image, in which time depends on movement to create meaning within the coherent and unified whole of classical cinema. The experience of classical cinema follows a commonsense logic of images controlled by the sensory-motor schema, that is, everyday life perceptions of space-time relations, achieving the illusion of verisimilitude. Time is contingent on processes of montage. Movement-images indirectly represent time as linear and chronological, as physical movement through space. The musical comedy became one of the principle genres of classical cinema because it served the ends of the medium. Performers such as Fred Astaire and Charles Chaplin used cinema to make dance and mime, respectively, actions that responded to environments and functions of space and time, turning an art of posed figures into a continuity of movement (7).

The thrust of Deleuze's argument in *Cinema 1* is most evident in his section on the "crisis of the action-image" (205), a particular type of movement-image comprised of the forces that propel action and reaction and produce realist narrative. This exegesis paves the way for his meditation on the time-image of modern cinema in *Cinema 2*. Deleuze reflects, "This crisis which has shaken the action-image has depended on many factors which only had their full effect after the war, some of which were social, economic, political, moral and others more internal to art, to literature and the cinema in particular" (206). Among the contributing factors after World War II to which he alludes are the deferment of the American Dream, the stronger voice and visibility of minority populations, a more pervasive visual media culture, the influence of literary modernism on cinema, and the decline of the Classical Hollywood studio system along with its old genre formulas that would soon be revised.

The crisis of the action-image is constituted by "dispersive" situations, ambiguity of action, passivity of characters, a weakening of causal narrative links, and a worlds of "clichés":

1. "Dispersive" situations: the single protagonist with whom we identify in classical storytelling has become multiple characters spread across multiple storylines. No longer do we have Chaplin's Tramp hero, from whose actions springs a globalizing situation. Instead we have vignettes that diffuse action, as—Deleuze suggests—in Robert Altman's ensemble films (such as *Nashville* [1975] and *A Wedding* [1978]). Spaces and crowds took on a "collective and unanimist character" in the classical film (as we can see in the films of King Vidor), but "the upright city" has now become "the recumbent city." Skyscrapers and low-angle shots of city centers have given way to horizontal geography of urban sprawls shot at human height, inhabited by alienated or anonymous dwellers (*Cinema 1* 207).

2. Ambiguity: the emphasis on more ambivalent urban characters undoes the cause-and-effect coordination of action in moral or psychological ambiguity and inconsistent actions. We assume Travis Bickle (Robert De Niro) in Martin Scorsese's *Taxi Driver* (1976) will commit either suicide or a political assassination, but instead he undertakes a massacre with vigilante violence that surprises even himself. Delays, idle periods, silences, and chance occurrences may contribute to what Deleuze calls "white events, events which never truly concern the person who provokes or is subject to them" (*Cinema 1* 207).
3. Passivity: characters undertake ballad-like trips out of "the need for flight," and their directions and choices are vague rather than goal-oriented (*Cinema 1* 208). Narrative has become governed by "the stroll," in Deleuze's words, "the voyage and the continual return journey" (208). Consider Sidney Lumet's aimless, real-life characters played by Al Pacino: NYPD officer Frank Serpico in *Serpico* (1973) and bank robber Sonny Wortzik in *Dog Day Afternoon* (1975), who "behave like windshield wipers" (208).
4. Weak links, and 5. Clichés: The diegetic worlds of classical cinema preserved a totalizing continuity of action with causal narrative links. With the crisis of the action-image, and the weakening of those links, diegetic worlds are made up by only mediations or "clichés," what Deleuze defines as "a monopoly of reproduction" operated by the mass communication technologies of television, radio, and microphones, which allows filmmakers to reflect critically on the medium of cinema. In Lumet's *The Anderson Tapes* (1971), burglar John Anderson (Sean Connery) is the subject of "systems of reception, surveillance and transmission"; and in his *The Prince of the City* (1981), NYPD officer Daniel Ciello (Treat Williams) "records the whole city on magnetic tape" (*Cinema 1* 210) to expose police corruption. *Network*, Lumet's 1976 satire on the corporate broadcasting industry, makes this point even more explicitly, focusing on a fictional television network that turns a disgruntled former news anchor (Peter Finch) into its own celebrity "mad prophet of the airwaves."

By contrast, the time-image was most fully realized by post–World War II European art cinemas. As Deleuze explains it in *Cinema 2*, "Time is no longer subordinated to movement, but rather movement to time" (*Cinema 2* xi). The timepiece and schedule, in short, were now dominant, whereas in earlier culture behavior, habit, routine, and the rhythm of everyday life structured a sense of the day, of the life cycle, of urgency, of tranquility. This new temporal structure of "time in the pure state" generates false movements and also false continuity in film, or editing that seems irrational, destabilizing the pragmatics of narrative, reality, and subjectivity while eschewing teleological history to bring the past, present, and future into coexistence. Time-images render time and thought visible, audible, and perceptible, loosening the sensory-motor linkage of movement-images. The spaces of time-images are "any-spaces-wherever," or "deserted but inhabited" environments that "we no longer know how to describe" and to which "we no longer know how to react," such as "disused warehouses, waste ground, cities in the course of demolition or reconstruction." Occupying these disconnected spaces are "a new race of characters" whom Deleuze describes as "kind of mutant: they saw rather than acted, they were seers" (xi). Exhausted, waiting bodies show and develop the passage of time rather than acting as subjects of movement or instruments of action (xi). By extension, Deleuze notices "a new type of actor," not necessarily nonprofessional but "professional non-actors," or "'actor-mediums,' capable of seeing and showing rather than acting, and either remaining dumb or undertaking some never-ending conversation, rather than of replying or following dialogue" as it is written in the script to advance the plot (20). Italian neo-realism is perhaps the best exemplar of these trends.

The movement-image shifts into the time-image. What leads this to happen is the pure optical-sound image, in which viewer identification with a character is inverted, as "the character has become a kind of viewer." Deleuze continues, "He records rather than reacts. He is prey to a vision, pursued by it or pursuing it, rather than engaging in an action" (*Cinema 2* 3). One might recall Luchino Visconti's heroine (Clara Calamai) "possessed by an almost hallucinatory sensuality" in the proto-neorealist *Ossessione* (1943), whom Deleuze compares to "a visionary, a sleepwalker"; or, more obviously, the unresponsive maid (Maria Pia Casilio) in *Umberto D* (1952), whom Vittorio De Sica films robotically cleaning a kitchen and grinding coffee (an ordinary, everyday event of domesticity presented as a series of smaller mechanical events in real time) (*Cinema 2* 3). In the absence of plot, Deleuze asserts, the pure optical-sound image shows "what a character *is*" and "what he *says*" (13; emphasis in original). He goes on: "The important thing is always that the character or the viewer, and the two together, become visionaries" (19). Put in art-historical terms, time is "still life," unchanging even as things change over time (17), and "white spaces" reify the image by emptying it of sensory–motor perceptibility (21). Evacuating the image of its conventional subjects drains it of what we assume makes it complete, but we can reconstruct the image, filling voids and holes with what is present by its very absence.

The importance of visual description over motor action makes the real and the imaginary indiscernible, one reflecting the other. Deleuze notes, "We no longer know what is imaginary or real, physical or mental, in the situation, not because they are confused, but because we do not have to know and there is no longer even a place from which to ask" (*Cinema 2* 7). Contrasting the flattened perspectives of subjectivity and objectivity in the films of Michelangelo Antonioni and Federico Fellini, Deleuze muses how Fellini's mental recollections and fantasies are indeed subjective, but they are transformed into "the reality of spectacle, of those who make it, who live from it, who are absorbed in it" (7). In *8½* (1963), Fellini reveals filmmaker Guido Anselmi's (Marcello Mastroianni) "inter-mental" world to be "'a neutral, impersonal vision" of "all our world," taking us "behind the scenes" of the character's life and art as he struggles to imagine what his next film might be (8). On the other hand, states Deleuze, Antonioni's objective images of reportage "are not formed without becoming mental, and going into a strange invisible subjectivity" (8). The couple in *L'Avventura* (1960), for instance, searches for a missing woman, but, feeling as if they are the objects of an "indeterminable gaze," they flee and only pretend to continue their investigation (8).

There is also something akin to the sublime that Deleuze finds in the pure optical-sound image, "something intolerable and unbearable" (*Cinema 2* 18) that lies even further beyond the movement-image. He submits, "It is a matter of something too powerful, or too unjust, but sometimes also too beautiful, and which henceforth outstrips our sensory–motor capacities" (18). This claim bears particular relevance for cinema of the immediate postwar moment, which was marked by emergent widescreen technologies, greater use of color, new young stars and acting styles, and the aesthetics of documentary realism that mobile equipment and cost-effective location shooting made possible. One of the most visually striking phenomena of postwar cinema was a group of highly stylized films that contemporary critics have retroactively labeled film noir, which owed their look in part to evolutions in faster film stock and lenses that gave cinematographers greater flexibility in their manipulation of light and depth of field, facilitating visual contrast and chiaroscuro lighting (see Schatz).

Touch of Evil

A black-and-white B-film produced by Universal Pictures at the end of the classical studio system, Orson Welles's *Touch of Evil* (1958) is a film noir set in a nocturnal urban wasteland of police corruption and cultural prejudice on the U.S.–Mexico border. Welles, who wrote and directed the film, plays Texas police captain Hank Quinlan, who for thirty years has harbored a deep-seated hatred for Mexicans after a "half-breed" murdered his wife and was let free for lack of evidence. Vowing to see all criminals convicted, Quinlan has since covertly planted evidence and framed suspects, earning a reputation for his uncanny "hunches" and "intuition." But with only a small turkey ranch to his name, he is left lonely and embittered. Mike Vargas (Charlton Heston) is his counterpart, a Mexico City narcotics officer, who over his honeymoon joins Quinlan's investigation into the murder of construction tycoon Rudy Linnekar and his girlfriend (a bomb was planted in Linnekar's car on the U.S. side of the border, but it exploded on the Mexico side).

The organization of time and movement is largely classical in that it unfolds through a forward momentum of action, driven by the clear motivations and objectives of Vargas as the protagonist with whom we are meant to identify (the handsome idealist to Quinlan's bloated ex-alcoholic). One character spells out this straightforward trajectory in a key scene, remarking to Vargas, "Gonna do it alone, huh? All you gotta do is solve the murder and also prove that the idol of the police force is a fraud. Amigo, you've got your work really cut out for you." While investigating the murder, Vargas comes to believe that Quinlan framed the prime suspect, a young Mexican named Sanchez who married Linnekar's daughter in secret. (Indeed, Quinlan planted sticks of dynamite in Sanchez's apartment.) After consulting the Hall of Records, Vargas notices a series of past cases in which either Quinlan or his loyal partner, Pete Menzies (Joseph Calleia), uncovered principal evidence, the existence of which the defense denied in each case. Vargas makes criminal accusations to the district attorney, but Quinlan retaliates by setting up Vargas's American wife Susie (Janet Leigh) as a junkie who murdered local druglord Joe Grandi (Akim Tamiroff). When, to his disillusionment, Menzies discovers Quinlan's guilt, he agrees to wear a wire and elicit a confession. Meanwhile, Vargas tracks them with the receiver to capture the recording that will incriminate Quinlan and clear Susie of her charges.

Throughout this progression Welles keeps the audience oriented dramatically but also spatially and temporally, beginning with the celebrated long take—running over three minutes—that opens the film. A shadowy figure plants a bomb in a car, which the camera then follows through the seedy border town of Los Robles where the film's action will take place. Yet, the graceful, almost balletic movement of the camera as the car crosses the border is at once in the service of continuity, and, by turns, in excess of it, relinquishing the sensory-motor capacity of the image by calling attention to something "too powerful" or "too beautiful" for the gaze to bear. The viewer is both held in suspense and swept into a state of ecstasy, of bedazzled excitement over what the filmmaker can do with elaborately complex blocking, lighting, and crane-mounted camerawork.

Los Robles, as the viewer will soon realize, is a horizontal expanse of "any-spaces-wherever": dive bars and burlesque clubs; haunted, empty streets lit by neon signs and strewn with blowing debris; an old curio shop/bordello overseen by an aging fortuneteller/prostitute named Tana (Marlene Dietrich), who sells chili and listens to sad pianola music. Sleazy hotels and motels are particularly significant locations: the Mirador Motel outside the city limits, where Vargas stashes Susie away and she is terrorized by Grandi's nephews; and the ironically named Ritz, where Quinlan strangles Grandi to death in an almost expressionistic set piece. Never before was Welles more theatrical or carnivalesque in his sensibility, and the odd angles and lens distortions threaten to throw the viewer off balance. Populating Los Robles is a group of eccentrics including the nervous night clerk at the Mirador, a butch lesbian biker who conspires with the Grandi gang, and a blind shopkeeper who blinks and grimaces in the foreground of a deep-focus shot while Vargas places a phone call to Susie in the background. Grandi is the most grotesque of these figures, with his oversized cigars, sweaty face, and bad toupee. Beyond the classical ways in which Welles configures action, space, and character, Los Robles is a borderland of blurred legal and ethnic boundaries, impinged upon by sexual desires, ambivalences, and frustrations, where memory and nostalgia are in constant tension with the march of time.

The climax of the film occurs in a desert landscape of oil derricks, a nightmare vision of institutional greed and power that renders even Quinlan insignificant. It is the film's bleakest "any-space-wherever," permeated with an atmosphere of the "cliché," as Vargas pursues Quinlan and Menzies to record their conversation on tape. At the same time, this sequence most explicitly demonstrates the film's workings of the movement-image through montage and action. We view events in deep-focus, but also in quick cuts between shots of Vargas spying in shadows from the derricks and under a bridge as he moves through this maze to grab Quinlan's confession to Menzies as they walk past the oil pumps. Vargas's action as the noir investigator creates narrative action, to which the camera, the editing, and Heston's performance give movement as he traverses the space of the sequence.

Although the film ends with some return to order and normalcy, with Menzies shooting Quinlan as the authorities arrive and Susie's innocence is restored, there is a tragic irony to the final revelation. Unbeknown to Quinlan,

FIGURE 13.1 Vargas's action as the noir investigator creates narrative action, to which the camera, the editing, and Charlton Heston's performance give movement in *Touch of Evil* (Orson Welles, Universal International, 1958). Digital frame enlargement.

Sanchez was, in fact, guilty (by chance, he admitted to the bombing moments earlier). Tana confirms the falseness of harmonious closure with an enigmatic question that speaks to the anxiety over knowledge and truth at the core of modern cinema: "What does it matter what you say about people?" Like much of classical film noir, *Touch of Evil* reflected the European modernisms of the 1950s and anticipated the modernisms of the 1960s and 1970s (it was Welles's last film as a director in Hollywood). But it is also symptomatic of Hollywood's postwar commercial practices at the intersections of classical and modern aesthetics, on an affective spectrum between the movement-image, in which event and human action are central, and the time-image, which abandons motive and impulse for a world of external controls.

The Straight Story

For comparison, let us now turn to a film far removed from *Touch of Evil* at the levels of time, space, and geography, in addition to genre, production conditions, and cinema history. David Lynch's *The Straight Story* (1999) is an independently produced road film, distributed by Walt Disney Pictures at the end of the twentieth century, set in the rural American Midwest aglow with warm colors and bright sunlight. Based on a true event, the film chronicles a 240-mile, six-week trip from Laurens, Iowa, to Mount Zion, Wisconsin, on a 1966 John Deere lawn tractor. The traveler is a seventy-three-year-old World War II veteran named Alvin Straight (Richard Farnsworth), who struggles with failing eyesight, hip problems, and difficulties with circulation (his doctor warns him that he may be in the early stages of emphysema and diabetes, suggesting he give up smoking and change his diet, although Alvin refuses to undergo tests and x-rays). Like Quinlan, he is an ex-alcoholic. At seventy-nine, Farnsworth battled cancer during the film's production and committed suicide a year after its release, imbuing Alvin's bittersweet journey with deeper poignancy ("Richard Farnsworth").

Unable to drive a car, Alvin hitches a trailer to his riding mower and sets out to visit his estranged brother Lyle (Harry Dean Stanton) after learning that he suffered a stroke. Lynch presents Alvin's experience as a kind of cathartic spiritual quest by which he takes stock in his life and identity before he dies. Yet, despite the purported "straightness" of his storytelling—a self-consciously provocative change of pace for the director of *Eraserhead* (1977), *Blue Velvet* (1986), and *Mulholland Dr.* (2001)—it is no less existential than what we find in films constructed out of alternate universes or maddened dream states and hallucinations. *The Straight Story* does not so much depart from the usual Lynchian metaphors and abstractions as it literalizes them.

Slightly surreal episodes interrupt Alvin's trek, such as when he encounters a distraught woman who continues hitting deer with her car on her daily commute, or when he is overtaken by cyclists in RAGBRI (the world's oldest, largest,

FIGURE 13.2 Montage of physical movement articulates linear, chronological time—the film's "straightness"—that Alvin (Richard Farnsworth) controls as the primary subject/instrument of action in *The Straight Story* (David Lynch, Asymmetrical/Canal+/Channel 4, 1999). Digital frame enlargement.

and longest bike ride, spanning the state of Iowa and organized by the *Des Moines Register*) ("RAGBRI history"). One night, he imparts advice to a pregnant young runaway who visits his campfire, and later he confides to a priest in a cemetery about his relationship with his stricken brother. When his drive belt and transmission give out, Alvin practically runs into a family watching a barn burning, who offer him a place to stay while his tractor goes in for repair (with the family's eldest member, he shares a traumatic war story describing how he accidentally killed a young man in his platoon). While *The Straight Story* may be Lynch's quietest film, his actors/characters speak deliberately, granting Lynch free range to play with the peculiar mannerisms and idiosyncrasies of everyday speech that these "professional non-actors" bring to the film with their "never-ending conversations" about birdhouses, Braunschweiger, lawnmowers, and reaching tools called "grabbers."

The laconic Farnsworth/Alvin, however, is one of Deleuze's tired, waiting "seers" of the world. We share in his visions of a lightning storm, a humming grain elevator, long country roads, sunrises and sunsets, and starry night skies (the film is bookended with credits over a field of stars). For all of its digressions and cosmic imagery, movement in the film ultimately determines time. While the cause of Alvin and Lyle's separation remains a mystery, Alvin's goal is transparent and he reaches it through perpetual (albeit leisurely) movement: "I want to make peace. I want to sit with him, and look up at the stars . . . like we used to do . . . so long ago." The evocative aerial photography and lap-dissolve sequences of cornfields verge on the "too powerful" or "too beautiful," and at the same time they are motivated by Alvin's trip.

Montage of physical movement articulates linear, chronological time—the film's "straightness"—that Alvin controls as the primary subject/instrument of action. Moreover, the action-image is dictated by the affect of perception. Frequent close-ups of Alvin are examples of the "affection-image," as Deleuze would say, which registers affect in the face as a corporeal expression of thought and emotion. Lynch often conflates Alvin's subjectivity with the point-of-view of the camera itself, a sort of free-indirect discourse that perceives the experience of perception. This "perception-image," invoking Deleuze again, ranges from Alvin's "solid" subjective perception (for example, the shaky view of the barn burning as his tractor careens down a steep hill) to the "gaseous," more purely cinematic perception of camera consciousness (the pastoral lap-dissolve sequences) and the "liquid," semi-subjective perception in between (shots of the stars at which Alvin gazes, that dissolve into objective shots of the morning after).

By looking at *Touch of Evil* and *The Straight Story* through a Deleuzian aesthetic framework, I want to suggest that commercial American cinema after World War II did not return to its classical origins, nor did it define itself in opposition to modernist international cinemas. Rather, it created a negotiated or "hybrid" practice of filmmaking. If, as Tom Gunning has taught us, the "cinema of attractions" before the mid-1910s did not disappear with the advent of classical narrative and editing techniques but went underground, as "a component of narrative films" (as with musical numbers) ("Cinema of Attraction" 64), the legacy of cinema's second modernity in the postwar era is underground, too—concealed in disparate films that with claims to artistic integrity and appeals to popular tastes relentlessly seek crossover audiences whose relationships to movement and time are done justice only by the cinema.

14

Stanley Cavell

The Contingencies of Film and Its Theory

DANIEL MORGAN

A philosopher by profession, Stanley Cavell (b. 1926) wrote three books on film. The first, *The World Viewed* (1971), is the one most explicitly involved in theories of cinema. Subtitled "Reflections on the Ontology of Film," it continues a tradition of approaching cinema by inquiring into its defining properties, mainly its photographic base, and seeing in that inquiry the source of a range of philosophical problems. The two other books, while explicitly works of interpretation, are likewise philosophically inclined. *Pursuits of Happiness* (1981) analyzes seven Hollywood comedies from the 1930s and 1940s, finding in them a genre Cavell calls "the comedy of remarriage." It is a revision of Shakespearean comedy: rather than getting a young couple together, the task is to get an older, more experienced couple *back* together. Cavell argues that this is done by presenting the institution of marriage as a special form of conversation, a way of taking pleasure in each other's company and of taking responsibility for each other's ongoing development. *Contesting Tears* (1994) explores the genre that operates as the dark side to remarriage comedies, the "melodrama of the unknown woman." The pathos of these films—and what Cavell argues are their feminist impulses—comes from the failure of a man and a woman to achieve a state of shared existence; their sadness and power comes from the woman's remaining unknown to the man. Cavell has also written essays on television and video as well as on specific films, and his late *Cities of Words* (2005) weaves philosophy and philosophical accounts of literature with studies of films to provide a moral articulation of a democratic society.

While these works do not form a strict and unified system, there are deep connections among them, resonating not only across themes and arguments in Cavell's philosophical work—a topic too broad for this chapter, involving issues of epistemology and ethics organized around a longstanding engagement with the legacy of skepticism—but also in the mode of analysis. Within film studies,

Cavell is frequently seen as the end of a tradition of classical film theory, a label that places him as the last major film theorist to write outside the academic study of film. It also carries two deep assumptions that have shaped how Cavell's work has been understood, first that the basic task of the study of film is an elucidation of the essential feature of the medium—here, its photographic basis; secondly that the films that matter, mainly narrative fiction films of the classical period of Hollywood cinema, directly and explicitly respond to that feature (see Carroll 9, 11ff). So understood, Cavell's writings on film can appear nostalgic in their taste and retrograde in their theoretical commitments (a charge made by Tania Modleski and others), a naïve and uncritical embrace of a bygone era of filmmaking and film theory. Yet, as I will argue, these assumptions miss the mark. Cavell's writing on film in fact provides a way of thinking about cinema marked by flexibility and openness; rejecting the idea that cinema is best understood through a single key feature, his approach is committed to ongoing developments in the fluid life of films. If we are to understand what Cavell is doing—what his arguments and methods are, and how they might matter to the contemporary situation of films and film theory—we need to change the framework in which he has been placed. My principal focus will be on *The World Viewed*, since it underlies his general approach to cinema.

Cavell does value and emphasize classical Hollywood cinema: *The World Viewed* begins by recounting his own experience of going to these movies, and from this experience launches into broader reflection on cinema. The two books of film criticism and interpretation bear this out, as Cavell not only claims the films as the best instances of American cinema but also defends their insights into questions of gender and cinema over and against instances of more explicitly political and modernist cinema. The specific powers of cinema, Cavell suggests, were most evidenced in the films made in the years when, as it happened, he had a "natural relation" to movies and movie-going.

Yet Cavell's critical interests are more complicated. The chapter that is at the center of *The World Viewed*—there are nine chapters before and nine after it—announces "The End of Myths," claiming that traditional forms of Hollywood cinema have lost their force. Where the first half of the book represents an attempt to account for cinema's past, to understand the conditions that allowed for a certain kind of cinema to emerge and thrive, the second half, by contrast, attempts to understand the filmmaking of Cavell's present, the rise of modernist cinema in the 1960s. Thus, of the films he discusses for any length of time, all are from the period *after* classical Hollywood cinema ended: *Vertigo* (1958), *L'Avventura* (1960), *The Children's Hour* (1961), *The Man Who Shot Liberty Valance* (1962), *Jules and Jim* (1963), *The Graduate* (1967), and *Rosemary's Baby* (1968), not to mention broad surveys of Jean-Luc Godard's films. Despite appearances to the contrary, *The World Viewed* is essentially a book about cinema under the condition of modernism (Rothman and Keane 217ff). Cavell is a theorist of cinema in crisis and transformation.

What makes Cavell's openness hard to recognize is his apparent commitment to a theory of cinema in which a film's fundamental feature is the relation to reality given by its photographic basis. There are several reasons for the prominence of this view of his work, not the least of which has been the reprinting of chapters 3–6 of *The World Viewed* in Gerald Mast and Marshall Cohen's popular *Film Theory and Criticism*. In that context, and with only those chapters reprinted, *The World Viewed* is positioned as a direct inheritor of a line of thinking that emerges from Erwin Panofsky and André Bazin and continues through Siegfried Kracauer's *Theory of Film*, according to which film emerges at the end of the nineteenth century as a technological solution to an increasing demand for realism across the arts. In Bazin's account, for example, whereas painting is always dependent on human skill, with photography "for the first time an image of the world is formed automatically, without the creative intervention of man" (13). The result is a medium uniquely oriented toward reality, whose emergence thereby "freed the plastic arts from their obsession with likeness" (12) and opened the way for abstraction in painting. Cinema is thus photography plus time, "change mummified as it were" (15).

Cavell certainly contributes to this reading, calling Panofsky and Bazin "the two continuously intelligent, interesting, and to me useful theorists" (*World Viewed* 16). And when the first chapter of *The World Viewed* ends with the question "What is film?" the second chapter begins by taking up the relation of film to reality. Nevertheless, Cavell sharply diverges from this tradition in three important ways.

1. Cavell resists the idea that photography and painting are competing solutions to a wish for realism. Instead, he argues, "so far as photography satisfied a wish, it [was] the human wish, intensifying in the West since the Reformation, to escape subjectivity and metaphysical isolation" (*World Viewed* 21), a problem of Cartesian doubt about the relation of self to world. This is, for Cavell, the beginning of modern skepticism, which resonates across philosophy, art, and literature. Painting negotiates skeptical doubt through an increasing emphasis on the act of painting itself, the romantic vision of "the acknowledgement of the endless presence of the self" (*World Viewed* 22). Photography, by contrast, takes the reverse approach, mechanically "overcoming" the role of the self in establishing the surety of the world—not defeating but escaping the terms of painting altogether.
2. Classical film theory often proceeds by way of a deduction: if film is twenty-four still photographs per second, then the thing to do is to ask what photography does; photography, it turns out, involves a relation to reality; hence film is about reality. Cavell rejects such views as making a fetish of

technology, arguing that the answer to the question "What is film?" cannot be determined simply by thinking about the technical means by which images are generated. This argument can be hard to see. When he writes, for example, "A photograph does not present us with 'likenesses' of things; it presents us, we want to say, with the things themselves" (*World Viewed* 17), it seems to be a straightforward claim about photography—and one that is obviously false. But the "we want to say" is crucial, not a rhetorical affectation but a central piece of method. Cavell is making an argument not about what photography, as a technology, is or does but about what we, as ordinary viewers of photographs, think and say about photography. This is the data on which he erects his entire argument.

What's at issue here is Cavell's commitment to a philosophical approach known as "ordinary language philosophy." Associated with J. L. Austin and Ludwig Wittgenstein, it holds that many philosophical puzzles arise because philosophers have removed language from its everyday contexts and uses. Paying attention, as Austin put it, to "what we should say when, and so why and what we should mean by it," provides the tools by which philosophical "field work" can be done (Austin 181, 183; see also Cavell, *Must We Mean* 97–114). This does not mean that solutions come readymade in language. When Cavell says that "we want to say" that photographs present us with "the things themselves," he offers not an end so much as a beginning. It's true that the position cannot be upheld, but it matters that we are tempted by it (as, for instance, when in looking at a photograph of the Eiffel Tower I say that I see the Eiffel Tower, not a representation of it). Part of his goal, Cavell says, is to get us, his readers, to recognize how "mysterious" photographs are by seeing how difficult it is to talk about them; their familiarity shouldn't mask their essential strangeness.

3. Criticism occupies a strikingly central place in Cavell's understanding of what theory consists in: "It is arguable that the only instruments that could provide data for a theory of film are the procedures of criticism" (*World Viewed* 12). Indeed, Cavell acknowledges that the appeal of the realist tradition of classical film theory, and the reason he begins with its terms, is the quality of the criticism it produced (*World Viewed* 166). But Cavell doesn't follow models of criticism usually found in film studies, whether that's ideological analysis, reading larger social and political meaning off the surface of films, or doing close readings on structuralist or neo-formalist terms. Instead, for him criticism involves finding words with which to account for *his own experience* of movies; criticism is empty, he argues, without this orientation. *Pursuits of Happiness* thus begins with a declaration that each chapter "contains an account of my experience of a film made in Hollywood between 1934 and 1949" (1). And the preface to *The World Viewed* speaks of technical details as mattering only "so far as they were relevant

to the *experience* of particular films" (xxi), and of his attempts to find "some words I could believe in to account for my experience of film" (xxiii).

What emerges is not another essentialist account of cinema but a way of thinking about cinema that is responsive to changes in technology, techniques, and the social forms of movie-going. As Cavell repeats over and over again, it is impossible to tell in advance what will count as a salient feature of the medium. It is only the production of films, the viewing of them, and the criticism, whether written in print or spoken in conversations, that can tell us what cinema is. Cavell's emphasis on criticism brings the openness and mutability of experience, of movie-going in general and of individual films, into the orbit of problems of film theory.

Cavell is certainly aware of, and at times anxious about, the fact that there is nothing to ground his arguments other than the contingency of his experiences and the conclusions he draws from them. "I hope I am not alone," he worries in the midst of a discussion of character actors (*World Viewed* 70); elsewhere, he wonders if he has "the *right* to speak" about contemporary trends in films (98). But, for Cavell, to speak for his own experience is necessarily to make a claim that others have a similar kind of experience, that they will recognize themselves in his words. As he puts it, "The alternative to speaking for myself representatively (for *someone* else's consent) is not: speaking for myself privately. The alternative is having nothing to say, being voiceless, not even mute" (*Claim* 28). In speaking of his own experience, Cavell is thereby speaking for us as well, assuming that the relations he had (or has) to movies are shared. We are invited, as readers, to go to the movies with him.

Based on his experience, Cavell defines cinema as a "succession of automatic world projections" (*World Viewed* 72). Three of the terms are relatively straightforward. "Succession" and "projection" cover the basic features of movement of things onscreen and the continuity of the image. "World" is the intuitive idea, and marks an explicit difference from a tradition of realist theory. Where Bazin says "the photographic image is the object itself" (14), a relation between a mechanical apparatus and the particular objects it records, Cavell argues that "what is manufactured is an image of the world" (*World Viewed* 20). Not this or that individual thing, but all the things that together comprise a world, that shape our experience of a film.

The difficult term is "automatic"—and the cognate "automatism." Mostly, Cavell uses this term to describe what happens "by itself" in photographic media: presenting the world automatically, without the intervention of human agency. "Reproducing the world is the only thing film does automatically" (*World Viewed* 103). But, as *The World Viewed* develops, new and more expansive genealogies of the term come into play. Automatism is cited as a feature of both surrealist and Abstract Expressionist painting; it is also, Cavell suggests, related to an ethical desire for autonomy (107–108). At its broadest, "automatism" comes to describe any part of a film that is *experienced* as "happening of itself": something that carries with it meanings shared by filmmakers and viewers alike (107). It's not just photography that is automatic but "artistic discoveries of form and genre and type and technique" (105). Film noir is an automatism, as we readily recognize its characters and visual style; so is Humphrey Bogart, who brings a set of tendencies, behaviors, and expectation to every role he inhabits. So, too, are things like shot/reverse-shot constructions, since their appearance allows us to recognize, without thinking, that we should be oriented around a specific character.

This argument is breathtaking in its scope, uniting under one label a range of radically disparate features of cinema. Cavell recognizes that each feature has its own history and its own specific meanings—at times, he describes each as its own "medium" (*World Viewed* 36)—but he brings them together because of the way we experience them; types, forms, and genres are as natural to cinema as photography is. Cavell's insight is that this idea of automatism explains how films work: plots progress and characters develop without the need for full psychological explanations simply because we expect certain actions, meanings, and implications from the types, genres, and conventions being used. We require no explanation that Jimmy Stewart behaves in a certain way other than the fact that he is Jimmy Stewart. That's part of the "natural magic" of Hollywood cinema. It's also the source of its flexibility: that a type or star functions as an automatism does not mean that it, he, or she is set in stone; filmmakers innovate within a tradition by producing variations on automatisms, playing with expectations they generate (as is done, for example, with Stewart in films like *The Naked Spur* [1953] and *Vertigo*). When Cavell spends several chapters uncovering precursors to cinematic types in Charles Baudelaire's *The Painter of Modern Life*, it is to find "stores of cinematic obsession" (43) that move beyond their original contexts. Thus, the Dandy is not an aristocratic character but a way of being in the world, a "hidden fire" that heroes from Alan Ladd in *Shane* (1953) to Peter Fonda in *Easy Rider* (1969) adapt to their own ends (55–60).

The Lady from Shanghai

Orson Welles's *The Lady from Shanghai* (1947) offers a lesson on how automatisms work. For example, Rita Hayworth's preexisting status as a pin-up girl, a star whose picture was produced in an alluring pose for mass consumption, is repeatedly evoked. One shot, taken from above, shows her lying full-length on the deck of a yacht, bathed in luminous light, her glamour simply called into being, part of the way she is constructed as an object of desire. A slightly later scene satirizes this function, as Hayworth wears a sailor's costume, jauntily taking the wheel while a fake advertising jingle plays on the radio: she is an image, as much a commodity as the product being hawked. Other automatisms are also present. The film employs an array of recognizable types: a rugged sailor with a violent past; a woman in need of saving; a shrewd lawyer whose brains make up for physical frailty; a duplicitous private detective; even a Shakespearean fool. Genres emerge with similar rapidity: an adventure yarn, doubling as a tour of exotic sights; a melodrama of romantic entanglements; a courtroom drama; and a crime thriller. These automatisms are part of the organizing logic of the film. Once we recognize Bannister (Everett Sloane) as a crooked lawyer, we know what he is doing; once we see his wife Elsa (Hayworth) as a femme fatale, her actions no longer need explanation. Psychological interiority is not a necessary postulate for understanding why things happen as they do.

Welles goes one step further. *The Lady from Shanghai* shows that, however natural automatisms feel, they are only conventions. Types and genres are not dispersed by the film to reveal, underlying them, some essential and defining quality. Each pattern opens only onto other patterns, other automatisms: Michael O'Hara (Welles) is not just a rugged sailor or hero but also a fool; Elsa is not just a woman in distress but also the organizer of the events. Neither of them is any one thing but all of their roles together: nothing is behind convention, no automatism proves viable on its own. The film teaches us to recognize the shaky ground on which we stand.

There are two further lessons about automatisms here. One has to do with modernism. Where Cavell argues that a successful use of automatisms is a way of being in a tradition (*World Viewed* 104), Welles holds the range of automatisms up to scrutiny to determine which still hold force. While this suggests a strategy of disillusionment, *The Lady from Shanghai* never wholly enters "the modernist predicament" (72) in which conviction in the viability of a technique or device must be secured at each moment. We may be aware that automatisms are being used but the absorptive pleasure of the film is never lost. Welles's game with realism, his virtuosity with forms, lies in maintaining the power of automatisms even as we recognize their contingent status. Even if they are no longer secure, the automatisms still work.

This is the tension in which Cavell is interested. One of his most impassioned arguments is that cinema's reflexivity predates its modernism, taking a more subtle and supple form (see *World Viewed* 130). Take his discussion of the "walls of Jericho" in *It Happened One Night* (1934), where the blanket hung by Clark Gable between his bed and Claudette Colbert's, "blocking a literal view of the figure, but receiving impressions from it, and activating our imagination of that real figure as we watch in the dark . . . [works] as a movie screen works" (*Pursuits* 82). Or the home movie placed within the narrative of *Adam's Rib* (1949), which works with the idea of the surface of the screen and the fundamental fact of projection: a fantasy of marriage appears not just as a fact of the world but in the guise of cinema (211–213). These devices are within the world of the film, never breaking its absorption while also being fully about the fact that we are watching a film.

A second lesson has to do with photography. A dance between reality and illusion runs throughout *The Lady from Shanghai*, from the scene where Michael and Elsa embrace in an aquarium and the tanks behind them resemble a film strip to the final (and much celebrated) mirror sequence in which reality becomes indistinguishable from illusion.

These are virtuosic moments of cinematic display that call on film's photographic power even while suggesting its inadequacy, that photography does not grant us privileged access to reality. In a sense, while Welles never explicitly questions photography in terms of its mechanical aspect, he suggests that it has no deeper grounding than any other automatism in the film.

This is the key ambiguity surrounding the automatism of photography in *The World Viewed*. Generally, Cavell treats film's relation to reality as constitutive of its identity as a medium, and goes so far as to say that while a celluloid film can succeed as art without engaging with its photographic base, "movies cannot so be made" (*World Viewed* 102–103). Thus, "cartoons are not movies" (168) because they evade the significance of the relation to reality that makes the movies what they are (on animation and automatism see Pierson). Yet he also puts forward an expansive model of automatisms—which he calls "perverse" at one point—that suggests something entirely different, that photography is merely

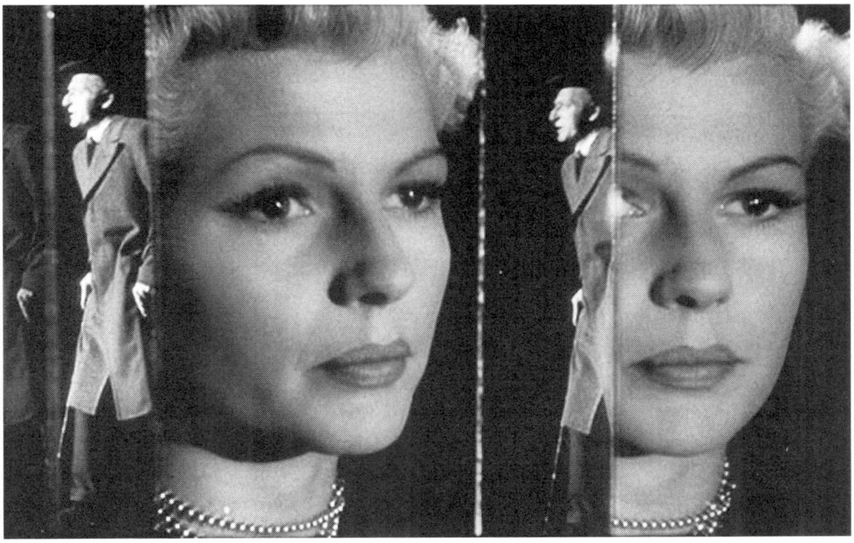

FIGURE 14.1 In the hall of mirrors, reality is indistinguishable from illusion. Rita Hayworth and Everett Sloane in *The Lady from Shanghai* (Orson Welles, Columbia, 1947). Digital frame enlargement.

one automatism among many, and not even a privileged one. Cavell connects this view to the rise of modernism in cinema: when what was taken for granted loses its binding force, not even "photographed reality" is spared such questioning.

Holy Motors

The openness of automatism is part of what has led to renewed interest in Cavell's work in an age where celluloid is increasingly rare, and digital technologies of image production and manipulation overwhelming present (see Krauss; Rodowick, *Virtual Life*). Cavell's relevance in this context is built into the structure of his engagement with modernism. For much of film history, photography was its central automatism, seemingly as essential as possible. The rise of new kinds of films in the 1960s, however, leads him to suggest that it was never more than a convention, its importance appearing as necessary but in reality historically contingent (*World Viewed* 83; on convention, see *Claim* 86–125, esp. 111). This recognition is what not only enables Cavell's theory to survive the emergence of digital media, a post-photographic condition, but gives it explanatory force in these new circumstances. We don't leave cinema, or its appeals, despite changes around them, even as those appeals are transformed.

Again, this comes down to criticism. For Cavell, the various factors that can produce changes—historical events, technological innovations—become meaningful only through the achievements of individual films. Although there is no shortage of recent films that make explicit, thematize, and even allegorize the shift from analog to digital technologies, there are fewer that join these allegories to reflections on the legacy of cinematic traditions, conventions, and automatisms to look at how new technologies of image production and manipulation fit within, and change or sustain, other cinematic appeals. Fewer still do so with such depth, care, and complexity as Leos Carax's *Holy Motors* (2012).

The narrative of the film is at once straightforward and baroque. It follows Oscar (Denis Lavant), an actor of sorts who goes through a range of "appointments" over the course of the day, driven in a white limousine by Céline (Édith Scob). Each appointment requires that he inhabit a particular character and engage in a scene taking place in the world. The scenarios get increasingly bizarre: from a banker at the beginning of the day, he becomes an elderly woman begging on the streets, an actor in a motion-capture suit, a violent tramp emerging from the sewers, a father disappointed in his daughter, an assassin (twice), a dying uncle, an ex-lover, and finally the father of a family made up of chimpanzees. After each scene, Oscar returns to the limousine to change into his next role.

A degree of reflexivity thus runs throughout *Holy Motors*, since it is to a large extent a reflection on the relation between actor and character. Part of this is the way that we pay heightened attention to performance, to the way Oscar manipulates his body into various roles (and thus to Levant's ability to do the same). In this, Carax seems to follow Cavell's insistence that the condition of acting in cinema is such that the actor does not wholly disappear into the character: "The screen performer is essentially not an actor at all; he *is* the subject of a study, and a study not his own" (*World Viewed* 28). Carax's attention to the actor's craft is given a contrast in the motion-capture scene, where the exertions of Oscar and a woman are rendered seamlessly onto a giant screen as an encounter between bizarre dragon-like creatures. Technological changes, the film suggests, affect not only the referential capacities of images but performance as well. Toward the middle of the film, an unnamed man, seemingly in a position of power, tells Oscar that his work lacks conviction; an unspecified audience is disappointed. Oscar notes that it's hard to perform for small digital cameras (like those on which *Holy Motors* itself was shot): they do not allow for the kind of satisfaction in performance as did older, larger cameras.

Carax's concern over a lost audience is not a sociological lament. *Holy Motors* stages an extended and virtuosic exploration of the minimum conditions necessary for the creation of an immersive fictional narrative world, stripping away seemingly necessary features of cinema. The necessity of each automatism for the creation of a successful film is tested and rejected. It's partly the way we are reminded of the presence of Oscar behind each character, so that the ontological boundary between actor and character seems porous but is firm: Oscar is killed twice while in character, for example, each time returning unharmed to the limousine to prepare his next role. In his dying-man scene, we are further astonished to realize that other characters may also be actors like him: the "niece" is performing on an appointment, too. Carax's great achievement is that despite what we know, what we cannot help but know, each time a scene begins we are drawn into it. Even when Oscar ends the day by going to a suburban home with "his" wife and daughters and they turn out to be chimpanzees—even when, in the film's final shot, all the limos are left alone for the night and proceed to have a "conversation"—we remain absorbed in and by this world.

Holy Motors shows that our relation to the world of a film can survive the disappearance of the conditions that seemed to make it possible, the drama of what happens to reality when it is filmed, screened, and projected. This does not come without a cost. The film opens with a man, played by Carax himself, waking up in bed and opening a door that leads into a packed movie theater: it's a scene not least about the natural conditions of movies, a way of experiencing cinema that is already lost. In its absence, Carax mobilizes a range of cinematic automatisms: familiar genres, the byplay between actor and character,

FIGURE 14.2 Even though we focus on the actor, we can't help but believe in the role. Denis Lavant in *Holy Motors* (Leos Carax, Pierre Grise/Théo, 2012). Digital frame enlargement.

recognizable stylistic devices, and the deployment of types. A history of obsolete cinematic form is also evoked as automatisms. There is an entr'acte, an extraordinary sequence in a church where Oscar plays an accordion with a group of musicians, itself introduced by a clip of a bird from the photographic experiments of Etienne-Jules Marey: both the entr'acte and the clip are residual automatisms, brought into this film to evoke a history. Actors and characters likewise appear from elsewhere: Oscar's tramp is from a short film Carax made as part of an omnibus collection, while Eva Mendes, Kylie Minogue, and Michel Piccoli bring their own star personas into the film. Most of all there is Scob in the role of Céline: famous for her role in Georges Franju's *Eyes without a Face* (1960), in Carax's final scene she dons her familiar mask—aquamarine now instead of white—and exits, either into or out of film history. These features *compensate* for the ease of absorption in "traditional" forms of cinema that is now gone (on compensation see *Pursuits* 28ff).

Holy Motors is a film made within what Cavell describes as the modernist condition: when "an art has lost its natural relation to its history [and] an artist . . . is compelled to find unheard-of structures that define themselves and their history against one another" (*World Viewed* 72). Cavell's central gamble in *The World Viewed* is that modernism, understood this way, is not merely a passing feature but the best way to understand cinema's ongoing changes and developments. *Holy Motors* suggests that such an account retains its power in the digital age. The film does this not through mere reflexivity but by creating scenarios that give significance to possibilities of the medium even as we learn about its (new) conditions. In *Pursuits of Happiness*, Cavell uses the metaphor of night and day to describe the complementary parts of a relationship: the explicitness of conversation and the mystery of desire. Discussing *The Lady Eve* (1941), he describes Jean's lesson to Charles, that of telling her entire (if fabricated) sexual past, as a threat: "I'll turn the night into an endless day for you" (65). The endless day is a danger for cinema, too, one represented for Cavell by any response to a crisis in cinema that seeks to render explicit all of its illusions. Against this threat, *Holy Motors* brings illusions into daylight, showing them to be only conventions, yet still keeps alive the night, the mystery of cinema. It returns us to the natural condition of being in wonder at the kind of thing movies are, the pleasures they afford, and the power of their appeals.

15

Michel Foucault

Murmur and Meditation

TOM CONLEY

Votaries of film theory will no doubt be surprised to find Michel Foucault (1926–1984) figuring in this anthology. Having never written explicitly on film, hardly associated with a given director or style, refusing to admit to a psychology of cinema, lacking usage of its lexicon, he would be outside of the purview of film studies. In the context of this volume, where bona fide film theorists are shown married to great movies past and present, Foucault would have little mettle. Yet, it will be argued here, much of his legacy informs a good deal of film theory and history, from his early writing, an unclassifiable *Raymond Roussel* (1963) and the first edition of *Madness and Civilization* (1965), all the way to the three volumes of his *History of Sexuality*, the last of which appeared at the time of his untimely death, at the age of fifty-eight. An unclassifiable "author" who called in question the status of the author—authors including himself as well as all of the "authors" in this book of essays—Foucault crafted ways of thinking that wed history, what is of shorter duration and calibrated in human time, to archaeology, the study of the formations that shape and determine history. Fastidious would be the task of sorting through books and essays on cinema of the last forty years that either build upon his hypotheses or make salient reference to his work. Cinema murmurs throughout the compendious oeuvre that counts ten major titles and now, numerous fascicules that record his lectures and seminars at the Collège de France along with shorter writings that Daniel Defert and François Ewald gathered and scrupulously edited, in four volumes of his *Dits et écrits, 1954–88*, counting approximately 3,500 pages, a sum roughly equivalent to Marcel Proust's *In Search of Lost Time*.

From the sum, a few operative concepts can be thought of as the hammers, screwdrivers, wedges, and chisels in a theorist's toolbox. First and foremost is the history and function of the author or *auteur*, a catchword in film studies that Foucault relentlessly calls into question. Second, given how he analyzes any number of objects—city plans, maps, prisons, novels, philosophy, works of anthropology, the Greco-Roman canon, theology, paintings, pornography, ephemera, the architecture of archives—he studies the languages of various "disciplines" from a spatial bias. He reveals how by its very nature language is "split" or comprised of different "tracks," that is, how it must be both seen and heard, thus how, in order that we may see how language works, signs must be cracked open to display in their ocular and aural form. Foucault makes us aware of the cinema whose strength and muscle conjugate language and image, in order to have us pose questions we often prefer not to ask. Then, third, Foucault innovates in showing how *power* is related to the relation of language to space. He studies how the form of an idiom shapes its meaning, thus how the latter ought to be studied in terms of what, borrowing from linguist Louis Hjelmslev, he calls the "form of content" of things and even of institutions. As a quasi-corollary, fourth, in the mode of what might be called a political philosophy of dissonance, Foucault crafts the idea of *heterotopia* to designate places and practices that escape the control of a legitimating source, be it any array of pass-me-down ideas concerning morality and proper human conduct, or more obviously the codes of ethics that a dominant political body imposes on its subjects.

Fifth—and here his writing on the painters Diego Velásquez, René Magritte, Edouard Manet, and Paul Rebeyrolle is keynote—Foucault communicates to his readers the effects of a *haptic eye* that, extramissively, touches what it sees. To be sure, this would be the sensuous eye that we associate with the way great filmmakers shoot close-ups. It can also change focus, turning into a powerful apparatus when it assumes a controlling distance in respect to what it holds in its field of view. Readers generally find the model for this eye of power in Jeremy Bentham's "panopticon" prison, that in *Discipline and Punish* Foucault made famous. Here, Foucault deals with the effects of incarceration and alienation on the mind and the body. The prison becomes a space in which "limit-experiences" are encountered through torture, detention, and sensory deprivation. Sixth, and in consort with writers who think about what and why it means to think—Michel de Montaigne, René Descartes, Friedrich Nietzsche, Sigmund Freud, Maurice Blanchot—in his later writings Foucault studies the *technologies of the self.* How does the "self" get to the point where it can possibly imagine itself to "be" what it is and, further, where it might figure in a dubious order of things? We often ponder this nagging question, that runs from Montaigne's "Apology for Raimond Sebond" to Descartes's *Meditations* and from there to Maurice Merleau-Ponty and Gilles Deleuze, when, as we linger in relative solitude (be it in the movie house or before a computer screen), films seem to be asking us why in God's name (or even in Hell's) we are looking at them.

It almost goes without saying that in the oral and written fictions we construct to make order of our lives (believing that we were born where we were told we were) we wonder why we happen to be alive, and when and how we will die. Thinking in this manner belongs to what Foucault titles *Le Souci de soi*, the care for self. He looks closely at the "technologies"—modes of writing and reading, sexual conduct and deviance—and "practices"—cooking, conversing, walking, activities of everyday life—that have to do with the constitution (and not quite, as Stephen Greenblatt has argued through his study of the Elizabeth Age, the "fashioning") of the self. Over the last century cinema has undeniably played a vital role in shaping the self. We often map our lifelong itineraries according to films whose memories we carry with us: seeking to recall our first movie, we see cavalcades of confused images passing before our eyes. We bond with the world when we appreciate a film from "the first time" and onward, when we see it differently. And likewise, in recalling how we squirmed or slept through movies whose titles (unfortunately perhaps) resist oblivion, we remember how our eyes took a critical distance from what had brought us to the theater or before a television screen: a sense of relation, a new take on symbolic forms, perhaps a sense of conduct, came with the movies. We configure "phases" of our lives according to emblematic films that mark them. For entitled specialists certain filmmakers and theorists have viatic and vatic, even biblical, virtue: Griffith for contributor Tom Gunning, Hitchcock for editor Murray Pomerance, Kracauer for contributor Johannes Von Moltke, Balázs for Steven Woodward, Bazin for Dudley Andrew. How, as they do, the rest of us—amateurs as we are—work and live with movies has much to do with what Foucault called these same "technologies" of the self. Along this very line, Jean Louis Schefer, fellow writer of the same generation, generally opaque or unknown among Anglophones, in alluding to Georg Simmel and Walter Benjamin asserted that whoever we are, in everyday life we are "the ordinary people of cinema."

In 1969, in the closed space of a seminar (attended by Jacques Lacan), Foucault delivered his landmark essay, "What Is an Author?" Crafting a history of identity and anonymity in the context of proper names attached to works of philosophy from antiquity until then, he also brought a deeper perspective to "auteur theory" that at that very moment was in its waning hours. In 1971, new editors of *Cahiers du cinéma* took Foucault's cue to the quick in publishing a collectively ("anonymously") authored study of John Ford's *Young Mr. Lincoln* (1939). Pantheon director and demi-urge John Ford quickly went from icon to peon, from luminary to purveyor of ideology. The stupendous historical scope of Foucault's work, indeed his long take on the fabrication of self-identity from the pre-Socratics to Marx, provided foundations for and perspectival depth to what the new critics of "apparatus theory" (Jean-Louis Baudry, Jean-Louis Comolli, et al.) were developing to politicize film analysis. Foucault and film were suddenly consubstantial. As François Truffaut's watchword of 1954, borrowed from playwright Jean Giraudoux, "There are no more works, only authors," suggested, the *auteur* had become an agent of classification that offered historians and theorists a way of reordering what in the postwar years

(1946–1968) was becoming an unmanageable archive of cinema. With it, the notion of a signature and a style could be understood within the industrial matrix of cinema as such. In turn, in 1983, when Deleuze published the first of a two-volume philosophy of cinema, he avowed, in harmony with the author of *The Archaeology of Knowledge*, that his was "not a history of cinema, but an essay in classification," a mode of theory without which history could not be countenanced (*Cinema 1* 7). In 1986, two years after Foucault's death, he avowed that in all of his writing Foucault was "singularly close to contemporary cinema" (*Cinema 2* 213).

Foucault's way of "seeing" and "reading" things along different tracks bears directly on film analysis. The cinematic latency of his work is notably found in *This Is Not a Pipe*, a meditation on Magritte, where he spells out the difference between words and letters as they are read, seen, and spoken, in the context of a media—especially painting—whose modes of figuration would be alien to them. A work of art is studied in terms of its *tracks*: the "title" of Magritte's representation of a curved pipe, a legend or supertitle within the field of the image, begins to resemble a supine comma, what in old French was called a *point-queue* (a period-tail or, obscenely, as Foucault implies tongue-in-cheek, given that in slang a *pipe* is a blow-job, a period-cock, a sign harmony with *virgule*, from *virgula*, a virile coda). To say "this is not a pipe" is not to discern what the painting is not, but what it happens to imply in language that cannot be separated from it. Foucault's reflections inform viewers of cinema about how sound, graphic material, and images inflect one another, be it directly or differentially. Tracked, the sights and sounds of cinema, autonomous in respect to one another, become functions of the machinery of ideology when they are "synched." Filmmakers who play on the disruptive effect of voiceover or of things heard off-frame (Fritz Lang, Jean Renoir, Jean-Luc Godard, but by all means Robert Bresson) draw attention to the facticity of the medium and, at once within and without a given narrative or documentary frame, to the grain and texture, analog or digital no matter, of the medium. Herein, as discussed at the beginning of *The Order of Things*, where Foucault studies coordinated distributions of space, light, reflection, and bodies (in Velásquez's *Las Meniñas*), the analyst's eye has haptic virtue: now to dolly in to touch the pigment, then to draw back to gain a view that accounts for the form of the painting's content, much of which deals with how regal power in the Baroque Age is tied to the representation of the monarch. In this tableau the king and queen, subjects of the portrait the artist is commissioned to paint, and upon whom he casts his gaze, are seen in a mirror in the background, that stands exactly where the ideal viewer would be. The containing force of the painting when it is seen from afar counters the painterly details Foucault describes in a close view. From Balázs to Benjamin, and from Kaja Silverman to Laura Marks, the alternately haptic and distanced eye is that of the theorist and historian. Along the diagonal line he draws between painting and language Foucault makes manifest the enabling virtues of film analysis.

The setting of Foucault's major reflections on the contemporary world is the prison. Within its walls (components of its form), in guise of a mission to amend, redress, and "correct" its inmates (its content), the push-and-pull of reason and violence are played out. Published in 1975, *Discipline and Punish* marked a turning point, a sudden politicization, too, in Foucault's research and writing. A denizen of the Bibliothèque Nationale when it was located on the rue de Richelieu, Foucault spent his diurnal hours under Henri Labrouste's airy vaults in the main reading room. While researching the history of torture and incarceration in the confines of the library the author could have been an extra in Alain Resnais's incomparable *All the Memory of the World* (*Toute la memoire du monde*, 1956), a painterly meditation on the Bibliothèque (in this film Piranesi's *Prisons* seem to inspire the many takes, in chiaroscuro, of the elevators, shafts, inner stacks, and dimly lit corridors) that figures as the right panel of a diptych with *Night and Fog* (*Nuit et brouillard*, 1955). In the latter, the horror of the camps, revived as the camera approaches what has become a museum in slow tracking shots on rails, finds a counterpoint in the heterotopia of the library, a place where anxiety and pleasure are mixed, and through which the camera glides like a zombie from one cloistered chamber to another. A product of the same library, *Discipline and Punish* implies that the *prison* can be emblematic of certain cinematic spaces. Films dealing with incarceration and escape are many, but so also are reflections, from Antoine Artaud to Jean-Paul Sartre, on the isolation of the spectator in the *huis-clos* or closed space of the theater, on occasion a site where viewers find themselves visually tortured and even traumatized.

The heterotopia, that in Foucault's world spins off Sebastian Brant's *Stultifera navis* (in the late fifteenth and early sixteenth centuries an immensely influential satire of texts and woodcut images), a beacon for the discourse on madness at the outset of *Madness and Civilization*, might include the library and movie theater and be thought of through Foucault's work on prisons. We can surmise that his extensive work on the practical dimension of meditation ("the soul, the technique of the body," he writes in *Discipline and Punish*) belongs to a technology of the self that pertains to film theory. Films become objects of meditation that inspire self-consciousness, when they prod us to consider, beyond the frame of narrative design, their latent or manifest political virtue: how they craft the pleasure they are designed to yield, and how they themselves build their ambient worlds and work or think through what they do. Films that *represent* sentience and meditation tend to be marginal, while those that succeed often use exiguity or confinement to advance englobing agendas. A past master, a director of indelibly Foucaldian signature is Robert Bresson, notably in *A Man Escaped* (1956). The feature, it will be argued in the remaining paragraphs, gives force and reason to J. C. Chandor's *All Is Lost* (2013). In the former, incarcerated and seen in close-up as he copes with what is around him, the hero cogitates issues of fate, hope, and destiny that help him engineer his escape. In the latter, alone, a sailor manning a crippled yacht tries to survive on an endless and often cruel sea. Both protagonists seek to survive through *doing*, which for both is related to *thinking*: thinking practically, without losing time in ruminating over abstraction, but melding matters of life and time in meticulous labor. In their solitude both protagonists qualify as existential heroes, one young and the other grizzled, who look at the conditions in which they are found and use to the best of their efforts practical means—guile and writing—to live and to die.

A Man Escaped

Bresson's screenplay and dialogues for *A Man Escaped* (in French, *Un condamné à mort s'est échappé, ou le vent souffle où il veut*—A Condemned Man Escaped, or the Wind Blows Where It Wishes) finds inspiration in André Devigny's eponymous short story that recounts the Nazis' apprehension and confinement of the Resistance fighter Fontaine (played by nonprofessional actor François Leterrier) who, captured in Lyons in 1943, against all odds engineers an escape from a heavily guarded prison. The plot is as barren and forbidding as the setting: while being driven with another detainee to the prison (where Germans put 11,000 inmates to death) Fontaine attempts to escape when the vehicle stops before an unexpected obstacle. Apprehended and pistol-whipped, bloodied and dazed, he is thrown into a cell where he slowly comes to his senses. When day breaks, he climbs to a barred window looking over the courtyard and notices three older men taking a daily walk from one end of the yard to the other. From them he obtains their confidence, and soon after a safety pin (allowing him to open his handcuffs) and a pencil (with which *writing* becomes a wherewithal of survival). Fontaine filches a spoon, which he sharpens to dismantle the panels of the door and, eventually, finding egress from a transom near the rooftop, plans a daring escape. He fashions a cord from cloth wrapped about wire taken from the bedstead and a hook from the metal frame of the transom shutter at the top of the cell. At the Hotel Terminus Nazi agents inform Fontaine that he will soon face a firing squad. Distraught, returning to his cell, he discovers a young man (malodorous, wearing a German jacket, ridden with fleas), aptly named "Jost" (Charles Le Clainche), consigned to share his cell. After gaining his confidence Fontaine includes him in the escape that brings them over the walls of the prison and, after harrowing trials, to what seems to be freedom.

The traits of Bresson's sensuously austere cinema convey a gripping narrative despite its outcome being known before the film begins: shots take care to depict the texture of forbidding walls and the spare interiors of what could be both prison and monastery. Close-ups prevail of the hero who turns away from the camera when thinking or when protecting himself from the guards' gaze. As

FIGURE 15.1 Meditating, Robert Bresson's hero (François Leterrier) raises doubt about his plan to escape in *Un condamné à mort s'est échappé* (Gaumont, 1956). Digital frame enlargement.

if to show that the space of the prison is of importance equal to its inhabitants—hence insisting on the form of the content of the cloister—and in a mode of editing entirely alien to narrative, the lens holds on the décor after the characters have exited. Fades in and out isolate the sequences that seem bookended by long moments of black screen asking the spectator to countenance the very nature of visibility and how the film is designed as a mosaic of *tableaux*. Given, from the beginning, the bloodied shirt that Fontaine wears throughout the film, he appears much as a painter in a virtual studio that would be in consort with the milieux of Georges de la Tour and Philippe de Champaigne. Fontaine's voiceover (in an aorist tense), that we hear redundantly describing what we see onscreen, alternates now and again with voice-in (in an existential present) whenever he murmurs with cellmates during their collective ablutions or, staring out of the barred window, converses across the wall with the older, fragile Blanchet (Maurice Beerblock), a wizened man occupying the adjacent cell. A sense of places other or *off*, embodying what Foucault calls the *dehors*, other heterotopias perhaps, is felt where nondiegetic sounds punctuate the film: distant cackle of children who might be at recess in a nearby schoolyard; toots and whistles of locomotives that in every viewer's imagination are hauling victims eastward in cattle cars to death camps; the bark of a dog that might belong to a resident outside the walls; short bursts of gunfire suggesting that the Germans are putting Fontaine's comrades to death.

The plot is woven with reflections, doubt, faith, hope, community, and, above all, an array of the "techniques" that tie body and soul. Action, what in the *Poetics* Aristotle deems worthier than human psychology, punctuates meditation. And if meditation there is, it is a function of practical guise and guile. To a priest who tells Fontaine to think of Scripture he murmurs, "I don't have the Bible, but I have a pencil." Before launching his escape project, Fontaine shares some last comment with Blanchet, who hears fear in his words. Blanchet, seen so very obliquely through the barred window that his voice is disembodied: "You think too much, you're no longer scheming" [*tu ne figures plus*]. Soon Fontaine responds-*in*, looking outward, toward the viewer or skyward: "In this life where we are we must believe" [*il faut croire*]. Blanchet—who could as well be Maurice Blanchot—retorts: "Believe first of all in your [ropes and] hooks, but within yourself, you're doubting [*tu doutes*]," to which Fontaine whispers in response, in what could be an aphorism from existential theology, "Making up one's mind [*Se décider*] is what is hard." Pensive, the words weigh heavily. *Décider* (from *de + caedere*, to cut off or away), and *doute* (from *dubitare*, that also means to fear), a verb at the bedrock of existential philosophy, inspires creative belief. The style of Bresson's film brings forward the force of these words, murmured in the confines of the prison walls, in stark sensuousness. Paradoxically—paradox is of Bresson's essence—the abstraction of these exchanges queues on the long sequences in which Foucault studies the techniques of body and soul. As he shows in the pages of *Discipline and Punish* where the public spectacle of torture and death by retribution gives way to corrective isolation, "techniques of the self" become vital to survival. In Bresson's film they are anchored in the hero's *bricolage*, his mode of engineering destiny in the way he fashions ropes woven with fabric and reflections on fate.

All Is Lost

Few recent films are of the same stuff, but one could be Chandor's *All Is Lost*. In the beginning, in darkness (what else?), to the sound of splashing and clanking, a title-card announces, "1700 nautical miles from the Sumatra Straits." The film fades in to a calm sea in crepuscule, the background over which the title appears (in white upper-case, sans-serif characters set slightly above the sea line) before the camera pans left where the side of a great black triangle, what seems to be a metallic iceberg, comes into view. Voiceover:

> 13th of July, 4:50 P.M. (. . .) I'm sorry. I know that means little at this point. But I am. I tried . . . I think you would all agree . . . that I tried. To be true,

> to be . . . strong. To be kind. To love. To be right. But I wasn't. And I know you knew this. In each of your ways. And I *am* sorry. All is lost here . . . [the camera reveals the slope of the object on the left] . . . except for soul and body, that is, what is left of them, and a half-day's ration. It's inexcusable really. I know that now. How long it took to admit that I'm not . . . sure, but I did. I fought till the end. I'm not sure what that is worth, but know that I did. I have always hoped for more for you all. [Fade to black] I will miss you. I'm sorry. [Title-card appears to the sound of creaking: "8 Days Earlier": holds and then fades to black for a duration of twenty seconds before a cut to Robert Redford, seen head to waist upside down in a navy blue tee shirt, chest and torso visible, his right arm on his chest displaying a wrist watch. The splintering of a cracking hull is heard.]

The words resemble a confession addressed to an unidentified authority, perhaps to a jury enjoined to deliver a last judgment, or even to the spectator upon whom a power of attorney seems conferred. Spoken beyond time, from a space *outside* of what can be represented, the words come from someone having undergone a limit-experience. As in a great deal of medieval literature, they could be spoken by a dead soul swimming in the limbo of the second circle of Hell or by a modern mystic who reports having died and, now, disembodied, returns to tell of his experience.

The film registers in flashback a solitary man's attempt to survive perdition on the high sea. Possibly having fled an untenable situation, the upside-down man sleeps in solace in the hold of a well-equipped yacht: a collision with a derelict shipping container suddenly breached the fiberglass nacelle. From there he uses every practical measure in his means to survive. After repairing the gash in the hull (and later another on his head), he encounters raging storms inundating the craft with seawater. It capsizes, turns topsy-turvy, loses its mainmast, and becomes flotsam before sinking only seconds after he has abandoned ship and taken refuge in an inflated life raft. The latter catches fire and succumbs to the sea when, on point of drowning, the hero sees the searchlights of a rescue vessel arriving at the site of his conflagration. Stunning underwater photography of the final shots underscores the metaphysics: seen from below, only minutes after it had drawn away in cosmic zoom-out, the raft set ablaze turns into a dying planet at the limit of a watery empyrean in twilight. After all his trials and inventive means to survive the hero looks upward to sight his place in cosmic oblivion.

In strong contrast to Fontaine in *A Man Escaped*, the hero never thinks aloud. He murmurs, mutters, groans, and heaves, but swears (voice-in) only once. Far from the painterly effects around the edges of the close-ups in Bresson's black-and-white film, Frank G. DeMarco's digital photography softens

FIGURE 15.2 The solitary hero (Robert Redford) of *All Is Lost* (J. C. Chandor, Before The Door/FilmNation, 2013) confronts uncertain destiny. Digital frame enlargement.

its edge only when, under the direction of Peter Zuccarini, the underwater photography catches a mottled and fluid light cast upon the sea above. When the camera records the turmoil of storm the spectator is *there*, engulfed, light-years from painterly thoughts of J.M.W. Turner or Winslow Homer. Consideration of fate and destiny devolves upon the spectator who witnesses—in the best biblical sense—the *passion* of the voyager's struggle to survive, recorded, as if with structural resemblance to Bresson's film, in *tableaux* marked by the passage of night and day.

Serendipitously: where the final shot of *A Man Escaped* shows Fontaine and companion Jost from behind, briskly walking away over a bridge and disappearing in a puff of steam that washes the frame with light, *All Is Lost* follows Redford swimming upward from the depths where he is drowning toward the beacon of a rescue boat where, before he reaches the surface, the film cuts from the dark waters to a brief shot of a hand—the hand of God?—extending from off-frame, that he grasps before the film cuts to an absolutely white frame. Death? Salvation? Essence? Illumination? No one can know for sure.

The ending begins when a faint light on the horizon and the distant whir of a craft inspire the hero to start and then nourish a fire with crumpled paper torn from his log and notebooks. Just before, in rehearsing the romantic literary *topos* of the forlorn soul tossing an "ms. in a bottle" (that resurfaces in Michael Powell's *Edge of the World* [1939]), he pens some last words on paper, inserts the message into a bottle, seals it, and tosses it into the sea. Writing gives way to incineration and, possibly the man's survival. *A Man Escaped* begins with the shot of the concrete wall of a prison over which appear inscriptions, some handwritten, others chiseled in stone, and soon afterward, the epigraphy of the title itself. Given that Fontaine's salvation owes to what he does with a pencil, the plot implies that the film is of scriptural gist and maybe a piece of secular scripture: writing cues action, and when successful, writing evanesces into light. So, too, with *All Is Lost:* Redford's hope comes on the heels of writing a memorial and an SOS before putting paper and writing to fire. Like the filmmakers who set them onscreen, both Fontaine and the man who is lost are, finally, authors: authors of our experience of them, authors of their two fates.

Readers of Foucault will recall how for him, in oblique homage to Blaise Pascal's memorial that the mystical philosopher had sewn into his vest, illumination comes with writing, in "My Paper, My Body, This Fire," an addendum to *Madness and Civilization* (1972). His words speak volumes for the role that, at once present and absent, *écriture* or self-writing plays in the technology of the self. Words help us grasp the relation of writing and light, of dream and cognition and, in their portrayals of limit-experiences, in a strong existential sense, the meditative and creative virtues of the seventh art. May they serve as an invitation to engage the wondrous and endless venture of reading, living, and seeing with Michel Foucault.

16

Jean Douchet

La Politique Hitchcockienne

R. BARTON PALMER

One of the founders of postwar French film culture, Jean Douchet (b. 1929) continued into his eighties to be a telegenic and energetic spokesman for the seventh art, as the cinema came to be called in the course of the 1950s. Trained at the Sorbonne in philosophy, and with a cinephilia shaped by the ciné-club scene in the 1940s and early 1950s, Douchet began a career as a film critic in his twenties, then in 1957 joined the staff of *Cahiers du cinéma* (which began in 1951) after the journal's founder, André Bazin, died and Eric Rohmer became the editor. Given the freedom to pursue his different interests, he there began a long association with many of the major critics and filmmakers of the era, including Rohmer (Maurice Schérer), Jean-Luc Godard, Jacques Rivette, Claude Chabrol, Alexandre Astruc, and François Truffaut, as rapidly evolving critical fashion put *Cahiers*, by the end of the decade, firmly established as the leading organ of international film culture, through a dizzying series of changes.

But Douchet remained faithful to his initial understanding of the cinema. Throughout his long career, he has been a forceful promoter of the *politique des auteurs*, a slippery term that means both "author policy" (a critical protocol or form of reading) and also "author politics," or advocacy for a production strategy emphasizing directorial personal expression over the roles played by screenwriters and their literary sources (see Bordwell, *History* ch. 3). Auteurism, it needs emphasizing, is not a theoretical position as such; it offers no explanation for any of the various workings of the cinema (formal, technical, or psychological), nor does it connect, except indirectly, with various forms of cultural theory. However, auteurism is without doubt the most important critical protocol that has emerged in international film culture, guiding most research into and writing about the cinema. If not a theory per se, it has shaped the field in the manner of one.

Along with his younger colleagues at *Cahiers*, Douchet did much to establish this essentially neo-Romantic view of the film "author," developing with that team a particular fascination with and admiration for British/American director Alfred Hitchcock. Among the staff writers at *Cahiers*, he belonged to the party informally known as the "Mac-Mahonists," fervent admirers of the American cinema who haunted a Parisian cinema of that name that exclusively screened Hollywood films. Best known for his work on the relentlessly self-promoting "Master of Suspense," in 1967 Douchet published his influential monograph *Hitchcock*, which will be the main focus of this chapter. Although he makes no reference to the identically titled book published a decade earlier by Chabrol and Rohmer, Douchet engages in a productive dialogue with their view that through the director's acknowledged technical expertise "a complete moral universe reveals itself" (Chabrol and Rohmer 154).

Phrased a bit stridently perhaps, John Hess's summary of the *politique* is far from inaccurate: "a justification, couched in aesthetic terms, of a culturally conservative, politically reactionary attempt to remove film from the realm of social and political concern" (Hess 19). With its bracketing off of politics, the *politique* somewhat paradoxically demands to be read politically. An "engaged" approach to the cinema had held sway in France following the continuing national trauma during the 1940s of sudden military collapse, occupation by a hated enemy, and then liberation by yet another foreign power, followed by paroxysms of guilty national self-examination and the perversely self-congratulatory mythlogizing of the *Résistance*, which for some years promoted an enthusiastic collectivism that saw the French public through years of economic desperation. As Dudley Andrew suggests, not long into the postwar era "the Liberation faded in vividness, and as the social and economic structures upholding French life reasserted themselves, the feeling of progress and brotherhood were not so easy to maintain" (Andrew, *Bazin* 132). Among the *Cahiers* group, it was André Bazin who developed and held most tenaciously to an idealizing view of the cinema and its social importance. An adherent of Emannuel Mounier's version of Personalism, with its hopes for human betterment, both individual and collective, Bazin found ameliorative energies in film's extraordinary representational capacity: its ability to show spectators, as Andrew describes, "a world alive with possibilities that ask for recognition and response" ("Introduction" xxi).

Bazin's younger colleagues at the journal, including Douchet, found such transformative realism less compelling, if not irrelevant. They were, Bazin once gently admonished, "fierce partisans" for Hitchcock, not willing to heed the caveats about the director's supposed artistry that Bazin issued after a careful reading of Hitchcock's own statements and a measured assessment of his films' production histories (Bazin, "Hitchcock contre Hitchcock" 25). With their inevitable revelations of involuntary compromises, flagging energies, and ironic detachment from a process stained by the original sin of commercialism, these production histories pointed to a quite different concept of authorship, which emerges as a light that burns brightly at times, but flickers and goes dim at others. Gorgeous images of the charismatic figures who populated the entertainment business that was the cinema filled the fanzines of the era. The pages of *Cahiers* similarly overflowed with fevered discussions of such individuals, suitably illustrated by stills and punctuated by earnest interviews, as in the now-legendary special Hitchcock number of the journal (No. 39, 1954). The auteurists assumed that films were important in and of themselves, a view that they were inclined to take as given. They did not prize movies that could be reduced to social criticism or comment, though Douchet, for one, occasionally reads Hitchcock politically, as in the following passage devoted to the American notion of economic self-fashioning in *The Wrong Man* (1956). With this film, so he says:

> We find ourselves confronting the most vigorous denunciation that this auteur ever launched against the deadly appeal, as much social as individual, of the mythology upon which advanced capitalist societies are based. . . . Son of immigrants . . . [the main character] strives at all costs to find his place in an era of abundant wealth, never realizing that he is in fact the one designated to be exploited by such a system. (*Hitchcock* 99)

The critics at friendly rival *Positif* (which began in 1952) were more inclined to promote this kind of socially based commentary, to value directors who refused to "exalt the values of the Eisenhower era," as its long-time editor Michel Ciment proudly proclaims (Ciment and Kardish 10). *Cahiers*, in general, showed little enthusiasm for the likes of cineastes such as Richard Brooks (and, for example, the social reformism of his *Blackboard Jungle* [1955]).

Attracted instead to filmmakers who were not *engagé* in the sense of a Gillo Pontecorvo (*The Battle of Algiers* [1966]) or Costa-Gavras (*Z* [1969]), the *Cahiers* auteurists were hardly formalists, at least in the usual sense of that term. Instead, they tended to promote the significance of moral or metaphysical interpretations. Watching Hitchcock films, proclaims Alexandre Astruc, reminds him of reading William Faulkner or Feodor Dostoevsky, and there finding a "universe both aesthetic and moral" (5). Commenting on Hitchcock, Chabrol makes this point more elegantly: "I should say that his moral ideas point toward the metaphysic that subsumes them. It is clear enough that in human terms Morality in capital letters constitutes the only workable metaphysic, and that man's salvation, which is the very stuff of Hitchcock's artistic fabric, in the end is closely connected to his sense of dignity" (18).

Needless to say, the formal details of Hitchcock's cinema tend to disappear from view when confronted with this idealizing approach. The salvation of which Chabrol speaks is Christian and individual, disconnected from any collective political project. For Hitchcock, at least as Chabrol sees him, the notion of dignity is hardly public but instead the sense of self-worth that comes from some *dilemme morale* successfully traversed. If crime or international intrigue figures centrally in the plot, these social facts do not prove meaningful in and of themselves. Chabrol provides readings that emphasize the instrumentality of all experience, whose real point is the testing of the individual soul, which is thereby provided the opportunity for the spiritual development to whose dramatizing the Hitchcock text is devoted (20). According to Chabrol, the "Catholic conception of existence, which is Hitchcock's . . . considers man as perfectly free . . . it's up to him to win through or sink to defeat" (20). Saint Augustine could not have put the matter more succinctly, especially if he wished to outline an eminently repeatable plot line for directors inclined toward a Christian form of high seriousness. Throughout Hitchcock's body of work, Chabrol suggests, "the heavy breath of Satan never ceases to make itself felt . . . but the signs, the traces of this are revealed through symbols that are more and more perfectly precise. . . . [Hitchcock] suggests an infernal presence without ever finding it necessary to designate it literally" (Chabrol 19–20). The foundational opposition of Light to Darkness thus takes on a variety of forms, providing the materials for a lifetime of filmmaking and affirming the importance of a cosmogenic narrative for their interpretation.

If Hitchcock is primarily a metaphysician, it is hardly a leap to read his films as embodying central themes within Western intellectual and religious traditions. Douchet represents the extreme form of this developing culturalist approach among the *Cahiers* group (Rohmer's five-part discussion of "Celluloid and Marble" is also worthy of note in this regard). Chabrol and Rohmer begin their celebrated monograph on Hitchcock, which appeared in 1957, with a detailed biographical account and their readings of his films pay due attention to production history. In contrast, Douchet ignores the materiality of the director's career, suggesting simply that Hitchcock entrances filmgoers with illusion, which allows him to "make real his own mental universe." Each film, then, represents "the victory of the creator over his material, of his soul over his emotions, of his reason over his unconscious" (9). Douchet's opening critical gesture is as challenging as it is unexpected: to connect this body of films to the mystical writings of the third-century Greek thinker Plotinus. As Douchet sees it, Hitchcock's embrace of a metaphysics founded on exploring the idea of a hierarchical continuum between spirit and matter explains the elemental opposition in the films of virtue to villainy:

> The One, the Monad, God and the essence of existence. The Monad acts through the creative force of the Dyad, for as soon as God manifests Himself he is double, with poles both positive and negative, principles both masculine and feminine. This Dyad engenders the world, or the visible expansion of God through space and time. . . . The conflict

> between the light and the shadows of darkness, dreamed of in their all-powerful hiddenness. This conflict becomes for the artist the expression of the struggle between the imagination and the spirit, and, for all men, the struggle between impulse and rationality. . . . The vision of the conflict between the Darkness and the Light directs the cinematic imagination of Hitchcock. It is the source of his most beautiful gestures of form. It gives order to even as it supports the *mise-en-scène* of the Idea. . . . Life ceases to be a nightmare, a necessary passage across the realm of shadows. It gives way to the Light. The One triumphs . . . . The Idea becomes flesh, developing in three orders . . . the occult . . . the logical . . . and the psychological or everyday. (10–11)

Douchet here writes an interesting version of the self-consciously mandarin prose that by the end of the 1960s had become the house discourse of *Cahiers*. His refusal to see these films within their immediate cinematic context is striking, and this surely begs for a symptomatic reading. Beyond its inherent interest (which is considerable), his invocation of classical metaphysics seems a response to the problem that enthusiasm for Hitchcock posed to his *Cahiers* supporters. However worthy, Hitchcock was a Hollywood employee in the 1950s, not a sage pondering existential subtleties at the Academy. So how could the "dream factory" be a realm that sponsored the production of the most moving and profound forms of art when filmmaking was also a business catering to the essentially insignificant desires of filmgoers for affect, for the arousing and satisfying of different forms of emotion?

In evaluating his moralism, Chabrol boldly suggests that Hitchcock succeeds in presenting embodied evil where great writers (Honoré de Balzac, Dostoevsky, and Georges Bernanos are suggested as examples) partly failed. Is this a testimony to the English director's genius? Of course, but this artistic triumph was also made possible because of the medium in which he worked, with its reliance on images inescapably replete with undecodable messages and thus worth many thousands of words:

> He held in his hands a medium with the greatest possible resources, whose miraculous powers he was one of the very few to realize. . . . It is useful to stop and reflect upon . . . fleeting indications [such as] the missing digit of Professor Jordan [in *The 39 Steps*] . . . the amnesia of Gregory Peck in *Spellbound* . . . whatever it is that makes Father Benoît's bicycle wobble and fall in *I Confess*. (Chabrol 20)

Douchet takes this *homage* a step further. For him, the Hitchcock oeuvre finds its value through a deep consonance with the most elemental of Western moral themes, even as, in a verbal gesture approaching blasphemy, the director's films are imagined as issuing from something analogous to the materializing creative process invoked in the first verse of John's gospel.

Yet was such thematic profundity consistent with Hitchcock's evident popularity? Chabrol advised that the critic disregard the "misleading superficial aspects" of the films, especially their arousing of "suspense," which he regarded as a singular form of artificiality. The plot is merely a device to test the main character's moral self. For Chabrol, Hitchcock was both a slick professional, able to entertain filmgoers with the essentially meaningless play of affect he called suspense, and also, perhaps in spite of this pleasant form of Aristotelianism, a moralist who compelled to provide portrait after portrait of dignity-conferring trial, evoking, if not depicting, the workings of the universal principle of nothingness and lack, which the Bible personifies as Satan. But there is perhaps a more satisfactory solution to this supposed duality. Hitchcock is only in some ways an artist, as Bazin and Chabrol agree, if he can be understood as catering in part to vulgar and banal desires. As Douchet sees it, however, this view of his supposed "commercialism" is dead wrong. Safer to erase any claim that the industry might be said to have on him. It could easily be explained away:

> The title "Master of Suspense," willingly adopted by Alfred Hitchcock is rarely understood in a positive sense. It underlies not only the reservations that have long been expressed by almost all critics regarding a suspect talent, but, even worse, a kind of scorn for a genre [i.e., the thriller] long considered much too Grand Guignol. But, rather than refute this title, it is appropriate to consider it as offering a fundamental definition of the Hitchcock oeuvre. . . . To say that suspense is based on the eruption of sudden brutality into the daily order of things is in fact a truism. . . . Suspense then expresses the most ancient philosophical attitude possible. (9)

Through suspense, narrative form expresses the unimpeachable truth that disaster haunts every minute of every life, with the ultimate loss—death—an unavoidable conclusion for one and all. The Sword of Damocles (to borrow Douchet's telling image) does eventually fall everywhere.

Hitchcock's genius in giving "fleshly" expression to this elemental theme can be imagined, moreover, as marked by a maturational trajectory: his later films (those produced through the middle 1960s) are more profound than his earlier forays. In the films preceding the second version of *The Man Who Knew Too Much* (1956), Douchet finds that the hero's double, embodying the infernal opposition of shadow to light, is the source of threatening betrayal and thus can be defeated in a series of external actions that burnish the virtues of the main character (see, for example, Richard Hannay [Robert Donat] in *The 39 Steps* [1935]). The films that follow reveal a form of treason that is subtler and more serious. In *The Wrong Man* (1956), as Chabrol and Rohmer had earlier emphasized, the everyman main character, Manny Balestrero (Henry Fonda) is forced to "inhabit a body, an outer form, a semblance that does not belong to him, to assume an identity that is not his" (86):

> The trial imposed on Balestrero . . . consists in making him conscious, by each successive form of loss, that the only true goods in life are those that are moral and spiritual and move us emotionally; these cannot, under any circumstances, be understood as depending on material possessions alone; and of these goods, the most precious is that of our spirit, whose watchfulness and strength alone allow us to triumph over the difficulties that existence presents. (100)

Douchet does not explicate the deep cultural resonances of Hitchcock's evolving view of human experience. He probably expected his first readers to recognize that this turn toward the spirit and away from material goods (always inadequate and impermanent) is the intellectual center of a work that was required reading for every Western intellectual: Boethius's *The Consolation of Philosophy* (ca. 524), a meditation on existential disaster and spiritual redemption made memorable by its portrait of an unreliable Lady Fortune, the author of the kind of bad luck that, for a time, brings Balestrero low. Like Boethius, Manny must confess to his powerlessness in the world before he is delivered. He must experience "the true emptiness" of his life (Douchet 101) through what Chabrol and Rohmer had previously identified as his being brought face to face with the "fundamental abjection of human existence," that he is simply "one object among other objects" (Chabrol and Rohmer 149). Manny is subject in the end only to the irresistibility of the Grace he summons to his rescue, the choice that determines his fate. Nothing else matters. The anxiety we are made to feel about the injustice that objectifies him, and the suspense the film arouses about its final rectification, implicates the viewer in the "peeling away of a surface at once deceptive and traitorous," as the ever-present, and truly horrifying, possibility that one might be reduced to thingness is made as mundane as a casual visit to an insurance office to borrow money (Douchet 92).

Obsession: A Difficult Moral Passage

Appropriations, Julie Sanders suggests, are unlike adaptations properly speaking in that they offer "a more decisive journey away from the informing source into a wholly new cultural product and domain" (26). Most of Brian De Palma's early films feature self-conscious borrowings from Hitchcock, especially from *Vertigo* (1958) and *Psycho* (1960). And this is certainly true of *Obsession* (1976), whose remade appropriations from *Vertigo* constitute the bulk of the film. Disturbed perhaps at the pervasive reuse of themes, characters, and narrative elements from an honored auteur, critics have been inclined to treat films like *Obsession*,

Dressed to Kill (1980), and *Body Double* (1984) as clumsy homages at best and, at worst, as little better than plagiarism. Douchet, however, might well be inclined with Julie Sanders to analyze *Obsession* as a "wholly new cultural product," on the assumption that as an auteur, De Palma would dominate his material creatively; as he says of Hitchcock: "Every narrative, reduced to its lines of force, finds itself filled with the imaginings of the artist" (Douchet 10–11). One way to see *Obsession* as Hitchcockian, then, would be to understand De Palma as connecting, through a confrontation with essential moral questions, to the same deep metaphysical structures as his model. With Douchet, we would resist the temptation to see De Palma's film as secondary, as either the product of a complex production history (including a much-revised screenplay by the Bressonian Paul Schrader) or a radical remaking of an honored classic, by whose standards it should be judged.

Obsession begins where a classic Hollywood film might end, but with a thoroughgoing disaster rather than triumph for the protagonist, whose power to affect the course of events is revealed as a mirage. A tenth wedding anniversary celebration at his sumptuous Garden District home acknowledges the personal and professional success of developer Michael "Court" Courtland (Cliff Robertson), who smugly accepts the praise his guests shower on him, not recognizing that what he now "has" is also due to good fortune. A recently concluded partnership with friend Bob LaSalle (John Lithgow) holds out the prospect of immense profits, as a huge tract of New Orleans property, now purchased by them, is ready for the building of homes. Court's wife Elizabeth (Geneviève Bujold) is beautiful, and they are shown to be deeply in love, and to enjoy, with mutual satisfaction, their love for their daughter Sandra. But does Court really possess anything? That same night, his wife and child are suddenly abducted from their bedrooms while, close by yet unaware, he does nothing. Asked to pay a huge ransom, Court refuses on the advice of the police, sending the kidnappers a suitcase filled with bundles of paper. This gesture, the kidnappers angrily suggest to their terrified captives, signifies perfectly what Court thinks they are worth. Surrounded, the gang tries to escape with mother and daughter as hostages, but their car crashes, bursts into flame, and all within are apparently killed.

It seems that Court has failed the test that is life, agreeing too quickly to the demands of the police that the ransom not be paid, perhaps because he does not want to give up what he has earned. The difficult question of what to do in response to the demands of the abductors gets only short shrift in the quick resolution of the challenge it poses to Court. Give them the money and they have every reason to kill their victims, the argument runs; refuse payment and increase the chance of a successful rescue. Years pass, but for Court time has stopped. He devotes himself to building a memorial to the dead, where he often stands vigil, reflecting for two decades on his impotence to remake the past, immobilized as he is like some victim of a fairy-tale bewitching. No longer the object of Court's desire for profit, the prime real estate remains undeveloped except for his memorial, and the narrative, as if trapped in a nightmare, elides twenty years of inaction and stasis.

If, as Douchet suggests, suspense consists in "the prolongation of a present situation trapped between two contrary possibilities of resolution in an imminent future," then De Palma at first refuses to prolong a present in which everything is suddenly at stake and in which there is an insistent need to choose between alternatives and act. But that need is foreclosed when the worst happens. When the narrative resumes, Court is caught up in circumstances that seem, by happy chance, to promise deliverance. Bob encourages him to visit Florence, where the firm often does business, and there he meets a young woman, Sandra Portinari, who is the very image of his dead wife. She is reluctant, but he successfully romances her. They return to New Orleans to marry, but before their relationship can be consummated the past again grabs hold of Court, confirming the sense he had already felt of living through a new life or second chance. In the precise manner of the original kidnapping, Sandra is abducted. He is again encouraged to pay a ransom in exactly the same fashion. This time, he chooses to pay, eager to take the second chance that he is seemingly so generously offered to make good his earlier failure, if that is what it was.

As instructed, Court borrows a briefcase full of money from Bob LaSalle, signing over his interest in their company as collateral. He delivers it. But the money is not there. Court has been betrayed by LaSalle, who has replaced the bills with paper bundles. Confronted, Bob tells Court that he planned the original kidnapping out of jealousy and its repeat performance in order to seize control of their business. What has just happened, however, is playacting, as he proudly proclaims, involving the participation of Court's own daughter, now grown up (Geneviève Bujold in the twin roles of mother and daughter). Sandra (Court's hitherto unnamed daughter) did not die in that failed escape attempt, but had been sent by LaSalle to Florence, where she grew up hating the father who she thought betrayed her. Court confronts and kills LaSalle, but Sandra has already left to return to Rome, convinced by LaSalle that her father had once again refused to pay the ransom and thus, in her mind, express his love for her.

Angry at her betrayal, and resolved to kill her, Court rushes to the airport still carrying the ransom money, which he has retrieved from LaSalle. But there he must confront his daughter, on a gurney after having slit her wrists out of despair for her betrayal. Brought together by their mutual connection, in a reunion almost polluted by LaSalle's wickedness, father and daughter find their ways out of this moral abyss. Seeing the money, she embraces him as her father, and, overwhelmed by this display of love, he forgives what she has done. Evil of the most unreasoning kind has in the deceptive form of the charming LaSalle done its best to destroy what matters most, the bonds of natural affection that join us to each other. LaSalle has succeeded, however,

FIGURE 16.1 Court Courtland (Cliff Robertson) and his new paramour, Sandra Portinari (Geneviève Bujold), in *Obsession* (Brian De Palma, Columbia, 1976). Digital frame enlargement.

only in providing his would-be victims with the opportunity to become most fully human. In *Obsession*, as in Hitchcock's films, we are forced to "suffer the terrors of a soul torn between good and evil," the metaphysical form of a suspense that can be resolved only by the operations of grace and human will (Douchet 8).

If, as Douchet argues, the essence of Hitchcock's moral seriousness consists in the "peeling away" (he uses the word *dépiauter*, literally meaning "to flay") of false appearances to reveal the often distressing truths of life and experience, we might credit De Palma with having achieved something similar in *Obsession*. The film begins with an image of power, accomplishment, and possession that, while not discredited by the narrative, is substantially reconfigured, with money revealed in the end as indispensably disposable, relevant only for the decision it indexes. A profound sense of love suffuses the final scene, something quite distinct from the relatively easy domestic affection evident in the Courtland mansion before disaster strikes. This love is measured by the loss and absence that precedes the reunion of father and child. And it can be achieved only through the forgiving of deep betrayal. Deliverance from the evil unleashed by LaSalle's treachery is no easy thing.

For Douchet, the Hitchcockian thriller depends on the affective power, and moral resonance, generated by the resolution of suspense, as an indeterminate present gives way to a reality stripped of what has prevented its truths from being revealed. Identities are fixed, plots are uncovered, gaps in the information provided by the narrative are filled, justice assigns one and all their proper fates. The protagonist solves the mysteries of his experience and is delivered by that knowledge, but this passage has transformed him. Suspense, Douchet writes, thus finds its "origin and meaning in the vastness of the religious imagination," with its initiation into mysteries and journeys of self-discovery, from which the protagonist emerges forever altered (8).

Side Effects: Vindicating Male Power

Moral seriousness—such is the implication of the *Cahiers* line on Hitchcock—is the criterion by which thrillers might be judged, turning an exercise in the arousal and deflection of elemental existential fears toward an understanding of the human condition, defined as the struggle between good and evil, the drive to preserve life and virtue when faced by forces determined on their destruction. The Augustinianism (for Hitchcock, perhaps Jansenism) of this moral trajectory is proudly proclaimed by the Mac-Mahonists, Douchet included. So judged, Steven Soderbergh's *Side Effects* (2013), though well-made, suspenseful, and emotionally affecting, must be found wanting, an inferior form of the Hitchcockian wrong-man formula. Here there is no form of the "exchange" (*échange*) that links the hero to his double (or to some previous form of selfhood), a reminder of the original sin, the great leveler that is the foundation of human brotherhood. A faux transcendence of evil restores the status quo ante, as a psychiatrist, Jonathan Banks (Jude Law), involuntarily made central to a murder plot carefully calculated to create great wealth, faces professional ruin and rejection by his family because of what seems to be his bad medical advice. In part, his troubles stem from his acceptance of a substantial subvention from a drug company, whose product figures centrally in the plot, but this interest in a substantial supplement to his regular earnings responds clearly to the upscale New York City lifestyle that Banks, his wife, and stepdaughter are now living and are shown to have no intention of forsaking. As it turns out, Banks's lapse of professionalism in prescribing for his patient Emily Taylor (Rooney Mara), perhaps inappropriately, the drug he has been paid to study turns out to be a mirage as, in a stunning reversal at the narrative's center, she only faked the sleepwalking stupor in which she "accidentally" stabbed her husband Martin (Channing Tatum) to death. Banks, not Emily, is the victim, as he is instrumentalized (but not reified like Manny Balestrero) by Emily and her psychiatrist-turned-lover, Victoria Siebert (Catherine Zeta-Jones). But poor Jonathan does not lose everything, even temporarily, nor is he forced to acknowledge the false allure of material goods compared to those of the spirit. It is all just a bad dream from which he awakes untransformed.

Pelagius was the great opponent of Augustine, believing that we are all born innocent (sans Original Sin) and have only to exercise our divinely provided virtue in order to achieve salvation. Along with the other committed Catholics at *Cahiers*, Douchet might well have objected strongly to the Pelagian self-sufficiency of the protagonist in *Side Effects*, as Banks expertly takes charge of "reading" the plot correctly and then turning it around on the perpetrators,

FIGURE 16.2 Drs. Bank and Siebert (Jude Law; Catherine Zeta-Jones) are doubles, one good and the other evil, in the Hitchcock tradition, in *Side Effects* (Steven Soderbergh, Endgame/FilmNation, 2013). Digital frame enlargement.

ensuring in the end that Victoria and Emily are both punished for their perfidy, with the one off to serve a long sentence for murder and the other, because of double jeopardy, tricked into indefinite confinement in one of Manhattan's seedier mental hospitals. Banks reconstructs his practice, while the final shot captures a distraught Emily confessing to her doctor that she feels "much better" even though a faux cure for her faux psychosis will not open the doors of the ward and set her free. Banks has met the enemy and discovers, in the most un-Hitchcockian of finales, that it is not immaculate him.

17

Christian Metz

Dreaming a Language in Cinema

STEVEN RYBIN

The key works of Christian Metz (1931–1993) on film language and the psychoanalysis of the spectator—collected, in English translation, in *Film Language: A Semiotics of the Cinema* (1974) and *The Imaginary Signifier: Psychoanalysis and the Cinema* (1982)—enjoy canonical status as essential reading for students of film. And yet, for film lovers working in academia, the question of how to apply Metz's work to problems of cinema is vexing. There exist fine dialogues with Metz in recent years, of course; Kevin Fisher cites him to explore the viewer's pleasure in computer-generated special effects (179–180), and Jason Sperb quotes Metz in an essay on digital cinephilia (141–143). Yet these uses run up against Metz himself, who, in *The Imaginary Signifier*, separates the cinephile from the institutionally situated film scholar. In contrast to the enraptured cinephile, Metz's scholar puts himself "into a regime of maximal wakefulness, a work regime" (138)—a distinction between passive and active ways of viewing that Stephen Heath, in a 1973 article on Metz in *Screen*, would define as the difference between reading film in an "immediate" way, on one hand, and an "analytical" way, on the other (7).

Film and Desire

Metz thus remains for many a sign of a position that developed at one moment in the history of film theory that is now to be discarded, a "cold," rational-scientific discourse that erects false binaries between film spectators and film theorists. For many, this is a discourse that is no longer relevant, given the exciting ways cinephile-theorists in the last decade have integrated their passion for film with the "work regime" of the traditional scholar (see, for example, Ray; Richards). However, in this chapter, before weaving together some of Metz's concepts with some thoughts on two particular films, F. W. Murnau's

Sunrise: A Song of Two Humans (1927) and Martin Scorsese's *Hugo* (2011), I want to suggest that Metz indeed offers a framework for writing about the pleasures movies offer us and, perhaps surprisingly, a model for a rigorous theoretical prose that occasionally glimmers with signs of the writer's desire for film.

In his study of cinephilia, Christian Keathley cites a passage in *The Imaginary Signifier*, "Loving the Cinema," as emblematic of the historical turn away from film pleasure in 1970s academic work (27–28). Metz writes:

> To be a theoretician of the cinema, one should ideally no longer love the cinema and yet still love it: have loved it a lot and only have detached oneself from it by taking it up again from the other end, taking it as the target for the very same scopic drive which had made one love it. Have broken with it, as certain relationships are broken, not in order to move on to something else, but in order to return to it at the next bend in the spiral. Carry the institution inside one still so that it is in a place accessible to self-analysis, but carry it there as a distinct instance which does not over-infiltrate the rest of the ego with the thousand paralyzing bounds of a tender unconditionality. Not have forgotten what the cinephile one used to be was like, in all the details of his affective inflections, in the three dimensions of his living being, and yet no longer be invaded by him: not have lost sight of him, but be keeping an eye on him. Finally, be him and not be him, since all in all these are the two conditions on which one can speak of him. (15; translation by Ben Brewster)

In these words Keathley observes a dialectical ambivalence between "cinephilia and anti-cinephilia" rather than an outright repudiation of love for film (28). The writing that came in the wake of Metz was mostly of the anti-cinephilic variety, however, the kind of work unwilling to admit that the film lover might be wakefully engaged and active while watching movies. But when cinephilia returned, as a discourse, to the academy in the mid-'90s (see Willemen), the viewer's delight in moments of film pleasure was recuperated. George Toles articulates the fate of a thinker like Metz in an academic climate more amenable to cinephilia: "The critical language that Metz and others devised to protect us from pleasure, beauty, and the power of the senses was suitably dry, abstract, and cold—eerily remote from the slip and slide of sensation, and the emotional texture of aesthetic detail" (160).

It is true that the Metz (in translation) in *Film Language* and *The Imaginary Signifier* tends to mask signs of desire in a text that aims for rigor and general applicability. He writes *about* film (and *about* cinephilia); but mostly he does not write under the spell of it. Nevertheless, the effort of some writers (Toles, but also Metz himself, and other academic cinephiles; see Ray, especially 66–70, and Sperb 143) to draw a firm distinction between cinephilic (passionate, writerly, explorative) and noncinephilic ways of writing (cold, rigorous, scientific) is threatened by the sheer contingency of the *reading* of theory, an experience wherein certain passages of "rigor" can delightfully give way to the reader's discovery of more writerly passages buried within them. There are moments in Metz's oeuvre (mostly in *Film Language*) in which a turn of phrase, couched in what is otherwise an ostensibly dry theoretical text, strikes, perhaps even moves, the reader. I, for one, am continually affected by a passage that appears late in *Film Language*, in an essay entitled "The Modern Cinema and Narrativity." There, Metz is attempting to account for the international art cinema, and the sense that this cinema is different from classical narrative form. He cites as an emblematic example of the modern cinema the "almost-danced" scene amid the pines of a forest in Jean-Luc Godard's *Pierrot le fou* (1965), featuring a singing Anna Karina ("My life line . . . your hip line . . .") twirling about Jean-Paul Belmondo, and writes the following:

> No other film passage, however—unless perhaps, to a lesser extent, the silent seduction scene during the parade in Stroheim's *Wedding March*—had portrayed with an accuracy as fundamentally direct, as superbly careless of the external probabilities of time and place, the mute corporeal agreements that love produces and by which it is produced, the ambience of gestures and smiles, the thousand minor acceptances of a docile receptiveness that is no mere obedience and that mold the woman's sunny face in the succeeding directions her lover's ballet of active, amused, and moving tenderness describes around it, impelling it. (197–198; translated by Michael Taylor)

One can perhaps imagine better, or more detailed, ways to describe this scene—other modes of writing that would glean more vividly the sort of "pleasure, beauty, and power" (to quote Toles again) of this moment from *Pierrot le fou*. Yet the very compression of Metz's affective experience of *Pierrot le fou* into economic phrases—"the mute corporeal agreements that love produces"; "the ambience of gestures and smiles"—creates an evocative chain of words that might inspire his reader to return to the film with the surrounding concepts of his theoretical corpus in mind. Tantalizing phrases here—like "ambience of gestures and smiles"—might be unpacked into a more detailed, more satisfyingly descriptive criticism; how do the beaming smiles and enticing gestures of Karina and Belmondo find their way into, perhaps even inflect or constitute, the ambience of Godard's film? Metz does not push his observations on this particular film very far; he is frying larger fish. Nevertheless, the effort of a theorist to economically and creatively describe this scene within an essay which is otherwise concerned with the larger theoretical question of "what modern cinema is" should not go unnoted, for the theoretical question Metz is attempting to answer is only interesting, as his writing suggests, because there are particular film moments such as the previous one which provoke, or inform, larger-level conceptual thinking.

If Metz's own work provides evidence that the attempt to strictly separate the scholar and the cinephile, on the levels of institutional position or even finally of writing, is less than persuasive, the theoretical concepts he develops offer further indication of a shared experience between the two positions. In *The Imaginary Signifier*, Metz discusses, at length, the parallels between watching films and daydreaming; in both, he suggests, the "unconscious manifestations of phantasy . . . [cross] the thresholds of consciousness and thus [become] accessible," in an active and conscious way, to the subject (131). In watching a film, Metz goes on, we have the opportunity to see whether our private daydreams might find connection with the daydreams of the filmmaker:

> [A film's] profound conformity to one's own phantasy is never guaranteed, but when chance permits this to a sufficient degree, the satisfaction—the feeling of a little miracle, as in the state of shared amorous passion—derives from a sort of *effect*, rare by nature, which can be defined as the temporary rupture of a quite ordinary solitude. This is the specific joy of receiving from the external world images that are usually internal . . . of seeing them inscribed in a physical location (the screen), of discovering in this way something almost realizable in them, which was not expected, of feeling for a moment that they are perhaps not inseparable from the tonality which most often attends them, from that common and accepted yet slightly despairing impression of the impossible. (136; translated by Alfred Guzzetti)

For Metz, cinema, or at least particular films, can manifest, in both physical (the screen) and social ("the temporary rupture of a quite ordinary solitude") terms, images, and thoughts we usually keep private, hidden away.

Cinema brings us close to our dreams not only in those films explicitly about dreams and dreaming, but also through its very operation as a medium, one which involves a curious tension between wakefulness and dream. For Metz, the "primary identification" the viewer establishes through the film camera (rather than one's "secondary identification" with characters), may be the stuff of dream as we watch a film, but it becomes the stuff of analytical reflection once we awaken. As Richard Rushton writes in an essay on Metz, "At the cinema we perceive and understand, as it were, in a manner that is like that of a camera; we both introject and project, passively receive and actively impose forms on what we see and hear" ("Christian Metz" 273). If our private dreams find social communion in cinema, these dreams "at the cinema" become manifest through the twin poles of character identification and camera identification—and for Metz, our tendency to identify with the camera, and its position of visual mastery in the dream world of the film, is most fundamental to film's operations as a medium. But always in Metz there is the ability, in turn, to "actively impose forms"—to think about the dream, to organize it, to reflect upon it.

For Metz, then, the ability to actively reflect upon what one has dreamt, alongside the camera, is fundamental to the viewer's operations as a social being; already the distinction between the dreaming cinephile and the responsible scholar is breaking down. The dream of film is itself, for Metz, the necessary precondition for the tough theoretical work of carving out film concepts. But if Metz's concepts of primary and secondary identification make an important distinction between our secondary connection to characters and our more transcendent view through the camera, what is produced, existentially and socially, through this complex immersion in and reflection upon two forms of identification becomes an important question.

Crucial here is Metz's emphasis, in his later work, on the film viewer's social and linguistic production. In *The Imaginary Signifier*, Metz defines the signifiers of cinema as "imaginary" in part because they do not exist in any grammar or syntax of film that exists prior to specific film instances; they exist only in the semi-conscious relationship between viewer (half active, half dreaming) and film screen. There is no language of film that exists before particular instances of film (unlike in literature, where codes do exist, in the form of grammar and syntax); rather, a viewer's thoughtful and active sense that there is a signifier in cinema emerges from particular films, and, from there, extends to the desire to account for those signifiers in critical prose and theoretical argument. Metz says film possesses nothing like morphemes or words *prior* to the act of speech itself; because cinema lacks the filmic equivalents of phonemes, morphemes, and words, film can never be reduced to a language system prior to or beyond the experience of existing films (62–63). Metz admits that a paradigmatic body of conventions and iconographies does exist (the black and white hats of villain and cowboy in the western, for example), images that viewers can readily "read." Yet these conventions are not evidence that there exist minimum units of communication in film as in a spoken language. The shot remains the smallest unit of cinema (rather than the iconographies within it); the sequence within which the shot appears drives the viewer toward meaning above and beyond the particular iconographic properties *within* the shots themselves. Metz thus argues that in cinema, the *syntagmatic* chain—the pull of the viewer along arranged lines of images across the continuous, linear experience of a film—is often much stronger than the *paradigmatic* content that occasionally appears in those images, such as the cowboy hat in a western. What fascinates in cinema is thus "the richness, exuberance even, of the syntagmatic arrangements possible in film" (*Film Language* 67) and the ways these arrangements can become inflected by especially imaginative filmmakers.

When syntagms, or ways of arranging the linear flow of images, repeat often enough, they become something like codes, or established methods of arranging images. Yet even these codes never "settle" into a finalized lexicon; crucially, they are only ongoingly recognized as a "language" as long as there are viewers—writers, thinkers, theorists, film lovers—alive to them, and filmmakers who continue to reimagine them. That is, in cinema, the act of "speech" (the filmmaker's film) and the "syntax" that results from it (a product of the perception of the particular arrangement of images) cannot exist apart from the viewer's active engagement with a given film. We can say, following Metz, that it is the viewer's immediate connection to the screen which to a great extent *produces* whatever we might call film language and an understanding of its codes, and which accounts for the way in which films from earlier epochs of cinema can continue to remain vital to and relevant for us. For Metz, syntagms in film form "that current of induction that refuses not to flow whenever two poles are brought sufficiently close together, and occasionally even when they are quite far apart. . . . It is not because the cinema is language that it can tell such fine stories, but rather it has become language because it has told such fine stories" (*Film Language* 47). Whenever a fine story is viewed, the syntagm comes alive again.

For Metz, Soviet montage was one "current of induction" that fascinated and continues to fascinate viewers, who, in turn, making sense of its current, produce a language; classic Hollywood and German Expressionism are other examples. And like Metz's compacted phrase in describing *Pierrot le fou*, "the ambience of gestures of smiles," "current of induction" is one of those phrases that tantalizes the cinephilic reader, perhaps inspiring further writing for how one might write *within* rather than only *about* (as Metz tends to do) whatever current of cinematic flow one presently finds fascinating, while keeping Metz's concepts in mind. Indeed, in writing within the affects of that current—in effect, taking one's cue from Metz without quite writing just like him—the cinephilic writer can explore the way any particular film code works: how it works on viewers, yes, but also how those viewers might actively engage with the imagination of its signifiers in writing.

The Dream of Movies: *Sunrise* and *Hugo*

Now, two films that are *about* the dream of movies and that induct us, and their characters, into especially imaginative currents: F. W. Murnau's *Sunrise* and Martin Scorsese's *Hugo*. Both are enchanted with the possibilities of cinema, its various ambiences (the long take, the special effect, the rhythm of cities), and its "gestures and smiles." Both tell stories about human beings in love: dangerously in and out of love with one another, in *Sunrise*, and in love with the automatisms of cinema itself, in *Hugo*. For Murnau, the delight in cinema came through his conscious discovery of new ways to push camera and image in the creation of expressionistic film worlds. Scorsese's cinephilia, meanwhile, takes flight from a desire to preserve the cinema he loves, which in *Hugo* is dramatized through a narrative about the rediscovery and restoration of the precious films of a forgotten filmmaker. Both *Sunrise* and *Hugo* not only confirm their unique employment of preexisting codes as well as their search for new chains of imaginary signifiers, they also parallel, on the level of character experience, the viewer's own tendency to both introject and project at the cinema, to submit to a fantastical involvement with images while at the same time actively and consciously shaping a sense of the form and meaning of those images.

Sunrise tells the story of a rural Man (George O'Brien) who is tempted by the Woman from the City (Margaret Livingston) to murder his pure Wife (Janet Gaynor) so he may leave the country and join an imagined urban utopia. But he is even more lured by a dream of cinema. The Woman from the City entices the Man into her plan by shaking her hips and body sinuously, like a flapper girl; these movements then give way, on the backdrop of a rural sky which serves as something of a movie screen (see Fischer, *Sunrise* 62–65), to exciting images of a city which produces girls like her. It is a montage of city lights: busy cars, skyscrapers, crashing cymbals, all unfolding in together not unlike the sort of city symphonies directed by Dziga Vertov (*The Man with a Movie Camera*, 1927) and Walter Ruttmann (*Berlin: Symphony of a Great City*, 1927). This is a dream of cinema that enthralls the characters as much as it does us. We delight in Murnau's creation of a new visual code for the "cinematic dream" (a shot of two characters watching a dream image unfold in their mind's eye, made manifest through superimposition on the diegetic sky before them). So the Man will lure the Wife onto a boat, ostensibly for a vacation to the city, with the plan to murder her before they get there. Yet something snaps in him. He cannot bring himself to do it. The two complete their journey to the city, the site of their reconciliation in the last half of the film.

In *Hugo*, meanwhile, we find characters whose dream of cinema compels them to make social meaning. In the film, young Hugo Cabret (Asa Butterfield), an orphan who lives in the clock-tower of the Gare Montparnasse, clings to an automaton given him by his departed father (Jude Law). The father also shared with him memories of cinema, one of which involved a spaceship crashing into the eye of the moon. Hugo, in turn, shares his love and knowledge of movies with bookish friend Isabelle (Chloë Grace Moretz); she knows what a good story is, but has she ever seen a great image? It is not enough to simply tell her about movies. She must see one, and learn to dream with the camera. So Hugo takes Isabelle to a local Parisian theater. The film they sneak into is Harold Lloyd's *Safety Last!* (1923). They join this silent comedy as bespectacled Lloyd hangs breathtakingly from the side of a building. Scorsese emphasizes the impact Lloyd's movie has on young Isabelle (this is the first movie she has ever seen) by tracking in close to her face and capturing her reaction, which is one of astonishment and disbelief: she is *dreaming* with the movies, yet still wide awake. How is such magic possible? Before the two kids can know if Lloyd survives his climb up the building, however, the dream is rudely interrupted by the theater manager, who has caught them having sneaked in without paying (in a sense, Lloyd remains forever suspended above that city street in their imaginations). The impact this movie moment has made on the two kids spills out onto the rest of the narrative: shortly after seeing the Lloyd picture, they discover Hugo's automaton has been engineered to reproduce illustration of frames from Georges Méliès films. The two kids find Méliès and try to convince him to restore his films to public view—to take his dream of cinema back into the light of the social world.

Both films allegorize their own efforts to engage the viewer in their cinematic dream-making with characters who serve as diegetic spectators. The characters actively try to make their dreams manifest in some socially recognizable form (in *Sunrise*, through a renewal of the vows in the rite of marriage; in *Hugo*, the form of the cinema institution itself). As we watch Murnau's tracking camera, his use of superimposition and matte painting, and his rhythmic cutting and expressionistic lighting, and as we immerse ourselves in Scorsese's striking use of 3-D, his orchestration of color and music, and his own digitally enhanced tracking shots, we are ourselves engaged with a very special manifestation of film's primary means of imagination, and our primary means of identification with film: the camera itself, produced in each case through two historically situated codes ("Expressionism," "Digital 3-D") given freshly imagined purposes.

But we are also watching a story about characters, our points of "secondary identification" with film narratives, who are themselves transfixed by the camera (in *Sunrise*, the imaginary camera which produces the mystical images of the city that the Man and the Woman from the City see across the night sky; and in *Hugo*, the camera belonging to Harold Lloyd and, later, Georges Méliès, whose films, when projected, cause waves of delight to pass across the faces of Hugo and Isabelle). These diegetic dreams of cinema, notably, do not keep the characters in a state of passive stasis. The dreams cinema gives them impel them to move forward: in *Sunrise*, to reach the dream the city offers through, first, a murder plot, and then, the reconciliation of the couple in a (no less dreamlike) real city; and in *Hugo*, to rehabilitate the oeuvre of Méliès himself, which is discovered, restored, and exhibited to an appreciative audience in the film's happy ending. In all of these instances, *Sunrise* and *Hugo* synthesize the means of fantasy described by Metz in his work on cinema. What Metz called "the secondary identification" with characters and their goals is tightly bound up in both works with the "primary" camera.

To identify with the camera in either film is to inhabit a shared fantasy with the characters, whose desires are not wholly separate from the camera's own elegant embodiment in either film. And the forward movement, the current of induction, in both works, compels both viewer and character to take this fusion of primary and secondary identification forward into social meaning that might actively synthesize the fantasies one has experienced while viewing, with the real world to which one must return upon leaving the cinema. To be the cinephile and yet be able to distance oneself from one's imaginary immersion in cinema so as to be able to speak of those experiences, and make them valuable to others; this is part of what Metz meant in *The Imaginary Signifier* when he asked us to not forget "what the cinephile one used to be was like, in all the details of his active inflections, in the three dimensions of his living being. . . . Finally, be him and not be him, since all in all these are the two conditions on which one can speak of him" (15).

I want to end by offering two still shots from these selected films, two images as if snatched from dream. The first still, from *Sunrise*, arrives after the Man and his Wife walk through the city streets, holding one another and narrowly avoiding the trams, cars, and trolleys that spin right by them across pavement. After a dissolve to an imaginary space, they walk through a field of tall grass, flowers, and trees, with a horizon line just off in the distance, and above that, a ribbon of bright light. In the still, the couple are about to be brought out of dream by the rude interruption of those trams, cars, trolleys, and buggies that nearly crash into them—about to be brought out but not quite yet, given that the shot is still a superimposition

FIGURE 17.1 The Wife (Janet Gaynor) embraces the Man (George O'Brien) before traffic breaks them out of their dream in *Sunrise: A Song of Two Humans* (F. W. Murnau, Fox Film Corporation, 1927). Digital frame enlargement.

and thus still retains some of the dreamlike quality of their earlier stroll (they remain oblivious, clenched in an embrace). What revives this couple's renewed commitment are less the church vows they will utter and more the vitality of this larger cinematic world, the more primary means of identification Murnau is striving to create through rhythmic cutting, superimposition of image, and tracking camera. After all, the reconciliation of the couple in *Sunrise* happens not at the end but halfway through the film, and so the film emerges as ultimately being less about the spiritual reconciliation itself and more about the question of whether or not that private reconciliation, presented by Murnau as a dream of cinema, can be sustained once the couple enter the city in the film's third act. *Sunrise* is the story of Murnau's vivid cinematic energy, and of a couple that serves as a figural metaphor for the affects this brilliant new flow might have on an audience. The screen might be a city street, or a rural sky. The challenge is to sustain, in a social form, the magic one has found there.

In the still from *Hugo*, we see Méliès standing in front of a movie screen covered by a curtain, onto which are projected new restorations of his classic films. "Come and dream with me," he tells us, and the audience in the film. Putting on a top hat and bringing a cigarette to his lips, Méliès steps back and becomes part of the projection. The ensuing flow of images is a montage of cherished moments from Méliès films (in which he almost always starred), quite similar to what one would expect to find, for example, at the celebration of a lifetime achievement award. The chain of signifiers Scorsese is using here is not unfamiliar; there is a somewhat similar sequence at the end of Richard Attenborough's *Chaplin* (1992) when Charlie (Robert Downey Jr.) weeps as

FIGURE 17.2 Georges Méliès (Ben Kingsley) invites an audience to share his dream of cinema in *Hugo* (Martin Scorsese, Paramount/GK, 2011).

images from his classic films unfold on a screen behind him. But in *Hugo* Scorsese achieves something Attenborough does not: he synthesizes viewer involvement with character experience, through his creative use of 3-D and his astonishing dissolve of Kingsley into the frame of the Méliès film, turning the private dream of cinema, and the primary identification with the camera, into one which is socially shared, and paralleled with character experience. To emphasize this larger social dimension of film dream, Scorsese will cut, throughout the sequence, to shots of an appreciative diegetic audience watching the Méliès films. As we identify with Scorsese's camera and its blissful gaze at the Méliès images flowing before our eyes, we are also identifying with the characters, who view the images no less rapturously and whose psychological motivations now seem altogether subservient to the dream of cinema flowing before them. And they will wake up, and will tell about it. When the film ends on a long tracking shot which includes all of the characters we have come to know during the film, it will pause briefly on Isabelle, now writing of her experience with Hugo and Méliès, ready to share a dream with a future social world of readers.

Both *Sunrise* and *Hugo* show us dreams of cinema, offering us visions that correspond, if not to every viewer's deepest private fantasy, then at least to our shared love of film. They also induct us into a flow—of narrative, and of image—that takes that dream and, through our demand that we imagine a language and a form to describe it, pushes it into our social world, the only place where dreams can be shared.

18

V. F. Perkins

Aesthetic Suspense

ALEX CLAYTON

The sad intellectual sidelining of the work of V. F. Perkins (b. 1936) in film studies can be ascertained simply by observing the absence of his name in the index of most film textbooks. Where it appears, the reference tends to be cursory. This is unjust because Perkins is responsible for our most developed theory of film evaluation, the centerpiece of which is *Film as Film* (1972). The neglect of *Film as Film* among most film academics can perhaps be explained by the timing of its initial publication at the moment the burgeoning discipline was turning decisively away from criticism for the first but not the last time (see Clayton and Klevan 1–26). This chapter does not undertake to recapitulate the argument of *Film as Film*, since the book itself is succinct, lucid, and splendidly illustrated with examples. Instead I want to explore the pertinence and value of a single theoretical idea, named by Perkins just once: "aesthetic suspense" ("*Johnny Guitar*" 226). It is hardly surprising, in one sense, that the term has not been taken up—it is tucked away in the midst of a piece of criticism appraising a 1954 western, Nicholas Ray's *Johnny Guitar.* Perkins is reflecting on Victor Young's musical score. He notes how

> it regularly goes to the limit of seemingly naïve pictorialism by duplicating the image or mickey-mousing its movement. Characters struggle uphill to a background of effortfully stepped rising chords. Falls to earth are marked with tumbling or crashing descents into the bass. Qualities of movement are closely described and thus boldly displayed by an accompaniment that exerts itself to turn action into choreography. . . . [It] can seem to be counting off the shot changes, as if on the fingers of one hand, with jabbing chimes to greet the arrival of each new image. . . . In a literal spirit, too, it takes upon itself to echo processes of thought with stinging shifts in the musical line to signal each fresh realization: there

> is a lovely one when a floored and cornered Vienna spots a possibly handy gun lying nearby. (225)

What could sound like a catalogue of complaints about the score's apparent lack of subtlety or finesse ("effortfully," "exerts," "jabbing," "naïve"—checked only by "seemingly") turns out to be a listing of qualities that show the score as "masterly in its comprehension of and contribution to the film's peculiar idiom," with its "precisely graded exaggeration of effects" and "unusual overtness of construction" ("*Johnny Guitar*" 225). Perkins continues: "The hyperbolic quality of Young's score is appreciated even as it contributes to the urgency of conflict and the vividness of emotional depiction. Intensification is calculated to arrive at, but not to pass, the edge of absurdity. The daring in this process constructs an aesthetic suspense that defines the film's special thrill" (226).

Perkins's writing prepares us for the term "aesthetic suspense," and relieves itself of the need for definition, by repeatedly incorporating a "nearly-but-not-quite" sense and syntax—as in "calculated to arrive at, but not to pass the edge of absurdity" (226), "an ironic attitude informs but does not undermine the construction of effects" (225) and "[the] inspiration [of comic-book composition] inflects but does not contradict the film's quest for eloquence and beauty" (226). We have already been told that leading lady Joan Crawford's "intensity [as Vienna] was always at the edge of the grotesque and needed only an element of play to become parodic," implying both the proximity of easy options that would prove hazardous to conviction, and their skillful avoidance. Later in the essay, Perkins identifies the intriguing decision to have Robert Osterloh sidle up to the camera to deliver a line down the barrel as another way the film narrowly skirts a comic-absurdist register. His apparent address to camera threatens to "compromise the integrity of the fictional world" (226) until the subsequent shot saves the day by retrospectively situating the viewpoint as Tom's (John Carradine) eye line. Perkins finds the film repeatedly courting incredulity with "brazen moments [that] are not safely hived off into special sectors of the film." Such moments punctuate without quite puncturing the film's drama and invitation to emotional investment.

Perkins's emphasis on aesthetic risk taking here can be understood as a revision or development of themes in *Film as Film*, published several decades earlier. There is a distinction to be made between "early" and "late" Perkins as a theorist of movie achievement. In his earlier work, *Film as Film*, Perkins was inclined to emphasize more secure and proportionate forms of balance, such as he finds between credibility and significance in the films of Otto Preminger, for example. Interestingly, such a quality is also found exemplified by *Johnny Guitar*:

> Our first sight of Emma was when she rode on an earlier errand of persecution. She arrived outside the heroine's saloon during a dust storm, the wind driving behind her so that she had to clutch on to her hat.

> As she reined in her horse she seemed in danger of being carried away on the storm. The organization here impressed us with the feeling, confirmed and developed by her later actions, that Emma had almost lost control over the pressures that drove her.
>
> The impression of dangerous instability was developed from the action by the image. Emma's arrival was observed by the heroine and by us, from an upstairs window. The solid stillness of its frame set off the turbulence and insecurity of her movements: Emma's difficulty in holding her ground was emphasized for us by the fact that if she failed to do so she would disappear from sight. (*Film as Film* 78)

Perkins calls this shot "a beautiful example of the balance between action and image that skill can achieve," praising the way "a single image is made to act both as a recording, to show us what happens, and as an expressive device to heighten the effect and significance of what we see" (78). The contrast between stillness and turbulence emerges organically from the choice to shoot through the window, which itself is, as Perkins notes, "contrived to seem natural, almost unavoidable" (79) since it follows Vienna's interest in the commotion outside. Even the fact that Emma's arrival coincides with the dust storm seems not contrived to imply her psychological instability but to issue from her haste to accuse Vienna (which no mere dust storm is going to delay). Indeed, *Johnny Guitar* is identified in *Film as Film* as one of a handful of great movies whose elements "do not operate solely to maintain or further the reality of the fictional world, nor solely to decorative, affective or rhetorical effect" (131). There is an inherent tension between these functions, Perkins notes, and "at any point short of collapse, the tension is a source of strength and energy" (124). Yet for the Perkins of *Film as Film*, "the hallmark of a great movie is not that it is without strains but that it absorbs its tensions; they escape notice until we project ourselves into the position of the artist and think through the problems which he confronted in his search for order and meaning" (131). What the later Perkins alerts us to is the "special thrill" of a movie like *Johnny Guitar* that goes right to that point "short of collapse," where a relationship between elements is more acutely felt as delicate because it is on the verge of upset.

This later apprehension may clarify Perkins's choice of directors to service his claims in *Film as Film*. Nicholas Ray and Alfred Hitchcock would seem curious examples for a theory of value that is apparently inclined toward films where labors of realization "escape notice" (*Film as Film* 131). Hitchcock particularly would seem to contradict an ideal of authorial self-effacement. Few filmmakers are as stylistically emphatic. Recognizing this, Perkins defends what he calls the "Hitchcock tendency"—the tendency to assert significance and call attention to directorial control—by recourse again to balance: "the correlation of emphasis assigned with importance perceived" (130). Perkins's example is from *Rope* (1948). The camera is made to hold on the housekeeper (Edith Evanson) as she clears the surface of a corpse-filled chest and prepares to open it. The selection of viewpoint markedly, and somewhat perversely, denies us a view of the murderers. Perkins claims the dramatic suspense is "heightened by the frustration of our desire to know whether either of the heroes is in a position to observe what is happening and so intervene to prevent catastrophe" (125). Nonetheless, in this instance "the effect of the restrictive viewpoint is in no way damaged by our awareness of the director's design" because the camera's fixation on the housekeeper is consonant with the "dramatic import" of her actions. Moreover, Hitchcock's establishment of the space of the apartment prior to this moment has anyway made the selection of viewpoint seem an either/or choice: there is no position within the walls of the apartment—as we have already come to know it—from which the camera could show both the heroes *and* the housekeeper *and* the chest (126–127).

The camera's inability to see through walls is surely a convention that Hitchcock could have overturned, as many directors do without damage to fictional involvement (Perkins even implies as much [*Film as Film* 122]). Besides, it is only a rule of Hitchcock's own making, and only for this particular film, that says he must sustain the long take and so "cannot" cross-cut between the housekeeper and the murderers. Hitchcock's rejection of this option has less to do with the requirements of dramatic suspense, I would say, than the instinct to manufacture aesthetic suspense, of which he also shows himself a master. Denying us knowledge by holding the shot of the housekeeper gives Hitchcock the chance to test, and marvelously not to break, our pact of tolerance with his self-imposed rule. The notion of aesthetic suspense may better define the *audacity* of Hitchcock's technique as an integral part of its address.

Where the earlier Perkins values the aptness of particular filmmaking decisions that viewers could easily overlook (his essay "Moments of Choice" is a sparkling catalog of great calls), later Perkins finds himself drawn especially to the daring choice that declares itself. Modesty as the foremost ethic is supplanted, then, by courage, avoidance of the easy and compromising option. So Perkins will praise Jean Renoir for his "refusal of continuity editing [which] puts on screen, and makes us feel, the difficulty of the choice between simultaneous and competing lines of action" (*Règle* 92). Similarly, Orson Welles is admired for his "refusal of the easy rhetoric of emotional and psychological exposure that analytical editing makes available" (*Magnificent Ambersons* 59). The fact of choice is so discernible in Welles's *The Magnificent Ambersons* (1942) that the film can even "joke with us about its own selections" (41). Whereas early Perkins can find the pronounced *choice* an intrusion, a potential threat to immersion in a film's dramatic happenings, later Perkins finds the viewer's perception of choice a vital part of the texture of movie involvement. In his book on Renoir's *La Règle du jeu* (1939), he describes film as "a medium that insists on choice frame by frame. . . . The camera demands placement; each image declares its angle of vision. The availability of the cut means that the decisive moment occurs once every fraction of a second" (94). Parallel to, and crucially without damage to, our involvement in the film's drama, we follow the stream of perceivable choices embodied in its presentation onscreen; we judge these choices in terms of what they offer, what they refuse, what they claim, and what they betray, and urge the rare film that strikes an electrifying balance to sustain it a little further, not to blow it. This is the vision of the spectator invoked by the concept of aesthetic suspense.

Johnny Guitar

A prime instance of aesthetic suspense may be found in *Johnny Guitar*'s second half, when Emma and her mob have returned to Vienna's saloon to accuse her of harboring the Dancing Kid and arrest her for complicity in his crimes. Vienna's blocking tactic on this occasion is to construct a performance of "minding my own business" that involves her playing a meditative nocturne at the stage piano. Small search parties rove around the saloon while the main pack, headed by Emma, confront Vienna in the main hall. Perkins observes how "her [piano] playing develops through the interrogation as an emotional commentary. Its hesitations and resumptions, its changes of key and dynamic, inflect what is said and articulate what is unspoken" (226). These qualities form part of the rhetoric of Vienna's performance of calm control designed to deflect and embarrass the intruders by contrast, showing up their intervention as rash and undignified. But for a brief passage after she has declared the saloon closed, there is also a conspicuous rhythmic coordination between certain phrases in the music she is playing and the appearance of successive search parties as they return empty-handed to the saloon's landing. The match between music and action here goes beyond commentary and seems more like synchronization, as if the men are now working to Vienna's rhythm, having failed to impose their own. The feel of choreography is greater still in the next moment, when Emma and her posse advance toward Vienna's position. To trivialize the situation at this dramatic point would be to undercut one of the film's climactic confrontations, yet the arrangement starts to tip the film dangerously in the direction of dance musical. Emma is flanked to either side by identically dressed men so that she constitutes the tip of a V-formation. When she advances toward Vienna, her several dozen minions move with her as a single body. The high-level camera tilts down to accommodate their progression so that they fill the frame, growing and spreading like a fungus. More returning search parties filter down into the mob's body and hit marks to assume their positions in the advancing triangle.

What stops this short of becoming simply laughable? Aesthetic suspense results from the perception that we are only a whisker away from risibility.

FIGURE 18.1 Emma (Mercedes McCambridge) and her mob advance on Vienna in *Johnny Guitar* (Nicholas Ray, Republic, 1954). Digital frame enlargement.

All it would take, perhaps, would be for the dialogue to cease, or for the footsteps to synchronize, or the composition to become too symmetrical, and the intensity would collapse. Our acceptance is sustained, I think, because the film has carefully won our assent to several key facts: the members that make up the posse obediently follow Emma's lead; they stand around in configurations that reflect the group hierarchy; they are all dressed in matching black suits (having come directly from a funeral); and (as the film's eponymous hero [Sterling Hayden] has put it) "a posse is an animal—it moves like one and thinks like one." The film can now cash in on this gradual acceptance of individually credible facts which only *now* in combination and degree border on the ludicrous.

Elephant

A very different kind of aesthetic suspense can be encountered in Gus van Sant's *Elephant* (2003). The film is built around a series of lengthy Steadicam shots that follow various pupils through corridors, cafeteria, and classrooms in the lead-up to a high school shooting (in invocation of the Columbine High School massacre). In the absence of any extended interaction between these pupils, the use of traveling shots conspicuously links them, suggesting a common structure of feeling across the diversity of student types. This extends across victims and perpetrators of the massacre, the device being used to present both the ordinary journeys of pupils around the school premises and the armed stalking of the killers. The film's challenge is to capture this common feeling without the definition that would make it diagnostic. The sensitivity of the subject matter naturally charges stylistic decisions with moral significance, but this is not exactly the root of *Elephant*'s aesthetic suspense. It derives rather from the way the film undertakes to walk the line between aestheticism and naturalism, mystification and cliché, subjective alignment and autonomy of viewpoint. Aesthetic suspense occasions in those passages where the tension between these facets is held in precarious balance.

One such sequence, five or so minutes in duration but comprised of only two extended takes, starts with an unfussy eye-level view of the sports field, where a group of teenage boys are practicing football plays. The camera is oddly unresponsive to their movements—for instance, there is a long throw but the camera does not budge to take in the trajectory and catch, which happens just out of frame. The perception that this camera is handheld—slight wobbles, not fixed—makes the act of choosing not to follow the action more conspicuous than it would have been if the camera were mounted on a tripod. Even more pronounced is the accompaniment of nondiegetic piano music whose triplet figurations in minor key we are likely to recognize as constituting the opening movement of Beethoven's Moonlight Sonata. The use of music forces a tone of meditative melancholy to an energetic but otherwise mundane scene of team sports activity. The assertion of mood is held in check from swamping the image only by the even-handed sound mix. The quiet music is made to blend with, not to overwhelm, the distant ambient sounds of the sports field. Just at the point it seems the image can support it no longer, a female pupil appears in foreground and pauses for an instant to gaze up at the sky. Her gangly appearance, with glasses and oversized sweatshirt, and above all her whimsical gesture—underlined by the use of slow-motion, which picks out a exhalation of breath—briefly harmonizes with the Romantic perspective embodied by camera and music: dreamy, delicate, disengaged from surrounding activity. A moment earlier the relation between sound and image seemed almost too insistent in its mismatch; now the risk is of an alignment too cozy, clichéd even, where the camera's curious outlook could be simply explained away as an effort to convey the daydreaming perspective of the sensitive loner who has more interest in clouds than sports. This would be confirmed, and the interest would dissolve, if only we were now to cut to a reverse shot of the sky. Yet the film's viewpoint retains its autonomy from that of any single figure. The girl leaves the shot, and we continue to hold on the irregular, uneventful image of the sports field.

Eventually another figure, one of the football players, appears individuated in shot. We watch him put on a red sweatshirt and, having remained still for the better part of two minutes, the camera now turns and floats to follow this young man as he walks away from the field. A Steadicam shot follows him for the entirety of his journey over to the main school building, and then, after a cut to the school's interior, in real time and closer proximity through the maze-like corridors of the precinct and eventually to the school reception area, where he greets his girlfriend. The persistence of this traveling shot creates a hypnotic effect that vividly evokes the feeling of being in a bubble, alone in one's own head, cut off from the world. This is heightened further by the soundtrack, where familiar school noises are rendered strange and distant through a reverberation filter, presenting unsettling disharmonies with the clean, soft notes of the Moonlight Sonata—which by contrast now seems to express the pupil's inner life as we study the back of his head in vain. What is he thinking? What is he feeling? Such a strident effect would be serious overkill if the figure we were following was obviously troubled and friendless. Yet of all the high school types invoked by *Elephant*, the chosen type—the attractive, popular "jock"—would seem least amenable to this characterization. As he departs from the sports field, for instance, he gives one of his buddies a playful slap on the back. Later in the sequence, he passes some pupils break-dancing and is interested enough to glance over to their activity. Greeting the girlfriend at the end of the

FIGURE 18.2 The camera follows Nathan (Nathan Tyson) on his journey from sports field to school precinct in *Elephant* (Gus Van Sant, HBO/Fine Line, 2003). Digital frame enlargement.

sequence he shows no sign of disillusion. What we can see and surmise about this figure, who seems for all the world popular and engaged in his surroundings, is put in provocative tension with the insinuation of existential loneliness.

The significance of this implication would be less profound if it came at the expense of the other half of the film's project, to give a lucid sense of a real school environment. What balances out the ultra-formalism of the film's style is the meticulous attention to detail in the costume, casting, performance, and blocking of bit players. We are almost never given to suspect that these are extras waiting around for the Steadicam to arrive so they can perform their moment of business. The vivid impression of a lived world provides ballast, just enough, for stylistic gestures that in other films might seem pretentious. Maybe they still seem so for the viewer—that is a matter of judgment. Better that than the denial of judgment, or the relativistic belief that any one choice is as good as another, that appears to underpin the skeptical attitude toward evaluation which prevails in academic film studies. The notion of aesthetic suspense that I have tried to sketch out here describes a form of pleasure unavailable to those who are unwilling to judge, viewers for whom, effectively, anything goes. For, as V. F. Perkins has taught us to see, creative risk can be admired and enjoyed as risky only by a viewer attuned to the balance between competing elements and the ever-present possibility of a misstep.

19

Jacques Rancière

Equality and Aesthetics

GILBERTO PEREZ

Jacques Rancière's (b. 1940) recent *Aisthesis* carries jacket blurbs from two noted contemporary artists. "Rancière shows a way out of the malaise," says Liam Gillick, and he means the malaise of postmodernism. "It's clear that Jacques Rancière is relighting the flame that was extinguished for many," says Thomas Hirschhorn, and he means the flame of aesthetic sensibility, the animating flame of art. To a postmodern way of thinking, aesthetic experience is mere illusion, seductive deception in line with the ruling ideology, so that the task prescribed for art is a critique of aesthetic illusion and social and political ideology. Rancière criticizes the critics, however, and freshly reconsiders aesthetics, putting renewed emphasis on its eye-opening capacity, its liberating potential.

Avant-garde art characteristically takes issue with received aesthetics. But the futurist contention that a roaring car is more beautiful than the Victory of Samothrace, the surrealist call for convulsive beauty or none at all, proposed a new aesthetic to replace the old. Postmodernism—which is not so much an art movement as an academic initiative, not so much an approach to artistic practice as a theory of what's wrong with art—would do away with aesthetics *tout court*. No wonder artists have welcomed Rancière's renewed case for the defense.

Aisthesis is the Greek word for sense perception, and aesthetics began in the eighteenth century as the philosophy of art, of beauty, and more broadly of sensory experience. It has had its vicissitudes in the past half century. Theodor Adorno's aesthetics renounced pleasure, but then Roland Barthes reaffirmed the pleasure of the text. In 1971 the art historian Otto Karl Werckmeister published a book called *Ende der Ästhetik*—End of Aesthetics—but the following year the literary scholar and reception theorist Hans Robert Jauss answered with *Kleine Apologie der ästhetischen Erfahrung*—Little Apology for Aesthetic Experience. In

1983 a young art historian, Hal Foster, made a splash in the academy with a book he edited, *The Anti-Aesthetic: Essays on Postmodern Culture*; but a decade later the art critic Dave Hickey made a counter splash with *The Invisible Dragon: Four Essays on Beauty*, whose egalitarian and subversive claims for aesthetics ("the vernacular of beauty, in its democratic appeal, remains a potent instrument for change" [17]) anticipated Rancière's similar claims. The sociologist Pierre Bourdieu studied taste as a function of social class and challenged Immanuel Kant's conception of disinterested aesthetic judgment; but Rancière defends aesthetic disinterestedness because he feels it offers us imaginative freedom, and he objects to class taste because he fears it keeps us stuck in our place in the established order.

Plato's Republic is for Rancière the prime example of what he calls the *ethical* arrangement of social relations. *Ethos*, the Greek word for character, originally meant abode, he tells us, the place where one lives and the way one lives there, so he uses the term *ethical* to designate the kind of social order that assigns to everyone a set place in life and a set way of life—the mind sovereign at the top and the working hands at the bottom, in the Platonic scheme. By sleight of etymology Rancière equates the ethical with the hierarchical. Politics he construes as the endeavor to unsettle hierarchy and foster equality. Running a city or nation according to ethical law and order is for him not politics but the police: politics is allied not with power but with freedom, not with ethics but with aesthetics. For him, Bourdieu's class-bound taste is the police, and the aesthetic experience of alternative possibilities is politics. Plato banned not only poets from the Republic but also politics, as Rancière observes: an early indication of the close link he sees between aesthetics and politics. He makes clear he doesn't mean the mass rallies and spectacles of power that Walter Benjamin had in mind when he said that fascism aestheticizes politics. What, then, does Rancière mean?

Rancière has a vocabulary of his own, and in each of his books, which are many and mostly short, he goes over his terms at some length. He has often explicated the special way in which he uses terms like aesthetics, ethics, or politics, and the meaning of such coinages as *dissensus* (a counter to consensus) or *le partage du sensible*. "The distribution of the sensible" is the usual translation of this last, which in *Disagreement*, Rancière's most incisive (and best translated) treatment of politics, is rendered as "the partition of the perceptible" (24–27 and passim). "Sensible" doesn't carry in English a sort of pun Rancière wants: he means the partition, among people in different social places and occupations, of things perceptible to the senses and invested with sense. *Le partage du sensible* is the social order as manifested in sensory experience, the aesthetic dimension of the social order, and in *Disagreement* Rancière puts it in apposition with *aisthesis*. He seems to regard it, however, as not just an aspect but the crux of politics: "Politics consists in reconfiguring the distribution of the sensible," he writes in *Aesthetics and Its Discontents*, as if politics were mainly a matter of the view you get out your window (25). The close connection Rancière sees between politics and aesthetics may be seen as a matter of terminology, of the special way he defines politics and aesthetics.

"Politics," as he defines it, "is that activity which turns on equality as its principle" (*Disagreement* ix). Politics disputes police order but ceases being politics if it seeks to establish order of any kind: "Equality turns into the opposite the moment it aspires to a place in the social or state organization" (34). For him there is no order but police order. Politics as he construes it is an activity of disorder, and this is key to its alliance with aesthetics as he construes it: "Aesthetics is the thought of the new disorder" (*Discontents* 13). For most of us, I daresay, politics can work on the side of either hierarchy or equality, and aesthetics can serve to endorse or to dispute an established order. Beauty is rhetoric, as Dave Hickey says, a means of persuasion that can be put to different ends. I think Benjamin was wrong to single out fascism for aestheticizing politics: every politics in one way or another enlists aesthetics for its purposes. Aesthetics belongs in politics, as Rancière argues, and only a prejudice against the senses would argue otherwise. But the marriage he makes is between his kind of politics and his kind of aesthetics, other kinds being ruled out by definition.

While drawing a sharp distinction between politics and the powers that be that he calls the police, he recognizes that politics requires some sort of transaction with the police: "For politics to occur, there must be a meeting point between police logic and egalitarian logic" (*Disagreement* 34). Such a meeting "is never set up in advance," he says: "anything may become political if it gives rise to a meeting of these two logics. . . . Equality is not a given that politics then presses into service . . . or a goal politics sets itself the task of attaining. It is a mere assumption that needs to be discerned within the practices implementing it" (32–33). This sounds like we have to play it by ear. Let me propose something more precise, the American frontier as a meeting point between the two opposing logics, the frontier as understood by the historian Frederick Jackson Turner and as represented in John Ford's westerns. In *Stagecoach* (1939), the Law and Order League that has the prostitute Dallas and the alcoholic Doc Boone thrown out of town can be taken as the police in Rancière's sense, the police coming to the frontier from the East with advancing civilization and its strictures and hierarchies. Turner, and Ford after him, saw the frontier as "the meeting point between savagery and civilization" (Turner 3), the scene of a transaction between civilized order and the loosening, leveling wilderness, a continual new beginning for American society with a continually renewed tendency toward liberty and equality.

The "meeting point between savagery and civilization" may raise eyebrows—the Native Americans had their own civilization, and the European settlers inflicted plenty of savagery—but Turner's frontier thesis puts the stress on freedom rather than conquest ("The most significant thing about the American frontier is, that it lies at the hither edge of free land" [3]), on indigenously democratic rather than manifestly destined America. And in any case Turner's thesis doesn't rest on what you deem savagery and what you consider civilization: it is enough for his argument that the encounter with so-called savagery disturb the order of so-called civilization—just what politics in Rancière's account does to the order of the police—and open it to the prospect of greater liberty and equality.

Stagecoach

Stagecoach was Ford's first western in sound—he made many silent ones but none through a decade that saw westerns mostly relegated to grade-B pictures—and it is at once distinctively the director's work and a dyed-in-the-wool genre film. It enacts both the Indian attack and the gunfight showdown, the two climactic scenes most typical of the western—though by setting them back to back, resolving one thing only to move on to another, it holds off narrative closure and conveys a sense of beginning again on the frontier. Its characters are generic types, the tough sheriff, the shady gambler, the drunken doctor, the gallant outlaw, the good-hearted saloon girl—but generic with a difference, a suggestion or at least a hint that social roles and positions aren't fixed on the open frontier.

The western is a political genre—it is about the building of towns, the formation of social order, the founding of a nation—and in *Stagecoach*, as for Rancière, the central political issue is equality. The two main characters are the saloon girl and the outlaw, Dallas and Ringo, the lowest in the social hierarchy and the highest in our esteem. Ringo isn't the typical rugged individualist roaming the wilderness but has ties to frontier society and wishes to regain a place in it. And Dallas departs even more from type. The typical whore with a heart of gold endears herself to us but usually dies to spare us the embarrassment of her irredeemability. This saloon girl doesn't die in the hero's arms after taking a bullet meant for him: she rides off by his side at the end, a fellow pioneer of better things, a fallen woman not merely good but as good as anyone. Nor should Dallas and Ringo be seen as "natural aristocrats": even if they are the best people in the film, the best hope for the future, they are still very much of the common people. David O. Selznick wouldn't take on *Stagecoach* as producer because he saw it as "just another western" with no big stars, and he would have wanted Marlene Dietrich and Gary Cooper in the leads. But Ford insisted on Claire Trevor and John Wayne (who wasn't a star until this movie made him one). Dietrich and Cooper would have turned Dallas and Ringo into the natural aristocrats that Ford didn't want; Trevor and the young Wayne bring to their roles a plebeian nobility assuming no superiority. And sharing the stagecoach with Dallas and Ringo are several other travelers given almost as much importance in the movie: there is social inequality but dramatic equality among the characters in this group portrait.

The aristocrat in the movie is Lucy, a southern army wife traveling out West to meet her officer husband. Recognizing a true lady the moment he sees her, the gambler, himself a southerner with an aristocratic air—gone disreputable in his case—offers Lucy his protection and rides by her side on the stagecoach. This haughty patrician couple adjoins the plebeian frontier couple of Ringo and Dallas. At a way station the travelers decide by vote—a bit of frontier democracy—whether to keep going through Apache country without an army escort. The sheriff first asks the lady, Lucy, but then Ringo reminds him of the other lady, Dallas. Before resuming their journey, which nearly all vote to continue, the passengers sit down for a meal. Lucy sits at the head of the table, as befits her social position. Ringo invites Dallas to sit beside him, bringing the saloon girl he treats as a lady too close to the recognized lady who would keep her distance. We watch this from Lucy's viewing angle, at the slant of her disapproving point of view, the camera moving in and accenting the slant, the line of her weighty censorious gaze, from which Dallas averts her eyes ashamedly.

In an article on *Stagecoach* and the position of the spectator, Nick Browne attentively focuses on this passage and accurately notes that we put ourselves in Dallas's place even though we view her from Lucy's position. Browne aims to show how a "classical" Hollywood movie like *Stagecoach* conceals the author or narrator behind the adopted point of view of a character such as Lucy. Here, however, Ford's authorial point of view unmistakably comes across in opposition to Lucy's. Let's examine the rest of this sequence.

What matters here, rather than her individual point of view, is the social hierarchy that places Lucy at the head of the table. Seeing her perturbed by Dallas's proximity, the gambler approaches her: "May I find you another place, Mrs. Mallory? It's cooler by the window." As Lucy and the gambler, followed by the banker who turns out to be a thief, move to the other end of the table, Ford holds a shot of the whole table from the point of view of the seat she has vacated at the head. At the other end she could still be at the head, but by taking the perspective of her empty place, pointedly no character's position, Ford implies that it should remain empty, that no one should be sitting there passing judgment on others. Through that vacancy the author speaks against hierarchy. Then he cuts to a frontal two-shot of Dallas and Ringo seated side by side and, we feel, freed of the slant laid on them by the view from the head of the table. And now the camera, in another authorial gesture, pulls back behind them and, at an angle, moves past them toward the patrician couple at the other end of the table, recalling and reversing the earlier slanted movement toward the plebeian couple and slyly suggesting that we can now lay the slant on Lucy and the gambler and compare them unfavorably with Dallas and Ringo. Now there is no

FIGURE 19.1 Reversing the slant: Louise Platt and John Carradine in *Stagecoach* (John Ford, Walter Wanger Productions, 1939), with Claire Trevor and John Wayne in foreground. Digital frame enlargement.

censorious gaze, though, either from the characters or from the author: Dallas and Ringo are looking at each other and so, at the other end, are Lucy and the gambler; and Ford respects both couples and appreciates the gallantry and solicitude they have in common even as he rejects the intolerance of the patricians and favors the larger-hearted plebeians as an improved, egalitarian, democratic frontier couple.

At the next way station Lucy goes into labor and gives birth to a baby. The social outcasts rise to the occasion: the doctor sobers up for the delivery, and Dallas takes care of the baby while Lucy is unwell—the saloon girl as apt mother. Some object that Dallas acts like a servant to Lucy, but that's just what a woman in her position would do. Ford gets social relations right and he asks us to recognize the saloon girl as equal to the lady, the servant as equal to the master, the whore as equal to the mother, the social distance between them notwithstanding. Though grateful to Dallas for her help, Lucy still holds back from her, and some are disappointed to find no class reconciliation, no personal acknowledgment on Lucy's part of Dallas as her equal. But again that's true to life, and it does not imply resignation to inequality. *Stagecoach* depicts a break in hierarchy, an opening toward equality on the frontier, without pretending that this could settle the matter for good. It knows that equality is difficult to secure.

Rancière hasn't, as far as I know, said much about Ford. I suspect he mistrusts Ford's social sense for the same reason he faults Bourdieu's, because he thinks that to place people socially is to keep them stuck in place. But Ford takes a dialectical view and sees social class as amenable to contradiction and open to change—while Rancière, like Michel Foucault and Jacques Derrida, wants to leave dialectics behind.

The Romantic movement, as we learned in school, broke with the classical tradition. Rancière argues that the succeeding movements we also learned about—realism, symbolism, modernism—all respond to the same principle. He's not the first to consider the romantic break with the classical the founding moment of modern art. I, for one, agree with him on that. But he proposes a great divide between an *ancien régime* of art, going all the way back to Aristotelian times, and the art of modern times: he may not be a dialectician, but he's big on binary oppositions. The classical he calls the "representative" regime of art; the romantic-cum-modern he calls the "expressive" or more often the "aesthetic" regime of art. In two words: *mimesis* versus *aisthesis.*

As an example of the representative regime he offers Pierre Corneille's version of *Oedipus Rex.* Sophocles's play had to be substantially revised for the French classical stage. It was found wanting as a detective story, the murderer being too clearly Oedipus himself, so Corneille changed the plot for the sake of mystery and suspense. To please the ladies in the audience he added a love story, he explained, and to avoid upsetting them he omitted "the eloquent and curious description of the way the unhappy prince puts out his eyes—and the spectacle of the blood from those same dead eyes dripping down his face, which occupies the whole fifth act" (Pierre Corneille qtd. in Rancière, *Unconscious* 12). For Rancière, however, Sophocles's Oedipus doesn't merely upset the ladies, doesn't merely breach the decorum of classical French theater: "What he upsets, in the end, is the order of the representative system" (17). Why not just say that Sophocles and Corneille wrote for different audiences, worked under different *conventions* of dramatic representation? Are we to suppose that Sophocles worked not under the representative but under the aesthetic regime, a romantic-cum-modern back in ancient Greece? It is evident that the "representative regime" means to Rancière the conventions and decorum of French neo-classicism.

He sees Aristotle as the founding theorist of the representative tradition, but what he traces back to Aristotle is what the neo-classicists took Aristotle to mean. Aristotle did give primacy to the plot, and did say that it should proceed according to probability or necessity, but not, as Rancière assumes, that it had to be a linear concatenation of cause and effect. Why, in Aeschylus's play, does Clytemnestra murder her husband Agamemnon on his return from Troy? Because he had their daughter Iphigenia killed as a sacrifice so that his ships could sail for Troy? Because Clytemnestra has a lover, Aegisthus, who feels entitled to her husband's throne? Because Agamemnon brought the enslaved princess Cassandra back from Troy as his concubine? All these motivate the murder: no linearity here but a multiplicity of causation. Plots are more various and can be more subtle and complex, and causality is more various and can be more subtle and complex, than the linear chain of events allows. *Stagecoach* might be called linear for the way it follows the path of the stagecoach, but it is not cause-and-effect linear: each scene (look at the one at the dinner table) stands on its own rather than leading to the next, and even the final showdown between Ringo and the bad guys is not a linear affair but one complicated by his walking Dallas home and seeing that she lives in the red-light district of town.

Rancière is right to point out how the romantic-realist-modern turn often gives the setting, the material environment, the social situation, precedence over the plot. He brings up the example of Victor Hugo's novel *Notre-Dame de Paris*, in which the cathedral isn't just the background but the true protagonist and "Hugo's sentences animate the stone, make it speak and act" (*Mute Speech* 43). In *A Grammar of Motives* Kenneth Burke set forth a dramatistic scheme with five key terms: act, scene, agent, agency, purpose (xv–xxiii). If act is plot and agent is character, scene, the place and time, would come under what Aristotle called *opsis*, spectacle, which he deemed the least of tragedy's parts. Since the time of the romantics—and not only in our art but in our sense of history and of the world we inhabit—scene, the where and when of act and agent and purpose, has gained unprecedented consequence. *Notre-Dame de Paris* is a scenic novel: it tells the story of the cathedral as the story of Paris. The western is a scenic genre, not just on account of the scenery, the landscape and the horses, the dust and the buttes and the sky, but because the background comes to the fore, the scene largely determines the sense. The scene is the frontier: the western tells the story of the frontier as the story of America.

But I speak of stories, which for Rancière belong to the old order. For him *mimesis* means the representation of actions, the supremacy of plot, and *aisthesis* comes into its own with the liberation of art from the tyranny of storytelling. He posits that, under the representative regime, stories conform to genres defined by the subject represented—tragedy for the high and mighty, comedy for the common people—and genres conform to a hierarchical system enforced by decorum, the appropriate, the fitting: an elevated style for a lofty subject, a plain style for a lowly one. Made subordinate to the subject under the representative regime, style under the aesthetic regime "becomes the very principle of art" (*Mute Speech* 51). As he sees it, the new order democratically does away with genre and with the generic hierarchy built into narrative. But isn't that paradigmatic new form, the novel, eminently a narrative form? "The novel is the genre of what has no genre," he maintains: "it has no principle of decorum" (51). No notion of suitability, of what goes together? He seems to think that in a novel anything goes. "For some forty years now literature has been dominated by the contrast between the gravity of the expression and the frivolity of the subject (a result of *Madame Bovary*)," he quotes Proust as saying (145). But if there is no decorum, no sense of the fitting, how can there be a sense of the incongruous, how can there be a contrast between the expression and the subject?

Decorum endures, even if notions of the noble and the vulgar have loosened. Modern taste may prefer Dutch paintings of ordinary life to grand battle pictures, but it sees Rembrandt's style as appropriately ennobling his humble subject. Genres endure, even if now they are more apt to be mixed. Concurrently with the novel, and frequently entering into it, another genre was born, melodrama, which flourished in the popular theater of the nineteenth century and in opera—second only to the novel among the century's art forms—and continues to flourish down to this day. Melodrama makes much of plot, so Rancière yokes it with the old order, but it is a new genre in which the sorrows traditionally represented in tragedy befall ordinary people traditionally represented in comedy. Though often held in disdain, melodrama demands to be taken seriously as a broad genre that has produced its share of estimable art. If Rancière took it seriously—which he should, since he repudiates the snobbish split between popular entertainment and high art—he might be led to revise his view of the movies as split in another way: between stories, hangovers from the old order, and images harboring the new.

Nouvelle vague

Such a split fits one filmmaker particularly well. The image, which in most movies is a vehicle for the story, is separated from the story, set at odds with it, in the work of Jean-Luc Godard. In his early films Godard did a parody, a parody without mockery, of generic stories, the gangster melodrama in *Breathless* (1960), the fallen-woman melodrama in *Vivre sa vie* (1962), the fugitive-couple melodrama in *Pierrot le fou* (1965); and he already endowed the image with a will of its own to move or cut, skip forward or linger on, interrupt or digress. A bit later he dwindled narrative down to extracted moments, fragments joined together circumstantially rather than dramatically, thus freeing the image to slight the action and look into the situation—French youth mixing politics and pop culture in *Masculin Féminin* (1966) and embracing leftist activism in *La Chinoise* (1967), a Parisian neighborhood undergoing in *2 ou 3 choses que je sais d'elle* (1967) massive modernization in line with consumer society—films you could call scenic essays. From the start Godard was loosely called an essayist rather than a storyteller, but these films of his late *nouvelle vague* period adopted a form more truly essayistic. This has more or less been his preferred form since. No exponent of the pure image, he uses plenty of words but words that give pause, mostly not the words of characters in action but words arresting action and stirring reflection. *Histoire(s) du cinéma* (1997–1998), an extended video essay on the history and the stories of film, is for Rancière Godard's way of rescuing the images of other filmmakers from the stories they served to tell under the representative regime and lending them the autonomy they enjoy under the aesthetic regime.

The rather neglected film Godard titled *Nouvelle vague* (1990) is an amazing scenic essay. The scene is a Swiss lakeside country estate, a site of both pastoral beauty and propertied privilege, and the film enacts a conflict between that beauty, which it lyrically exalts, and that privilege, which it incisively exposes. It disallows the complacency both of those who would simply enjoy beauty without looking into the conditions that make for it, and of those who would simply dismiss it as the plaything of a privileged few without recognizing its capacity to transcend and even subvert their claim to ownership.

Except for a few years during which, after 1968, he subscribed to the equation of the anti-aesthetic with the political, Godard has always been devoted to beauty. In his early films Anna Karina personified it, and the available light of the *nouvelle vague*—the actual light of an actual place, uncorrected by concealed lamps and reflectors normally used to light a scene for the camera—gave it a special radiance. Godard has remained pledged to that light, which visibly comes from reality yet at the same time yields an image visibly artificial, prone to being overexposed (when the daylight is too bright) or underexposed (when the light indoors or in the streets at night is too dim). Rancière describes Godard's images as "icons of pure presence" conveying the sense that (as Novalis said in the days of German romanticism) "everything speaks" (*Film Fables* 178). Above all, what conveys that sense is that light coming from things themselves, which is, however, also the artificial light of the image, the beauty in the eye of the beholder.

You might think that the beauty of nature is there for everyone to enjoy. But you have to have money to own a country estate in which to enjoy it; you have to have the requisite social standing to belong as a guest there. Pastoral presupposes privilege. Social order shapes sensory experience. That's *le partage du sensible* for you. The corporate rich in *Nouvelle vague* are a new breed, however: they're not the old idle rich, they don't sit back and enjoy their privileges, they take no pleasure in the pastoral beauty all around them. Even by the pretty lake, even under the luxuriant trees, even in the handsome rooms of the country mansion, they keep at the incessant business of making money and leave aesthetic experience to their hangers-on and their servants—a maid partial to Schiller, a philosophical gardener—and to us in the audience. The great beauty of *Nouvelle vague* isn't just a rebuke to these insensitive rich, isn't just a salute to the appreciative servants taking care of the estate: it is a disturbance of the peace, a challenge to the established order.

The owner of the lakeside estate, and the head of a multinational corporation, is an Italian countess (Domiziana Giordano), a beauty with hair the color

FIGURE 19.2 The philosophical gardener: Roland Amstutz in *Nouvelle vague* (Jean-Luc Godard, Vega/Sara/Canal+, 1990). Digital frame enlargement.

of autumn leaves who could be taken to personify the old aristocratic pastoral relinquished to the callous new capitalism. On the road she rescues from the traffic a vagrant who becomes her lover (Alain Delon), a soulful unshaven type personifying something like the bohemian artist, and so out of place in her estate that after a while she lets him drown in the lake. But he, or his twin brother, comes back as a ruthless entrepreneur and runs her business with smashing efficiency: like Berthold Brecht in *The Good Woman of Setzuan*, here Godard reverses the Jekyll-and-Hyde scheme of the double and portrays the *bad* self as the one that thrives in society. The entrepreneurial twin has enough in him of the sentimental twin, though, to rescue in his turn the aristocratic beauty from drowning in the lake: the bohemian allied with the aristocrat against corporate capitalism, you could say, except that the forceful reborn man has shed the vagrant's self-pitying nostalgia, and the aristocrat seems ready to shed her privilege.

"The positive is given to us." We hear this on the soundtrack as the camera travels along the windows of the country mansion in the evening and peers into the lamp-lit rooms. "It remains for us to make the negative." The reborn man can be seen through a window next to the countess, both standing immobile as the camera keeps moving. This extended traveling shot may be the most beautiful shot in *Nouvelle vague*, perhaps in all of Godard. The camera reverses direction and now travels with a servant who is going from room to room turning out the lights: a symbol of the negative that remains for us to make. It is a beautiful mansion, and it is beautiful to see its lights extinguished in the night. It is a stirring beauty, not merely a contemplation of things as they are but of things that could be changed. *Nouvelle vague* eloquently illustrates the role aesthetics can play in politics.

20

Michel Chion

Listening to Cinema

JONAH CORNE

Critical work devoted to film sound typically and justifiably sets out from a complaint about the distortingly ocularcentric everyday terms that we use to describe our interactions with movies. "Do you want to *watch* a movie tonight?" "Have you *seen* this actor's or that director's latest?" The situation is no better within academic discourse, where "the viewer" and "the spectator" serve as the most common default expressions for referring to the impersonal third-person singular subject of cinema. Of course, our reception of movies is hardly sensorially exclusive and restrictive. We hear movies, too; and, more obscurely, feel, smell, and taste them. As the composer and influential French critic of film sound Michel Chion (b. 1947) proposes, we are "audio-viewers," a pointedly hyphenated, hybrid term that not only recognizes the role of hearing in our experience of movies but also insists upon the inextricably, mutually interactive ways that hearing and viewing influence each other.

Attempting to rectify film theory's historic privileging of visuality, and unable to draw on image-focused work for usable models—as he points out, there exists no basic unit of film sound such as the shot, nor any corresponding aural equivalent to the frame—Chion has introduced a veritable lexicon of neologisms for taxonomizing audio-visual phenomena. (Let's call him the Linnaeus of film sound, the field's core classifier.) Among such terms, the one for which Chion is best known is "the acousmêtre," the main focus of his first book of film criticism, *The Voice in Cinema* (1982). Chion coins the term by mashing the noun "*être* [being]" with the rare adjective "*acousmatique* [acousmatic]," which his mentor Pierre Schaeffer, the inventor of *musique concrète* (a form of experimental or "new" music based on recording and remixing everyday sounds), brought into currency in the 1950s after being introduced to it by the writer Jérôme Peignot. "Acousmatic, specifies an old dictionary," Chion explains, "'is said of a sound that is heard without its cause or source being seen'" (18), the word etymologically tracing back to "a Pythagorean sect whose followers would listen to their Master speak *behind a curtain*, as the story goes, so that the sight of the speaker wouldn't distract them from the message" (19). Similarly, the tape-recorder mobilized as the central means of instrumentation in *musique concrète* divorces sounds from their sources, or "acousmatizes" them, thus enabling listeners to attend to sounds in-themselves, as "concrete" objects in their own right. As Chion discriminates, however, the acousmatic sounds of recording and communication media that involve only an audio channel and thus that acousmatize "by nature" (18)—for instance the phonograph, the tape-player, the telephone, and the radio (one could add the CD and the MP3 player)—operate differently from acousmatic sounds in the mixed, audio-visual medium of the cinema. In the case of the former there exists no possibility for the source of a sound to become seen, whereas in the case of the latter a sound whose source we do not see can and might penetrate the frame and enter into visibility.

According to Chion, such lurkingly ever-present involvement with the image invests acousmatic sounds in the cinema with a distinctive, mysterious quality of "being in the screen and not, wandering the surface of the screen without entering it" (*Voice* 24); a quality, he maintains, that "when the acousmatic presence is a voice, and especially when this voice has not yet been visualized" (21), generates an almost supernatural being. Take, for examples (and these are the three that Chion spends the most time examining): (a) the titular, telepathic criminal mastermind in Fritz Lang's *The Testament of Dr. Mabuse* (1933); (b) Norman Bates's psychically incorporated and administering mother in Hitchcock's *Psycho* (1960); and (c) the super-computer Hal 9000 in Kubrick's *2001: A Space Odyssey* (1968). Evocatively linking the acousmêtre to such formidable archetypes as the God of Islam and Judaism (around whom there is a prohibition against looking), the psychoanalyst (who in the classic Freudian set-up is positioned so that the analysand lying on the couch can't see him/her), and the Mother (whose voice the child hears before being able to see her), Chion enumerates its fourfold powers as "ubiquity, panopticism, omniscience, and omnipotence" (24). However, he also reflects on the proneness of the acousmêtre to what he calls "de-acousmatization," where the voice-being enters the visual field, assuming a body and a concrete point in space, and is thus robbed of its special powers—deflated, mortalized—as in the famous scene near the end of *The Wizard of Oz* (1939).

As Chion observes of his own text, the emphasis in *The Voice in Cinema* falls on "what may be called *the complete acousmêtre*, the one who is not-yet-seen, but who remains liable to appear in the visual field at any moment" (*Voice* 21). Partial cases are different. Concerning these, wishing to keep his central term as flexible and wide-ranging as possible, Chion offers only a brief, albeit intriguing, aside: "The already visualized acousmêtre, the one [only] temporarily absent from the picture, is more familiar and reassuring—even though in the dark regions of the acousmatic field, which surrounds the visible field, this kind can acquire by contagion some of the powers of the complete acousmêtre" (21). If such a transference is possible, however, on what grounds can complete and incomplete acousmêtres essentially be differentiated? Further, how exactly does the process of transference work, and across a range of movies, where one might well expect to find the interim, less rigorously formalized, "incomplete" acousmêtre instead? As one can deduce from the resonances of his language (cf. "dark," "contagion"), Chion in his writing on the acousmêtre inclines especially toward manifestations within horror (see Silverman). Indeed, *The Testament of Dr. Mabuse*, *Psycho*, and *2001* are all, in their ways, horror movies.

In what follows I want to examine a fascinating example of the incomplete acousmêtre—this underexplored, undermapped species—and from there move to an equally fascinating example of what can be considered its counterpart: namely, the temporarily voiceless body. Along the way, we will encounter some other valuable Chionion concepts—these having mostly to do with temporality. My two filmic examples come respectively from Ernst Lubitsch's 1932 Hollywood romantic comedy *Trouble in Paradise* and the Israeli director Eran Kolirin's 2009 *The Band's Visit*.

Trouble in Paradise

Ernst Lubitsch's first nonmusical sound comedy, *Trouble in Paradise*, routinely ranks high if not highest on people's lists of favorite films by the émigré, Berlin-born director. Again and again the film displays Lubitsch's often noted and admired penchant for indirection and innuendo, perhaps nowhere more daringly so than in what might be termed "the clock sequence." Elaborating the development of a love triangle between the film's three main characters—the partners in crime Lily and Gaston (Miriam Hopkins, Herbert Marshall) and a young widow who owns a giant perfume empire, Madame Mariette Colet (Kay Francis)—the sequence consists almost entirely of close-up images of clocks combined with offscreen voices and sounds. Taking place in Colet's stylish art deco Parisian mansion, where the pair of crooks have become employed (Gaston as Colet's personal secretary, Lily as an assistant to him) with the aim of cleaning out Colet's safe, it begins by dissolving between four images of a desk clock, made up of three circles emblematically arranged into a (love) triangle, taken at four different times. Although such a screen convention for showing temporal change would be highly familiar to viewers of silent cinema—indeed, Chion cites the surrealist Jacques Brunius writing in the 1920s about "the epidemic of symbolic clocks and calendars that has spread like wildfire through cinema" (*Sound Art* 16), a trend that emerged out of an attempt to reduce reliance on intertitles, and yet that doesn't effectively differ very much from textual narration—Lubitsch reinvigorates the convention by implanting it creatively within a sound context. To begin, we hear, along with each clock image, a different bit of aural business occurring within the vicinity but invisibly to us: Lily taking leave of Gaston with a mixture of fragility and jealous rage (five o'clock); Mariette coquettishly come to invite Gaston out for dinner (twelve minutes later); the telephone ringing unceasingly, signaling that Gaston and Mariette aren't yet back from their evening out (is it Lily making the call, attempting to check up on Gaston?) (five minutes past nine); Mariette and Gaston returning in a flurry of mutual compliments and deciding to continue the night by heading downstairs for a drink (five minutes before ten).

In the sequence's next and middle interval, the film dissolves to the living room and a different clock reading ten o'clock and resembling an empty picture frame, a resemblance that subtly gestures at the sequence's own technique of evacuating the film frame of bodies. Starting out from a close-up of this clock sitting on the extreme right edge of a table, the camera pans left toward an uncorked bottle of champagne lounging aslant in a steel, decoratively ribbed ice bucket. Now the film repeats the dissolve-and-pan: dissolving to a window through which we can see in the distance a steepled clock-tower featuring a glowing face on one side, and panning over to a second window through which

FIGURE 20.1 Voices without bodies in *Trouble in Paradise* (Ernst Lubitsch, Paramount, 1932). Digital frame enlargement.

we can see a full moon suspended in a gracefully lewd crack between treetops. All we hear throughout these two shots is the chiming of the two clocks, the little one inside and the huge one far away, striking the hour. Lubitsch gives us no voices, no banter between Mariette and Gaston, who are presumably in the room drinking the champagne and conversing. Given that Mariette suggested that they retire to the living room to "talk it over," their offscreen voices ironically appear to go, as it were, offscreen from themselves, scrambling Christian Metz's seemingly sensible formulation that "sound in itself is never 'off': either it is audible or it doesn't exist" ("Aural Objects" 28–29). Transfiguring such an either/or situation, Lubitsch allows for Mariette and Gaston's offscreen voices to be inaudible *and* somehow existing at the same time.

Transitioning to the third and final interval, the film dissolves to one more image of a clock: a free-standing, hyper-modern grandfather model with a transparent glass body, resolving at the top into a kind of phallic capsule. Two o'clock. Again a left-panning trajectory to arrive at a three-quarter shot of Mariette, her hand on the bedroom door handle. Sexily glancing offscreen she says to Gaston (employing what she has not yet learned is his pseudonym), "Goodnight, Monsieur Laval." In his own three-quarter shot, Gaston returns the desirous glance and with ironic overformality replies, "Goodnight, Madame Colet." Now a master shot giving the alignment between Mariette, Gaston, and the clock. The device occupies an almost exact midpoint between the doors of the two respective rooms, thus establishing again the sequence's thematic crux of triangulation. As Mariette switches off a fluorescent light on the wall and they say goodnight one more time—in near complete darkness, and consequently under conditions of disembodied aurality not substantially different from those in the first part of the sequence (how tenuous this restoration to synchrony has been!)—Gaston gestures as though to try, one final time, to extend the evening but then thinks twice, stops at the clock, switches off its lighting by pulling a cord, and retreats. Now visibility in the space is dangerously low. The camera tracks forward to catch in frame the clock and Gaston's door, while we hear the acousmatic sound of him turning the deadbolt on the opposite side. Again the camera pans left, arriving at Mariette's door. The acousmatic sound of her turning her deadbolt, but more forcefully than he did, as if in one-upmanship or to say, in a kind of nonlinguistic sound language, "So! You won't venture to come after me! Well, too late! And if you try later on, you can't, this lock is violently fastened."

Although Mariette and Gaston, already amply seen, technically qualify only as incomplete acousmêtres, since they and their voices pass in and out of the visual space of the film, this sequence gives them opportunity to take on the magical ambiance of the complete acousmêtre if perhaps not of its particular divine potencies. Their incomplete acousmetricality is made complete. The question, however, is how? The answer, I think, is by falling in love. The film delivers them over to the magically electrified acousmatic field as both cause and effect of their mutually coming under the influence of each other's charms. Moreover, once they are in this acousmatic field, and each time they return to it, the fact that we've already seen them becomes less and less important, since the persons we have seen constitute their everyday selves and since the enchantment they are experiencing offscreen, like all enchantment, disorganizes the self. Consequently, we *can't* assign their hovering, enamored and enamoring voices retroactively to entities previously known to us, or even to themselves. Under the influence of romance, and even though we know what they look like generally, Mariette and Gaston as incomplete acousmêtres assume a quality of not-yet-seenness, in a diffuse characterological sense, that effectively blurs them with, transforms them into complete acousmêtres.

What to make of the clocks, the items we *do* see—emphatically—throughout the sequence? Irresistibly, these connect to the film's more general fixation on time. The phrase "in times like these," referring to the direness of the Depression (when the film is set), is repeated several times by different characters to the point of becoming a kind of leitmotif or refrain. Further, in a scene that comes late in the film, Mariette says to Gaston, as they embrace in her bedroom, "We have a long time ahead of us, Gaston: weeks, months, years," Lubitsch cutting on each of the last three words and showing the two first as reflections in mirrors (two differently sized circular ones that recall clock-faces) and then as shadows thrown on the sheets of the immaculately made bed. This sudden outbreak of montage punctuates and calls special attention to Mariette's line; and indeed a "long time ahead" is precisely what the characters *don't* have together, as Gaston's ruse is in the process of inexorably unraveling.

Encompassing socioeconomic and existential aspects, such time pressure also places the film within the relatively early sound period. As Chion discusses in *Sound on Screen* (1990), one of the most important consequences of the coming of sound was the subjection of the cinematic image to a multifaceted process of "temporalization" (13). He writes:

> One important historical point has tended to remain hidden: we are indebted to synchronous sound for having made cinema an art of time. The stabilization of projection speed, made necessary by the coming of sound, did have consequences that far surpassed what anyone could have foreseen. Filmic time was no longer a flexible value, more or less transposable depending on the rhythm of projection. Time henceforth had a fixed value; sound cinema guaranteed that whatever lasted *x* seconds in the editing would still have this same exact duration in the screening. In the silent cinema a shot had no exact internal duration; leaves quivering in the wind and ripples on the surface of the water had no absolute or fixed temporality. Each exhibitor had a certain margin of

> freedom in setting the rhythm of projection speed. Nor is it any accident that the motorized editing table, with its standardized film speed, did not appear until the sound era. (16–17)

In their first scene together, a first date in Gaston's hotel suite, Lily pickpockets his pocket watch and when she returns the object to him deadpans: "It was five minutes slow, but I regulated it for you." With this line, it's almost as if Lily is speaking as, or on behalf of, sound cinema itself, announcing what its advent has wrought.

What Chion means by temporalization is not restricted to the newly regularized—stabilized, standardized—speeds or "tempos" of shooting and projection. If the "weeks, months, years" mini-montage were in a silent film, for instance, we might very well interpret the shots, which show the characters from different vantages, as occurring simultaneously. Once you add the dialogue, as Chion writes more generally, the shots all of a sudden "fall into a linear time continuum" (*Sound on Screen* 18). There is no longer any way they all occupy the same moment, or that, say, the "years" shot could precede the "weeks" shot. This aurally generated sense that the activity in shot B comes *after* the activity in shot A, and *before* the activity in shot C, Chion refers to as "temporal linearization" (17). Here I diverge from William Paul, whose more strictly visual reading of the montage as an instance of temporal warping and suspension eliminates precisely this effect of the dialogue. As he writes in *Ernst Lubitsch's American Comedy*: "The method of shooting turns this brief sentence about the passage of time into something of an eternity as it is stretched out over four separate shots. But as it elongates time, it also stops it for each shot freezes the lovers into a series of static images with no movement in the image as there is virtually no movement from the lovers themselves" (66).

Relatedly, under the conditions of silent film, shots of certain repetitious actions might be played forward or backward, and the audience isn't likely to be able to tell which. Here Chion gives the example of a shot from a hypothetical film set in the tropics where a woman dozes and deeply respires in a rocking chair on a veranda bedecked with wind-blown bamboo chimes. Add a soundtrack, however, and "if we now play the film in reverse, it no longer works at all, especially the windchimes. Why? Because each one of these clinking sounds, consisting of an attack and then a slight fading resonance, is a finite story, oriented in time in a precise and irreversible manner. Played in reverse, it can immediately be recognized as 'backwards'" (19). As Chion adds, "aural phenomena are much more characteristically vectorized in time, with an irreversible beginning, middle, and end, than are visual phenomena" (*Audio-Vision* 19), and therefore when combined with visual phenomena tend to "vectorize" such phenomena, pointing the activity of shots along a specific temporal axis—namely, forward, toward the future.

To return to the acousmatic clock sequence with such reflections in mind, then, we can appreciate Lubitsch doing something intriguingly, richly ambivalent. On one hand, the shots featuring clocks raise awareness of the new clock-like dimension of cinema occasioned by the assimilation of synchronous sound. We become hyper-conscious not only of exactly what time it is in the narrative of the film, but that such a regularized, ordered, forward-directed temporality exerts an influence over the functioning and perception of the apparatus more generally. On the other hand, Lubitsch employs throughout the sequence a patently nonsynchronous or asynchronous, offscreen audio-visual strategy proper to the acousmatic, that upends sound cinema's much-hyped, purportedly chief use, the matching of sounds with sources, spoken words with moving mouths. In short, emphatically asserting and disrupting a particular organization, he stages a dialectic, inscribes a tension across the audio-visual field, and, in doing so, ingeniously prefigures and distills all of the foreclosing pressure and permissive transitory bliss of Mariette and Gaston's romantic relationship. In such a context, it is interesting to note that Chion over the years has refined his position on "temporalization," adjusting in order to accommodate more variegated formulations about the workings of time in sound cinema. Justifiably concerned that he should be promoting a too rigid divide between the so-called silent and sound eras, he writes in *Film, A Sound Art:* "It seems to me inaccurate to say that one mode of cinema came to replace another. Rather, a splitting and doubling, a coexistence developed: silent film lives on *beneath* sound film" (263–264). Disrupting standard synchronous configurations while being a phenomenon of sound film more broadly, the acousmatic of course doesn't equate with silent film; and yet Lubitsch's clock sequence gives us something highly akin to such a vision of the constitution of film after the advent of sound as collidingly mingled and multiple.

The Band's Visit

A polyglot, melancholy-suffused comedy that might be regarded as a kind of neo-Lubitschean enterprise, Eran Kolirin's *The Band's Visit* tells the fictional story of a long-running, fiscally endangered Egyptian police band, the "Alexandria Police Ceremonial Orchestra," who wind up lost in a bleak, middle-of-nowhere Israeli town while on their way to perform at an Arab cultural center in Israel. The whole plot-generating muddle arises out of a slight discrepancy in Hebrew pronunciation, a minor consonantal difference upon which major geographic differences hinge: namely, the town *Petah Tikva*, where the Arab cultural center is located, and *Beit Hatikva*, whither the band ends up taking a bus. The band is forced to spend the night variously billeted with the residents, and so the two groups enter into a period of intimate contact fraught by the specters of the Arab-Israeli conflict (see Shohat). Speaking among themselves in their native

Arabic and Hebrew, they can converse only in English, a situation that reflects not a concession to the ages-old Hollywood convention where all the denizens of non-English-speaking countries somehow miraculously speak English, but rather the reality of today's globalized world in which English has emerged as the dominant lingua franca (see Shohat and Stam, esp. 52).

In one of the most memorable scenes in the film, the band's handsome young violinist, Haled (Saleh Bakri), joins some Israeli youth for a night on the town at a roller rink. Meanwhile, one of these locals, the hapless, scruffy Papi (Shlomi Avraham), finds himself in a romantic muddle. Set up with a girl named Yula (Rinat Matatov), whom he sees as gloomy, Papi completely fails to make any sort of connection. "I don't know what to say, what to do . . . . I want to talk, but I hear the sea in my ears," he confides to Haled. By the end of the night, as the DJ plays the last song, a schmaltzy, Euro-vision-ish slow number in Hebrew with an asemic, tra-la-la-ing chorus, Yula is in tears, sitting on a chair that's she forced to surrender to an indifferent janitor performing his closing duties. With seemingly no place else to go, Yula sits next to Papi, albeit tellingly angling herself away from him. At this point, flanking Papi on the other side, Haled embarks on a much-needed intervention, serving as a mediator between Papi and Yula by effectively puppeteering Papi, supplying him with gestures or "moves" designed to salvage the disastrous evening. In a nearly wordless single extended shot composed in static tableau, pulling objects of astonishingly Don Juanish preparedness out of the jacket pocket of his baby-blue uniform, Haled passes Papi a giant white handkerchief; whispers something in his ear only half-audible to us about a drink proposal; passes him a mini-bar-sized liquor bottle; gently massages his knee; puts an arm over his shoulder—all of which actions Papi repeats with Yula as the recipient. Brilliantly choreographed, the shot moves us from the anxiety of blundering sexual awkwardness to rambunctious laughter (especially when the chain of transmission unexpectedly switches direction, and Yula's reciprocating placement of her hand on the hand Papi has placed on her knee causes Papi to place his hand, reportingly, on the hand Haled has placed on his knee) to a fragile sense of release and relief. The scheme finally enables a kiss, Papi moving in to embrace Yula as Haled, apprehending that his guidance has bestowed the requisite confidence or momentum for (apparently) independent action, slides his arm away from Papi's shoulder and looks on smilingly at the successful recovery that he has contrived.

Treating intricate romantic triangulation via heavily stylized audio-visual play, the shot brings us forcefully back to Lubitsch, indeed embodies a kind of yin to the yang of the clock sequence in *Trouble in Paradise*. For whereas Lubitsch's sequence of clocks and offscreen sounds is structured around the acousmêtre or bodiless voice, Kolirin's shot is structured around what Chion describes in *The Voice in Cinema* as the acousmêtre's "counterpart" (100)—that

FIGURE 20.2 Bodies without voices in *The Band's Visit* (Eran Kolirin, July August/Bleiberg, 2007). Digital frame enlargement.

is, the "cinematic mute" or "voiceless body," which at once functions as a revenant or memory trace of silent film and possesses a crucial feature particular to sound film. Drawing on Bresson's famous axiom in his *Notes on Cinematography* that "the soundtrack invented silence" (21), Chion explains:

> By endowing the film with a synchronized 'sound track' and bringing the voice to this added track, the talkies allowed us not only to *hear silence* (until then, on occasions when the continuous musical accompaniment was interrupted, there was no true silence within the fiction itself, but only a silence imposed on the filmgoer by the deaf cinema), but also to have truly silent, mute characters. The deaf cinema, having presented them in among speaking but voiceless characters, wasn't able to *make their silence heard.* (*Voice* 95; emphasis original)[1]

Of course, none of the three characters in *The Band's Visit* is grappling with an overriding condition of muteness or mutism—they are rather merely conditionally, circumstantially mute, fallen silent for the prolonged duration of the shot, and even then not fully, if we count the few little stray words and phrases that leak out from them, such as Haled's half-audible whisper, Yula's hushed (and significantly unsubtitled) "*toda* [thanks]," or Papi's flailing "What now?" Embodying silence in a more fugitive, fickle, non-absolute way than characters coded as "mute," they serve as counterparts to the incomplete acousmêtres of Lubitsch's clock sequence, and, as in the earlier film, garner a great power.

Emplotted within a voiced, audible world, the silence of Haled, Papi, and Yula is (following Chion) pronouncedly, paradoxically *heard*, and participates in the film's larger obsession with silence, which emerges and operates in a variety of ways. Silence, or one kind of silence, is what happens when linguistic communication breaks down, which frequently occurs throughout the film, as one might well expect when so much of what is said must be conveyed awkwardly. Working with and within a non-native language, one either can't find the right word or isn't quite sure of it, and so submits to saying nothing. Hence the several impasses that transpire between the Israelis and the Egyptians as they try to communicate with one another in their thickly "accented," terse, sometimes nakedly "broken" English. Yet it's also crucial to note that Kolirin doesn't reduce communicative failure merely to something that happens between people divided, or ostensibly divided, by language, nation, and culture. Hence Papi's blockage in trying to talk to Yula; or the band leader Tawfiq's (Sasson Gabai) disclosure to Dina (Ronit Elkabetz), the Israeli woman who billets him—and with whom he has a complex, emotionally and even erotically charged yet nonphysical dalliance—about his tragic past involving the deaths of his son and wife: "I was hard with him. I didn't understand him. He was gentle, fragile, like her. I didn't understand him. He took his life. He broke her heart." The silences between Papi and Yula, and between Tawfiq and his son, represent debacles or avoidances of speech with frustrating, even fatal, costs, and they occur between people of the same "people."

Potentially destabilizing, silence in *The Band's Visit* also provides unexpected possibilities for connection. Tawfiq defends the presumable boredom of his favorite activity, fishing, to Dina by describing—à la the Zen-inspired composer John Cage—how it enables a kind of world-communing encounter with silence, or rather with all the normally hidden or unacknowledged noises that silence brings into aural focus. "In the early hours at sea you can hear the whole world, like . . . like . . . symphony," Tawfiq remarks, inverting Papi's pathologization of the sea as paralyzing, distressing noise,[2] and indeed sounding a little bit like Cage who, like Pierre Schaeffer, considered the everyday life world to be an illimitable fount of what could expansively be called music (see Cage; Schafer). Silence functions generatively, too. At the roller rink, Papi and Yula connect via the virtually wordless puppeteering engineered by Haled; a highly theatrical and internally theatricalizing series of actions in which the film's fairy-tale-ish airs becomes especially marked. Indeed, as Chion points out in elaborating the kinship between the acousmêtre and cinema's silent characters, the latter are also often treated as if invested with exceptional, magical powers: "The mute is the guardian of the secret" (*Voice* 96) as well as "the witness, the eyes that were there when it happened" (97), possessed of abnormally vast powers of seeing as if in compensation for the inability to speak. Tapping into similar associations, *The Band's Visit* in the roller rink scene aligns silence with a marvelous secret, with confidential knowledge—namely, the concatenated pattern of externally supplied gestures that are able to dispel Yula's aggravated gloom, reclaim (unlock) her heart, and prepare a seemingly impossible moment of union.

As Lubitsch does in *Trouble in Paradise*, Kolirin exploits an "incomplete" form of a figure of audio-visual dissociation in order to conjure up the powerful magical energies of romantic enchantment. Conscripting the bodiless voice and the voiceless body, the two filmmakers offer up a convenient précis of Chion's attraction to limiting cases of the audio-visual rupture or monstrosity that he finds inherent in even the most normative moments of synchronized sound film. "If the talking cinema has shown anything by restoring voices to bodies," he writes, "it's precisely that it doesn't hang together; it's decidedly not a seamless match" (*Voice* 125). Citing the French journalist and writer Alexandre Arnoux's 1929 remarks on the oddity that "the voice always comes from the same spot no matter which character is speaking [viz. from the loudspeaker]" (131), and thus noting how easy it is to slip into the mindset that one is in the presence of ventriloquism, Chion claims that all speech in the sound film is technically ventriloquism (see also Altman). It is a point that invests Haled's puppeteering of Papi with added resonance and a dose of strange irony given the virtual speechlessness of the act. Ironic, too, is the fact that the examples of stressed audio-visual rupture in Lubitsch and Kolirin serve as sites of intense bonding across subjects, even if just for the moment and not without complicating factors at work. Love doesn't tear us apart, the examples suggest in their Chionian gravitation to the disjunctive potential of sound film, but rather, never are we so in love as *when* we are torn apart.

NOTES

1. Chion's use of the term "deaf cinema" derives from his desire to correct the phrase "*cinéma muet* [mute cinema]," the standard French translation of the English "silent cinema." Chion's point is that the characters in "silent cinema" (itself an obviously imperfect term) aren't mute—indeed they speak profusely; it's just that we, the audience, can't hear them, are deaf to them.
2. Interestingly, the English (and Old French) word "noise" etymologically relates to seasickness. "Nausea and *nausée* are derivatives of the Latin *nauseam*, and the root is originally from the Greek *naus*. *Naus*, ship, noise, and the French words *noise, nausée, nautique, navire*, belong to the same etymon. In short, they are related to the sea, so noise is a sea of sound, pure frequency, uncontaminated by symbolization—or sound waves" (Yasunao Tone, *Parasite/*Noise 101).

21

Judith Butler

Sex, Gender, and Subject Formation

KRISTEN HATCH

With its publication in 1990, Judith Butler's *Gender Trouble* helped to shift the direction of feminist theory and quickly became one of the founding texts of queer theory. *Gender Trouble* was released at the moment when the New Queer Cinema was just beginning to emerge and AIDS activism was at the center of gay and lesbian politics. Prior to the book's publication, feminist theories of gender and the body rested on an understanding that there is a relatively stable relationship between sex and the material body—that genitalia determine one's sex—and between sex and gender—that females are feminine, males are masculine. Rather than challenging these categories, feminist scholars were interested in understanding how femininity and womanhood are experienced and represented within patriarchy. Within the field of film and media studies, much feminist debate centered on questions of spectatorship that had arisen from Laura Mulvey's "Visual Pleasure and Narrative Cinema"—focusing on the degree to which the cinematic gaze was "male," for example, and whether "female" spectatorship is characterized by too close a relationship to the image—and struggled over the question of what Mulvey termed "transvestite" spectatorship.

Gender Trouble helped to reshape feminist debates and spark queer theory by interrogating the stability of such categories as sex and gender and their relationship to one another, thereby challenging the very foundations of feminist theory and LGBT studies. Drawing on Michel Foucault's understanding of the relationships between discourse and power, *Gender Trouble* seeks to understand gender in relation to subject formation. Butler (b. 1956) examines how we come to understand ourselves as distinct individuals, how "I" come to occupy the position indicated by that pronoun, arguing that in recognizing ourselves as "male" or "female," "masculine" or "feminine," we begin to constitute ourselves as subjects. Further, we cannot exist as subjects without having assumed an understanding of ourselves in relation to sex and gender, regardless of what that relationship might be. Therefore, the production of sexed and gendered bodies appears natural and immutable, though in fact this is a product of discourse and the workings of power, particularly in relation to heterosexuality.

Sex and gender are not willed into being but are produced, according to Butler, by a prohibition against homosexual desire. Whereas Sigmund Freud and Jacques Lacan posit the incest taboo as foundational for the formation of the ego, Butler argues that the taboo against homosexuality is at the heart of identity; "the resolution of the Oedipal complex affects gender identification through not only the incest taboo," she writes, "but, prior to that, the taboo against homosexuality" (*Gender* 63). Butler draws on Freud's understanding of the role of melancholia in the formation of the ego in order to understand how subjectivity is produced. According to Freud, in order to contend with the loss of a loved object, we internalize the forbidden other, taking the lost object into ourselves in order to contend with the loss. Butler draws on this understanding of ego formation to argue that heteronormativity is foundational to identity:

> If feminine and masculine dispositions are the result of the effective internalization of [the taboo against homosexuality], and if the melancholic answer to the loss of the same-sexed object is to incorporate and, indeed, *to become* that object through the construction of the ego ideal, then gender identity appears primarily to be the internalization of a prohibition that proves to be formative of identity. Further, this identity is constructed and maintained by the consistent application of this taboo, not only in the stylization of the body in compliance with discrete categories of sex, but in the production and "disposition" of sexual desire. (*Gender* 63)

Therefore, one important project for queer activism will be to draw attention to what Butler terms the "heterosexual matrix"—the seemingly natural relationship between sex, gender, and sexuality whereby masculine men desire women and feminine women desire men.

Gender, according to Butler, is performative, produced by our behavior rather than causing it. Gender is not "a stable identity or locus of agency from which various acts follow." Rather, it is "the repeated stylization of the body, a set of repeated acts within a highly rigid regulatory frame that congeal over time to produce the appearance of substance, of a natural sort of being" (*Gender* 33). Butler argues against the understanding that one's preexisting masculinity or femininity causes one to act in a certain manner—to sit with knees splayed far apart, or legs demurely crossed, for example. Rather, these stylized behaviors are what produce our masculinity or femininity. And because gender is produced through behavior rather than causing behavior, because it is something we do rather than who we are, it is inherently unstable. No matter how many times I have kept my knees together, there is always the possibility that I will let them splay next time I sit down.

Feminist scholars have long recognized that gender is socially constructed. Simone de Beauvoir, for instance, famously claimed that "one is not born but rather becomes a woman" (283). However, Butler argues that it is not only gender that is socially constructed but sex as well. We are accustomed to understanding the body—which, barring illness or accident and subject to the passage of time, remains relatively stable and reassuringly concrete—to be the basis of our sexed identity. I am female because I have female body parts. However, Butler suggests, the assignment of identity on the basis of reproductive function is no less the product of a "ritualized repetition of norms" than is gender. Although reproduction may play little or no part in our lives, we are assigned one of two sexes—male or female—according to our genitalia. Until recently, in the case of infants whose reproductive function was ambiguous, the medical community routinely intervened to surgically produce a "male" or "female" body, even if such surgery ensured that the child would become infertile or experience a reduction in genital sensation. This is because sex, as Butler argues, "is not simply a static description of what one is but one of the norms by which one becomes visible at all, that which qualifies a body for life within the domain of cultural intelligibility" (*Bodies* 15).

However, this is not to say that gender or sex is entirely within an individual's control. Gender is not produced through any single act but through countless daily actions, most of which are done without a thought. Nor can we call a halt to "doing" gender, since there is no subjectivity without it. And, rather than drawing from an infinite variety of behaviors in the production of gender, we draw on a narrow set of options that have been produced over time (wearing pink or blue, high heels or loafers, etc.). Further, unlike a consciously enacted performance, there is no actor who precedes the performance of gender. Rather, the act of gender is what helps to constitute the actor; "gender is always a doing, though not a doing by a subject who might be said to pre-exist the deed" (*Trouble* 25). Nonetheless, Butler sees in the instability of gender the potential for destabilizing heteronormativity.

Alfred Hitchcock's *Rebecca* (1940) and Sally Potter's *Orlando* (1992) both point to the subject's limited agency in relation to gender identity even as they explore the relationship between gender and subject formation. In the case of *Rebecca*, gender is ultimately naturalized, although we witness the central character's struggles to assume an adult, feminine identity. *Orlando*, however, tests the bonds between sex and gender in its exploration of the relationship between sex, gender, and artistic practice.

Rebecca

Rebecca traces the development of an adult, feminine subject. Based on Daphne Du Maurier's 1938 gothic novel, the film tells the story of a sheltered young woman, whose name is never given (Joan Fontaine), who marries a wealthy older man, Maxim De Winter (Laurence Olivier). The two meet in Monte Carlo, and after a hasty courtship and marriage arrive at Maxim's grand family estate, Manderley, which seems haunted by memories of Rebecca, the first Mrs. De Winter, who died in a boating accident. The young bride struggles to play the role of mistress of the estate, though she is undermined by the strange housekeeper, Mrs. Danvers (Judith Anderson), who remains devoted to Rebecca. And she is rebuffed by her husband, who is given to violent mood swings at any mention of his first wife. When Rebecca's body is discovered at the bottom of the sea, Maxim breaks down and confesses that Rebecca did not drown but hit her head during a quarrel in which she revealed that she was pregnant by another man, and that it was he who put her in the boat that now rests at the bottom of the ocean. He did not love his first wife, as his young bride had imagined, but hated her for taunting him with her aberrant sexual behavior, which is left largely to the viewer's imagination. During the inquest, the new Mrs. De Winter finally assumes her role as the ideal wife when she provides support to her husband, who is ultimately exonerated.

In many ways, the new Mrs. De Winter can be understood in relation to subject formation. She is repeatedly referred to as a child, and Maxim, who is notably older than his young bride, is more father than husband: he tells her to eat up "like a good girl," to stop biting her nails, blow her nose, and put on an overcoat ("one can never be too careful with children"). The fact that she remains nameless contributes to our sense that she is without an identity. The film begins with a voiceover narration in Fontaine's voice: "Last night, I dreamt I went to Manderley again . . . ." The narrator's "I" and her ability to speak and, in speaking, to produce the film image (a tracking shot along the drive to Manderley) suggests that she has completed the journey toward becoming a subject. Further, the dream seems to describe her transformation: "It seemed to me I stood by the iron gate leading to the drive, and for a while I could not enter, for the way was barred to me. Then, like all dreamers, I was possessed of a sudden with supernatural powers and passed like a spirit through the barrier before me." The film, then, describes her passage through a sort of barrier, her trajectory from unformed and unnamed child to an adult woman.

In *The Women Who Knew Too Much*, Tania Modleski argues that the film addresses the "problem" of women's inability to differentiate self from other, the tendency toward over-identification that Freud discussed in relation to the female Oedipal trajectory. Like the boy, the girl is attached to the mother and views her father as a rival. Eventually she recognizes the mother as castrated and shifts her love to the father. This Oedipal crisis is never completely resolved, however, and she remains in a sort of limbo, identifying too closely with the mother whom she also desires. Modleski sees *Rebecca* as being about the daughter's persistent competing desire for mother and father. "In *Rebecca*, the heroine continually strives not only to please Maxim, but to win the affections of Mrs. Danvers, who seems herself to be possessed, haunted by Rebecca and to have a sexual attachment to the dead woman. Finally, it becomes obvious that the two desires cannot coexist: the desire for the mother impedes the progress of the heterosexual union. Ultimately, then, the heroine disavows her desire for the mother, affirming her primary attachment to the male" (51–52).

Instead of reading the film in terms of the narrator's recognition of her status as castrated, we might consider how she seeks to become a subject by observing the prohibition against homosexuality. As Butler argues, gender is not the result of subjectivity but its foundation. In order to become a speaking subject, the narrator must become a gendered subject. In doing so, she struggles to incorporate competing models of femininity, models that are produced through history, literature, art: through discourse, in other words. The narrator is constantly threatened by the possibility that she will not achieve an identity as a woman, that Maxim will send her away and she will remain a nonentity, like the woman who was rather conveniently washed ashore shortly after Rebecca's death. This unnamed woman is also marked by her failure to be Rebecca; "the woman that is now buried in the family crypt, that was not Rebecca," explains Maxim during his confession. "That was the body of some unknown woman, unclaimed, belonging nowhere."

The narrator's repudiation of Danvers and, by extension, the Rebecca Danvers loved, suggests that her recognition of the prohibition against homosexuality is the prerequisite for her entering into subjectivity. Like nearly every other character in the film, the new Mrs. De Winter is fascinated by Rebecca, who is characterized by her sexuality and desirability. Penetrating Rebecca's bedroom, the young wife is entranced by the remaining traces of Rebecca's body which Danvers exhibits to her—her hairbrush, her clothing and undergarments. When she escapes the room, however, the spell is broken, and rather than succumb to her desire for Rebecca she repudiates Danvers and seeks to displace Rebecca. Refusing any further "help" from Danvers, she orders her to dispose of Rebecca's things in her first, tentative step toward becoming the "lady of the house."

In *Bodies That Matter*, Butler argues that the subject "assumes" a sex not only through the process of identification—as with the narrator's initial identification with Rebecca—but also through the disavowal of other identifications. "The abject . . . will constitute that site of dreaded identification against which—and by virtue of which—the domain of the subject will circumscribe its own claim to autonomy and to life" (16). Danvers is most dramatically repudiated in the process of the narrator's establishing her subjectivity; she is last seen engulfed in flames in Rebecca's bedroom, having set fire to Manderley. But before the second Mrs. De Winter can assume her position as subject, she must also repudiate Rebecca. Significantly, then, this repudiation comes in the wake of the revelation of Rebecca's unnamed queer proclivities, the sexual peccadillos that she has described to Maxim and that he vows he will repeat to no living soul. She recognizes Rebecca's death not as a tragedy but as a just end.

In order to become a woman and a speaking subject, she must do more than repudiate homosexual desire. She must also assume an adult, gendered identity. As Butler argues, the subject is not free to invent the gendered behaviors that will help usher her into subjectivity, though the narrator certainly tries. Rather, gender is produced through discourse and shaped by power. As the film makes clear, femininity is shaped by heterosexuality. From the beginning, the girl understands her role as Mrs. De Winter to be shaped by her husband's desires. The difficulty arises when these desires appear contradictory. On the one hand, she seems inclined to the role of caregiver. But this role is already taken by the estate manger, Mr. Crawley (Reginald Denny), whom Maxim dismisses as a "mother hen," and by Mrs. Danvers, who shames

FIGURE 21.1 The unnamed narrator draws on images from a magazine to shape her body to the requirements of heterosexuality in *Rebecca* (Alfred Hitchcock, Selznick International, 1940). Digital frame enlargement.

the narrator with her efficiency. Alternately, the narrator envisions an ideal femininity defined relative to an imagined male sexual desire. However, Maxim rejects this model. While the narrator might wish to become a sexualized woman—to be "a woman of thirty-six, dressed in black satin with a string of pearls"—Maxim demands that she promise never to wear black satin or pearls, or be thirty-six years old. And when she does appear in a black evening gown, he laughs at her attempt at assuming the role of sophisticate.

Ultimately, the narrator's maturation arises out of Maxim's need for her. In this manner, the film works to produce the illusion that gender arises naturally out of sexual difference, that it is not a matter of behavior as the narrator had imagined. Rather than self-consciously stepping into the position of Mrs. De Winter, she unselfconsciously assumes the role of Maxim's wife by looking after his needs during the inquest. Indeed, her most helpful action is to lose consciousness; as Maxim is being questioned and seems on the verge of confessing in an angry outburst, she faints, bringing the court proceedings to a halt.

Orlando

Orlando is also concerned with the relationship between sex, gender, and subjectivity, in this case subjectivity as it is expressed through artistic practice. The film is an adaptation of Virginia Woolf's 1928 novel, a fantastical biography of the title character, whose youth and beauty win the favor of Queen Elizabeth I. The aging queen gifts the boy an estate, which is his "on one condition: Do not fade. Do not wither. Do not grow old." And, indeed, Orlando does not age over the course of the film, though he does lose his inheritance due not to the passage of time but to his transformation into a woman. After a long sleep, Orlando awakens in a new century and a new sex; "Same person," she says to herself, "no difference at all," and then to the camera: "Just a different sex." But of course, this small difference makes all the difference.

The film is divided into seven sections, each corresponding to a different time period and exploring a different theme: 1600: Death; 1610: Love, 1650: Poetry; 1700: Politics; 1750: Society; 1850: Sex; and Birth, which viewers will recognize as occurring in the twentieth century. In addition to the intertitles, shifting cultural styles mark time's passage in a way that destabilizes our understanding of what constitute "masculine" and "feminine" behaviors. Orlando is played by a woman, Tilda Swinton, though in voiceover the narrator (Swinton) assures us "there can be no doubt about his sex, despite the feminine appearance that every young man of the time aspires to." The aging Queen Elizabeth is played by a man (Quentin Crisp), in part, because she embodies masculine power in her role as England's ruler. As the queen arrives at Orlando's grand estate, she is serenaded by Jimmy Somerville, whose falsetto points to a gay male identity in the twentieth century but was normatively masculine to Elizabethan audiences. In the eighteenth century, the male Orlando appears in extravagant curls and a large plumed hat, his feet in high heels, his legs revealed beneath a knee-length skirt in the tradition of a courtier.

The film consistently identifies gender as arising not merely out of one's choice of clothing but more significantly through the subject's relationship to power. Again, according to Butler, gender is performative, arising not as a result of an invisible core identity but produced by our behaviors. For Potter, as for Butler, these behaviors are always shaped by the workings of power. In the film, powerlessness is associated with visibility. Initially, Orlando seeks royal favor by reciting lines from Edmund Spenser's *The Faerie Queen* that reflect on time's ravishment of female beauty—a provocative reminder to the aged queen of her status as woman and the consequent instability of her relationship to power. While she might reign as England's sovereign, she remains female, thus secondary to man. To reassert her authority she reminds Orlando's father that everything in his possession by rights belongs to her.

With a queen as ruler, the youthful Orlando becomes an object of visual delight. The queen is charmed by the boy's youth, and she ties her garter to his knee. Later, she beckons the nervous youth to her bed and presses his face to her lap; "Ah!" she exclaims, "this is my victory": while she may not enjoy a victory over time her status as queen gives her power over this youth. And in payment for this access to his youthful beauty, she tucks the deed to the estate into his garter. Here, the conventions that would associate a woman with beauty, a man with desire, are reversed.

Orlando's later transformation from man into woman will be produced not through a change in her genitalia but through her increased visibility. A first inkling of the change comes when Orlando wakes and washes her face in a bowl of water, her breast briefly entering into the frame. Then she examines herself before a full-length mirror, and we are offered an unfettered view of her naked body. Her posture—weight on the left leg, right leg slightly bent as she stands next to the wash basin—echoes countless images of the nude female form in painting and photography. Sex, the film seems to imply, is constituted by the body's visibility. Indeed, she repeatedly gazes at herself in the mirror in a manner unfamiliar to the male Orlando.

Throughout the film, Potter explores the ways in which artistic expression shapes and is shaped by gender. As we have seen, the female body is often taken as the proper object of art produced by men. And as a man, Orlando enjoys an uncritical appreciation of literature, devoting himself to writing poetry. Further, Orlando's privileged status permits him to indulge in an idealistic and romantic view of love. We see this as Orlando falls in love with Sasha (Charlotte Valandrey), the daughter of a Russian ambassador, when he is already engaged

FIGURE 21.2 Orlando's (Tilda Swinton) transformation from man to woman is produced by the visibility of her body, which is shaped by the history of images of the nude female form (*Orlando*, Sally Potter, Adventure, 1992). Digital frame enlargement.

to be married to an English woman. The infatuation begins at an ice-skating party, which Orlando attends with his fiancée. There, he catches sight of the beautiful Russian princess and breaks away from the courtly dance in order to join her. The fiancée is humiliated but powerless to do anything about it, while Orlando—by virtue of his wealth and gender—is free to throw over one woman in favor of another. "It would never have worked," he tells the camera. "A man must follow his heart."

What Orlando fails to recognize is that a woman does not enjoy the freedom to follow her heart. Orlando has jeopardized the fiancée's economic and social standing, which depend on her ability to make an advantageous match. Nor does he notice that Sasha flirts with him because her family is penniless. She must secure a wealthy husband, though she is in love with a Russian sailor. While Orlando indulges in an extravagant melancholy after he shares a kiss with Sasha, saddened "because I can't bear this happiness to end," Sasha and Orlando's fiancée are required to submerge their feelings because marriage is their only means to status and wealth. Later, in the nineteenth century when Orlando is a woman, she will recognize that her lover Shelmerdine's (Billy Zane) pursuit of high ideals—"the pursuit of liberty" and of being a "free spirit, unfettered by position or possession"—similarly rests on his status as a man.

Notably, these indicators of masculine privilege also signal Orlando's class status. His callousness toward his fiancée is mirrored by the callousness of the aristocrats toward the peasants, the film suggesting a correspondence between the way that power works in relation to gender and to class. While the aristocracy enjoys the extreme cold of winter as an occasion for skating parties and ice tableaux, for the peasants the winter weather is disastrous. A low-angle shot of a group of men looking down toward the camera, for example, leads to a reverse shot revealing that they are laughing at the sight of a girl trapped beneath the ice, drowned, presumably, while carrying a basket of apples, which float toward the surface.

Art seems to speak directly to the male Orlando's experience, which only serves to affirm his privileged status. Jilted by Sasha, he comes across a performance of *Othello*, in which the Moor has killed Desdemona and turns the blade upon himself, uttering the well-known line, "One that loved not wisely but too well." The famous tragedy of a general's jealousy seems to echo Orlando's situation, and he turns to the camera to describe this as a "terrific play." To be a man, the film implies, is to enjoy a privileged relationship to artistic expression, whereas after Orlando has become a woman, she finds herself excluded from the realm of letters. In the eighteenth century, despite her butler's admonishments that a lady should not venture out unaccompanied by a man, Orlando eagerly attends a literary salon, where she meets the leading writers of the era—Alexander Pope, Joseph Addison, and Jonathan Swift. Expecting to enjoy their wit and erudition, she instead finds herself alienated by their barbs against women; "Women have no desire," declares Swift, "Only affectation." "Indeed," replies Pope," "women are but children of larger growth." Having experienced life as a man, she is not prepared to be interpellated as an ornament for men's amusement. When she objects to their disparagement, Swift dismisses her aspirations to personhood: "The intellect is a solitary place, and therefore quite unsuitable a terrain for females who must discover their natures through the guidance of a father or husband."

A century later, she will find herself among women who have entered into the world of letters. The film indirectly links the emergence of the female writer to the development of science as a discipline distinct from philosophy. At the eighteenth-century salon, the Archduke Harry (John Wood) expressed the emerging spirit of Enlightenment when he told the assembled guests, "I believe science to be more interesting than poetry. The systematic study, exploration and taming of the material world is surely a proper occupation for a man [unlike] the introvert art of scribbling." Science does win out in the end, as witnessed by the locomotive that appears in the next chapter of the film. With science emerging as the more "manly" method of taming the material world, literature is opened to the scribblings of women. When Orlando steps out of eighteenth- into nineteenth-century England, she emerges onto the misty moors described by the Brontë sisters. In a scene evocative of Jane Eyre's initial meeting of Mr. Rochester, she meets her future lover, Shelmerdine, when he is thrown at her feet by his startled horse. And it is as a woman in the twentieth century that Orlando will finally achieve success as a writer.

Even as *Orlando* works to destabilize the relationship between the material body and one's assigned sex, and to identify the relationship between power and gender expression, the film suggests that there is an absolute difference between the sexes, lying in their relationship to life and death. As an ambassador to an unnamed country in "the East," Orlando is enjoined to enter into battle. A soldier lies dying, and the archduke urges him to ignore the man's fatal injuries. "This is a dying man," objects Orlando. "He's not a man," replies Harry, "he's the enemy." But Orlando cannot accept this dehumanization of the enemy; heroism in battle is not a masculine behavior he is willing to embrace. After this crisis of identity, he falls into a deep sleep, from which she awakens as a woman.

Later, as a woman, Orlando tentatively explores the relationship between killing and masculinity with her lover, Shelmerdine. "If I were a man," Orlando suggests, "I might choose not to risk my life for an uncertain cause. I might think that freedom won by death was not worth having." For Shelmerdine, a "freedom fighter," this means that "you might choose not to be a real man at all"; this would be the equivalent of a woman choosing "not to sacrifice my life caring for my children nor my children's children. Nor to drown anonymously in the milk of female kindness." Orlando's relationship with Shelmerdine ends when Orlando proposes they have a child together, but Shelmerdine leaves instead to fight for "liberty" in America. The film jumps ahead to the twentieth century, with Orlando pregnant and, inexplicably, stumbling through a battlefield, bombs exploding around her, as though to suggest that both her pregnancy and the war are the natural outcomes of her preoccupation with giving life and Shelmerdine's with fighting. However, unlike the relationship between gender and power or sex and the visibility of the body, the film never examines the basis of these gendered ideologies.

Further, the film works to naturalize the idea that humankind can be divided into two distinct sexes, which, Butler argues, is one of the basic tenants of the heterosexual matrix. *Orlando* has a doubled structure that arises out of the title character's experiences as both man and woman. Events occurring when Orlando is a man are echoed in her life as a woman, giving the character and the audience an opportunity to reflect on how gender shapes experience. As a man, for example, he misreads Sasha's jilting as a sign of female treachery, while as a woman she jilts a man and is herself accused of perfidy. This dyadic structure suggests that there are only two perspectives—male and female—through which one might interpret such experiences.

The film ends with Orlando's daughter turning a video camera on her mother. In the sky, Jimmy Somerville appears as an angel, intoning a celebratory song: "At last I am free." However, while the film might end on this note of optimism, suggesting a new gender identity that is not dependent on male power or female submission, it has also shown us that sex and gender are not "free" from history but shaped by it. As Butler argues, "the act that one does, the act that one performs is, in a sense, an act that's been going on before one arrived on the scene" ("Performative Acts" 277).

WORKS CITED

Abel, Richard. "Photogénie and Company." *French Film Theory and Criticism, Vol. 1: 1907–1929*. Ed. Richard Abel. Princeton, NJ: Princeton UP, 1988. 94–124.

Adorno, Theodor W. "Nach Kracauers Tod," in *Vermischte Schriften I: Theorien und Theoretiker, Gesellschaft, Unterricht, Politik*, Vol. 20.1 of *Gesammelte Schriften*. Frankfurt am Main: Suhrkamp, 1986. 194–196.

Altman, Rick. "Moving Lips: Cinema as Ventriloquism." *Yale French Studies* 60 Cinema/Sound (1980): 67–79.

Ames, Eric. "The Image of Culture—or, What Münsterberg Saw in the Movies." *German Culture in Nineteenth-Century America: Reception, Adaptation, Transformation*. Ed. Lynne Tatlock and Matt Erlin. Rochester, NY: Camden House, 2005. 21–42.

Andrew, Dudley. *André Bazin*. New York: Oxford UP, 1978.

———. "André Bazin and His 'Ontology of the Photographic Image.'" *The Routledge Encyclopedia of Film Theory*. Ed. Edward Branigan and Warren Buckland. New York: Routledge, 2013. 333–339.

———. "Foreword." André Bazin, *What Is Cinema?* Trans. Hugh Gray. Berkeley, CA: U of California P, 1967. ix–xxiv.

———. *The Major Film Theories: An Introduction*. Oxford: Oxford UP, 1976.

———. *What Cinema Is! Bazin's Quest and Its Charge*. Malden, MA: Wiley-Blackwell, 2010.

Arendt, Hannah. "Introduction." Walter Benjamin, *Illuminations*. Ed. Hannah Arendt. New York: Schocken, 1968. 1–51.

Arnheim, Rudolf. "Art Today and Film." *Film Essays and Criticism*. Trans. Brenda Benthien. Madison, WI: U of Wisconsin P, 1997. 23–28.

———. *Film as Art*. Berkeley, CA: U of California P, 1977.

———. "Zum Geleit [für Hugo Münsterberg: Das Lichtspiel]." *Montage/AV* (Sept. 2000 [1981]): 55–57.

Astruc, Alexandre. "Quand un homme . . . ," *Cahiers du cinéma* 39 (1954): 5.

Aumont, Jacques. *Montage Eisenstein*. Trans. Lee Hildreth, Constance Penley, and Andrew Ross. Bloomington, IN: Indiana UP, 1987.

Austin, J. L. *Philosophical Papers*. New York: Oxford UP, 2000.

Ayfre, Amédée. "Néo-Réalism et Phénoménologie." *Cahiers du cinéma* 17 (Nov. 1952): 6–18.

Babener, Liahna, "De-feminizing *Laura:* Novel to Film." *It's a Print!: Detective Fiction from Page to Screen*. Ed. William Reynolds and Elizabeth Trembley. Bowling Green, OH: Bowling Green State U Popular P, 1994. 83–102.

Balázs, Béla. "The Spirit of Film." *Béla Balázs: Early Film Theory–Visible Man and the Spirit of Film*. Ed. Erica Carter, trans. Rodney Livingstone. Oxford: Berghahn, 2010.

———. *Theory of the Film*. Trans. Edith Bone. London: Dennis Dobson, 1952.

———. "Visible Man." *Béla Balázs: Early Film Theory–Visible Man and the Spirit of Film.* Ed. Erica Carter, trans. Rodney Livingstone. Oxford: Berghahn, 2010.

Barthes, Roland. *Camera Lucida: Reflections on Photography.* Trans. Richard Howard. London: Vintage, 2000.

———. *Image, Music, Text.* Trans. Stephen Heath. London: Fontana, 1977.

———. *Mythologies.* Trans. Annette Lavers. London: Vintage, 1993.

———. *S/Z: An Essay.* Trans. Richard Miller. New York: Hill & Wang, 1991.

———. *Writing Degree Zero.* Trans. Annette Lavers and Colin Smith. New York: Hill & Wang, 1990.

Baudrillard, Jean. *Simulacra and Simulation.* Trans. Sheila Faria Glaser. Ann Arbor, MI: U of Michigan P, 1994.

Bazin, André. "The Death of Humphrey Bogart." *Cahiers du cinéma the 1950s.* Ed. Jim Hillier. Cambridge, MA: Harvard UP, 1985. 98–101. Originally published in February 1957.

———. "Grandeur et décadence du gangster." *Radio-Cinéma-Télévision* 92 (Oct. 21, 1951): n.p.

———. "Hitchcock contre Hitchcock." *Cahiers du cinéma* 39 (1954): 25–32.

———. "Les Passagers de la nuit," *Parisien Libéré* 1191 (July 14, 1948): n.p.

———. "A Saint Becomes a Saint Only After the Fact." *Bazin at Work.* Ed. Bert Cardullo. New York: Routledge, 1997. 205–210. The original, "Un saint ne l'est qu'après . . ." appeared in *Cahiers du cinéma*'s second issue, May 1951.

———. *What Is Cinema?* Vol. 1. Trans. Hugh Gray. Berkeley, CA: U of California P, 1967.

Benjamin, Walter. "Little History of Photography." *Walter Benjamin: Selected Writings.* Vol. 2. Ed. M. W. Jennings, H. Eiland, and G. Smith. Cambridge, MA: Harvard UP, 1999. 507–530.

———. "On Some Motifs in Baudelaire." *Illuminations.* Ed. Hannah Arendt. New York: Schocken, 1968. 155–194.

———. "The Work of Art in the Age of Mechanical Reproduction." *Illuminations.* Ed. Hannah Arendt. New York: Schocken, 1968. 217–251.

Bogue, Ronald. *Deleuze on Cinema.* New York: Routledge, 2003.

Bordwell, David. *On the History of Film Style.* Cambridge, MA: Harvard UP, 1997.

———. *The Way Hollywood Tells It: Story and Style in Modern Movies.* Berkeley, CA: U of California P, 2006.

Bowie, Malcolm. *Lacan.* London: HarperCollins, 1991.

Brant, Sebastian. *Stultifera navis.* London: Richard Pynson, 1509.

Braudy, Leo, and Marshall Cohen. *Film Theory and Criticism.* 7th ed. New York: Oxford UP, 2009.

Bresson, Robert. *Notes on Cinematography.* Trans. Jonathan Griffin. New York: Urizen Books, 1977.

Browne, Nick. "The Spectator-in-the-Text: The Rhetoric of Stagecoach." *Film Quarterly* 29.2 (Winter 1975–1976): 26–38.

Bruno, Giuliana. "Film, Aesthetics, Science: Hugo Münsterberg's Laboratory of Moving Images." *Grey Room* 36 (Summer 2009): 88–113.

Bulgakowa, Oksana. "The Evolving Eisenstein: Three Theoretical Constructs of Sergei Eisenstein." *Eisenstein at 100: A Reconsideration.* Ed. Al LaValley and Barry P. Scherr. New Brunswick, NJ: Rutgers UP, 2001. 38–51.

———. *Sergei Eisenstein: A Biography.* Trans. Anne Dwyer. Berlin: Potemkin Press, 2001.

Burke, Kenneth. *A Grammar of Motives.* Berkeley, CA: U of California P, 1969.

Butler, Judith. *Bodies That Matter: On the Discursive Limits of Sex.* New York: Routledge, 1993.

———. *Gender Trouble: Feminism and the Subversion of Identity.* New York: Routledge, 1990.

———. "Performative Acts and Gender Constitution: An Essay in Phenomenology and Feminist Theory." *Performing Feminisms: Feminist Critical Theory and Theatre.* Ed. Sue-Ellen Case. Baltimore, MD: Johns Hopkins UP, 1990. 270–282.

Cage, John. *Silence*. Middletown, CT: Wesleyan UP, 1961.

Cahiers du cinéma. "John Ford's *Young Mr. Lincoln*: A Collective Text by the Editors of *Cahiers du cinema*." *Screen* 13.3 (1972): 5–44.

Carroll, Noël. *The Philosophical Problems of Classical Film Theory*. Princeton, NJ: Princeton UP, 1988.

Carter, Erica. "Introduction." *Béla Balázs: Early Film Theory–Visible Man and the Spirit of Film*. Trans. Rodney Livingstone. Oxford: Berghahn, 2010. xv–xlvi.

Casetti, Francesco. *Eye of the Century: Film, Experience, Modernity*. New York: Columbia UP, 2008.

Cavell, Stanley. Cities of Words: Pedagogical Letters on a Register of the Moral Life. Cambridge, MA: Belknap Press, 2005.

———. *The Claim of Reason: Wittgenstein, Skepticism, Morality, and Tragedy*. New York: Oxford UP, 1979.

———. *Contesting Tears: The Hollywood Melodrama of the Unknown Woman*. Chicago: U of Chicago P, 1994.

———. *Must We Mean What We Say?* New York: Cambridge UP, 1976.

———. *Pursuits of Happiness: The Hollywood Comedy of Remarriage*. Cambridge, MA: Harvard UP, 1981.

———. *The World Viewed: Reflections on the Ontology of Film*. Cambridge, MA: Harvard UP, 1979.

Chabrol, Claude. "Hitchcock devant le mal." *Cahiers du cinéma* 39 (1954): 18–24.

Chabrol, Claude, and Eric Rohmer. *Hitchcock, the First Forty-Four Films*. New York: Ungar, 1979.

Chion, Michel. *Film, A Sound Art*. Trans. Claudia Gorbman. New York: Columbia UP, 2009. Originally published as *Un art sonore, le cinéma*. Paris: Éditions de l'étoile, 2003.

———. *Guide des objets sonores: Pierre Schaeffer et la recherche musicale*. Paris: Institut National de L'audiovisuel & Éditions Buchet/Chastel, 1983.

———. *Sound on Screen*. Trans. Claudia Gorbman. New York: Columbia UP, 1994. Originally published as *L'Audio-Vision: son et image au cinéma*. Paris: Éditions Nathan, 1990.

———. *The Voice in Cinema*. Trans. Claudia Gorbman. New York: Columbia UP, 1999. Originally published as *La voix au cinéma*. Paris: Éditions de l'étoile, 1982.

Ciment, Michel, and Lawrence Kardish. *Positif: Fifty Years*. New York: Museum of Modern Art, 2003.

Clayton, Alex, and Andrew Klevan, eds. *The Language and Style of Film Criticism*. London: Routledge, 2011.

Colman, Felicity. *Deleuze and Cinema: The Film Concepts*. New York: Berg, 2011.

Comolli, Jean-Louis. "Machines of the Visible." *The Cinematic Apparatus*. Ed. Teresa de Lauretis and Stephen Heath. New York: St. Martin's Press, 1980. 121–142.

Cook, David A. *A History of Narrative Film*. 4th ed. New York: W. W. Norton, 2004.

Dalle Vacche, Angela. "André Bazin's Film Theory and Philosophy." *Cambridge Encyclopedia of Film and/as Philosophy*. Ed. Bernd Herzogenrath, New York: Cambridge UP, 2015.

Dargis, Manohla. "This Is How the End Begins." *New York Times* (Jan. 1, 2012): MT1.

Dargis, Manohla, and A. O. Scott. "How the Movies Made a President." *New York Times* (Jan. 18, 2009). Online at nytimes.com

De Beauvoir, Simone. *The Second Sex*. Trans. Constance Borde and Sheila Malovany-Chevallier. New York: Random House, 2011.

Deleuze, Gilles. *Cinema 1: The Movement-Image*. Trans. Hugh Tomlinson and Barbara Habberjam. 1986. Minneapolis, MN: U of Minnesota P, 2003.

———. *Cinema 2: The Movement-Image*. Trans. Hugh Tomlinson and Robert Galeta. 1989. Minneapolis, MN: U of Minnesota P, 2003.

Del Río, Elana. *Deleuze and the Cinemas of Performance: Powers of Affection*. Edinburgh: Edinburgh UP, 2008.

Denning, Michael. *The Cultural Front: The Laboring of American Culture in the Twentieth Century*. London: Verso, 1996.

Deren, Maya. *Essential Deren: Collected Writings on Film*. Ed. Bruce McPherson. Kingston, NY: Documentext, 2005.

———. Letter to Sonya Dorman, November 3, 1953, Box 5, Folder 12, Maya Deren Collection, Howard Gotlieb Archival Research Center, Boston U.

———. "Symposium on Poetry and the Film." *Film Culture Reader*. 2nd ed. Ed. P. Adams Sitney. New York: Cooper Square Press, 2000. 171–186.

Descartes, René. *Méditations*. Trans. Laurence J. Lafleur. New York: Liberal Arts Press, 1951.

Dorman, Sonya. Letter to Maya Deren, October 29, 1953, Box 5, Folder 12, Maya Deren Collection, Howard Gotlieb Archival Research Center, Boston U.

Douchet, Jean. *Hitchcock*. Paris: Éditions de l'Herne, 1967.

Eaton, Mick. "The Production of Cinematic Reality." *Anthropology—Reality—Cinema: The Films of Jean Rouch*. London: BFI, 1979.

Eisenstein, Sergei M. "Beyond the Shot." *The Eisenstein Reader*. Ed. Richard Taylor. London: British Film Institute, 1998. 82–92. Translated elsewhere as "The Cinematographic Principle and the Ideogram" and published earlier in Jay Leyda, ed. and trans., *Film Form: Essays in Film Theory*. New York: Harcourt Brace and Co., 1949. 28–44.

———. "The Dramaturgy of Film Form (The Dialectical Approach to Film Form)." *The Eisenstein Reader*. Ed. Richard Taylor. London: British Film Institute, 1998. 93–110.

———. "Eisenstein on Disney." Trans. Alan Y. Upchurch, ed. Jay Leyda. *The Eisenstein Collection*. Ed. Richard Taylor. London: Seagull Books, 2006. 85–175.

———. "The Fourth Dimension in Cinema." *The Eisenstein Reader*. Ed. Richard Taylor. London: British Film Institute, 1998. 111–123.

———. "How I Became a Director." Trans. William Powell. *Writings, 1934–47, Selected Works*. Vol. 3. Ed. Richard Taylor. London: British Film Institute, 1996. 284–290.

———. Letter to Alexander Korda, October 3, 1943, Box 2, Orson Welles mss. Lilly Library, Indiana U, Bloomington, IN.

———. "The Montage of Attractions." Trans. Richard Taylor and William Powell. *The Eisenstein Reader*. Ed. Richard Taylor. London: British Film Institute, 1998. 29–34.

———. "The Montage of Film Attractions." *The Eisenstein Reader*. Ed. Richard Taylor. London: British Film Institute, 1998. 35–52.

———. *Nonindifferent Nature*. Trans. Herbert Marshall. Cambridge: Cambridge UP, 1987.

———. "The Problem of the Materialist Approach to Form." *The Eisenstein Reader*. Ed. Richard Taylor. London: British Film Institute, 1998. 53–59.

Elsaesser, Thomas. "Kracauer's Affinities." *Necsus: European Journal of Media Studies* (April 2014): n.p. Online at www.necsus-ejms.org/siegfried-kracauers-affinities/

Epstein, Jean. *Bonjour cinéma*. Paris: Éditions de la Sirène, 1921.

———. *Le Cinéma du diable* (*Devil's Cinema*). Paris: Éditions Jacques Melot, 1947.

———. *Le Cinéma vu de l'Etna* (*The Cinema Seen from Etna*). Paris: Les Écrivains Réunis, 1926.

———. "The Close-Up of Sound." *Jean Epstein: Critical Essays and New Translations*. Ed. Sarah Keller and Jason N. Paul. Amsterdam: Amsterdam UP, 2012. 365–372.

———. *Ésprit de cinéma* (*The Spirit of Cinema*). Geneva: Éditions Jeheber, 1955 (posthumous).

———. *L'Intelligence d'une machine* (*The Intelligence of a Machine*). Trans. and intro. Christophe Wall-Romana. Minneapolis, MN: Univocal, 2014. Originally published Paris: Éditions Jacques Melot, 1946.

———. *La Lyrosophie*. Paris: Éditions de la Sirène, 1922.

———. "Magnification." *French Film Theory and Criticism, Vol. 1: 1907–1929*. Ed. Richard Abel. Princeton, NJ: Princeton UP, 1988. 235–241.

———. "On Certain Characteristics of Photogénie," in *French Film Theory and Criticism, Vol. 1: 1907–1929*. Ed Richard Abel. Princeton, NJ: Princeton UP, 1988. 314–318.

———. *Poésie d'aujourd'hui: un nouvel état d'intelligence* (*The Poetry of Today: A New State of Intelligence*). Paris: Éditions de la Sirène, 1921.

Esnault, Philippe. "Jean Rouch—Les aventures d'un nègre blanc." Interview with Jean Rouch, *Image et Son* 249 (April 1971): 56–79.

Farocki, Harun, and Kaja Silverman. *Speaking about Godard*. New York: New York UP, 1998.

Fischer, Lucy. "'The Shock of the New': Electrification, Illumination, Urbanization, and the Cinema." *Cinema and Modernity*. Ed. Murray Pomerance. New Brunswick, NJ: Rutgers UP, 2006. 19–37.

———. *Sunrise: A Song of Two Humans*. London: BFI Publishing, 1998.

Fisher, Kevin. "Cinephilia as Topophilia in *The Matrix*." *Cinephilia in the Age of Digital Reproduction: Film, Pleasure and Digital Culture*. Vol. 1. Ed. Scott Balcerzak and Jason Sperb. London: Wallflower Press, 2009. 171–190.

Foucault, Michel. *The Archaeology of Knowledge*. Trans. A. M. Sheridan Smith. New York: Routledge, 2002.

———. *Discipline and Punish: The Birth of the Prison*. Trans. Alan Sheridan. New York: Pantheon, 1977.

———. *Dits et écrits, 1954–1988*. Ed. Daniel Defert and François Ewald. Paris: Éditions Gallimard, 1994.

———. *History of Sexuality*. 3 vols. Trans. Robert Hurley. New York: Vintage, 1980.

———. *Madness and Civilization: A History of Insanity in the Age of Reason*. Trans. Richard Howard. New York: Pantheon, 1965.

———. "My Body, This Paper, This Fire." Trans. Geoff Bennington. *Aesthetics, Method, and Epistemology*. Ed. James D. Faubion. New York: New Press, 1998. 393–417.

———. *The Order of Things: An Archaeology of the Human Sciences*. New York: Pantheon, 1970.

———. *Raymond Roussel*. Paris: Éditions Gallimard, 1963.

———. *This Is Not a Pipe*. Trans. James Harkness. Berkeley, CA: U of California P, 1983.

———. "What Is an Author?" *Language, Counter-memory, Practice*. Ed. Donald F. Bouchard. Ithaca, NY: Cornell UP, 1977. 113–138.

Freud, Sigmund. *An Outline of Psychoanalysis*. Trans. Helena Ragg-Kirkby. Wiltshire: Penguin, 2003.

Gilbert, Morris. "Paris Cinema Chatter." *New York Times* (April 20, 1930): 14–15. Rpt. *Sternberg*. Ed. Peter Baxter. London: BFI, 1980.

Godard, Jean-Luc. *Histoire(s) du cinéma*. Paris: Gallimard, 1998.

Greenblatt, Stephen. *Renaissance Self-Fashioning: From More to Shakespeare*. Chicago: U of Chicago P, 1980.

Griffith, Richard. "Foreword." Hugo Münsterberg, *The Film: A Psychological Study*. Mineola, NY: Dover, 1970. v–xv.

Grosz, Elizabeth. *Jacques Lacan: A Feminist Introduction*. Sydney: Allen & Unwin, 1990.

Gunning, Tom. "An Aesthetic of Astonishment: Early Film and the (In)Credulous Spectator." *Viewing Positions: Ways of Seeing Film*. Ed. Linda Williams. New Brunswick, NJ: Rutgers UP, 1995. 114–133.

———. "The Cinema of Attraction: Early Film, Its Spectator, and the Avant-Garde." *Wide Angle* 8.3 (1986): 63–70.

Hale, Matthew, Jr. *Human Science and Social Order: Hugo Münsterberg and the Origins of Applied Psychology*. Philadelphia: Temple UP, 1980.

Hansen, Miriam. *Babel & Babylon: Spectatorship in American Silent Cinema*. Cambridge, MA: Harvard UP, 1991.

———. *Cinema and Experience: Siegfried Kracauer, Walter Benjamin, and Theodor W. Adorno*. Berkeley, CA: U of California P, 2012.

Hayes, Kevin J., ed. *Charlie Chaplin Interviews*. Jackson, MS: UP of Mississippi, 2005.

Heath, Stephen. "The Work of Christian Metz," *Screen* 14.3 (1973): 5–28.

Hergé. *The Secret of the Unicorn*. New York: Little, Brown, 1974.

Hess, John. "La Politique des Auteurs: Part One," *Jump Cut* 1 (1974): 19–22.

Hickey, Dave. *The Invisible Dragon: Essays on Beauty*. Rev. and enl. ed. Chicago: U of Chicago P, 2009.

Higgins, Scott, ed. *Arnheim for Film and Media Studies*. New York: Routledge, 2011.

Irigaray, Luce. *Speculum of the Other Woman*. Trans. Gillian C. Gill. Ithaca, NY: Cornell UP, 1985.

Irwin, John T. *American Hieroglyphics: The Symbol of the Egyptian Hieroglyphics in the American Renaissance*. Baltimore, MD: Johns Hopkins UP, 1980.

Iverson, Erik. *The Myth of Egypt and its Hieroglyphs in European Tradition*. Princeton, NJ: Princeton UP, 1993.

Jones, Janna. "The Library of Congress Film Project: Film Collecting and a United State(s) of Mind." *The Moving Image* 6.2 (2006): 30–51.

"Josef von Sternberg Interview." Supplementary material. *The Docks of New York*. Dir. Josef von Sternberg. 1928. DVD. Criterion, 2010.

Kasson, John. *Amusing the Million: Coney Island at the Turn of the Century*. New York: Hill and Wang, 1978.

Keathley, Christian. *Cinephilia and History, or The Wind in the Trees*. Bloomington, IN: Indiana UP, 2006.

Keller, Phyllis. *States of Belonging: German-American Intellectuals and the First World War*. Cambridge, MA: Harvard UP, 1979.

Keller, Sarah. *Maya Deren: Incomplete Control*. New York: Columbia UP, 2014.

Kennedy, Barbara. *Deleuze and Cinema: The Aesthetics of Sensation*. Edinburgh: Edinburgh UP, 2000.

Kirtland, Katie. "Introduction to La Lyrosophie." *Jean Epstein: Critical Essays and New Translations*. Ed. Sarah Keller and Jason N. Paul. Amsterdam: Amsterdam UP, 2012. 281.

Kleiman, Naum. Introduction to "Eisenstein on Disney." *The Eisenstein Collection*. Ed. Richard Taylor. London: Seagull Books, 2006. 79–83.

Koch, Gertrud. "Béla Balázs: The Physiognomy of Things." *New German Critique* 40 (Winter 1987): 167–177.

———. "Rudolf Arnheim: The Materialist of Aesthetic Illusion: Gestalt Theory and Reviewer's Practice." *New German Critique* 51 (Summer 1990): 164–178.

Kracauer, Siegfried. *From Caligari to Hitler: A Psychological History of the German Film*. Princeton, NJ: Princeton UP, 2004.

———. *History, the Last Things before the Last*. New York: Oxford UP, 1969.

———. "Hollywood's Terror Films." *Commentary* (Aug. 1946): 131.

———. *The Mass Ornament: Weimar Essays*. Trans. Thomas Y. Levin. Cambridge, MA: Harvard UP, 1995.

———. "A New Book on Film" (1930). *Béla Balázs: Early Film Theory–Visible Man and the Spirit of Film*. Ed. Erica Carter, trans. Rodney Livingstone. Oxford: Berghahn, 2010. 231–232.

———. "Photography." *The Mass Ornament: Weimar Essays*. Trans. Thomas Y. Levin. Cambridge, MA: Harvard UP, 1995. 47–64.

———. *The Salaried Masses: Duty and Distraction in Weimar Germany*. London: Verso, 1998.

———. *Siegfried Kracauer's American Writings: Essays on Film and Popular Culture*. Ed. Johannes von Moltke and Kristy Rawson. Berkeley, CA: U of California P, 2012.

———. *Theory of Film: The Redemption of Physical Reality.* Princeton, NJ: Princeton UP, 1997. Originally published in 1960.
———. "Those Movies with a Message." *Harper's Magazine* (June 1, 1948): n.p.
Krauss, Rosalind. *"A Voyage on the North Sea": Art in the Age of the Post-Medium Condition.* London: Thames and Hudson, 1999.
Kretzschmar, Laurent. "Is Cinema Renewing Itself?" *Film-Philosophy* 6.1 (2002). Online at http://www.film-philosophy.com/index.php/f-p/article/view/679
Lacan, Jacques. *Écrits: A Selection.* Trans. Alan Sheridan. London: Tavistock, 1977.
———. *The Four Fundamental Concepts of Psycho-analysis.* Trans. Alan Sheridan. London: Penguin, 1991.
Leclaire, Serge. *A Child Is Being Killed: On Primary Narcissism and the Death Drive.* Trans. Marie-Claude Hays. Stanford, CA: Stanford UP, 1998.
Liebman, Stuart. "Novelty and Poesis in the Writings of Jean Epstein." *Jean Epstein: Critical Essays and New Translations.* Ed. Sarah Keller and Jason N. Paul. Amsterdam: Amsterdam UP, 2012. 73–91.
Lindsay, Vachel. *Adventures Rhymes and Designs.* New York: Eakins Press, 1968.
———. *The Art of the Moving Picture.* Intro. Stanley Kaufmann. New York: Livewright, 1970. Originally published in 1915.
———. "Back Up Your Train to My Pony." *The New Republic* (March 10, 1917): 166–167.
———. "The Movies." *The New Republic* (Jan. 13, 1917): 302–303.
———. "Photoplay Progress." *The New Republic* (Feb. 17, 1917): 76–77. Online at www.unz.org/Pub/NewRepublic-1917feb17-00076
———. *The Progress and Poetry of the Movies.* Ed. and with commentary by Myron Lounsbury. Lanham, MD: Scarecrow Press, 1995.
———. "The Queen of My People." *The New Republic* 11 (July 7, 1917): 280–281. Online at www.vachellindsay.or/EssaysandStories/queen_of_my_people_1917_.pdf
———. "Venus in Armor." *The New Republic* 10 (April 28, 1917): 380–381.
MacCormack, Patricia. *Cinesexuality.* London: Ashgate, 2008.
Manovich, Lev. *The Language of New Media.* Cambridge, MA: MIT Press, 2001.
Marks, Laura U. *The Skin of the Film: Intercultural Cinema, Embodiment, and the Senses.* Durham, NC: Duke UP, 2000.
Martin-Jones, David. *Deleuze and World Cinemas.* London: Continuum, 2011.
———. *Deleuze, Cinema, and National Identity.* Edinburgh: Edinburgh UP, 2006.
Mast, Gerald, and Marshall Cohen. *Film Theory and Criticism.* 3rd ed. New York: Oxford UP, 1985.
Metz, Christian. "Aural Objects." Trans. Georgia Gurrieri. *Yale French Studies* 60 Cinema/Sound (1980): 24–32.
———. *Film Language: A Semiotics of the Cinema.* New York: Oxford UP, 1974.
———. *The Imaginary Signifier: Psychoanalysis and the Cinema.* Bloomington, IN: Indiana UP, 1982.
———. *Psychoanalysis and Cinema: The Imaginary Signifier.* Trans. Celia Britton, Annwyl Williams, Ben Brewster, and Alfred Guzzetti. London: Macmillan, 1985.
Modleski, Tania. "Editorial Notes: A Reply to Stanley Cavell." *Critical Inquiry* 17.1 (1990): 237–244.
———. *The Women Who Knew Too Much: Hitchcock and Feminist Theory.* New York: Methuen, 1988.
Montaigne, Michel de. *An Apology for Raimond Sebond.* Trans. M. A. Screech. London: Penguin, 1987.
Moore, Rachel O. *Savage Theory: Cinema as Modern Magic.* Durham, NC: Duke UP, 2000.
Morin, Edgar. *The Stars.* Trans. Richard Howard. Minneapolis, MN: U of Minnesota P, 2005.

Mulvey, Laura. "Visual Pleasure and Narrative Cinema." *Screen* 16.3 (1975): 6–28.

Münsterberg, Hugo. *Das Lichtspiel: Eine psychologische Studie (1916) und andere Schriften zum Kino.* Ed. Jörg Schweinitz, trans. Jörg Schweinitz. Vienna: Synema, 1996.

———. Letter to Abbott Lowell, May 3, 1916, Mss. Acc. 2499b (572), Hugo Münsterberg Collection, Rare Books & Manuscripts, Boston Public Library.

———. *The Photoplay: A Psychological Study.* New York: D. Appleton and Company, 1916.

———. "Why We Go to the 'Movies.'" *Cosmopolitan* 60.1 (Dec. 1915): 22–32.

Münsterberg, Margaret. *Hugo Münsterberg: His Life and Work.* New York: D. Appleton and Company, 1922.

Murray, Timothy. *Digital Baroque: New Media Art and Cinematic Folds.* Minneapolis, MN: U of Minnesota P, 2008.

Nancy, Jean-Luc. *L'évidence du film: Abbas Kiarostami.* Trans. Christine Irizarry and Verena Andermatt Conley. Bruxelles: Yves Gevaert, 2001.

Nichols, Bill, ed. *Maya Deren and the American Avant-Garde.* Berkeley, CA: U of California P, 2001.

Nochimson, Martha P. *David Lynch Swerves: Uncertainty from "Lost Highway" to "Inland Empire."* Austin, TX: U of Texas P, 2014.

Paul, William. *Ernst Lubitsch's American Comedy.* New York: Columbia UP, 1983.

Perkins, V. F. *Film as Film.* Harmondsworth, Middlesex: Penguin Books, 1972.

———. *"Johnny Guitar." The Movie Book of the Western.* Ed. Ian Cameron and Douglas Pye, London: Studio Vista, 1996.

———. *The Magnificent Ambersons.* London: BFI, 1999.

———. "Moments of Choice." *Movie Book of the Fifties.* Ed. Ann Lloyd. London: Orbis, 1982.

———. *La Règle du jeu.* London: BFI, 2012.

Petersson, Dag, and Erik Steinskog, eds. *Actualities of Aura: Twelve Studies of Walter Benjamin.* Svanesund, Sweden: Nordic Summer UP, 2005.

Pierson, Ryan. "On Styles of Theorizing Animation Styles: Stanley Cavell at the Cartoon's Demise." *The Velvet Light Trap* 69 (2012): 17–26.

Pisters, Patricia. *The Matrix of Visual Culture: Working with Deleuze in Film Theory.* Stanford, CA: Stanford UP, 2003.

———. *The Neuro Image: A Deleuzian Film-Philosophy of Digital Screen Culture.* Stanford, CA: Stanford UP, 2012.

"The Pixar Story." Supplementary material. *WALL-E.* Dir. Andrew Stanton. DVD. Walt Disney, 2008.

Pomerance, Murray. *Johnny Depp Starts Here.* New Brunswick, NJ: Rutgers UP, 2004.

Powell, Anna. *Deleuze, Altered States, and Film.* Edinburgh: Edinburgh UP, 2007.

———. *Deleuze and Horror Film.* Edinburgh: Edinburgh UP, 2005.

Proust, Marcel. *Swann's Way.* Trans. Lydia Davis. New York: Penguin Books, 2002.

Pudovkin, Vsevolod. "The Film Director and Film Material." Trans. Richard Taylor and Evgeni Filippov. *Selected Essays.* Ed. Richard Taylot. London: Seagull Books, 2006. 65–119.

"RAGBRAI history." RAGBRAI: The Register's Annual Great Bicycle Race Across Iowa. 2014. Online at http://ragbrai.com/about/ragbrai-history/

Rancière, Jacques. *Aesthetics and Its Discontents.* Trans. Steven Corcoran. Cambridge: Polity Press, 2009.

———. *The Aesthetic Unconscious.* Trans. Debra Keates and James Swenson. Cambridge: Polity Press, 2009.

———. *Aisthesis: Scenes from the Aesthetic Regime of Art.* Trans. Zakir Paul. London: Verso, 2013.

———. *Disagreement: Politics and Philosophy*. Trans. Julie Rose. Minneapolis, MN: U of Minnesota P, 1999.

———. *Film Fables*. Trans. Emiliano Battista. Oxford: Berg, 2006.

———. *Mute Speech*. Trans. James Swenson. New York: Columbia UP, 2011.

Ray, Robert B. *How a Film Theory Got Lost, and Other Mysteries in Cultural Studies*. Bloomington, IN: Indiana UP, 2001.

Redner, Gregg. *Deleuze and Film Music: Building a Methodological Bridge between Film Theory and Music*. Bristol: Intellect, 2011.

Ricciardi, Alessia. "Cinema Regained: Godard between Proust and Benjamin." *Modernism/modernity* 8.4 (Nov. 2001): 643–661.

"Richard Farnsworth, Stunt Man and 2-Time Oscar Nominee, 80." *New York Times* (Oct. 8, 2000): 46.

Richards, Rashna Wadia. *Cinematic Flashes: Cinephilia and Classical Hollywood*. Bloomington, IN: Indiana UP, 2013.

Rodowick, David N. *Gilles Deleuze's Time Machine*. Durham, NC: Duke UP, 1997.

———. *The Virtual Life of Film*. Cambridge, MA: Harvard UP, 2007.

Rohmer, Eric. "La Celluloid et le Marbre," *Cahiers du cinéma* 44 (February 1955), 32–37; 49 (July 1955), 10–15; 51 (October 1955), 2–9; 52 (November 1955), 23–29; and 53 (December 1955), 22–30.

———. "La 'révolution' Bazin; le mystère de l'existence." *Le Monde* (Dec. 15, 1994): n.p.

———. Letter to Dudley Andrew, September 25, 2008.

Rosenzweig, Roy. *Eight Hours for What We Will: Workers and Leisure in an Industrial City 1870–1920*. Cambridge: Cambridge UP, 1983.

Rothman, William. *Hitchcock: The Murderous Gaze*. 2nd ed. Albany, NY: State U of New York P, 2012.

Rothman, William, and Marian Keane. *Reading Cavell's "The World Viewed": A Philosophical Perspective on Film*. Detroit, MI: Wayne State UP, 2000.

Rouch, Jean. "On the Vicissitudes of the Self: The Possessed Dancer, the Magician, the Sorcerer, the Filmmaker, and the Ethnographer." *Studies in the Anthropology of Visual Communication* 5 (1978): 2–8.

Rushton, Richard. "Christian Metz." *Film, Theory and Philosophy: The Key Thinkers*. Ed. Felicity Colman. Montreal: McGill-Queen's UP, 2009. 266–275.

———. *Cinema After Deleuze*. London: Continuum, 2012.

Sanders, Julie. *Adaptation and Appropriation*. New York: Routledge, 2006.

Sargent, Epes Winthrop. *The Technique of the Photoplay*. New York: Moving Picture World, 1912.

Sarris, Andrew. *The Films of Josef von Sternberg*. New York: Museum of Modern Art, 1966.

Schafer, R. Murray. *The Soundscape: Our Sonic Environment and the Tuning of the World*. New York: Knopf, 1977.

Schatz, Thomas. "The Hard-Boiled Detective Film." *Hollywood Genres: Formulas, Filmmaking, and the Studio System*. Boston: McGraw-Hill, 1981. 111–149.

Schefer, Jean-Louis. *L'Homme ordinaire du cinéma*. Paris: Éditions Gallimard/Cahiers du Cinéma, 1980.

Schweinitz, Jörg. "Psychotechnik, idealistische Äesthetik und der Film als mental strukturierter Wahrnehmungsraum: Die Filmtheorie von Hugo Münsterberg." Hugo Münsterberg, *Das Lichtspiel: Eine psychologische Studie (1916) und andere Schriften zum Kino*. Vienna: Synema, 1996. 9–26.

Scott, A. O. "'Lincoln,' by Steven Spielberg, Stars Daniel Day-Lewis." *New York Times* (Nov. 8, 2012). Online at nytimes.com

Scott, A. O., and Manohla Dargis. "'Lincoln,' 'Django Unchained,' and an Obama-Inflected Cinema." *New York Times* (Jan. 16, 2013). Online at blouinnews.com/44721/topic_item/lincoln-django-unchained-and-obama-inflected-cinema

Shaviro, Steven. *The Cinematic Body*. Minneapolis, MN: U of Minnesota P, 1993.

Shohat, Ella. *Israeli Cinema: East/West and the Politics of Representation*. London: I. B. Tauris, 2010.

Shohat, Ella, and Robert Stam. "The Cinema After Babel: Language, Difference, Power." *Screen* 26 (May–Aug. 1985): 35–58.

Silverman, Kaja. *The Acoustic Mirror: The Female Voice in Psychoanalysis and Cinema*. Bloomington, IN: Indiana UP, 1988.

Simmel, Georg. "The Metropolis and Mental Life (1903)." *The Nineteenth Century Visual Culture Reader*. Ed. Vanessa Schwartz and Jeannene Przyblyski. New York: Routledge, 2004. 51–55.

Sobchack, Vivian. "Animation and Automation; or, The Incredible Effortfulness of Being." *Screen* 50.4 (2009): 375–391.

Sperb, Jason. "Déjà vu for Something That Hasn't Happened Yet: Time, Repetition, and Jamais vu within a Cinephilia of Anticipation." *Cinephilia in the Age of Digital Reproduction: Film, Pleasure and Digital Culture*. Vol. 1. Ed. Scott Balcerzak and Jason Sperb. London: Wallflower Press, 2009. 140–157.

Sternberg, Josef von. *Fun in a Chinese Laundry*. London: Secker and Warburg, 1965.

Stoller, Paul. *The Cinematic Griot: The Ethnography of Jean Rouch*. Chicago: U of Chicago P, 1992.

Sutton, Damian. *Photography, Cinema, Memory: The Crystal Image of Time*. Minneapolis, MN: U of Minnesota P, 2009.

Toles, George. "Rescuing Fragments: A New Task for Cinephilia." *Cinema Journal* 49.2 (Winter 2010): 159–166.

Tomlinson, Hugh, and Robert Galeta. "Translators' Introduction." Gilles Deleuze, *Cinema 2: The Time-Image*. Minneapolis, MN: U of Minnesota P, 2003. xv–xviii.

Tomlinson, Hugh, and Barbara Habberjam. "Translators' Introduction." Gilles Deleuze, *Cinema 1: The Movement-Image*. Minneapolis, MN: U of Minnesota P, 2003. xi–xiii.

Tone, Yasunao. Statement on Parasite/Noise in Yokohama International Triennial, exhibition catalog ed. Nobuko Shimuta, et al. Yokohama: Yokohama International Triennial, 2001, quoted in Caleb Kelly ed., *Sound: Documents of Contemporary Art*. London: Whitechapel Gallery, 2011. 101–103.

Turner, Frederick Jackson. *The Frontier in American History*. New York: Henry Holt, 1921.

Vertov, Dziga. "Kino-Eye on Strike." Trans. Julian Graffy. *Lines of Resistance: Dziga Vertov and the Twenties*. Ed. Scott Balcerzak and Jason Sperb. Pordenone: Le Giornate del Cinema Muto, 2004. 125–126.

Von Moltke, Johannes. "2 February, 1956. Siegfried Kracauer Advocates a Socio-Aesthetic Approach to Film in a Letter to Enno Patalas." *A New History of German Cinema*. Ed. Jennifer M. Kapczynski and Michael David Richardson. Rochester, NY: Camden House, 2012. 359–364.

Whissel, Kristen. *Spectacular Digital Effects: CGI and Contemporary Cinema*. Durham, NC: Duke UP, 2014.

Willemen, Paul. *Looks and Frictions: Essays in Cultural Studies and Film Theory*. Bloomington, IN: Indiana UP, 1994.

Wollen, Peter. "Perhaps. . . ." *October* 88 (1999): 42–50.

———. *Signs and Meaning in the Cinema*. 3rd ed. Bloomington, IN: Indiana UP, 1972.

Žižek, Slavoj, ed. *Everything You Always Wanted to Know About Lacan (But Were Afraid to Ask Hitchcock)*. London and New York: Verso, 1992.

NOTES ON CONTRIBUTORS

DUDLEY ANDREW is the R. Selden Rose Professor of Film and Comparative Literature at Yale. Biographer of André Bazin, he extends Bazin's thought in *What Cinema Is!* and in his edited volume *Opening Bazin*. He published *Film in the Aura of Art* in 1984, then *Mists of Regret* and *Popular Front Paris*. He also coedited *The Companion to François Truffaut*. For these publications, he was named Officier de l'ordre des arts et des lettres by the French Ministry of Culture.

JEREMY BLATTER is a lecturer in the history of science at Harvard University. He is currently working on a book that explores Hugo Münsterberg and the relationship between psychology, modernization, and everyday life during the Progressive Era.

WILLIAM BROWN is a senior lecturer in film at the University of Roehampton, London. He is the author of *Supercinema: Film-Philosophy for the Digital Age* and, with Dina Iordanova and Leshu Torchin, of *Moving People, Moving Images: Cinema and Trafficking in the New Europe*. He is coeditor, with David Martin-Jones, of *Deleuze and Film* and, with Jenna P-S Ng, of a Special Issue of *animation: an interdisciplinary journal* on James Cameron's *Avatar*. He has also made several micro-budget feature films, including *En Attendant Godard* (2009), *Afterimages* (2010), *Common Ground* (2012), *China: A User's Manual (Films)* (2012), *Ur: The End of Civilization in 90 Tableaux* (2014), and *Selfie* (2014).

ALEX CLAYTON is senior lecturer in film and television at the University of Bristol. He is the author of *The Body in Hollywood Slapstick*, coeditor of *The Language and Style of Film Criticism*, and sits on the editorial board of *Movie: A Journal of Film Criticism*. Recent essays include "Why Comedy Is At Home on Television" (in Jacobs and Peacock, eds., *Television Aesthetics and Style*) and "*I Was Born But . . . : Film as Social Philosophy*" (forthcoming in Neale, ed., *Silent Features*).

TOM CONLEY is Abbott Lawrence Lowell Professor of Visual and Environmental Studies and of Romance Languages and Literatures at Harvard University. He is the author of *Film Hieroglyphs, Cartographic Cinema, The Self-Made Map: Cartographic Writing in Early Modern France, The Graphic Unconscious in Early*

Modern Writing, and other works, and the editor, with T. Jefferson Kline, of *A Companion to Jean-Luc Godard*. He has translated Michel de Certeau's *The Writing of History*, Marc Augé's *Casablanca: Movies and Memory*, and numerous other volumes.

JONAH CORNE is associate professor in the Department of English, Film, and Theatre at the University of Manitoba. His articles on film and literature have appeared or are forthcoming in *Literature/Film Quarterly*, *Film International*, *College Literature*, *Criticism*, and an anthology on new silent cinema. He is currently at work on a project on cinema and statelessness.

TOM GUNNING is the Edwin A. and Betty L. Bergman Distinguished Service Professor in the Department on Cinema and Media at the University of Chicago. He is the author of *D. W. Griffith and the Origins of American Narrative Film; The Films of Fritz Lang: Allegories of Vision and Modernity*; and, with Giovanna Fossati, Joshua Yumibe, and Jonathon Rosen, *Fantasia of Color in Early Cinema*; as well as over 150 articles on early cinema, film history and theory, avant-garde film, film genre, and cinema and modernism. With André Gaudreault he originated the influential theory of the "Cinema of Attractions." In 2009 he was awarded an Andrew A. Mellon Distinguished Achievement Award, the first film scholar to receive one; and in 2010 was elected to the American Academy of Arts and Sciences. He is currently working on a book on the invention of the moving image.

KRISTEN HATCH is an associate professor in the Department of Film and Media Studies and the Visual Studies Program at the University of California, Irvine. Her book *Shirley Temple and the Performance of Girlhood* was published by Rutgers University Press in 2015.

NATHAN HOLMES is a postdoctoral research fellow with the Michigan-Mellon Project on Egalitarianism and the Metropolis at the University of Michigan. He has taught at Loyola University, Truman College, and the University of Chicago and is currently working on a book entitled *Welcome to Fear City: 1970s Crime Film and the Urban Imagination.*

SARAH KELLER is assistant professor of art and cinema studies at the University of Massachusetts–Boston. She is coeditor of *Jean Epstein: Critical Essays and New Translations*, and her book *Maya Deren: Incomplete Control* examines the role of unfinished work through Maya Deren's filmography.

DOMINIC LENNARD is an associate lecturer in the Centre for University Pathways and Partnerships at the University of Tasmania, Australia. He is the author of *Bad Seeds and Holy Terrors: The Child Villains of Horror Film*, and has also previously published essays on film stars, Tim Burton, Batman on film, and the "bromance" phenomenon.

DANIEL MORGAN is associate professor in the Department of Cinema and Media Studies at the University of Chicago. He is the author of *Late Godard and the Possibilities of Cinema* and of a number of articles on topics in the history of film theory, problems of film aesthetics, and nonfiction film.

R. BARTON PALMER is Calhoun Lemon Professor of Literature and director of film studies at Clemson University. He is the author, editor, or general editor of nearly sixty volumes on various film and literary subjects. Most recently, he has edited (with Robert Bray) *Modern British Drama on Screen* and *Modern American Drama on Screen* as well as (with Murray Pomerance) *George Cukor: Hollywood Master* and *A Little Solitaire: John Frankenheimer and American Film*. Forthcoming are (with Amanda Ann Klein) *Multiplicities: Cycles, Sequels, Remakes, and Reboots in Film & Television* and (with William Epstein) *Invented Lives, Imagined Communities: The Biopic and American National Identity*, as well as (with Homer Pettey) *Film Noir* and *International Noir*.

GILBERTO PEREZ was the Noble Professor of Art and Cultural History and professor of film history at Sarah Lawrence College. He is the author of *The Material Ghost: Films and Their Medium* and *The Eloquent Screen: An Essay in the Rhetoric of Film* (forthcoming).

MURRAY POMERANCE is professor in the Department of Sociology at Ryerson University and the author, most recently, of *Marnie, Alfred Hitchcock's America*, and *The Eyes Have It: Cinema and the Reality Effect*. He is the editor of numerous volumes including *Cinema and Modernity* and, with R. Barton Palmer, *George Cukor: Hollywood Master*; and series editor of "Horizons of Cinema" at SUNY Press and "Techniques of the Modern Image" at Rutgers University Press, as well as (with Lester D. Friedman and Adrienne L. McLean, respectively), the "Screen Decades" and "Star Decades" series from Rutgers.

WILLIAM ROTHMAN is professor of cinema and interactive media at the University of Miami. His books include *Hitchcock: The Murderous Gaze, The "I" of the Camera, Documentary Film Classics, Reading Cavell's "The World Viewed," Jean Rouch: A Celebration of Life and Film, Three Documentary Filmmakers,* and *Must We Kill the Thing We Love? Emersonian Perfectionism and the Films of Alfred Hitchcock*.

STEVEN RYBIN is assistant professor of film studies at Minnesota State University, Mankato. He is coeditor, with Will Scheibel, of *Lonely Places, Dangerous Ground: Nicholas Ray in American Cinema* and author of *Gestures of Love: Performing Courtship in Classical Hollywood Cinema* (forthcoming), *Michael Mann: Crime Auteur*, and *Terrence Malick and the Thought of Film*.

WILL SCHEIBEL is an assistant professor of film & screen studies in the Department of English at Syracuse University. Currently, he is at work on a book about modernism and the reputation of film director Nicholas Ray. He is the coeditor, with Steven Rybin, of *Lonely Places, Dangerous Ground: Nicholas Ray in American Cinema* and has written articles for the *Journal of Gender Studies, Oxford Bibliographies, Celebrity Studies*, and *La Furia Umana.*

MATTHEW SOLOMON is associate professor in the Department of Screen Arts and Cultures at the University of Michigan, where he teaches film history and theory. He is the author of *Disappearing Tricks: Silent Film, Houdini, and the New Magic of the Twentieth Century* (winner of the Kraszna-Krausz award for best moving image book) and of a BFI Film Classics monograph on *The Gold Rush* as well as the editor of *Fantastic Voyages of the Cinematic Imagination: Georges Méliès's "Trip to the Moon."*

JOHANNES VON MOLTKE is professor of German and screen arts and cultures at the University of Michigan, where he also chairs the German Department. He is the author of *No Place Like Home: Locations of Heimat in German Cinema*, as well as numerous articles on film theory and German film history in journals such as *Screen, New German Critique, Cinema Journal, October, German Studies Review*, and others. He has coedited two volumes of writings on and by Siegfried Kracauer, respectively, and has recently completed a manuscript entitled *Manhattan Transfer: The Curious Humanism of Siegfried Kracauer's American Writings.*

COLIN WILLIAMSON is a visiting assistant professor of film and media studies at Franklin and Marshall College. He has published articles on early cinema, animation, and science films, and his book on film, wonder, and technology titled *Hidden in Plain Sight: An Archaeology of Magic and the Cinema* was recently published by Rutgers University Press.

STEVEN WOODWARD is professor at Bishop's University in Quebec, where he teaches courses on film and media. He is the editor of *After Kieslowski* and co-editor of *Kieslowski: Interviews* and researches and publishes on the subjects of film franchises, cringe comedy, and film adaptation.

INDEX

Abe, Kobe, 149
Abel, Richard, 68, 76
Abraham Lincoln Vampire Hunter (Timur Bekmambetov, 2012), 47
Abstract Expressionism, 166
Absturz (Ludwig Wolff, 1923), 34
Adam's Rib (George Cukor, 1949), 168
Adorno, Theodor W., 46, 52, 54–55, 65, 217
The Adventures of Tintin (Steven Spielberg, 2011), 85–88
Advertising League of New York, 11
Aesthetics and Its Discontents (Rancière), 219
Agamben, Giorgio, 65
A.I. Artificial Intelligence (Steven Spielberg, 2001), 62–64
Aisthesis (Rancière), 217–218, 223–224
Alexandrov, Grigori, 37
All Is Lost (J. C. Chandor, 2013), 178, 181–184
All the Memory of the World (Alain Resnais, 1956), 178
Althusser, Louis, 3, 49, 150
Altman, Rick, 240
Altman, Robert, 153
Ambara Dama: To Enchant Death (Jean Rouch, 1974), 125, 128, 133, 135
Amstutz, Roland, 227
amusement parks, 2, 56, 64
An Anagram of Ideas on Art, Form, and Film (Deren), 70
Anderson, Judith, 95, 244
Anderson, Paul Thomas, 123
The Anderson Tapes (Sidney Lumet, 1971), 154
Andrew, Dudley, 7, 136, 138, 142, 144, 146, 148–149, 176, 186
Andrews, Dana, 93
The Anti-Aesthetic: Essays on Postmodern Culture (ed. Foster), 218
Antonioni, Michelangelo, 155–156
"Apology for Raimond Sebond" (Montaigne), 175
Appleseed, Johnny, 20
The Archaeology of Knowledge (Foucault), 177
Arendt, Hannah, 52, 65
Aristotle, 141, 152, 181, 223–224
Arnheim, Rudolf, 4, 7, 44–45, 101–112
Arnoux, Alexandre, 240
Aronofsky, Darren, 90, 97
L'arrivée d'un train en gare de La Ciotat (1895, Lumière brothers), 101, 103
Artaud, Antoine, 178
The Artist (Michel Hazanavicius, 2011), 14, 17–18
The Art of the Moving Picture (Lindsay), 19, 21, 25, 27
Astruc, Alexandre, 185, 187
Attenborough, Richard, 206–207
Augustine of Hippo, 188, 195
Aumont, Jacques, 77
Austin, J. L., 165, 253
The Avengers (Joss Wheden, 2012), 46
Avraham, Shlomi, 237
Ayfre, Amédée, 149

Babener, Liahna, 94
Bacall, Lauren, 138–139, 141–142, 148
Backstairs (Leopold Jessner, 1921), 44
Badiou, Alain, 3
Bakri, Saleh, 237
Balázs, Béla, 13, 31–41, 45
Balzac, Honoré de, 113, 189
Bancroft, George, 35, 37
The Band's Visit (Eran Kolirin, 2009), 231, 236, 238–239
Barsacq, Yves, 106
Barthes, Roland, 113–117, 119–121, 123–124, 217
Batista, Fulgencio, 122
The Battle of Algiers (Gillo Pontecorvo, 1966), 187
Battleship Potemkin (Sergei Eisenstein, 1925), 27, 80, 148
Baudelaire, Charles, 55–56, 167
Baudrillard, Jean, 3, 64
Baudry, Jean-Louis, 176
Bazin, André, 4–5, 65, 103, 136–139, 141–145, 147–149, 164, 166, 176, 185–186, 190
Beerblock, Maurice, 180
Beethoven, Ludwig von, 76, 214
Being and Nothingness (Sartre), 149
Being and Time (Heidegger), 149
Bejo, Bérénice, 17
Bekmambetov, Timur, 47
Belmondo, Jean-Paul, 141, 199
Benjamin, Walter, 4, 41, 49, 51, 54–60, 62–65, 103, 176–177, 218–219
Bergman, Ingmar, 147, 152
Bernanos, Georges, 189
Bibliothèque Nationale (France), 178
Bicycle Thieves (Vittorio De Sica, 1948), 144

The Big Sleep (Howard Hawks, 1946), 143
The Birth of a Nation (D. W. Griffith, 1915), 48
Blackboard Jungle (Richard Brooks, 1955), 187
Black Swan (Darren Aronofsky, 2010), 90, 96–100
Blanchot, Maurice, 175, 181
Blonde Venus (Josef von Sternberg, 1932), 70
Blue Velvet (David Lynch, 1986), 159
Body Double (Brian De Palma, 1984), 192
Boethius, 191
Bogart, Humphrey, 138–143, 147–149, 167
Bogue, Ronald, 154
Bonjour cinéma/Hello, Cinema (Epstein), 66, 68, 70
The Book of the Dead (Egyptian text), 24
Bourdieu, Pierre, 218, 223
Bordwell, David, 56, 108
Bowie, Malcolm, 90
Brando, Marlon, 120–121
Brant, Sebastian, 178
Breaking the Waves (Lars von Trier, 1996), 73
Breathless (Jean-Luc Godard, 1959), 141, 144, 147, 225
Brecht, Berthold, 227
Bresson, Robert, 152, 177–183, 192, 238
Brooks, Richard, 187
Brown, Dan, 114
Browne, Nick, 221
Bruegel, Pieter (the Elder), 74–75
Brunius, Jacques, 231
Bruno, Giuliana, 7
Buddhism, 20
Bujold, Geneviève, 192–194
Bulgakowa, Oksana, 77–79, 81
Buñuel, Luis, 152
Burke, Kenneth, 224
Butler, Judith, 241–243, 245–252
Butterfield, Asa, 203

The Cabinet of Dr. Caligari (Robert Weine, 1920), 35, 44
Cage, John, 239
Cahiers du cinéma (journal), 3, 49, 144, 151, 176, 185
Calamai, Clara, 155
Calleia, Joseph, 157
Call Northside 777 (Henry Hathaway, 1948), 143
Camera Lucida: Reflections on Photography (Barthes), 115
Camus, Albert, 138
Carax, Leos, 170–172
Carradine, John, 209, 222
Carrey, Jim, 108, 111
Carroll, Noël, 56, 163
Carter, Erica, 31
Casetti, Francesco, 55
Casilio, Maria Pia, 155
Cassel, Vincent, 96–97
Castro, Fidel, 122
Cavell, Stanley, 162–173
"Celluloid and Marble" (Rohmer), 188
Chabrol, Claude, 185–191
Champollion, Jean-François, 23
Chandor, J. C., 178, 181, 183
Chaplin (Richard Attenborough, 1992), 206
Chaplin, Charlie, 11, 13–16, 18, 153, 206
The Children's Hour (William Wyler, 1961), 163
La Chinoise (Jean-Luc Godard, 1967), 225
Chion, Michel, 229–231, 233–240
Chronicle of a Summer (Jean Rouch, 1961), 125
Cine-Eye (Dziga Vertov, 1924), 79–80
Cinema 1: The Movement-Image (Deleuze), 150–154
Cinema 2: The Time-Image (Deleuze), 150, 153–156
The Cinematic Body (Shaviro), 150
cinéma vérité, 51, 125, 128, 130–131
Cities of Words (Cavell), 162
City Lights (Charles Chaplin, 1931), 14–18
Clark University and Teachers' College, 11
Clayton, Alex, 208, 210, 212, 214, 216
Clooney, George, 46
Close-Up (Abbas Kiarostami, 1990), 126–128, 131
Cœur fidèle (Jean Epstein, 1923), 67
Cohen, Marshall, 164
Colbert, Claudette, 168
Colman, Felicity, 152
Columbia University, 11
Comolli, Jean-Louis, 55, 176
Compson, Betty, 35
Coney Island, 64
"The Congo: A Study of the Negro Race" (Lindsay poem), 20
Connery, Sean, 154
The Consolation of Philosophy (Boethius), 191
Contesting Tears (Cavell), 162
Cooper, Gary, 220
Coppola, Sophie, 113, 117
Corneille, Pierre, 223
Cosmopolitan (magazine), 10
Costa-Gavras, Constantin, 187
Cousteau, Jacques-Yves, 103
Crawford, Joan, 209
Crisp, Quentin, 247
The Cyclist (Mohsen Makhmalbaf, 1987), 126, 128

Dadaism, 3
Dalle Vacche, Angela, 136
Dano, Paul, 123
Dargis, Manohla, 46–47, 73–74
Dark Passage (Delmer Daves, 1947), 138–145, 147, 149
Daves, Delmer, 138, 140, 143–145
Day-Lewis, Daniel, 42–43, 47–48, 123
De Beauvoir, Simone, 243
Debord, Guy, 65
Defert, Daniel, 174
Deleuze, Gilles, 65, 148, 150–157, 159–161, 175, 177
Delon, Alain, 227
Del Rio, Elana, 150
DeMarco, Frank G., 182
DeMille, Cecil B., 25, 27, 62
De Niro, Robert, 154
Denning, Michael, 83
Denny, Reginald, 246

De Palma, Brian, 191–194
Deren, Maya, 3, 70–72, 74
Derrida, Jacques, 3, 223
Descartes, René, 175
De Sica, Vittorio, 155
2 ou 3 choses que je sais d'elle (Jean-Luc Godard, 1967), 225
Devigny, André, 179
Dialectic of Enlightenment (Adorno and Horkheimer), 55
Dieterlen, Germaine, 125
Dietrich, Marlene, 70, 157, 220
digital 3-D, 204
Disagreement: Politics and Philosophy (Rancière), 218–219
Discipline and Punish (Foucault), 175, 178, 181
Disney, Walt, 39, 41, 78, 83, 85–86, 159
Dits et écrits (Foucault), 174
The Docks of New York (Josef von Sternberg, 1928), 35–37, 39
Dog Day Afternoon (Sidney Lumet, 1975), 154
Dogon of Mali, 125
Donat, Robert, 190
Dorman, Sonya, 70–71
Dostoevsky, Feodor, 187, 189
Douchet, Jean, 185–195
Downey, Robert Jr., 206
Dressed to Kill (Brian De Palma, 1980), 192
Dumbo (Disney, 1941), 83–85, 86
Dujardin, Jean, 17–18
Du Maurier, Daphne, 244
Dunst, Kirsten, 72–73, 117

Easy Rider (Dennis Hopper, 1969), 20, 167
Eaton, Mick, 126, 129
Edge of the World (Michael Powell, 1939), 183
Eggeling, Viking, 102
Eisenstein, Sergei, 4–5, 23–24, 29, 37, 41, 45, 77–85, 87–88, 152
Elephant (Gus Van Sant, 2003), 213, 215
Elkabetz, Ronit, 239
Elsaesser, Thomas, 148–149
Emerson, Ralph Waldo, 128, 135
Ende der Ästhetik (Werckmeister), 217
Enough Simplicity for Every Wise Man (Ostrovsky), 78, 79
Epstein, Jean, 66–76, 103
Eraserhead (David Lynch, 1977), 159
Ernst Lubitsch's American Comedy (Paul), 235
Esnault, Philippe, 126, 129
Eternal Sunshine of the Spotless Mind (Michel Gondry, 2004), 104, 108, 110–111
Europe, 2, 4–5, 8, 22, 31, 33, 41, 122, 151, 154, 159, 219
European modernism, 2, 159
Evanson, Edith, 211
L'évidence du film (Nancy), 149
Ewald, François, 174
Ewers, Hanns Heinz, 8
Eyes Without a Face (Georges Franju, 1960), 172

Face of Another (Hiroshi Teshigahara, 1967), 149
The Faerie Queen (Spenser), 248
Farnsworth, Richard, 159–160
Faulkner, William, 138, 187
Felix the Cat (cartoon), 39
Fellini, Federico, 155–156
Field, Sally, 42
Film as Art (Arnheim), 101–104, 106–107, 109, 111–112
Film as Film (Perkins), 208–211
Film, a Sound Art (Chion), 236
Film Language: A Semiotics of the Cinema (Metz), 197–199, 201–202
Film Theory and Criticism (Mast and Cohen), 164
Finch, Peter, 154
Fischer, Lucy, 56, 203
Fischinger, Oskar, 102
Fisher, Kevin, 197
Fonda, Henry, 49–50, 53, 191
Fonda, Peter, 20, 167
Fontaine, Joan, 244
Ford, John, 49–50, 52–53, 176, 219–223
Foster, Hal, 218
Foucault, Michel, 152, 174–181, 183–184, 223, 241
The 400 Blows (François Truffaut, 1959), 147
4 Months, 3 Weeks, and 2 Days (Cristian Mungiu, 2007), 145, 149
Frampton, Hollis, 3
Francis, Kay, 231
Franju, Georges, 172
Frankfurter Zeitung (newspaper), 44
Frankfurt School, 54
Freud, Sigmund, 72, 90, 92–93, 175, 230, 242, 244
From Caligari to Hitler: A Psychological History of the German Film (Kracauer), 44–47, 50–52
Funeral at Bongo: Old Anai (Jean Rouch, 1972), 125, 132

Gabai, Sasson, 239
Gable, Clark, 168
Gainsbourg, Charlotte, 72
Galeta, Robert, 151
Gance, Abel, 152
Gaynor, Janet, 203, 205
Gender Trouble (Butler), 241
"General Booth Enters Heaven" (Lindsay poem), 20
German Expressionism, 202
Germany, 2, 8–9, 23, 43–47, 49, 51, 54, 77, 102, 138, 179, 181, 202, 226
Germany, Year Zero (Roberto Rossellini, 1948), 138
The Ghost That Never Returns (Abram Room, 1929), 107
Gilbert, Morris, 37
Gilles Deleuze's Time Machine (Rodowick), 150
Giordano, Domiziana, 226
Giraudoux, Jean, 176
Godard, Jean-Luc, 28, 125, 144, 147, 152, 163, 177, 185, 199, 225, 227–228
Gondry, Michel, 104, 110–112
Gone With the Wind (Victor Fleming, 1939), 48

Goodis, David, 144
The Good Woman of Setzuan (Brecht), 227
"Gospel of Beauty" (Lindsay), 20, 24
The Graduate (Mike Nichols, 1967), 163
A Grammar of Motives (Burke), 224, 254
Great Depression, 19, 49, 234
Greed (Erich von Stroheim, 1924), 27
Greenblatt, Stephen, 176
Griaule, Marcel, 125, 133
Griffith, D. W., 22, 26–27, 152, 176
Grise, Pierre, 172
Grosz, Elisabeth, 90–91, 93, 98
Guattari, Félix, 152
Guggenheim Foundation, 44
Gunning, Tom, 19–30, 41, 56, 76, 161, 176
Guthrie, Woody, 19
Guys and Dolls (Joseph L. Mankiewicz, 1955), 113, 120–123

Habberjam, Barbara, 155
Hale, Matthew Jr., 8
Hammid, Alexander, 70, 72
Hansen, Miriam, 8, 22, 24, 55
Harvard Psychological Laboratory, 9–10
Harvard University, 8–9, 11
Hayden, Sterling, 213
Hayworth, Rita, 167–169
Hazanavicius, Michel, 14, 18
Heath, Stephen, 197
Heidegger, Martin, 148–149
Hello Dolly! (Gene Kelly, 1969), 40
Hemingway, Ernest, 138
Hershey, Barbara, 98
Herzog, Werner, 152
Hess, John, 186
Heston, Charlton, 156, 158
Hickey, Dave, 218–219
Higgins, Scott, 103
Hinduism, 20
Hirschhorn, Thomas, 217
Histoire(s) du cinema (Jean-Luc Godard), 225
The History of Sexuality (Foucault), 174, 176
Hitchcock (Douchet), 186
Hitchcock, Alfred, 28–29, 134–135, 147, 152, 176, 185–196, 210–211, 230, 243, 246
Hjelmslev, Louis, 175
Hoberman, J., 46
Holden, William, 59, 61
Holy Motors (Leos Carax, 2012), 170–173
Homer, Winslow, 183
Homo Viator (Marcel), 136
Hopkins, Miriam, 231
Hopper, Dennis, 20
Horkheimer, Max, 54–55
Hugo (Martin Scorsese, 2011), 198, 202–204, 206–207
Hugo, Victor, 224
Hunters in the Snow (Bruegel painting), 74
Hurt, William, 63

Image, Music, Text (Barthes), 116, 119
Imaginary, the (Lacan), 92
The Imaginary Signifier: Psychoanalysis and the Cinema (Metz), 197–198, 200–201, 203–205
Imagism, 29
Impressionism, 3, 34–36, 74
The Incredibles (Brad Bird, 2004), 88
Institute of Applied Psychology (Berlin), 11
L'Intelligence d'une machine (Epstein), 67, 69
Intolerance (D. W. Griffith, 1916), 27, 29
The Invisible Dragon: Four Essays on Beauty (Hickey), 218
Irigaray, Luce, 90
Irwin, John T., 23
It Happened One Night (Frank Capra, 1934), 168
Ivanov, Vlad, 146
Ivan the Terrible (Sergei Eisenstein, 1945), 82
Iverson, Erik, 23

Jackson, Samuel L., 46
James, William, 9
Jansenism, 195
Jauss, Hans Robert, 217
The Jazz Singer (Alan Crosland, 1927), 13
Johnny Guitar (Nicholas Ray, 1954), 208–210, 212–213
Jones, Janna, 46
Judith of Bethulia (D. W. Griffith, 1914), 27
Jules and Jim (François Truffaut, 1963), 163

Karina, Anna, 119, 226
Kasson, John, 64
Kaufman, Denis, 3
Kaufmann, Stanley, 23
Keathley, Christian, 198
Keaton, Buster, 62
Keil, Charlie, 56
Keller, Phyllis, 8
Keller, Sarah, 66, 68, 70, 72, 74, 76
Kerouac, Jack, 19
Kiarostami, Abbas, 126–128
Kinoks (film collective), 79
Kirtland, Katie, 67
Kleiman, Naum, 83
Kleine Apologie der ästhetischen Erfahrung (Jauss), 217
Klevan, Andrew, 208
Koch, Gertrud, 31, 41, 103
Kolirin, Eran, 231, 236–240
Korda, Alexander, 78
Koyaanisqatsi (Godfrey Reggio, 1982), 40
Kracauer, Siegfried, 4–5, 41–55, 164, 176
Krauss, Rosalind, 170
Kretzschmar, Laurent, 149
Kubrick, Stanley, 230
Kuleshov, Lev, 3, 138
Kunis, Mila, 98
Kurosawa, Akira, 152

Lacan, Jacques, 4, 49, 89–95, 97–100, 146, 150–151, 176, 242
Ladd, Alan, 167
The Lady Eve (Preston Sturges, 1941), 173

The Lady from Shanghai (Orson Welles, 1948), 167–169
Lady in the Lake (Robert Montgomery, 1947), 139
Lang, Fritz, 152, 177, 230
The Last Laugh (F. W. Murnau, 1924), 27
Laura (Otto Preminger, 1944), 90, 93–96, 100
Lavant, Denis, 170, 172
L'Avventura (Michelangelo Antonioni, 1960), 156, 163
Law, Jude, 195–196, 203
Le Clainche, Charles, 179
Leclaire, Serge, 99
Leigh, Janet, 157
Leterrier, François, 179–180
Liebman, Stuart, 69
Lincoln (Steven Spielberg, 2012), 42–43, 47–53
Lincoln Memorial, 49
Lindsay, Vachel, 4, 7, 19–30
Lithgow, John, 192
"Little History of Photography" (Benjamin), 55–56
Livingston, Margaret, 203
Lloyd, Harold, 203–204
Lounsbury, Myron, 19
Lubitsch, Ernst, 231–238, 240
Lumet, Sidney, 154
Lumière, Auguste and Louis, 7, 101, 115
Luxo Jr. (John Lasseter, 1986), 40
Lye, Len, 102
Lynch, David, 159–161
La Lyrosophie (Epstein), 66–69, 75

MacCormack, Patricia, 150
Mac-Mahonists, 186, 195
Madame Bovary (Flaubert), 225
Madness and Civilization (Foucault), 174, 178, 184
Magritte, René, 175, 177
Makhmalbaf, Mohsen, 126–128
Malick, Terrence, 29–30
A Man Escaped (Robert Bresson, 1956), 178–179, 182–183
Manet, Edouard, 175
Mankiewicz, Joseph L., 113, 120–122
Manovich, Lev, 102
The Man Who Knew Too Much (Alfred Hitchcock, 1956), 190
The Man Who Shot Liberty Valance (John Ford, 1962), 163
The Man with a Movie Camera (Dziga Vertov, 1927), 203
Mara, Rooney, 195
Marcel, Gabriel, 136, 147, 149
Marey, Etienne-Jules, 7, 172
Marie Antoinette (Sophia Coppola, 2006), 113, 117–119
Marinca, Anamaria, 145
Marks, Laura, 150, 177
Marshall, Herbert, 231
Martin-Jones, David, 150
Masculin Féminin (Jean-Luc Godard, 1966), 225
The Mass Ornament (Kracauer), 51
Mast, Gerald, 164
Mastroianni, Marcello, 156
Matatov, Rinat, 237
Materialtheorie (Arnheim), 102
Mayer, Carl, 44
McCambridge, Mercedes, 213
McLuhan, Marshall, 23
Meditations (Descartes), 175
Melancholia (Lars von Trier, 2011), 72, 74–75
Méliès, Georges, 204, 206–207
Mendes, Eva, 172
Las Meniñas (Velásquez painting), 177
Merleau-Ponty, Maurice, 3, 136, 175
Meshes of the Afternoon (Maya Deren, 1943), 70–71
mesmerism, 9
Metz, Christian, 4, 89, 103, 197–205, 207, 233
MGM (Metro-Goldwyn-Mayer), 139
Minogue, Kylie, 72
Mirror Stage, the (Lacan), 89–92
Mitry, Jean, 3, 7
"The Modern Cinema and Narrativity" (Metz), 199
modernism, 2, 31, 76, 150–151, 153, 155, 157, 159, 161, 163–164, 166, 170, 172, 217, 223
Modleski, Tania, 163, 244–245
Monroe, Harriet, 20
Montaigne, Michel de, 175
Montant, Georges, 106
"Moonlight Sonata" (Beethoven), 214–215
Moore, Pauline, 49
Moore, Rachel O., 22
Moorehead, Agnes, 139
Moretz, Chloe Grace, 203
Morin, Edgar, 60, 125–126, 129, 234
Mounier, Emannuel, 5, 186
Mozhukhin, Edmund, 138
Mulholland Dr. (David Lynch, 2001), 159
Mulvey, Laura, 89, 151–152, 241
Mungiu, Cristian, 145–146
Murnau, F. W., 43–45, 197, 202–206
Musée de l'Homme (Paris), 125
Museum of Modern Art (New York), 21, 44
Must We Mean What We Say? (Cavell), 165
Muybridge, Eadweard, 7
"My Paper, My Body, This Fire" (Foucault), 184
The Mystery of Being (Marcel), 136

The Naked City (Jules Dassin, 1948), 143
The Naked Spur (Anthony Mann, 1953), 167
Nancy, Jean-Luc, 148–149
Narboni, Jean, 3
Nashville (Robert Altman, 1975), 153
National Archives, 46
Nazi Party, 44–45, 47, 54, 62, 126, 128, 179
Network (Sidney Lumet, 1976), 154
New Age, 20
New Deal, 49
"The New Laocoön: Artistic Composites and the Talking Film" (Arnheim), 102
New Queer Cinema, 241
The New Republic (magazine), 19, 25, 27, 29

New Year's Eve (Lupu Pick, 1923), 44
Nichols, Bill, 70
Nielsen, Asta, 34
Nietzsche, Friedrich, 152, 175
Night and Fog (Alain Resnais, 1955), 178
Nilsson, Anna, 62
Northwestern University, 11
Nouvelle Vague (New Wave), 51, 125, 144–145, 225–228
Nouvelle vague (Jean Luc Godard, 1990), 226–228
Notes on Cinematography (Bresson), 238
Notre-Dame de Paris (Hugo), 224
Novak, Kim, 131–132, 135
Novalis, 23, 226

O'Brien, George, 203, 205
Obsession (Brian De Palma, 1976), 191–194
O'Connor, Frances, 62
Oedipus Rex (Sophocles), 223
Oedipus complex (Freud), 90–91, 242
The Old and the New (Sergei Eisenstein, 1929), 82
Olivier, Laurence, 244
Olson, Nancy, 59
On Dangerous Ground (Nicholas Ray, 1951), 144
"On Some Motifs in Baudelaire" (Benjamin), 55
On the Road (Kerouac), 19
"On the Vicissitudes of the Self: The Possessed Dancer, the Magician, the Sorcerer, the Filmmaker, and the Ethnographer" (Rouch), 129
"The Ontology of the Photographic Image" (Bazin), 103
original sin, 195
Orlando (Sally Potter, 1992), 243, 247–251
Ossessione (Luchino Visconti, 1943), 155
Osment, Haley Joel, 62–63
Osterloh, Robert, 209
Ostrovsky, Alexander, 78
Oswald the Lucky Rabbit (cartoon), 39
Oudart, Jean-Pierre, 3

Pacino, Al, 154
The Painter of Modern Life (Baudelaire), 167
Paisà (Roberto Rossellini, 1947), 145
Panofsky, Erwin, 164
Parade of Ostriches (Lumière brothers, 1895), 115
Paris Exhibition of Art and Industry (1925), 79
Paul, William, 235
Pelagius, 195
Perkins, V. F., 208–213, 215–216
Personalism, 5, 186
The Pervert's Guide to Cinema (Sophie Fiennes, 2006), 89
Petersson, Dag, 58
Petrograd Institute of Engineering, 78
Phallus, the (Lacan), 92–93
Phenakistoscope, 7
photogénie, 66, 68–69, 76, 103
The Photoplay: A Psychological Study (Münsterberg), 7–16, 18, 24
phrenology, 9
Piccoli, Michel, 172
Pickford, Mary, 11, 25
Pierce, Charles, 152
Pierrot le fou (Jean-Luc Godard, 1965), 199, 202, 225
Pierson, Ryan, 169
Pinocchio (Collodi), 63–64
Piranesi, Giovanni Batista, 178
Pisters, Patricia, 150
Pixar, 38–41
Plato, 152, 218
Platt, Louise, 222
Play Time (Jacques Tati, 1967), 104–108
Plotinus, 188
Poe, Edgar Allan, 23, 26
Poetics (Aristotle), 181
Poetry (magazine), 20
Poetry Today: A New State of Intelligence (Epstein), 66
politique des auteurs (auteur theory), 32, 151, 174, 176, 185, 187, 191–192
Pontecorvo, Gillo, 187
popular music, 2
Populism, 19
Portman, Natalie, 96–97
postmodernism, 64, 217–218
Potter, Sally, 243, 248–249
Pound, Ezra, 20, 23
Powell, Anna, 150
Powell, Michael, 183
Preminger, Otto, 90, 93, 96, 209
Price, Vincent, 95
The Prince of the City (Sidney Lumet, 1981), 154
Prisons (Piranesi etchings), 178
professional sports, 2
The Progress and Poetry of the Movies (Lindsay), 19, 27
Progressivism, 20
Prohibition, 20
Proletkult Theater (Moscow), 78, 81
Proust, Marcel, 73, 174, 225
Psycho (Alfred Hitchcock, 1960), 135, 139, 191, 230–231
psychology, 7–9, 11, 16, 22, 77, 102, 174, 181
Pudovkin, Vsevolod, 3, 37, 81
punctum (Barthes), 113, 115–116
Pursuits of Happiness (Cavell), 162, 165, 172

Queen Kelly (Erich von Stroheim, 1929), 60, 61

Radcliffe College, 8
Rancière, Jacques, 217–221, 223–227
Ray, Nicholas, 144, 208, 210, 213
Raymond Roussel (Foucault), 174
Real, the (Lacan), 91–92, 146
Rebecca (Alfred Hitchcock, 1940), 243–246
Rebeyrolle, Paul, 175
Red Army, 78
Redford, Robert, 182–184

Redner, Gregg, 150
Rembrandt, 225
Remembrance of Things Past (Proust), 73
Republic (Plato), 218
Resnais, Alain, 152, 178
Richter, Hans, 102
Rivette, Jacques, 185
Robertson, Cliff, 192, 194
Rockefeller Foundation, 44
Rodowick, D. N., 150–151, 170
Rohmer, Eric, 144, 149, 185–186, 188, 190–191
A Romance of the Redwoods (Cecil B. DeMille, 1917), 25, 27
Room, Abram, 107
Rope (Alfred Hitchcock, 1948), 211
Rose, Jacqueline, 3
Rosemary's Baby (Roman Polanski, 1968), 163
Rosenzweig, Roy, 22
Rosetta Stone, 23
Rossellini, Roberto, 137–138, 144–145, 152
Rouch, Jean, 125–135
Rules of the Game (Jean Renoir, 1939), 137
Rushton, Richard, 150, 200
Ruttmann, Walter, 203
Ryder, Winona, 97

Sabzian, Hossain, 126–128, 131
The Sacrifice (Andrei Tarkovsky, 1986), 74
Sade, Marquis de, 73
Safety Last (Fred Newmeyer and Sam Taylor, 1923), 203
The Salaried Masses (Kracauer), 44
Salvation Army, 20
Sanders, Julie, 191–192
Sarrasine (Balzac), 113
Saving Private Ryan (Steven Spielberg, 1998), 42
Sayre, Robert F., 20
Schaeffer, Pierre, 229, 239
Schafer, R. Murray, 239
Schatz, Thomas, 156
Schefer, Jean-Louis, 176
Schrader, Paul, 192
Scob, Edith, 170, 172
Scorsese, Martin, 154, 198, 202–204, 206–207
Scott, A. O., 46–48
Scott, Walter Dill, 11
Screen (magazine), 197
Selznick, David O., 220, 246
Serpico (Sidney Lumet, 1973), 154
Shane (George Stevens, 1953), 167
Sharits, Paul, 3
Shattered (Lupu Pick, 1921), 44
Shaviro, Steven, 150, 152
Shoot the Piano Player (François Truffaut, 1960), 144
Side Effects (Steven Soderbergh, 2013), 195–196
Silverman, Kaja, 177, 231
Simmel, Georg, 31, 55, 176
Sinatra, Frank, 120
Singer, Ben, 56
Skeleton Dance (Disney, 1929), 39
Sloane, Everett, 168–169
Snow, Michael, 3
Sobchack, Vivian, 65
Soderbergh, Steven, 195–196
Solaris (Andrei Tarkovsky, 1972), 74
Songhay of Niger, 125
Sound on Screen (Chion), 234–235
Spenser, Edmund, 248
Sperb, Jason, 197–198
Spielberg, Steven, 42–44, 47–50, 52–53, 62–65, 87
Stagecoach (John Ford, 1939), 219–224
Stanton, Harry Dean, 159
Steinskog, Erik, 58
Stern, William, 11
Sternberg, Josef von, 35, 37, 70
Stewart, James, 131, 135, 167
Stoller, Paul, 130
The Straight Story (David Lynch, 1999), 159–161
Strike (Sergei Eisenstein, 1924), 79–80, 82, 88
The Student of Prague (Paul Wegener, Stellan Rye, and Hanns Heinz Ewers, 1913), 8
studium (Barthes), 115
Stultifera navis (Brant), 178
Summer with Monika (Ingmar Bergman, 1953), 147
Sunrise: A Song of Two Humans (F. W. Murnau, 1927), 197, 202–207
Sunset Blvd. (Billy Wilder, 1950), 58–63
Surrealism, 3, 108, 166, 217, 231
Sutherland, Kiefer, 72
Sutton, Damian, 150
Swanson, Gloria, 59, 61
Swedenborgianism, 20
Swinton, Tilda, 237, 249
Sword of Damocles, 190
Symbolic, the (Lacan), 92, 95–100
Symbolic Order, the (Lacan), 92–94, 96–100
S/Z (Barthes), 113–114

Tamiroff, Akim, 157
Tarkovsky, Andrei, 74
Tati, Jacques, 104–108, 112
Tatum, Channing, 195
Taxi Driver (Martin Scorsese, 1976), 142, 154
Le Tempestaire (Jean Epstein, 1947), 69
Teshigahara, Hiroshi, 149
The Testament of Dr. Mabuse (Fritz Lang, 1933), 230–231
Theory of Film (Kracauer), 4, 51–53, 164
There Will Be Blood (Paul Thomas Anderson, 2007), 123
They Live by Night (Nicholas Ray, 1948), 144
The Thief of Bagdad (Raoul Walsh, 1924), 27
This Is Not a Pipe (Foucault), 177
Tierney, Gene, 91, 96
Tolstoy, Leo, 127
Tomlinson, Hugh, 151–152
Tone, Yasunau, 240
Toubiana, Serge, 152
Touch of Evil (Orson Welles, 1958), 156, 158–159, 161
Tree of Life (Terrence Malick, 2011), 29–30

Trevor, Claire, 220, 222
Tristan and Isolde (Wagner opera), 73, 75
Trouble in Paradise (Ernst Lubitsch, 1932), 231–232, 237, 240
Truffaut, François, 144, 147, 176, 185
Turner, Frederick Jackson, 219–220
Turner, J.M.W., 183
Turu and Bitti: The Drums of Yore (Jean Rouch, 1971), 129
Turvey, Malcolm, 56
2001: A Space Odyssey (Stanley Kubrick, 1968), 230

Umberto D (Vittorio De Sica, 1952), 155
University of Leipzig, 9
utopianism, 20, 30, 33, 41, 47, 52–53, 138, 203

Valandrey, Charlotte, 248
Van Sant, Gus, 213, 215
Vasiliu, Laura, 146
vaudeville, 2, 11, 20, 79–80, 203
Velásquez, Diego, 175, 177
Vertigo (Alfred Hitchcock, 1958), 131–132, 134–135, 163, 167, 191
Vertov, Dziga, 3, 79–80, 203
Vidor, King, 153
Vieux Colombier (Paris theater), 37
Virilio, Paul, 3
Visible Man (Balázs), 31–34, 37
"Visual Pleasure in Narrative Cinema" (Mulvey), 241
Vivre sa vie (Jean-Luc Godard, 1965), 225
The Voice in Cinema (Chion), 229–230, 237
von Trier, Lars, 72–76

WALL-E (Andrew Stanton, 2008), 38–40, 46
Wanger, Walter, 222
Wayne, John, 220, 222
Webb, Clifton, 94, 96
A Wedding (Robert Altman, 1978), 153
Weimar Republic, 44–47, 51–52, 102
Welles, Orson, 78, 88, 149, 152, 156–159, 167–169, 211
Werckmeister, Otto Karl, 217
What Cinema Is! Bazin's Quest and Its Charge (Andrew), 145
What Is Cinema? (Bazin), 65, 137
Whitney, Ryan, 111
Who Framed Roger Rabbit? (Robert Zemeckis, 1988), 88
"Why We Go to the 'Movies'" (Münsterberg), 10
Wilder, Billy, 59, 61
Williams, Treat, 154
Wilson, Woodrow, 20
Winslet, Kate, 108, 111
Wittgenstein, Ludwig, 165
The Wizard of Oz (Victor Fleming, 1939), 230
Wolff, Ludwig, 34
Wollen, Peter, 78–79, 81
The Women Who Knew Too Much (Modleski), 244
Wood, John, 250
Woolf, Virginia, 247
"The Work of Art in the Age of Mechanical Reproduction" (Benjamin), 54–55
World War I, 20, 44, 54, 62
World War II, 3, 32, 49, 54, 84, 149–150, 153–154, 159, 161
Writing Degree Zero (Barthes), 113
The Wrong Man (Alfred Hitchcock, 1956), 187, 190
Wundt, Wilhelm, 9
The World Viewed (Cavell), 162–172
World Without Sun (Jacques-Yves Cousteau, 1964), 103

Young, Victor, 208–209
Young Mr. Lincoln (John Ford, 1939), 49–51, 176

Z (Costa-Gavras, 1968), 187
Zaynalzadeh, Moharram, 126
Zeta-Jones, Catherine, 195–196
Žižek, Slavoj, 3, 89
Zoetrope, 7
Zuccarini, Peter, 183